THE STATE OF FOOD AND AGRICULTURE 1998

PER
HD
1401
.S73

ISSN 0081-4539

THE STATE OF FOOD AND AGRICULTURE 1998

Université d'Ottawa
BIBLIOTHEQUES
LIBRARIES
University of Ottawa

FOOD AND AGRICULTURE ORGANIZATION OF THE UNITED NATIONS

Rome, 1998

The statistical material in this publication has been prepared from the information available to FAO up to July 1998.

The designations employed and the presentation do not imply the expression of any opinion whatsoever on the part of the Food and Agriculture Organization of the United Nations concerning the legal status of any country, territory, city or area, or of its authorities, or concerning the delimitation of its frontiers or boundaries. In some tables, the designations "developed" and "developing" economies are intended for statistical convenience and do not necessarily express a judgement about the stage reached by a particular country or area in the development process.

David Lubin Memorial Library
Cataloguing in Publication Data

FAO, Rome (Italy)
The state of food and agriculture 1998.
ISBN 92-5-104200-4

(FAO Agriculture Series, no. 31)
ISSN 0081-4539

1. Agriculture	3. Food security
2. Food production	4. Non-farm income
I. Title	II. Series
FAO code: 70	AGRIS: E16 E80a

© FAO 1998

Printed in Italy

Foreword

Two years have elapsed since the conclusion of the World Food Summit and the pledge made to bring about a radical reduction in world hunger and malnutrition. To achieve this, policy actions must remain highly focused on fulfilling the Summit's commitments, and wide publicity must be given to the measures that have either been taken or still need to be taken by countries and institutions in order to enhance food security.

The need to be constantly informed and vigilant is all the more pressing given the rapid pace of world events, which present new situations and daily challenges directly or indirectly affecting agriculture and food security. Even the most enlightened and determined efforts to eradicate hunger can be frustrated by events that are beyond the control of policy-makers. This has been demonstrated recently by two features reported in *The State of Food and Agriculture 1998*: the financial crises that initially affected East and Southeast Asia; and the El Niño phenomenon.

The financial crises are a matter for concern, as they threaten to increase in scope and depth. While constituting an element of economic and political uncertainty for the coming years, these crises and their repercussions have already caused deeply depressed economic and food insecurity situations in some countries. For instance, the Russian Federation as well as other countries, especially in Latin America, have been seriously affected by financial turbulence.

A phenomenon of an entirely different nature, El Niño, has also been at the forefront of our concern. Unusually severe in its current cycle, its effects have resulted in massive losses in crop, livestock, forestry and fisheries production, causing severe food shortages in a large number of countries.

On a more positive note, recent encouraging developments are also reported. Despite the uncertainty arising from the Asian crisis, the overall economic situation remains generally favourable for much of the developing world. In particular, several consecutive years of overall improved economic conditions in Africa have strengthened our hopeful expectations of a new trend towards sustainable growth and development in this region. We also welcome the robust economic performances that many countries in Latin America and the Caribbean and in Asia exhibited during 1997, despite the fact that short-term growth prospects in both regions have been lowered by the financial crises. On the agricultural front, the cereal supply situation on the whole appears satisfactory, with global stocks that are within the minimum range considered to be safe for world food security. The weakening in international commodity prices will have opposite effects on net exporter and importer countries; nevertheless, lower food import prices provide much needed relief to many poor net food-importing countries. Indeed, this report highlights a considerably improved economic situation and outlook in those countries with the lowest capacity to finance food imports – and this is essential for their national food security.

It is appropriate to reiterate the importance of extending the benefits of economic growth to the poorest countries and to their entire populations. This year's report confirms that, in a long-term perspective, the poorest nations' populations have become increasingly poor and food-insecure, pointing out that this unacceptable trend has continued in recent years. The country policy reviews suggest that the promotion of rapid, equitable and broad-based growth remains a difficult challenge. However, growth and equity, far from being horns of a dilemma, are equally essential elements of a sound development strategy. Their achievement requires a genuine commitment to alleviating poverty and addressing social needs, and we must welcome all efforts that are being made in this direction by many countries, especially those in Africa. At the same time, in most countries growth-cum-equity can only be achieved by following a strong, rural-oriented development strategy involving large investments in rural infrastructure, human capital and social services.

Rural development and poverty alleviation are central issues of this year's special chapter, entitled "Rural non-farm income in developing countries". Rural non-farm activities represent a major component of rural household economies, and their crucial importance for development and food security cannot be underestimated. Incomes generated by such activities have a synergistic relationship with agriculture, as they provide farmers with financial resources to invest in productivity-enhancing inputs; and, vice versa, improved farm productivity increases rural incomes and lowers urban food prices. Furthermore, rural non-farm employment and income also have implications for the levels and distribution of overall rural incomes, the pace of urbanization, the incidence of rural poverty and natural resource use. It is my hope that this chapter will raise awareness of the fundamental importance of the topic, which is still inadequately comprehended by policy-makers, development agencies and the general public.

Two other selected themes with a direct bearing on food security are examined in Part I of this report: the problems and issues involved in ensuring a constant flow of food to satisfy the needs of cities; and the integration of fisheries and agriculture.

The task of feeding the world's cities adequately constitutes an increasingly pressing challenge, requiring the coordinated interaction of food producers, transporters, market operators and a myriad retail sellers. It also requires constant improvements in the quality of transport and distribution systems. Not least, it involves a shared understanding among city officials and national and international development agencies of the common problems and the potential solutions faced when seeking to feed cities on a sustainable basis.

As regards the integration of fisheries and agriculture, it is important to recognize the positive as well as the antagonistic interactions that arise from their common use of land and water resources. By maximizing synergies, significant contributions can be made to the enhancement of fisheries (coastal, inland and aquaculture) production, agricultural production and food security. Water use, integrated pest management and the recycling of nutrients should be optimized while negative interactions, such as those resulting from the excessive application of pesticides that may be harmful to acquatic organisms, must be minimized.

In presenting *The State of Food and Agriculture* this year, I am confident that a continuous flow of information on progress made and further efforts required to attain food security for all will heighten awareness of the fundamental importance of this goal. I also hope that it will help mobilize concerted action by all partners and enable us to report more convincing evidence of durable progress made in the years to come.

Jacques Diouf
DIRECTOR-GENERAL

Contents

PART II
Regional review

PART III
Rural non-farm income in developing countries

ANNEX TABLES

Boxes

Tables

Figures

Maps

Acknowledgements

The State of Food and Agriculture 1998 was prepared by a team from the Agriculture and Economic Development Analysis Division, led by F.L. Zegarra and comprising R. Nugent, J. Skoet and S. Teodosijevic. Secretarial support was provided by S. Di Lorenzo and P. Di Santo.

Contributions and background papers for the World review were prepared by

M. Palmieri (Forestry: production and trade), FAO Fisheries Department (Fisheries: catch, disposition and trade), L. Naiken and P. Narain (External assistance to agriculture), L.Wilhelm-Filippi (Feeding the cities) and R. Willmann (Integrating fisheries and agriculture to enhance food security and fish production). The sections on food shortages and emergencies, the cereal market situation, food aid and international agricultural prices were prepared by the staff of the Commodities and Trade Division units, supervised by J. Greenfield, P. Fortucci, W. Lamadé, A. Rashid and P. Konandreas.

Contributions and background papers for the Regional review were prepared by M. Allaya (Near East and North Africa), J. Budavari (Central and Eastern Europe and the CIS), N. Cochrane (Hungary and Poland), M. Cox (Chile), F. Dévé (the Islamic Republic of Iran), K. Dunn (Uganda) and A. Webb (Malaysia).

Part III, the special chapter (Rural non-farm income in developing countries), was prepared by T. Reardon (Michigan State University, USA), with substantial inputs from K. Stamoulis (FAO), M.-E. Cruz (MINAGRI, Chile), A. Balisacan (University of the Philippines), J. Berdegue (RIMISP, Chile) and B. Banks (East Lansing, Michigan, USA).

The State of Food and Agriculture 1998 was edited by R. Tucker; cover and design, graphics and illustrations were produced by G. De Pol – Studio Page; and project management was coordinated by J. Shaw.

Glossary

AMA	Agency for Agricultural Markets (Poland)
APA	Agricultural Property Agency (Poland)
APEC	Asian Pacific Economic Cooperation Council
AsDB	Asian Development Bank
ASEAN	Association of Southeast Asian Nations
CAP	Common Agricultural Policy
CEFTA	Central European Free Trade Agreement
c.i.f.	cost, insurance and freight
CIS	Commonwealth of Independent States
CMEA	Council for Mutual Economic Assistance
COMESA	Common Market for Eastern and Southern Africa
CONAGRO	National Council for Agricultural Production (Peru)
COPAGRO	Confederation of Commercial Grain Producers Cooperatives (Chile)
CPO	crude palm oil
DAC	Development Assistance Committee
DES	dietary energy supply
ECLAC	Economic Commission for Latin America and the Caribbean
EMU	European Monetary Union
EU	European Union
FDI	foreign direct investment
FELCRA	Federal Land Consolidation and Rehabilitation Authority (Malaysia)
FELDA	Federal Land Development Authority (Malaysia)
f.o.b.	free on board
GDP	gross domestic product
GNP	gross national product
HIPC	heavily indebted poor country
IBRD	International Bank for Reconstruction and Development
ICA	International Coffee Agreement
ICCO	International Cocoa Organization
IDA	International Development Association
IDB	Inter-American Development Bank
IDRC	International Development Research Centre
IEFR	International Emergency Food Reserve
IFAD	International Fund for Agricultural Development
IFPRI	International Food Policy Research Institute
IMF	International Monetary Fund
INDAP	Institute of Agricultural Development (Chile)
INIA	National Agricultural Research Institute (Chile)
IPM	integrated pest management
IRRI	International Rice Research Institute
ISA	International Sugar Agreement
IWRM	integrated water resources management
LIFDC	low-income food-deficit country

MERCOSUR	Southern Common Market
NEP	New Economic Policy (Malaysia)
NGO	non-governmental organization
ODA	Official Development Assistance
OECD	Organisation for Economic Cooperation and Development
PFE	permanent forest estate (Malaysia)
PROs	protracted refugee operations
RISDA	Rubber Industry Smallholders' Development Authority (Malaysia)
RNF	rural non-farm
UNDP	United Nations Development Programme
UNRISD	United Nations Research Institute for Social Development
WFP	World Food Programme
WTO	World Trade Organization

Explanatory note

Symbols
The following symbols are used:

- = none or negligible (in tables)
... = not available (in tables)
$ = US dollars

Dates and units
The following forms are used to denote years or groups of years:

1996/97 = a crop, marketing or fiscal year running from one calendar year to the next

1996-97 = the average for the two calendar years

Unless otherwise indicated, the metric system is used in this publication. "Billion" = 1 000 million.

Statistics
Figures in statistical tables may not add up because of rounding. Annual changes and rates of change have been calculated from unrounded figures.

Production indices
The FAO indices of agricultural production show the relative level of the aggregate volume of agricultural production for each year in comparison with the base period 1989-91. They are based on the sum of price-weighted quantities of different agricultural commodities after the quantities used as seed and feed (similarly weighted) have been deducted. The resulting aggregate therefore represents disposable production for any use except seed and feed.

All the indices, whether at the country, regional or world level, are calculated by the Laspeyres formula. Production quantities of each commodity are weighted by 1989-91 average international commodity prices and summed for each year. To obtain the index, the aggregate for a given year is divided by the average aggregate for the base period 1989-91.

Trade indices
The indices of trade in agricultural products are also based on the base period 1989-91. They include all the commodities and countries shown in the *FAO Trade Yearbook*. Indices of total food products include those edible products generally classified as "food".

All indices represent changes in current values of exports (free on board [(f.o.b.]), and imports (cost, insurance, freight [(c.i.f.]), expressed in US dollars. When countries report imports valued at f.o.b., these are adjusted to approximate c.i.f. values.

Volumes and unit value indices represent the changes in the price-weighted sum of quantities and of the quantity-weighted unit values of products traded between countries. The weights are, respectively, the price and quantity averages of 1989-91 which is the base reference period used for all the index number series currently computed by FAO. The Laspeyres formula is used to construct the index numbers.

PART I

WORLD REVIEW

WORLD REVIEW

1. RECENT DEVELOPMENTS IN WORLD FOOD SECURITY

Continuing the approach initiated in *The State of Food and Agriculture 1997*, this section presents an overview of the current world food security situation by region and by country. It provides the most recent FAO estimates of the number of undernourished people and their proportion in the population of their region and country; the relationship between income levels and trends, and the levels and composition of dietary energy supply (DES) and undernourishment; and a number of selected indicators relating to undernourishment[1] in defined country categories.

CURRENT SITUATION

The total number of chronically undernourished people in developing countries is now estimated to be 828 million for the 1994-96 period (Table 1). This figure represents a slight decline in the proportion of undernourished since the early 1990s, but also a slight absolute increase because of the growth in total population and the changes in age

Table 1

PROPORTION AND NUMBER OF UNDERNOURISHED IN DEVELOPING COUNTRIES, BY REGION, 1992-94 AND 1994-96

Region	Percentage of population undernourished		Number of undernourished (millions)	
	1990-92	1994-96	1990-92	1994-96
Sub-Saharan Africa	40	39	196	210
Near East and North Africa	11	12	34	42
East and Southeast Asia	17	15	289	258
South Asia	21	21	237	254
Latin America and Caribbean	15	13	64	63
All developing regions	**20**	**19**	**822**	**828**

Note: Owing to the omission of Oceania, numbers do not add up to the total.
Source: FAO.

Map I

DIETARY ENERGY SUPPLY LEVELS

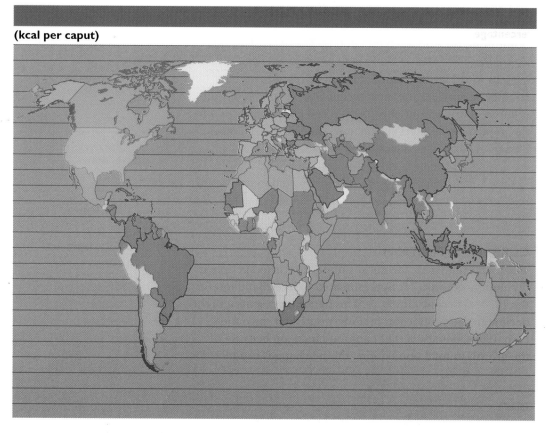

(kcal per caput)

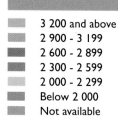

3 200 and above
2 900 - 3 199
2 600 - 2 899
2 300 - 2 599
2 000 - 2 299
Below 2 000
Not available

Source: FAO

composition which lead to changes in minimum dietary requirements.[2]

Table 1 confirms that the largest absolute numbers of undernourished people are in Asia, while the largest proportion of the population that is undernourished is in sub-Saharan Africa. Recent trends give no room for complacency, as progress in some regions has been more than offset by a deterioration in others. It has repeatedly been stated that these numbers are unacceptably high and must be drastically reduced. The World Food Summit Plan of Action is being implemented with the aim of halving the total number of undernourished no later than 2015.

Per caput dietary energy supply, the most important single indicator underlying estimates of food adequacy levels, measures the food available to each person on

Figure 1

SHARE OF FOOD GROUPS IN DIETARY ENERGY SUPPLY BY REGION AND COUNTRY GROUPS

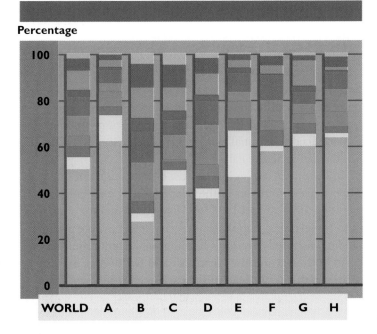

Percentage

Legend:
- Animal oils and fats
- Milk and eggs
- Meat and fish
- Other vegetable products
- Vegetable oils and fats
- Sugars
- Pulses and nuts
- Vegetables and fruits
- Roots and tubers
- Cereals

WORLD
A   Least developed countries
B   Industrialized countries
C   Countries in transition
D   Latin America and Caribbean
E   Sub-Saharan Africa
F   Near East and North Africa
G   East and Southeast Asia
H   South Asia

Source: FAO

average in a country. It is measured in kilocalories (kcal) per day. Map 1 shows the average DES of each country in the world and illustrates some of the variations within regions that are hidden by the regional aggregation in Table 1. Countries with an inadequate food supply – which are generally those with a higher proportion of undernourished people – are heavily concentrated in sub-Saharan Africa, with a relatively high number also in South and Southeast Asia.

In addition to kcal per caput, DES and food security are measured by access to a healthy and balanced diet. Figure 1 shows geographical differences in the composition of DES in the world. The differences are apparent from one region to another and are even more striking when the countries are grouped according to the level of economic development. Such differences are due to varying capacities to purchase food – people in richer countries can afford more livestock products and fats – and to the different availability of foods among countries. In general, the diets of richer countries seem to be more balanced nutritionally and also contain a

Figure 2

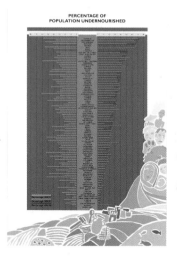

PERCENTAGE OF POPULATION UNDERNOURISHED

Drought-affected people

Drought can cause loss of crops and food availability.

greater proportion of protein, particularly of animal origin, than those of the poorer countries. Developing countries' diets are characterized by a high proportion of cereals. However, even at similar income levels, there are significant variations in diet among countries, reflecting differing production capabilities, access to food and tastes.

TRENDS IN UNDERNOURISHMENT

Figure 2 (presented in poster format in the inside back flap of this publication) shows recent changes in undernourishment in individual countries compared with their situation 25 years ago. The percentage of undernourished declined in the majority of countries in all regions, while a few countries experienced substantial increases owing to exceptional circumstances in the early 1990s.

In the entire subregion, almost half the countries experienced increases in the proportion of undernourished between 1990-92 and 1994-96. However, in many countries with fast-growing populations, even a lower proportion of undernourished translates into higher absolute numbers.

In both Asia and the Near East and North Africa, more than two-thirds of the countries achieved a decrease in

UN/FAO/12645

Figure 3

CHANGES IN DIETARY ENERGY SUPPLY LEVELS AND INCIDENCE OF UNDERNOURISHMENT BY INCOME* LEVEL IN DEVELOPING COUNTRIES

(1969-71 to 1994-96)

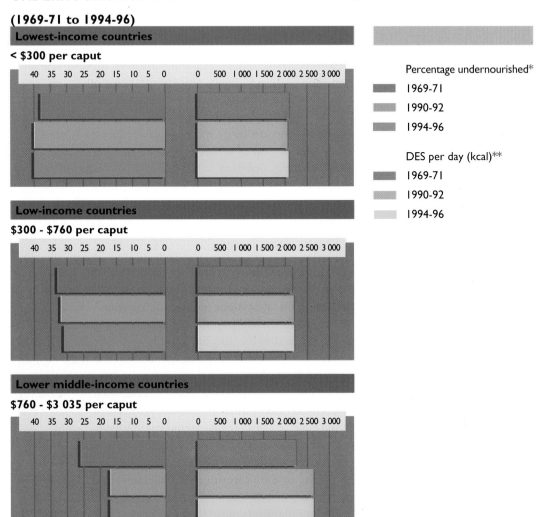

Percentage undernourished*
- 1969-71
- 1990-92
- 1994-96

DES per day (kcal)**
- 1969-71
- 1990-92
- 1994-96

*   Income in 1995 US dollars.
** Average of country groupings.

Note: The lowest income group consists of 20 countries, the low-income group of 32, the lower middle-income group of 31 and the upper middle-income group of 13.

Source: FAO

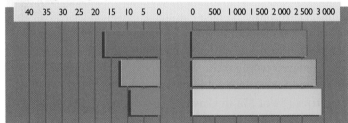

The poorest group of countries has not been able to reduce the number or percentage of undernourished since 1969-71.

undernourishment (in percentage terms) between 1990-92 and 1994-96. Only three out of 24 countries in the Latin America and Caribbean region show increase the proportion of undernourished during the same period.

One important aspect of undernourishment is its close association with people's financial capacity to purchase food. Figure 3 illustrates this aspect, showing four groups of countries, ranked by per caput income level in 1995, and the changes in both undernourished populations and per caput DES for the three periods 1969-71, 1990-92 and 1994-96. As expected, countries with a higher per caput income are those with a higher DES level and a lower proportion of undernourished in their population. More striking, however, is the fact that, contrary to the overall tendency in the developing countries as a whole, the poorest group of countries has not been able to reduce the number or percentage of undernourished since 1969-71.

Factors determining trends in undernourishment
Certain indicators are important in understanding past trends, and perhaps suggesting future trends, in the undernourished population. As indicators, they can be looked to for insights into the presence of undernourishment in a country or region, but they do not fully explain or predict it. This section discusses the relationship between selected indicators and undernourishment.

In order to highlight patterns better, 98 developing countries (comprising 96 percent of the population in the developing world) have been grouped into six categories according to the proportion of undernourished in the population in 1990-92. The percentage of undernourished in the population is more than 50 percent in Class 1 and declines to less than 10 percent in Class 6. Tables 2 and 3 show eight indicators corresponding to the six country groupings. Each indicator is discussed briefly in terms of how it relates to the proportion of undernourished in the country groupings.[3]

Table 2 shows that developing countries with a high proportion of undernourished tend to have the lowest income levels, while those with a low proportion of undernourished have relatively high incomes. Almost all the countries (34 of 37) in Classes 1 to 3 are below the low-income threshold of $765 per caput per annum (1995).

Table 2

SELECTED SOCIO-ECONOMIC INDICATORS ASSOCIATED WITH UNDERNOURISHMENT

Country groupings (by % of undernourished in 1990-92)	Number of countries	Population in 1992 (millions)	Per caput GNP in 1995[1] ($)	Share of rural population in 1995[1] (%)	Share of agriculture in GDP in 1995[1] (%)	Net food imports in 1993-95[2] (kcal/caput/day)
Class 1. > 50%	11	124	100 - 340	61-87	33-56	239
Class 2. 40-50%	10	126	180 - 800	42-87	15-42	314
Class 3. 30-40%	16	400	120 - 1 460	40-82	10-50	158
Class 4. 20-30%	25	1 216	240 - 3 490	14-79	5-51	-5
Class 5. 10-20%	17	1 631	620 - 7 040	21-73	0-26	172
Class 6. < 10%	19	606	1 120 - 17 400	10-47	6-20	464

[1] World Bank data.
[2] Negative figures indicate net food exports.
Note: Number of countries in each class:
Class 1:   11 (9 Africa; 1 Asia and Pacific; 1 Latin America and Caribbean; 0 Near East and North Africa)
Class 2:   10 (8 Africa; 0 Asia and Pacific; 2 Latin America and Caribbean; 0 Near East and North Africa)
Class 3:   16 (13 Africa; 2 Asia and Pacific; 1 Latin America and Caribbean; 0 Near East and North Africa)
Class 4:   25 (7 Africa; 8 Asia and Pacific; 8 Latin America and Caribbean; 2 Near East and North Africa)
Class 5:   17 (2 Africa; 5 Asia and Pacific; 7 Latin America and Caribbean; 3 Near East and North Africa)
Class 6:   19 (0 Africa; 4 Asia and Pacific; 5 Latin America and Caribbean; 10 Near East and North Africa)

Table 3

TREND INDICATORS RELATED TO UNDERNOURISHMENT

Country groupings (by % of undernourished)	Per caput GNP growth in 1985-95 (no. of countries)			Net agricultural trade surplus in 1985-95 (no. of countries)			Staple food production growth in 1985-95 (no. of countries)			Food price inflation in 1985-96 (compared with overall inflation)		
	+	0	-	+	0	-	+	0	-	+	0	-
Class 1. > 50%	0	7	2	1	5	3	9	0	2	1	5	0
Class 2. 40-50%	3	5	2	2	3	3	6	1	3	0	7	1
Class 3. 30-40%	5	5	6	3	10	3	14	0	2	0	11	0
Class 4. 20-30%	10	7	4	3	9	8	19	0	6	0	18	0
Class 5. 10-20%	13	1	2	4	6	7	11	1	5	1	13	0
Class 6. < 10%	9	1	5	4	4	10	13	3	3	0	10	1

Note: + = positive; 0 = negligible; - = negative.

Income distribution and ease of access to food have a major influence on a country's food insecurity situation.

There is a complex relationship between the prevalence of undernourishment and the agricultural/rural character of an economy.

Conversely, almost all the countries (28 of 31) in Classes 5 and 6 are above the low-income threshold. The range of income is fairly wide in each country class, however. Class 4 (consisting of 25 countries) is the most heterogeneous, including several countries with a per caput GNP below $300 and several others with a per caput GNP of more than $3 000 per annum. This demonstrates that other factors, such as income distribution, ease of access to food and other indicators discussed below, have a major influence on the food insecurity situation in a country regardless of the average level of income.

The dependence of a country's economy on agriculture is a significant factor in food security. This is shown in two ways in Table 2: by the proportion of rural population[4] and the share of agriculture in GDP. Developing countries are generally largely rural and heavily dependent on agriculture, especially those with a high prevalence of undernourishment. All of Classes 1 to 5 contain countries where 70 percent or more of the population is rural. Classes 1 to 4 include countries with a high share of agriculture in GDP. The data demonstrate, however, that the relationship between the prevalence of undernourishment and the agricultural/rural character of an economy is complex. In all classes, a fairly broad range of dependence on agriculture prevails, as measured by either indicator, although the upper and lower ends of each range do fall as the proportion of undernourished falls.

Food import dependence is measured as net food imports in terms of kcal per caput per day (see Table 2). Only one-quarter of countries have either a surplus or an approximate balance. Balance is defined as a surplus or deficit of less than 100 kcal per caput per day, i.e. 5 percent or less of per caput food availability.

For the food-deficit countries, which are the large majority, it is worth observing that a greater prevalence of high food deficits is found in classes with lower proportions of undernourished people; indeed, large food import volumes are generally associated with a higher per caput GNP and greater purchasing power.

Four different indicators are presented in Table 3 in order to demonstrate the effects of certain economic trends on the proportion of undernourishment in countries.

Per caput GNP growth reflects the economic conditions over the relevant period in each country and is closely related to the proportion of undernourished in the countries. In the group of 87, per caput GNP rose between 1985 and 1995 for 40 of these countries, declined in 21 and remained about the same in 26. All countries in Class 1 had a negligible or negative per caput income growth in the decade considered; two-thirds of countries in Classes 2 and 3 had a negligible or negative growth; in Class 4, one-half of the countries experienced positive growth during the period; and Classes 5 and 6 contain predominantly countries with positive growth in per caput GNP. The hypothesis that a high proportion of undernourished can itself be a handicap for economic development may be supported by this observation and deserves further investigation.

The net agricultural trade surplus is mainly of significance for countries with a higher dependence on agriculture. The indicator does not appear to be closely related to undernourishment. Table 3 shows that, overall, two out of five of the countries reviewed have approximately balanced agricultural trade over the period 1985-95; one country out of five had a positive surplus and two out of five a negative one.

Staple food production grew between 1985 and 1995 in the majority of countries in all classes and declined

A high proportion of undernourished can be a handicap for economic development.

Progress against hunger
The goal of the World Food Summit is to halve the number of undernourished by 2015.

G. BIZZARRI/FAO/17011

in fewer than one-quarter of them. Trends in staple food production do not show a strong relationship with the undernourishment classes. The majority of countries in Classes 1 to 3, those with the greatest prevalence of undernourishment, have increased their staple food production during the decade considered.

Food price inflation, measured as the differential between food price changes and overall inflation over the period 1985-95, has also been examined. It shows that there has been no general drift in real domestic food prices, with very few cases of either positive or negative real food price trends. It should be noted, however, that a trend analysis conceals short-term price fluctuations and provides no basis for understanding the difficulties resulting from price instability.

CONCLUSION

The complexity of hunger in the developing world is illustrated by the wide range of conditions prevailing among countries with similar levels of undernourishment.

The conditions and trends described tell a complex and serious story about the millions of people who experience undernourishment in the developing world today. Their common story is hunger. The complex part of the story is illustrated by the wide range of conditions prevailing among countries with similar levels of undernourishment. It is reflected in the multiplicity of factors that must contribute to a steady increase in food supplies for those countries where aggregate food availability is not enough to meet the needs of all; and to a much improved access to food by the poor in most countries, including those where aggregate food availability is now sufficient but inequalities maintain a significant level of food insecurity among parts of their population. The evolution in the first half of the 1990s, prior to the World Food Summit, showed a mixture of progress and setbacks. The Summit target of reducing by half the number of undernourished people by 2015 calls for continued emergency action.

In future years, The State of Food and Agriculture will continue to present the latest information available regarding food security conditions and the factors that can change those conditions, keeping in view the target set during the World Food Summit.

WORLD REVIEW

II. CURRENT AGRICULTURAL SITUATION – FACTS AND FIGURES

I. CROP AND LIVESTOCK PRODUCTION

• World crop and livestock production was estimated to have increased in 1997 by only 1.2 percent over the previous year, the lowest yearly rate of growth since 1993. However, the slowdown occurred after a particularly bountiful crop year in 1996, when world output had expanded by as much as 4.5 percent. The slowdown was widespread across both developed and developing country regions.

• For the developing countries as a whole, 1997 was a disappointing year for crop and livestock production. The 1.8 percent increase recorded was the lowest since 1979 and marked the end of five years of solid and accelerating growth, which by 1996 had reached an estimated 5.3 percent. The recorded rate in 1997 was only just in line with population growth. Thus, for the first time since 1987, the developing countries as a whole did not achieve any gain in per caput crop and livestock production.

The developing countries as a whole did not achieve any gain in per caput crop and livestock production during 1997.

• All developing country regions shared to varying degrees in the slowdown. The sharpest negative turnaround in agricultural performance in 1997 was recorded in the Near East and North Africa region, where agricultural output is estimated to have declined by close to 4 percent following a more than 9 percent expansion in 1996. Production shortfalls in this region reflected unfavourable weather, particularly in some Northern African countries where drought caused sharp reductions, mainly in cereal crops. However, production is also estimated to have declined in the Islamic Republic of Iran, Iraq and the Syrian Arab Republic.

• In sub-Saharan Africa also, agricultural production declined by 1 percent in 1997, implying a 4 percent decline in per caput terms and interrupting a four-year period of expansion in per caput agricultural output. Patterns of

Map 2

CHANGES IN CROP AND LIVESTOCK PRODUCTION, 1994-1997

(Percentage change from previous year)

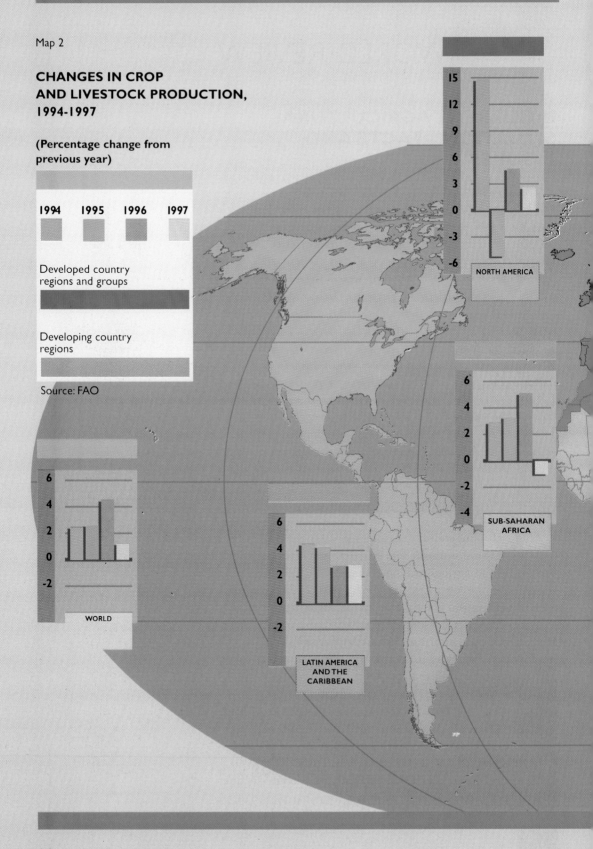

1994 1995 1996 1997

Developed country regions and groups

Developing country regions

Source: FAO

NORTH AMERICA

SUB-SAHARAN AFRICA

WORLD

LATIN AMERICA AND THE CARIBBEAN

WESTERN
EUROPE

COUNTRIES IN
TRANSITION

FAR EAST
AND
OCEANIA

NEAR EAST
AND
NORTH AFRICA

AUSTRALIA,
NEW ZEALAND
AND JAPAN

production performance in 1997 varied widely across the subregion, largely reflecting weather vagaries. Nevertheless, a majority of 36 countries experienced falls in per caput production, with the sharpest shortfalls occurring in southern Africa.

• In the Far East, agricultural output continued expanding but at a significantly reduced rate which estimates put at a mere 2.6 percent – the lowest rate in the 1990s and only the second time in the same period that output growth has fallen below 4 percent. Behind the decline are lower rates of output expansion in a majority of the region's larger countries. In particular, China's agricultural output growth slowed but remained substantial, while India's crops were hit by unfavourable weather in large parts of the country. Countries in Southeast Asia also suffered from droughts, partly associated with the El Niño phenomenon, causing a decline in agricultural production in Indonesia and a slowdown in the rate of expansion in Myanmar, the Philippines and Thailand. Although the effects of the region's financial crisis may influence planting decisions in some countries, the effects on output were not yet noticeable in 1997.

Although the effects of the Far East's financial crisis may influence planting decisions in some countries, the effects on output were not yet noticeable in 1997.

• In the Latin America and Caribbean region, agricultural output growth decelerated only marginally in 1997 to an estimated 2.9 percent. This is still slightly above the average of the previous five years and about 1 percent above the rate of population growth. The increase, however, was concentrated in a relatively small number of countries (including Argentina, Brazil and Peru), while several countries in Central America and the Caribbean, as well as Colombia and Paraguay, recorded declines in per caput production. In Latin America and the Caribbean, as in other regions, output shortfalls in many cases reflected the early effects of the El Niño phenomenon.

• In the developed countries, growth in overall agricultural output slowed to a mere 0.5 percent in 1997, following an estimated expansion of more than 3 percent in 1996. The most pronounced turnaround was in the European Union (EU), where production contracted by nearly 2 percent after having expanded by 4 to 5 percent the previous year. The contraction affected most EU member countries and concerned both crop and livestock production. Cereal production was slightly down from the record harvest of 1996, as delays caused by rains affected wheat yields in several countries.

- In North America, agricultural output in 1997 continued expanding at an estimated rate of 2.6 percent. While output contracted slightly in Canada for the first time since 1992, the United States recorded an expansion of 3 percent.

- Following record output levels in 1996, agricultural production in Australia declined by about 1 percent in 1997, while New Zealand's overall agricultural output continued to expand, posting an increase of 2 to 3 percent. In Japan, agricultural output in 1997 practically remained at the level of 1996, which followed two years of decline. Overall production levels are thus still about 7 percent below those prevailing a decade ago.

- Contrasting with the overall negative performances of the other regions, 1997 marked a positive turnaround for the transition countries. It was the first year since the beginning of the transition process in which overall agricultural production expanded, albeit by a relatively modest 1 percent. Cereal production expanded significantly while livestock production continued its downward trend. Production increased significantly in Ukraine and somewhat less in the Russian Federation and Kazakhstan. In the Central and Eastern European transition countries production patterns were uneven among countries, with Poland in particular experiencing a largely weather-induced decline and Romania a major expansion in cereal production.

In the transition countries, 1997 was the first year since the beginning of the transition process in which overall agricultural production expanded, albeit by a relatively modest 1 percent.

2. FOOD SHORTAGES AND EMERGENCIES

- The number of countries facing food emergencies rose from 29 in mid-1997 to 36 in mid-1998, mainly owing to the effects of the El Niño weather phenomenon.

- In East Africa, food supply difficulties stem from recent droughts followed by floods in most countries, coupled with civil strife in some. In Somalia, the food supply situation will remain extremely tight until the next harvest starting in August 1998, after the worst floods in decades sharply reduced the 1997/98 secondary "Dyer" crops. The floods also resulted in the loss of livestock and an outbreak of animal diseases. In eastern Kenya, food assistance continues to be distributed to the population affected by severe floods. In Uganda, emergency food assistance is still required for some 400 000 displaced people in the northern areas affected by continuing insurgency. In the United Republic of Tanzania, food difficulties are being experienced in areas where the 1997/98 secondary "Vuli" crop was reduced by heavy rains and floods. In Ethiopia, food aid is needed by more than 5 million vulnerable people, including those affected by a poor 1997 harvest. In Eritrea, following two successive reduced cereal harvests, the overall food supply in 1998 is tight and food prices have increased sharply in the past months. In the Sudan, despite an overall satisfactory harvest, the food situation is critical and assistance is required for some 2.4 million people affected by civil strife and drought. However, distribution is hampered by insecurity and poor road conditions. In Burundi, the food situation has deteriorated as a result of a decline in the 1998 first-season foodcrop production and the continuing economic embargo by neighbouring countries. The food supply situation is also tight in Rwanda owing to a reduced 1998 first-season harvest and insecurity in western parts of the country.

- In West Africa, despite above-average 1997 harvests in coastal countries, food supply difficulties are reported in several countries. In Liberia and Sierra Leone, rehabilitation programmes are under way and the agricultural sector is improving, but both countries remain heavily dependent on international food assistance. In Sierra Leone, the poor security situation in the east is causing large population displacements and is disrupting all agricultural activities. In the Sahel, several areas are facing localized food supply difficulties following poor harvests in

late 1997, notably in northern Senegal, Mauritania, the
Gambia and parts of Burkina Faso and the Niger.

- In central Africa, as a result of flooding, shortages of
inputs and civil unrest, crop prospects are poor in eastern
parts of the Democratic Republic of the Congo.

- In southern Africa, although the impact of El Niño on
crop production has been relatively limited, the food supply
situation in the subregion is anticipated to be tighter during
the 1998/99 marketing year than in the previous year. In
Zambia, cereal production is expected to be much below
average as a result of incessant rainfall and extensive
flooding in the northern areas, while the southern part of
the country experienced near drought conditions. In
Angola and Mozambique, production of food crops is
expected to improve this year, but relief assistance will be
required for the internally displaced, vulnerable people and
drought- or flood-affected population.

- In Asia, grave food supply difficulties persist in the
Democratic People's Republic of Korea, with continued
need for food aid. Severe drought in Indonesia, attributed
to El Niño, combined with the financial crisis, has seriously
undermined the food security of the population, resulting
in the need for considerable international assistance. In
Afghanistan, the overall food supply in 1998 is anticipated
to be tight as a result of ongoing hostilities and the recent
earthquake damage to the irrigation infrastructure in the
northern provinces. In Iraq, despite some improvement in
the overall food supply situation following the
implementation of the "oil for food" deal, malnutrition still
remains a serious problem throughout the country. In the
Lao People's Democratic Republic, adverse weather
conditions have caused crop damage in major rice-
producing areas, exacerbating food supply problems in the
country. In Mongolia, declining agricultural production and
problems of economic transition continue to have an
adverse effect on the food supply situation of vulnerable
groups. Serious food supply difficulties persist in Papua New
Guinea following reduced foodcrop production as a result
of El Niño-related drought.

- In Latin America, abnormally dry weather associated with
El Niño has delayed planting of the 1998/99 first-season

*In Asia, a combination of
adverse weather conditions,
the financial crisis,
earthquakes and hostilities
caused food emergencies in
several countries.*

Map 3

COUNTRIES EXPERIENCING FOOD SUPPLY SHORTFALLS
AND REQUIRING EXCEPTIONAL ASSISTANCE*

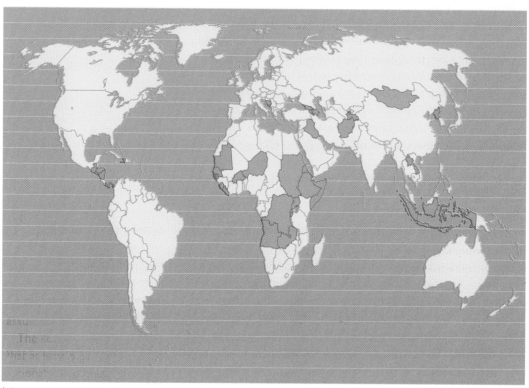

* *In current marketing year*

Source: FAO, Global Information
and Early Warning System,
June 1998

cereal crop in Central American countries. Food assistance
is being provided in Nicaragua, Honduras, El Salvador,
Guatemala and Panama and will be needed until the harvest
of the 1998 first-season crops. In the Caribbean, food
assistance distributions continue in Haiti.

• In the Commonwealth of Independent States (CIS),
some 16 percent of the population of Tajikistan is in need of
targeted food aid, following widespread damage caused by
floods and landslides. Vulnerable people in Armenia (about
13 percent of the resident population), Azerbaijan (11
percent) and Georgia (7 percent) continue to need relief
food assistance. In Eastern Europe, needy people in Bosnia-
Herzegovina are receiving food assistance.

3. WORLD CEREAL SUPPLY SITUATION AND OUTLOOK[5]

● World cereal production in 1997 reached a record
1 909 million tonnes (including rice in milled terms),
even though it increased only by a modest 1 percent,
or 17 million tonnes, from 1996. Global wheat output rose
to an all-time record of 615 million tonnes, 4 percent, or 25
million tonnes, higher than the good crop of 1996. Wheat
output increased in nearly all regions with the exception of
North Africa where severe drought reduced production in
several countries. By contrast, world coarse grain
production in 1997 fell by about 1 percent, or 8 million
tonnes, to 911 million tonnes, although it was still above the
trend. The decline in coarse grain production was mainly
on account of reduced maize crops in China, North
America and Africa, while much larger crops were
harvested in South America, Europe and the CIS. World
paddy production in 1997 remained at 571 million tonnes,
unchanged from the previous year's above-average level.
Slightly higher rice production in Australia, China, Egypt,
Pakistan, Nigeria and the United States almost entirely
offset reduced output in Brazil, the Democratic Republic of
Korea, Indonesia and Myanmar.

Global wheat output rose in 1997 to an all-time record of 615 million tonnes.

● Global cereal stocks for crop years ending in 1998 are
forecast to rise to 321 million tonnes, up by 8 percent, or
25 million tonnes, from their opening volume. Most of this
replenishment would be on account of larger wheat and
coarse grain inventories, reflecting good crops and slower
growth in feed utilization, despite weaker grain prices
during the season. By contrast, global rice stocks are
forecast to decline, especially in Indonesia, the Philippines
and Brazil where the 1997 outputs were adversely affected
by El Niño. Total cereal carryovers held by major exporters
would rise for the second consecutive year, approaching
39 percent of world total, compared with 34 percent at the
beginning of the season and only 28 percent in 1996.
However, cereal stocks held by other countries, particularly
the developing countries, are likely to remain unchanged
from the previous year. Globally, the ratio of end-of-season
stocks to expected utilization in 1998/99 would approach
16.9 percent, up by more than one percentage point from
the previous season and close to the 17 to 18 percent range
that FAO considers the minimum necessary to safeguard
world food security.

• The prospects for the 1998/99 marketing season point to further improvement in the global supply situation. Based on the condition of crops as of May 1998, and assuming normal weather for the remainder of the 1998 crop seasons, world cereal production in 1998 is tentatively forecast to reach 1 911 million tonnes, slightly higher than in 1997 and a new record. All of the anticipated increase in global cereal production would be on account of increased coarse grain production which, at 925 million tonnes, would be 1.6 percent higher than in 1997 and above the trend for the third consecutive year. However, wheat output is forecast to decline somewhat to 606 million tonnes, while global paddy output is also forecast to contract slightly to 567 million tonnes, following the bumper crops of the previous two years.

If current forecasts become a reality, cereal supplies will be sufficient to meet expected demand in 1998/99 and allow for further replenishment of global cereal reserves.

• If current forecasts become a reality, cereal supplies will be sufficient to meet expected demand in 1998/99 and allow for further replenishment of global cereal reserves. Early indications suggest that cereal carryovers for the crop years ending in 1999 could rise for the third consecutive year and reach 328 million tonnes, 2 percent, or 6 million tonnes, more than their estimated opening levels. Thus, for the first time in four years, the global stock-to-utilization ratio could return to within the 17 to 18 percent range. However, the likelihood of this forecast becoming a reality would hinge not only on the final outcome of 1998 production but also on the eventual size of cereal utilization during the 1998/99 season.

The forecast increase in cereal food intake in the developing countries would exceed their population growth by a small margin and result in their per caput food consumption rising.

• World utilization of cereals in 1998/99 is currently forecast to grow by about 1 percent to 1 904 million tonnes, which would be slightly above the long-term trend. Most of this increase is expected to be in the developing countries, particularly as increased food consumption is likely in those countries where most of the increase in production is expected. This increase in cereal food intake in the developing countries would exceed their population growth by a small margin and, hence, result in their per caput food consumption rising slightly. By contrast, the increase in global feed use of cereals is expected to be less pronounced despite the expected continuation of a period of weak grain prices. Most of the anticipated expansion in cereal stocks would be in the developed countries, especially in the major grain exporting countries, where the prospects of good crops and slower growth in feed use could result in a further replenishment of cereal inventories.

Figure 4A

SUPPLY / UTILIZATION TRENDS IN CEREALS

(Including rice on milled basis)

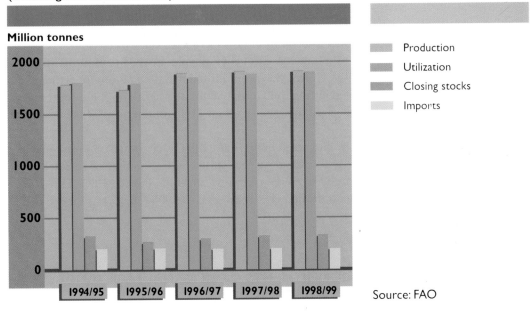

Million tonnes

Production
Utilization
Closing stocks
Imports

| | 1994/95 | 1995/96 | 1996/97 | 1997/98 | 1998/99 |

Source: FAO

Figure 4B

CEREAL CARRYOVER STOCKS*

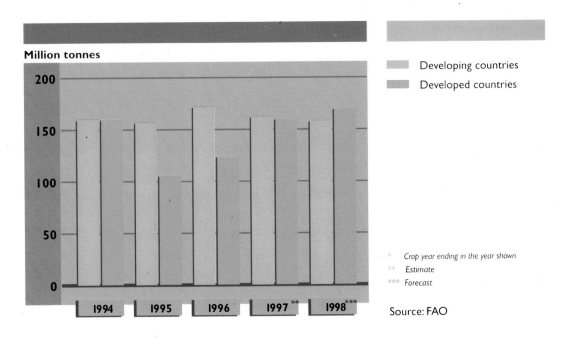

Million tonnes

Developing countries
Developed countries

* Crop year ending in the year shown
** Estimate
*** Forecast

| | 1994 | 1995 | 1996 | 1997 ** | 1998 *** |

Source: FAO

23

4. EXTERNAL ASSISTANCE TO AGRICULTURE

• Total commitments to agriculture (broadly defined)[6] made by bilateral and multilateral donors as official development assistance (ODA) in 1996 were estimated to be $10 985 million in current prices – $297 million less than the amount recorded in 1995. The figures, however, are not immediately comparable, as the estimate for 1996 does not include commitments in 1996 by the United States, for which data are not yet available. In 1995 commitments from the United States amounted to $400 million; therefore, excluding the United States, the figure for 1996 represents a slight increase of about $100 million over 1995.

• Measured in constant 1990 prices, total commitments in 1996 (excluding the United States) amounted to $10 363 million, compared with $10 446 million in 1995. Thus, commitments in real terms in 1996 remained at more or

Multilateral assistance was estimated to have declined slightly between 1995 and 1996.

Figure 5

COMMITMENTS OF EXTERNAL ASSISTANCE TO AGRICULTURE*

(At constant 1990 prices)

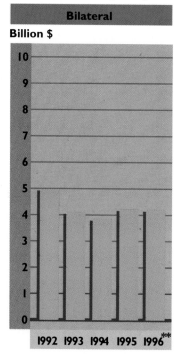

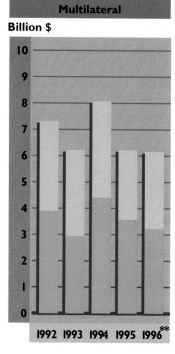

Concessional
Non-concessional

*   Broad definition
** Provisional

Source: FAO and OECD

less the same level as in 1995, and may even be slightly up when data for the United States are included. However, this can hardly be said to represent a turnaround in the declining trend in external assistance for agriculture during the 1990s, which brought total commitments measured in constant 1990 prices from a level of $12.2 billion in 1991 to $10.4 billion in 1995.

- The share of concessional assistance in total commitments has been oscillating around 70 percent throughout the 1990s, and stood at 72 percent of the total in 1996, with the share of grants at 47 percent. Most of the bilateral assistance (indeed more than 95 percent) is in grant form, while for multilateral assistance the share of grants is only 20 percent.

- In terms of bilateral commitments to agriculture, Japan remains the major donor and alone accounted for about half of the bilateral commitments of the Development Assistance Committee (DAC) countries in 1996. Among other DAC members, significantly increased contributions were made by Australia, Canada and Denmark. Australia, committed $300 million (in current prices) for the development of fisheries policies in developing countries.

- Multilateral assistance was estimated to have declined slightly (from $10 446 million in 1995 to $10 363 million in 1996). Among the multilateral donors, commitments in 1996 from the World Bank were down some $1.2 billion (27 percent in constant 1990 prices). The International Fund for Agricultural Development (IFAD) expanded its commitments from $276 million in 1995 to $405 million in 1996 (an increase of 50 percent in real terms), bringing its levels back to approximately those of 1994, following the sharp reduction of 1995. The regional development banks' commitments also increased by $869 million to $1 987 million, almost the same level in real terms as in 1994 after a sharp decline in 1995 similar to that recorded by IFAD.

- Provisional data for commitments by the World Bank group in 1997 indicate that contributions from the International Bank for Reconstruction and Development (IBRD) should be higher than in 1996 by about $1 billion, while those of the International Development Association (IDA) would remain at the same level.

Figure 6

COMMITMENTS BY MAIN PURPOSE

(At constant 1990 prices)

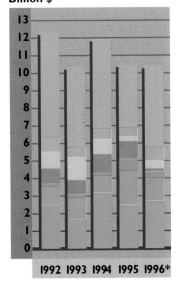

Billion $

1992 1993 1994 1995 1996*

- Research, training, extension
- Crop production
- Regional and river development
- Environment
- Rural development
- Land and water
- Others

* Provisional

Source: FAO and OECD

Figure 7

COMMITMENTS BY MAIN RECIPIENT REGIONS

(At constant 1990 prices)

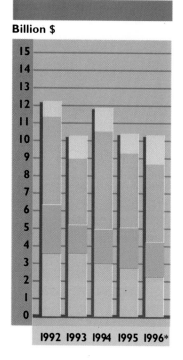

Billion $

1992 1993 1994 1995 1996*

Asia

Latin America and the Caribbean

Africa

Others**

* Provisional
** Including developed countries

Source: FAO and OECD

• In terms of the sectoral destination of assistance channelled to agriculture (narrowly defined),[7] commitments increased by 24 percent to $8 121 million in 1990 prices, but remained well below the peak level of 1992. The increase affected agriculture, fisheries, forestry and land and water development, the largest percentage increase being in the fisheries sector. Among the broadly defined subsectors, commitments increased only towards agro-industries, while contractions were recorded for environmental protection, rural development and, most sharply, regional and river development.

• With regard to the geographical distribution of flows, the share of the transition countries continued to increase and reached almost 7 percent in 1996, compared with 5 percent in 1995. Among the developing countries, no major changes in the shares were recorded with only a minor increase in that of Asia and a small decline for Latin America and the Caribbean. The share of Asia is still the largest, slightly above 40 percent, followed by Africa at 23 to 24 percent, and Latin America and the Caribbean at just below 20 percent. The share of nationally unallocated assistance, not destined to a specific country, had been increasing and reached 16 percent in 1996.

5. FOOD AID FLOWS[8]

- Total cereal food aid shipments under programme, project and emergency food aid in 1997/98 (July/June) are estimated to have reached at least 5.5 million tonnes. This represents an increase of some 3 percent from 1996/97, mainly on account of slightly larger shipments to low-income food-deficit countries (LIFDCs) resulting from more food emergencies, compared with the previous year, and additional food aid provisions in response to the Asian financial crisis. Cereal food aid shipments to LIFDCs in 1997/98 are estimated to have risen by 3 percent from 1996/97 to about 4.6 million tonnes. Food aid shipments of wheat in 1997/98 are estimated to reach 3.5 million tonnes, coarse grains to increase to 1.3 million tonnes and rice shipments to reach almost 700 000 tonnes, all three cereals together increasing by 3 percent over 1996/97.

Total cereal food aid shipments in 1997/98 are estimated to have increased by about 3 percent from the previous year.

- Estimates of shipments of non-cereal food aid, i.e. largely pulses and vegetable oils, show a further decline of about

Figure 8

RECIPIENTS OF SHIPMENTS OF FOOD AID IN CEREALS

(In grain equivalent)

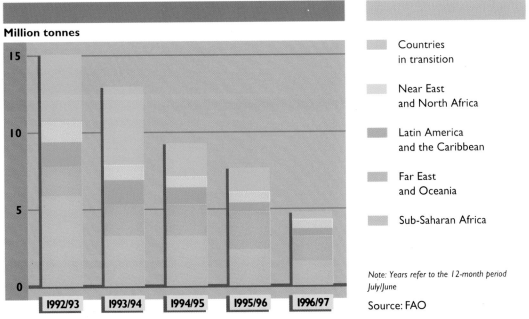

Million tonnes

Legend:
- Countries in transition
- Near East and North Africa
- Latin America and the Caribbean
- Far East and Oceania
- Sub-Saharan Africa

Note: Years refer to the 12-month period July/June

Source: FAO

30 percent in 1997 (January-December) to about 646 000 tonnes, compared with an estimate for 1996 of 948 000 tonnes.[9] This reduction affects most regions and also the LIFDCs. While the decline in 1997 is mostly reflected in reduced shipments of the two largest non-cereal food aid categories mentioned above, shipments of all other food products are also estimated to be down from the previous year.

- As of December 1997, contributions of cereals to the International Emergency Food Reserve (IEFR), administered by the World Food Programme (WFP), expanded by almost 12 percent in 1997 (January-December) to 993 000 tonnes, from 887 000 tonnes in 1996. These contributions are substantially above the minimum annual target of 500 000 tonnes set by the World Food Conference in 1974. For non-cereals, the contributions fell from 225 000 tonnes in 1996 to 167 000 tonnes in 1997. Furthermore, cereal contributions to the Protracted Refugee Operations (PROs), also administered by WFP, at 529 000 tonnes, were marginally higher in 1997 than in 1996. The PROs' contribution for non-cereals fell by about 20 000 tonnes to 70 000 tonnes in 1997.

6. INTERNATIONAL AGRICULTURAL PRICES[10]

● Bumper grain crops in the 1997/98 season and the
continuing increase in stocks kept grain prices significantly
below the previous year's levels for most of the 1997/98
season. In the absence of any major fundamental change in
international wheat markets and given the favourable crop
prospects and the seasonal harvest pressure, wheat prices
continued to decline during the second half of the 1997/98
season and by late May 1998 they were some 20 to 25
percent below the corresponding period the previous year.
Maize, barley and sorghum prices have also dropped
further, falling by the end of May by some 10 to 15 percent
from the corresponding period in 1997. The decline in
coarse grain prices is partly explained by larger supplies and
weaker import demand, especially from Asia, while
favourable crop prospects in all regions, with the exception
of southern Africa, have put even more downward pressure
on prices since April 1998. Looking ahead to the 1998/99
marketing season, and given the good crop prospects and a
likely decline in import demand especially for wheat, prices
for nearly all types of grains are expected to remain under
pressure at least through the first half of the next season.
Price development during the second half of the 1998/99
season will depend, as usual, on plantings and prospects for
the 1999 crops, while the economic situation in Asia may
also continue to affect international grain prices until the
end of the season.

● In contrast to recent
developments in grain markets,
international rice prices from
most origins continued on an
upward trend during the
months up to May 1998. As a
result, the FAO export price
index for rice (1982-84),
which has been rising since
December 1997, averaged 128
points in May, up from 125
points in March. The increase
in prices is attributable partly to
the strengthening of the Thai
baht against the US dollar and partly
to concerns about the availability of
exportable supplies, especially in Viet Nam

and Pakistan, following large purchases by Indonesia and the Philippines.

- The decline in international prices of oils since the 1994/95 season came to an end during 1997/98. The FAO price index of edible and soap fats and oils rose by about 14 percent compared with the 1996/97 season, from 135 to 154 (1990-92 = 100). The monthly average increase in the weighted prices of all types of oils and fats between August 1997 and May 1998 was about 2.5 percent, reflecting the tight market conditions for the commodities concerned, but especially for soft oils, for which the price increase was even steeper.

- At the same time, the rise in international prices of oilmeals since the 1994/95 season also terminated during 1997/98, and the FAO price index of oilcakes and oilmeals fell by about 7 percent in 1997/98 compared with the previous season, triggered by abundant supplies of the commodities concerned entering the market.

Oilseed production appears to have maintained its economic viability over other agricultural products.

- The divergent movement of prices, i.e. the increase in international prices of oils and the decrease in international prices of meals, coupled with other changes in market fundamentals, resulted in a 2.5 percent decline in international prices of oilseeds, as reflected by the FAO price index of oilseeds, over the same period. Despite this, oilseeds appear to have maintained their economic viability in production over other agricultural products and early indications are that global oilseed production will expand again in 1998/99. As a result, the downward pressure on the prices of oilseeds, oilcakes and oilmeals could continue well into the next season, while the upsurge in the prices of oils and fats could level off.

- World cocoa prices steadily increased during 1997, with an International Cocoa Organization (ICCO) average monthly price reaching 78 US cents per pound in December 1997, 11 US cents higher than in December 1996. In January 1997, the average monthly ICCO price was 65 US cents per pound. This corresponded with the end of a cycle of downward price movements from 1996 as large shipments from Côte d'Ivoire kept pressure on prices despite general expectations of a global deficit in supply. In March 1997, an upward trend in prices began as concerns over a continuing structural deficit in the global cocoa market resurfaced and weather-related concerns over crops in Indonesia emerged. In September 1997, the average ICCO price peaked at a ten-year high of 80 US cents per pound, and this was also underpinned by increased purchases by market speculators and grinders as a reaction to the El Niño phenomenon. In the last quarter of 1997, when an analysis of the El Niño impact became available and market concerns dissipated, prices began to stabilize. In December 1997, the average monthly ICCO price closed the year at 78 US cents. In the first quarter of 1998, prices fluctuated within the 75 to 80 US cents per pound range. The average 1997 ICCO monthly price was 73 US cents per pound, compared with the ICCO 1996 average of 66 US cents, representing an annual average increase of 8 US cents per pound, or 12 percent.

• World coffee prices rose dramatically during 1997, with the International Coffee Agreement (ICA) composite price increasing from 100 US cents per pound in January 1997 to 130 US cents per pound by December 1997, an increase of 30 percent. The peak of the market was reached in May 1997 when the ICA composite price reached 180 US cents per pound, its highest level since 1986. Unlike previous dramatic price increases in 1986 and 1995, which were caused by frosts in Brazil, the price increase of 1997 was driven by strong demand and tightness of supply of arabica coffee, particularly Colombian and other milds. Reflecting this tightness, the price of arabica coffee beans rose by over 100 percent between January 1997 and May 1997, compared with only 39 percent for robusta. As a result, the price differential between the arabica and robusta varieties increased by more than three times during this period. From its May 1997 peak, the composite price began to fall as production and exports were able to satisfy consumption needs. By December 1997, the price had fallen to 130 US cents per pound and remained near this level in the first quarter of 1998. It has since begun to fall again as crop prospects for the 1998 season appear favourable, particularly in Brazil where a very large crop is anticipated.

The peak of the market for coffee was reached in May 1997 when the ICA composite price reached 180 US cents per pound, its highest level since 1986.

• World cotton prices, as indicated by Cotlook A-Index, have trended downwards since July 1997, from 81.3 US cents per pound in July 1997 to 63.9 US cents per pound in

The Asian financial crisis and reduced imports from several major importing countries such as China have weakened the cotton market.

May 1998 (average for the first three weeks). The weaker market has been largely due to the Asian financial crisis and the reduction in imports from several major importing countries such as China. World production in 1997/98 (the marketing year begins on 1 August) is expected to be at the same level as that in 1996/97. Consumption, however, is expected to be lower than last year largely owing to a significant decline in consumption in several Southeast Asian countries. Thus, by the end of 1997/98, world stocks are expected to be slightly higher than at the same time the previous year. World trade is expected to contract by about 6 percent in 1997/98. Imports by China, Southeast Asia and the Republic of Korea are expected to decrease by 45, 20 and 21 percent, respectively, from their 1996/97 levels. Consequently, most exporting countries could expect to see their exports slightly lower than in 1996/97. Cotton prices are likely to continue to be under downward pressure in the

Figure 9

EXPORT PRICE INDEX FOR FOODSTUFFS

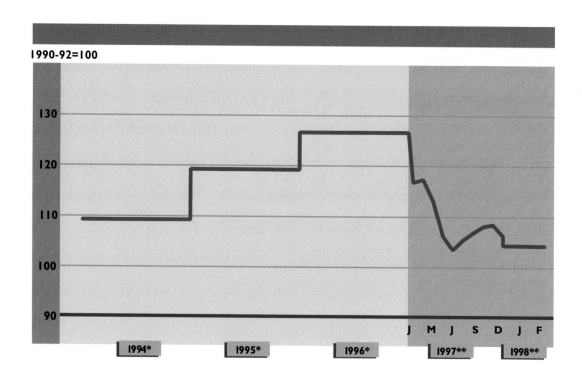

1990-92=100

*   *Annual average of prices*
**   *Monthly data*
Source: FAO

near future because of the ongoing competition from synthetic fibres and weaker import demand owing to the financial crisis in Southeast Asia.

- World sugar prices were relatively stable in 1997. The 1997 International Sugar Agreement (ISA) average price was 11.37 US cents per pound, compared with the 1996 ISA average price of 11.96 US cents per pound. The ISA price rose marginally throughout 1997 to reach 12.33 US cents per pound in the last quarter. The revised FAO estimate of world sugar production for 1997/98 is 123.6 million tonnes raw value, representing a marginal increase of about 100 000 tonnes over the previous year's output. The share of cane sugar remained substantially unchanged at about 70 percent of the total, or 85.6 million tonnes, compared with an output of 38 million tonnes of sugar from beet. World sugar consumption in 1998 is forecast by FAO to reach 123.1 million tonnes raw value, an increase of 1.6 percent compared with 1997. This represents a decline from the average growth rate in recent years of 2.5 percent, mainly owing to the economic downturn in Asia. World sugar trade is expected to decline by nearly 3 percent in 1997/98 with gross import demand amounting to 33.5 million tonnes compared with 34.5 million tonnes the previous year. World sugar stocks are expected to remain ample at more than 45 million tonnes, or 36 percent of consumption. In the first quarter of 1998, world sugar prices again began to decline, weakening to 9.77 US cents per pound in April 1998. This was attributed in part to lower global import requirements, in particular from Southeast Asia owing to the financial turmoil, from the Russian Federation owing to stock carryover in 1997, from China owing to increased internal production, and from India owing to increased internal production and the drawdown of stocks. Considering that sugar from the new crop in the Southern Hemisphere will soon be on the market, a substantial recovery in prices is not likely to take place in the short term.

World sugar trade is expected to decline by nearly 3 percent in 1997/98.

- World market prices of tea continued their upward trend in 1997, averaging $2 215 per tonne on the London market, 25 percent higher than in 1996, mainly owing to a further improvement in demand in the Russian Federation and CIS countries, and drought-reduced output in Kenya. Prices continued to be strong at the beginning of 1998, reaching

World market prices of tea continued their upward trend in 1997, averaging 25 percent more than in 1996.

Figure 10

EXPORT PRICES OF SELECTED COMMODITES, 1994-1998

($ per tonne)

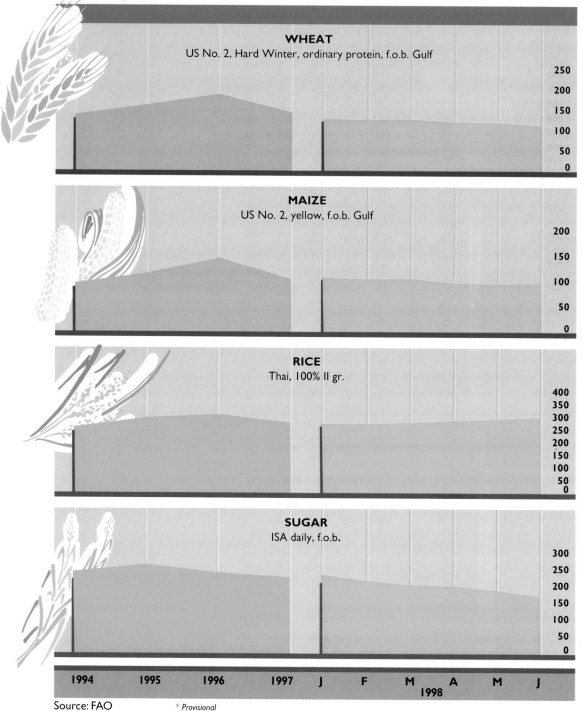

WHEAT
US No. 2, Hard Winter, ordinary protein, f.o.b. Gulf

MAIZE
US No. 2, yellow, f.o.b. Gulf

RICE
Thai, 100% II gr.

SUGAR
ISA daily, f.o.b.

1994 1995 1996 1997 J F M A M J
1998

Source: FAO   * Provisional

($ per tonne)

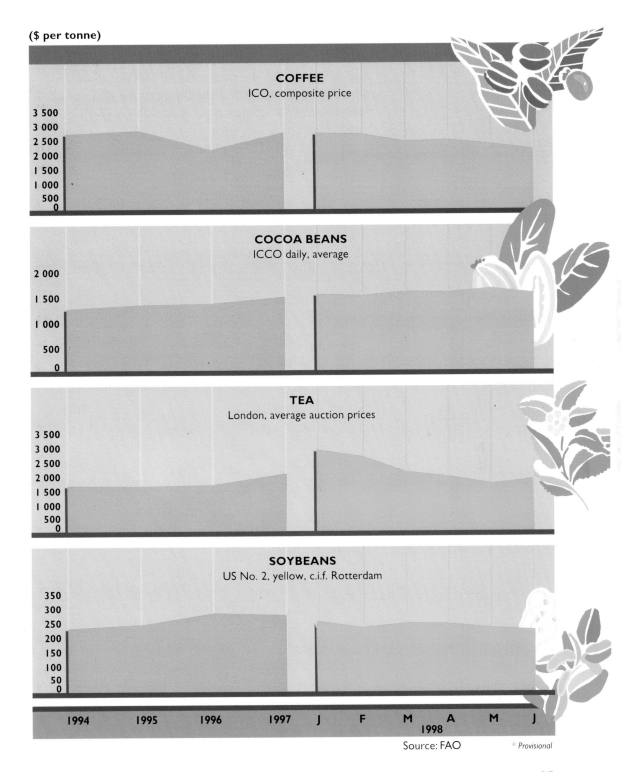

COFFEE
ICO, composite price

3 500
3 000
2 500
2 000
1 500
1 000
500
0

COCOA BEANS
ICCO daily, average

2 000
1 500
1 000
500
0

TEA
London, average auction prices

3 500
3 000
2 500
2 000
1 500
1 000
500
0

SOYBEANS
US No. 2, yellow, c.i.f. Rotterdam

350
300
250
200
150
100
50
0

1994   1995   1996   1997   J   F   M   A   M   J
1998

Source: FAO   * Provisional

35

$3 118 per tonne in January. After initial 1998 reports
indicated that production in major exporting countries
such as Sri Lanka, Kenya and India was significantly above
the previous year's level, tea prices declined rapidly to
$2 049 and $1 760 per tonne in April and May 1998,
respectively, and rose slightly in June. There is a strong
indication that for the remainder of 1998 the downward
pressure on prices might continue given the slow growth in
demand and the strong supply available in exporting
countries.

7. FISHERIES: PRODUCTION, DISPOSITION AND TRADE

• Production of fish, shellfish and other aquatic animals reached a record level of 121 million tonnes in 1996, an increase of 3.2 percent over 1995. Capture fisheries, at 94.6 million tonnes, increased by 1.7 percent and contributed 78 percent of the total volume. The remaining 22 percent was contributed by aquaculture production, which at 26.4 million tonnes recorded an increase of 8.2 percent over 1995. In addition, 9 million tonnes of aquatic plants (wet weight) were harvested, nearly 90 percent of which came from aquaculture production.

• Inland capture fisheries increased globally by 2.3 percent to 7.6 million tonnes; the increase occurred entirely in Asia while decreases were recorded in Africa, South America and Europe.

• Global catches from marine waters increased by 1.7 percent in volume for an estimated value of some $80 billion. This was as a result of higher landings from the Northwest Pacific – which accounts for nearly 30 percent of total marine capture fisheries – and, to a lesser extent, from the Eastern Central Atlantic and the Indian Ocean. These increases more than compensated for the lower landings reported for fisheries from some other marine areas, such as the Mediterranean and the Black Sea (where landings declined by 11 percent), the Western Central Pacific (a decline of 2 percent) and the Northeast Pacific (a decline of 5 percent). Small pelagic species, which represent 40 percent of the volume of specified captures, increased by nearly 3 percent to 39 million tonnes. Demersal fish, at 18 million tonnes, remained at the same level as in 1995, while salmons and tunas decreased by 10 percent and 2 percent, respectively. Increases relative to

Figure 11

WORLD FISH CATCH AND SUPPLY

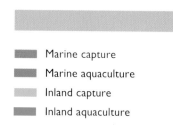

Marine capture
Marine aquaculture
Inland capture
Inland aquaculture

Source: FAO

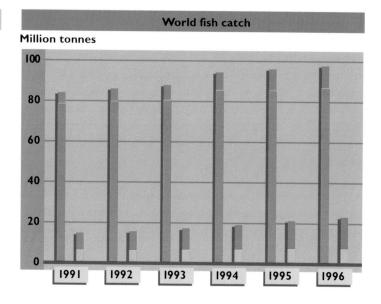

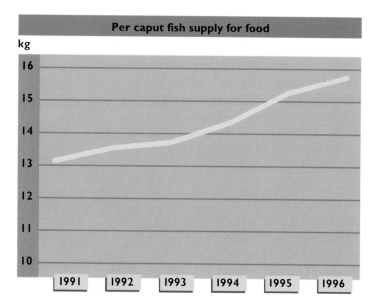

1996 were also recorded for captures of shrimps and prawns (8 percent), crabs (4 percent) and cephalopods (6 percent), while production of molluscs decreased by 13 percent.

Figure 12

TRADE IN FISHERY PRODUCTS

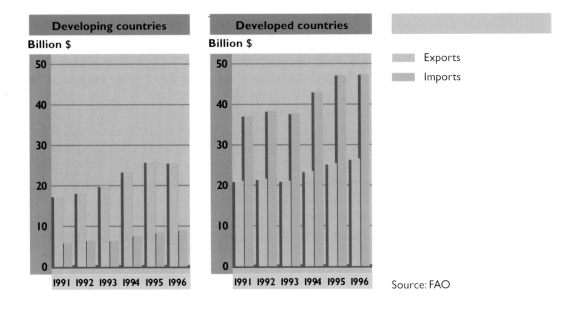

Source: FAO

• Output from aquaculture continued to expand at a faster rate than from any other food production sector. Between 1986 and 1996, global aquaculture production increased at an average annual rate of 10 percent in terms of both quantity and value, and in 1996 the value of total world output from the sector reached $46.6 billion (aquatic plants included). Asia, and in particular China, continues to dominate world production, and in 1996 Asia accounted for 91 and 83.5 percent of production in terms of volume and value, respectively. In contrast, Africa accounted for only 0.3 percent of volume and 0.6 percent of value, although since 1990 output in this continent has been increasing at an average annual rate of 5.4 percent.

Output from aquaculture continued to expand at a faster rate than from any other food production sector.

• Total fisheries exports amounted to $52.5 billion in 1996, virtually the same level as in 1995. Trade volumes increased, but as prices were lower for the most important fisheries commodities, the change in global value was insignificant. In value terms, just below half of total exports in 1996 originated from developing countries, compared with a share of 51 percent in 1995. Within this amount 36 percent was attributable to LIFDCs, compared with 39 percent the previous year. For many developing nations fisheries exports constitute a significant source of foreign currency earnings, with total net developing country receipts from fishery trade representing $16.6 billion in 1996, more than three times the total for 1986

- Twenty-two countries account for 75 percent of exports of fish and fisheries products in value, and the first 11 countries account for as much as 51 percent of the total. With export earnings of $4.1 billion in 1996 (9 percent of the world total), Thailand maintained its position, which it has held since 1993, as the leading world fisheries exporter, in spite of a 7.5 percent decrease compared with 1995. The second largest exporter, Norway, with total exports of $3.4 billion, increased its export value by 10 percent over 1995, while the third largest exporter, the United States, saw its exports decline by 7 percent to $3.1 billion. However, the United States is also the second largest importer of seafood products, with imports exceeding exports by $4 billion. Exports from mainland China amounted to $2.9 billion, showing no change compared with 1995, and those from Taiwan Province of China to $1.8 billion, preceded by

Export-oriented aquaculture activities on the Tonle Sap River in Cambodia

Aquaculture is the fastest-growing food production sector.

P. GIGLI/FAO/15685

Denmark and Canada showing exports of $2.7 and
$2.3 billion, respectively.

- The destination of most of the fisheries exports is the
developed economies. Industrialized countries accounted
for more than 80 percent of the value of imports, and Japan
alone (with $17 billion of imports) for nearly 30 percent of
the world total. The United States was the second largest
importer, with imports of $7 billion, followed by France and
Spain with just over $3 billion each. In 1996, however, all the
three largest importers recorded declining imports relative
to 1995. Developing country imports grew by 7.5 percent to
more than $9 billion, corresponding to 16 percent of the
world total, one-fourth of which was imported by the
LIFDCs. Some of these imports, however, were composed of
fishmeal for poultry, and aquaculture feed for the
production of high-value species for export.

*Industrialized countries
accounted for more than
80 percent of the value of
fisheries imports, and Japan
alone for nearly 30 percent
of the world total.*

- The major part of world fish and shellfish production
(75 percent in 1996) is destined for direct human
consumption and reaches consumers in a variety of end
uses, mainly as fresh or chilled products. In recent years, in
parallel with the upsurge of world aquaculture production,
the importance of fishery products marketed fresh has
increased in both absolute and relative terms. Indeed, in
1996 one-third of global production was marketed as
fresh/chilled with volumes nearly 70 percent higher than
ten years earlier. As a result of increased fishery production
and unchanged levels of its reduction to meal, world fish
availability for food increased from 15.2 kg per caput in
1995 to 15.7 kg in 1996.

- Early estimates for 1997 point to a lower level of fish
production, mainly owing to lower catches of small pelagic
species in South America as a consequence of the El Niño
phenomenon. Since such species are largely used in the
feed industry, it is likely that the availability of fish for food
has remained unaffected.

8. PRODUCTION AND TRADE OF FOREST PRODUCTS

In 1997, there was a general increase in output for all forest products.

- In 1997, world roundwood production increased by 1.6 percent to reach 3 410 million m³. In the developing countries, which account for about two-thirds of the total (64 percent in 1997), roundwood production increased by 2.3 percent, while in the developed countries output growth was limited to a modest 0.5 percent. Industrial roundwood production (which excludes fuelwood and accounts for 45 percent of the total) in its turn increased by 1.9 percent to 1 520 million m³. The developed countries are responsible for the larger share of industrial roundwood (70 percent) and expanded production by 2.2 percent to 1 060 million m³, with developing country production increasing by a more limited 1.5 percent to 460 million m³.

- Global production of solid wood products (sawnwood and sleepers and wood-based panels) showed an increase in 1997, with production of sawnwood and sleepers estimated to have increased by 2.3 percent to 439 million m³, and that of wood-based panels by 2-3 percent to 153 million m³. The bulk of this expansion again occurred in the developed countries, which account for more than two-thirds of the total output of these products.

- There was also a significant growth in world output of pulp and paper products in 1997, following the small decline experienced by the sector in 1996. Production of paper and paperboard increased by 6.3 percent. The strongest growth was recorded in the developed countries, at 6.8 percent, particularly in Western Europe where paper production went up by 8.5 percent, followed by the United States with an expansion of 5.2 percent, Japan with 3.3 percent and Canada with 3 percent. These producers account for some 75 percent of world paper production. The situation was less favourable in the developing countries, where the past strong growth of some major Asian producers slowed down considerably. As with paper products, production of wood pulp also grew considerably, at a rate of 5.7 percent, with international prices slowly recovering after the sharp fall experienced in 1996. Wood pulp inventories decreased from the 1996 high of 2.5 million tonnes to 1.6 million tonnes, which is considered to be closer to a balanced market. Because of the Asian financial crisis, analysts have predicted a decline in 1998 in Asian consumption, which is likely to depress world demand for pulp and paper products and lead to reduced prices.

A predicted decline in Asian 1998 consumption is likely to depress world demand for pulp and paper products and lead to reduced prices.

• Markets for other forest products were particularly favourable in Europe, where demand strengthened and consumption of nearly all forest products rose. However, because of highly competitive markets, European prices of wood products showed no increase in 1997. In North America, demand was favourable for most of 1997. In Canada, housing starts, the main economic indicator for the mechanical wood industry, increased by some 20 percent. In the United States, however, because of strongly reduced log prices caused by the diminished demand in Asian markets, domestic prices of sawnwood fell sharply in the second part of the year. Japan experienced a serious decline in starts of wooden houses in 1997, down by some 20 percent, reflecting the poor performance of its economy. This resulted in a marked reduction in its imports of processed wood products, both tropical and temperate, which had grown steadily in previous years.

• Prices for most forest tropical wood products such as logs, sawnwood and plywood decreased considerably in 1997, reflecting the weak demand of major Asian importers. The log exporters of Papua New Guinea and the Solomon Islands are reported to have experienced the worst market conditions in a decade. On the other hand, international prices for wood pulp and paper products rose marginally above the depressed levels of 1996.

• As a result of increased prices for pulp and paper products, 1997 saw an estimated increase of 2.2 percent in

Figure 13

MAIN FOREST PRODUCTS

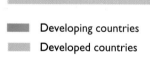

Developing countries
Developed countries

* *Sawnwood and sleepers and wood-based panels*
** *Wood pulp and paper and paperboard*

Source: FAO

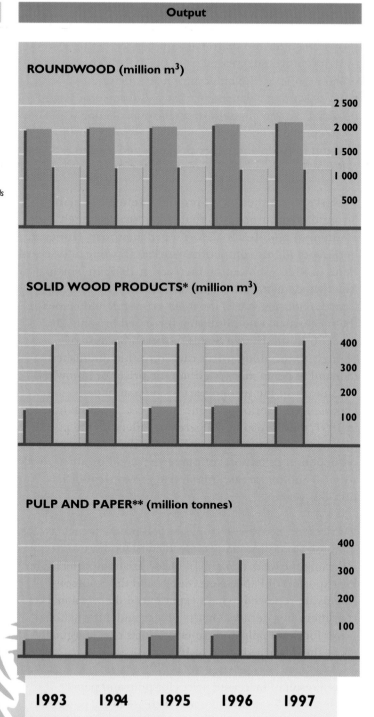

Output

ROUNDWOOD (million m³)

2 500
2 000
1 500
1 000
500

SOLID WOOD PRODUCTS* (million m³)

400
300
200
100

PULP AND PAPER** (million tonnes)

400
300
200
100

1993   1994   1995   1996   1997

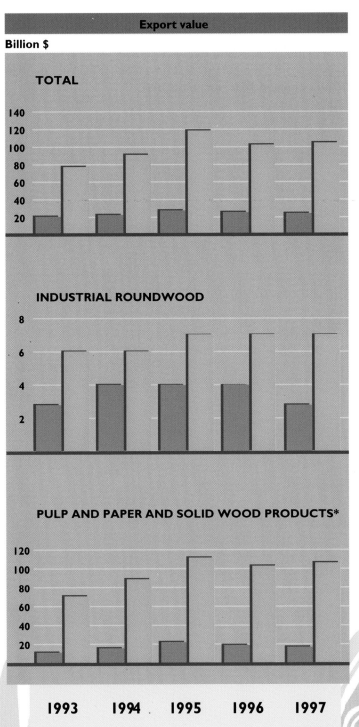

Export value

Billion $

TOTAL

INDUSTRIAL ROUNDWOOD

PULP AND PAPER AND SOLID WOOD PRODUCTS*

1993   1994   1995   1996   1997

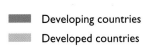

■ Developing countries
■ Developed countries

* *Wood pulp and paper and paperboard,*
  sawnwood and sleepers and wood-based panels

Source: FAO

45

the total value of exports of forest products. The increase was confined to the developed countries, which are the major producers and traders in pulp and paper products. On the other hand, the depressed prices of tropical wood products resulted in a 5 percent decline in developing country forestry exports and in a diminished weight of the developing countries in the total value of trade in forest products, with their share declining from 18 percent in 1996 to an estimated 16.5 percent in 1997.

WORLD REVIEW

III. OVERALL ECONOMIC ENVIRONMENT AND AGRICULTURE

WORLD ECONOMIC ENVIRONMENT

The sudden, severe and largely unexpected financial crisis that erupted in mid-1997 in East and Southeast Asia has since then been a dominant feature of the current world economic environment.

The crisis first hit several of the fastest-growing economies in the world, more severely Indonesia, the Republic of Korea and Thailand, and to a lesser extent Malaysia and the Philippines (see Regional review, Asia and the Pacific). Underlying the crisis were massive capital inflows into these economies (encouraged by their previous impressive performances and what appeared to be solid exchange rate guarantees), which were inadequately allocated and supervised by the domestic banking systems and authorities.

A re-evaluation by investors of the sustainability of exchange rates in these countries, triggered in particular by mounting current account deficits in several of them, led to a sudden withdrawal of funds and an attack on their currencies. The ensuing crisis deepened throughout the second half of 1997, becoming far more serious than initially expected and spreading negative influences on financial markets, economic activity and trade worldwide. Such influences manifested themselves in the form of reduced private foreign financing, falling stock market prices and pressure on national currencies. For the countries affected, the policy measures adopted to restore market confidence and halt the foreign exchange drain – tighter monetary and fiscal policies – translated into reduced domestic demand and imports, the latter also being negatively affected by currency devaluations. Considerable uncertainty remains over the evolution of the crisis in the countries most affected and the worldwide repercussions it could have.

On the one hand, there are a number of positive features in the overall economic fundamentals. Economic activity has remained dynamic and domestic demand conditions are

very favourable in much of the developed world – Japan
being the major exception. Only moderate contractionary
and disinflationary effects are to be expected from the crisis
in the developed countries, with such effects also
contributing to a reduced risk of overheating in several of
them. In general, the developing countries also showed
considerable resilience to the crisis after a severe initial
shock for those whose macroeconomic imbalances made
their economies vulnerable to speculation. For the five most
affected economies, some observers suggest that a
reasonably rapid export-led recovery may be expected,
given the outstanding record of these countries as successful
exporters; their strong currency depreciations; their excess
capacity for exports, resulting from depressed domestic
demand; and the fact that, for some of these five economies,
a large share of total trade is accounted for by foreign
multinationals, implying that a large part of their trade is
sheltered from the financial turmoil.

On the other hand, fears remain concerning a possible
extension of the crisis and, in the longer term, the
likelihood of similar situations occurring with increasing
frequency as a result of the growing globalization of
financial markets and the often overreactive behaviour of
investors and speculators. There is a danger that countries
threatened by such speculative behaviour might adopt
defensive policies countering previous reform efforts,
thereby exacerbating the risks of financial turbulence, loss
of investor confidence and depressed growth. These risks
appear all the more serious for developing countries where
the process of economic stabilization and reform is not yet
fully consolidated.

*Downward revisions of IMF
forecasts for world economic
growth in 1998 were greater
for the developing than for the
developed countries.*

Largely because of the Asian crisis, prospects for world
economic growth have weakened significantly. The
International Monetary Fund (IMF) is forecasting world
economic growth in 1998 to be barely more than 3 percent
(a year earlier, projections for 1998 were 4.25 percent),
compared with 4.1 percent in 1997.[11]

Downward revisions were greater for the developing than
for the developed countries, as the former generally
suffered more from adverse terms of trade, capital outflows
and more restrictive policy stances.

Despite the trade-depressing effects of the financial
turmoil in Asia, according to estimates by the World Trade
Organization (WTO), in 1997 the volume of world
merchandise trade accelerated to 9.5 percent, the highest

Figure 14A

GROWTH IN WORLD ECONOMIC OUTPUT*

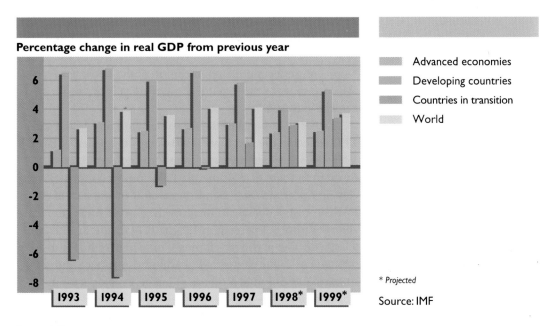

Percentage change in real GDP from previous year

Advanced economies
Developing countries
Countries in transition
World

1993 | 1994 | 1995 | 1996 | 1997 | 1998* | 1999*

* Projected

Source: IMF

Figure 14B

ECONOMIC GROWTH IN DEVELOPING COUNTRY REGIONS

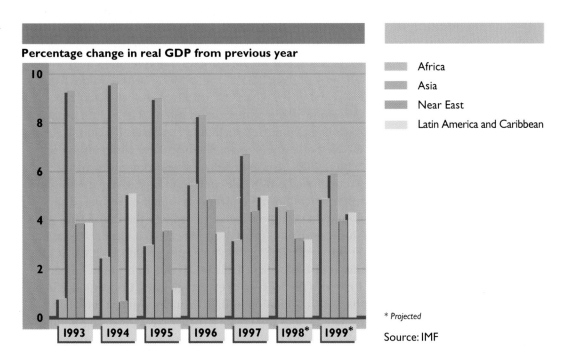

Percentage change in real GDP from previous year

Africa
Asia
Near East
Latin America and Caribbean

1993 | 1994 | 1995 | 1996 | 1997 | 1998* | 1999*

* Projected

Source: IMF

rate recorded in more than two decades, with the exception of 1994. Much of this strong increase reflected the dynamism of economies in North and South America. Thus, in line with a well-established historical trend, merchandise exports expanded much faster than world output (see Figure 15). Measured in current dollar terms, however, world trade growth decelerated between 1996 and 1997, from 4 to 3 percent, reflecting the appreciation of the US dollar *vis-à-vis* the currencies of the major trading nations in Western Europe and Asia.

The limited impact of the Asian situation on world trade in 1997 reflected the fact that the crisis only deepened in late 1997 and there had not been time for its effects to filter through to trade developments. Trade prospects for 1998 remain uncertain but a significant slowdown appears likely. IMF forecasts a decline in the growth of world trade (in volume) from 9.4 percent in 1997 to 6.4 percent in 1998, with a large decline in the developing countries (from 12.1 to 5.2 percent). One source of uncertainty is the pace and strength of economic recovery in Japan, a major actor in world trade.

Growth of world trade is forecast to fall from 9.4 percent in 1997 to 6.4 percent in 1998, with a large decline in the developing countries (from 12.1 to 5.2 percent).

For the IMF-defined advanced economies, growth in 1997 was 3 percent and is projected to slow down to 2.4 percent in 1998. The United States staged a very favourable economic performance in 1997, with the fastest growth in nine years, the lowest inflation rate in three decades, the lowest unemployment level in over two decades and virtually a federal budget balance for the first time since the early 1970s. Prospects for 1998 are for a deceleration in growth to 2.9 percent from 3.8 percent in 1997. Growth in the EU was less dynamic – 2.6 percent in 1997 and a projected 2.8 percent in 1998 – with wide divergences in cyclical positions. A group of countries, including Denmark, Finland, Ireland, the Netherlands, Norway, Spain and the United Kingdom, achieved fast growth in 1997, while economic activity strengthened only moderately in France, Germany and Italy, where unemployment problems remained serious. The dominant economic issue in Europe is the European Monetary Union (EMU). In May 1998, it was decided that 11 out of the 15 EU Member States would join EMU at its outset in 1999. Stage 3 of EMU is due to begin in January 1999 with the locking of exchange rates. Convergence in the areas of inflation, public finances, interest rates and exchange rates will create a firmer basis for strengthening the economic performance of prospective EMU members,

Convergence in the areas of inflation, public finances and interest and exchange rates should help strengthen the economic performance of prospective EMU members.

but structural rigidities in labour markets remain a major challenge in several countries.

In Japan, the depressed economic conditions in 1997 are expected to accentuate in 1998, current prospects being for zero growth this year. The signs of recovery that had been seen in Japan in 1996, after four years of stagnation, proved short-lived. A number of largely interrelated factors – fragilities in the financing system, weakening asset prices and budgetary cuts – contributed to this outcome. Reduced demand from, and competitiveness *vis-à-vis*, neighbouring trading partners affected by the crisis also contributed to a weakening in Japanese exports.

For the developing countries as a whole, growth is estimated to decelerate from a robust 5.8 percent in 1997 to 4.1 percent in 1998, the lowest rate since 1990. All the developing country regions are expected to share in the slowdown, with the notable and encouraging exception of Africa. Other than the Asian economic crisis, negative movements in commodity prices and terms of trade, factors contributing to the slowdown included the effects of the El Niño phenomenon and strengthened measures to stabilize

With the encouraging exception of Africa, the developing countries are expected to share in an estimated deceleration of growth, recording the lowest rate since 1990.

Figure 15

GROWTH IN WORLD OUTPUT AND VOLUME OF TRADE

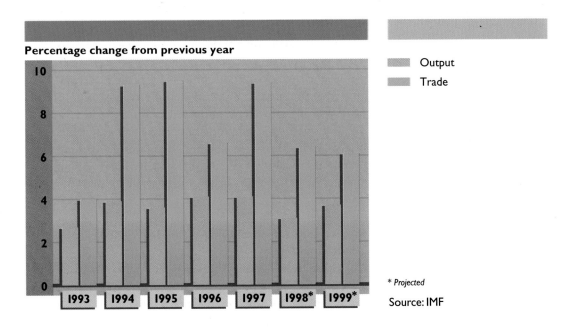

Percentage change from previous year

Output
Trade

1993 1994 1995 1996 1997 1998* 1999*

* Projected

Source: IMF

domestic and external balances. Merchandise trade remained dynamic in 1997, growing in volume by nearly 11 percent on the side of exports and by 12 percent on the side of imports. Nevertheless, exports and, more markedly, imports are expected to be less dynamic in 1998, and a deterioration in terms of trade is also expected this year after three years of improvement. After three years of dramatic decline, developing countries' inflation rates are forecast to increase from 8.5 in 1997 to 10.2 percent in 1998, mainly reflecting sharp price increases in the Asian countries hit by the crisis. In both Africa and Latin America and the Caribbean, on the other hand, the increase in consumer prices is forecast to decelerate further in 1998. Many developing countries have also achieved considerable progress in restoring fiscal balances; for these countries as a whole, central government deficits fell from more than 3 percent of GDP in the early 1990s to 2.2 percent in 1997, although some increase in the deficits is expected in 1998 (see Regional review).

The economies in transition also experienced financial market difficulties associated with the Asian crisis, since the currencies of several countries came under attack and required tightened fiscal and monetary measures. The most affected were Estonia, the Russian Federation and Ukraine. However, for the group as a whole, economic activity remained on an upward trend. The Russian Federation and the other economies in transition showed positive growth in 1997 (1.7 percent) for the first time in eight years. Prospects for 1998 are for an acceleration in growth, to around 2.9 percent, with none of these economies experiencing a decline in economic activity. Higher interest rates and reduced access to foreign capital are expected to lower growth in the Russian Federation and Ukraine, but growth prospects appear to have improved in Hungary and Poland, thanks in particular to strong export growth. Consumer price increases are also expected to decelerate further, most dramatically in Bulgaria and Romania, although inflation rates in these and many other transition economies remain very high.

For the first time in eight years, the economies in transition as a whole showed positive growth in 1998.

Implications for developing countries' agricultural growth and trade

The above trends and features suggest a generally favourable economic environment for agricultural output and trade. As already mentioned, however, major uncertainties remain regarding the course of events in East and Southeast Asia and repercussions worldwide. Developments in this region are important to agriculture, not only for their indirect effects on world economic activity but also because of their immediate implications for commodity markets. Indeed, the Republic of Korea and ASEAN-4 countries (Indonesia, Malaysia, the Philippines and Thailand) account for a sizeable share of world consumption of some commodities. The general reduction in import demand in these and other countries affected by the crisis, together with higher import

Developments in East and Southeast Asia are important to agriculture because of their immediate implications for commodity markets.

Box 1

EXTERNAL DEBT AND FINANCIAL FLOWS TO DEVELOPING COUNTRIES

According to preliminary estimates, the external debt stock of developing countries totalled an estimated $2 171 billion at the end of 1997, a 3 percent increase in nominal value from $2 095 billion in 1996. Outstanding debt stock increased in all regions except sub-Saharan Africa, where debt decreased from $227 billion in 1996 to $223 billion in 1997 as interest arrears on long-term debt dropped by $5 billion. Total private long-term debt reached $46 billion in 1997, a rise of 4 percent over 1996, while official debt totalled $133 billion, down by $2 billion from 1996. Total short-term debt stock (with a maturity of one year or

less) of developing countries went up from $286 billion at the end of 1994 to $361 billion in mid-1997. More than 50 percent of the rise was accounted for by East Asia and the Pacific.

The ratio of debt to export earnings of all developing countries fell from 137 percent in 1996 to 134 percent in 1997, mainly owing to improved export performances. The ratio declined in all regions except the Near East and North Africa where, because of the sharp rise in private borrowing in 1997, it increased to 115 percent against 111 percent in 1996. The debt-service ratio (the ratio of total debt service to

the value of exports of goods and services, including workers' remittances) declined marginally for all developing countries, to 17 percent in 1997. To service all their long-term and short-term external liabilities, the developing countries paid $269 billion in 1997, which was $7 billion more than in 1996.

In 1996, IMF and the World Bank jointly developed a programme of action to provide exceptional assistance to heavily indebted poor countries (HIPCs) that follow sound policies designed to help them reduce their external debt burden. This exceptional assistance will entail a reduction in the net present value of the future claims on the indebted country and will help provide incentives for investment and broaden domestic support for policy reforms. In 1997, seven countries that had established the required record of good economic performance were considered for additional debt relief under the initiative. Agreements were reached with Bolivia, Burkina Faso, Côte d'Ivoire, Guyana and Uganda, and preliminary discussions were started with Guinea-Bissau and Mali. The programme should reduce the debt of these countries by a total of $1.5 billion in present value terms.

Since 1989 the debt to commercial banks has mainly been rearranged through buybacks supported by the IDA's Debt Reduction Facility for low-income countries and through officially supported debt and debt-service reduction programmes (Brady operations) for middle-income countries. In 1997, nine debt-reduction agreements with commercial bank creditors were concluded, restructuring $19 billion in debt and reducing outstanding debt by $7 billion.

Aggregate net resource flows to developing countries rose to an estimated $300 billion in 1997, up from $282 billion in 1996. For the twelfth year in a row, net long-term flows from private sources reached a new record, totalling $256 billion against $247 billion in 1996. Private capital flows to developing countries, which represent 85 percent of total net flows, continued to outpace by far official flows. In the last quarter of 1997 however, private flows fell sharply, reflecting the growing dimension of the crisis in Asia and a general retreat from new investments in emerging markets.

The largest form of net private flows in developing countries continue to be foreign direct investment (FDI), estimated to be $120 billion in 1997, followed by bonds at $54 billion, commercial bank lending at $41 billion and portfolio equity at $32 billion. Net flows of FDI, five times their 1990 level, again touched a record level in 1997 but growth rates were markedly lower than in previous years. The ratio of FDI to GDP in developing countries increased from 0.8 percent in 1991 to 2 percent in 1997. More than 70 percent of net FDI flows have been concentrated in ten countries. Most of the recipients are middle-income countries (with the exception of China and India in 1997), reflecting their large markets and rapid growth in recent years.

Deepening financial problems in Asia had severe repercussions on FDI flows during the last quarter of 1997. The decline in FDI flows to the two largest East Asian recipients, China and Indonesia, were compensated by increased flows to Latin America in response to privatization transactions (primarily with Brazil) and improved economic performance. While FDI flows to East Asia and the Pacific declined by 9 percent in 1997, totalling to $53 billion, flows to Latin America and the Caribbean rose by 10 percent, reaching $42 billion. Large privatization projects in infrastructure as well as a better economic performance and strong flows into and within the Southern Common Market (MERCOSUR) all contributed to Latin America's increased FDI in 1997.

Figure 16

COMPOSITION OF EXTERNAL DEBT OUTSTANDING

Billion $

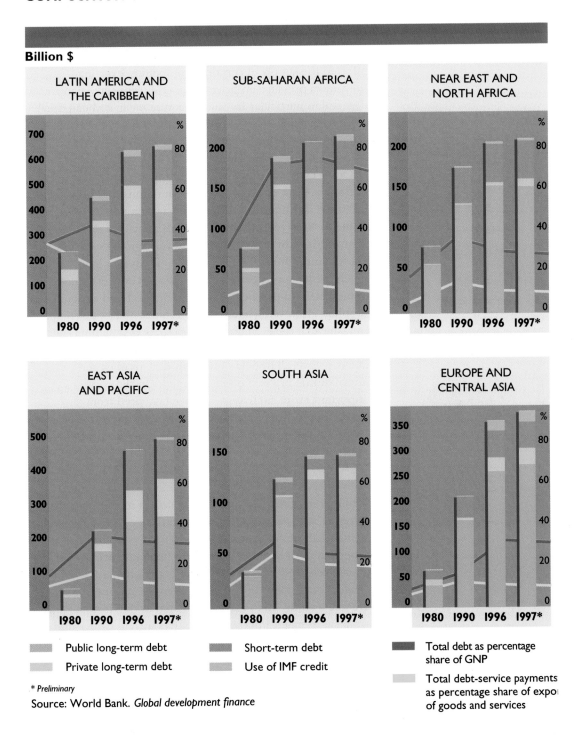

Public long-term debt
Private long-term debt

Short-term debt
Use of IMF credit

Total debt as percentage share of GNP
Total debt-service payments as percentage share of expor of goods and services

* Preliminary

Source: World Bank. *Global development finance*

55

costs resulting from devaluations and reduced credit for financing imports, were important factors contributing to the decline in commodity prices during much of 1997/98 (see Current agricultural situation – facts and figures, 6. International agricultural prices). Export incentives arising from currency depreciations, along with larger export supplies arising from reduced domestic demand, also affected the supply of certain commodities, exerting downward pressure on prices. The crisis reduced Asian demand in particular for maize, bovine meat, soybean meal, temperate fruits, cotton and hides and skins, while boosting the region's exports of tropical fruits and rubber (see Regional review, Asia and the Pacific).

Other current features determining the agricultural outlook are the unusual weather conditions that have prevailed during much of 1997/98, largely as a consequence of the El Niño phenomenon, and an agricultural situation characterized by ample supplies in relation to demand for many commodities. The El Niño phenomenon has attracted much media coverage and raised general concern about its immediate and prospective impact on food and agricultural supplies. However, while the phenomenon has caused considerable losses in crop and livestock production and created food emergency situations in various parts of the world, its overall impact on commodity supplies and international prices has been limited. On the contrary, important crops such as grain have benefited from favourable weather conditions in 1997/98 and prospects for 1998/99 also appear favourable, suggesting downward pressure on prices as seen above.

Overall, prices of major foodstuffs and raw materials are likely to be weak throughout 1998, followed by a gradual stabilization of markets and resumption of moderate price increases at a later stage. Prices of coffee are expected to be substantially below the peak levels of 1997 owing to expectations of larger crops in 1998/99; sugar prices could remain relatively low because of an expected increase in production in 1998/99 and slower growth in import demand in some leading Asian markets affected by the financial crisis as well as in major importing countries such as China and the Russian Federation. However, over the long term, import demand is expected to be stimulated by the lower price levels. Cotton prices, which declined in 1997/98, are expected to stabilize in 1998/99 while natural rubber prices are expected to be depressed in dollar terms, at least in the short term. On the other hand, prices of jute may be expected to rise from the exceptionally low levels of 1997/98 and market conditions should remain generally tight for cocoa.

Over the medium term, the expectations are for a general pattern of economic stability and resumed economic and trade growth.[12]

Project LINK projections[13] for agricultural growth and trade for 1998-2002 in the developing country regions suggest the following:

- After a temporary slump in the course of 1998, agricultural output in the developing countries as a whole is expected to regain dynamism in the coming years. Overall, the average growth rate of agricultural output during the period 1998-2002 is forecast to be about 3.9 percent, close to that of 1991-97 and above longer-term trends (3 percent during the 1970s and 3.5 percent during the 1980s).

- All the developing country regions except Asia and the Pacific are forecast to raise average growth rates above those of the 1990s. The improvement would be more pronounced for Latin America and the Caribbean, where agricultural output would rise by an average yearly rate of nearly 4 percent annually, up from the mediocre 2.8 percent recorded during the period 1990-97. For sub-Saharan Africa, following two bad crop years in 1997 and 1998, production is expected to rebound to rates comparable with those of 1993-96, a period of relatively high growth for the region's agriculture. Forecasts for the Near East and North Africa region also suggest somewhat better average performances than during 1990-97. For Asia and the Pacific, the projected slowdown to 3.8 percent (from about 4.6 percent during 1991-97) would largely stem from depressed performances in East and Southeast Asia, particularly in 1998 and 1999.

- After having expanded at a vigorous 9 percent yearly rate during the first half of the 1990s, developing countries' agricultural export earnings are estimated to lose momentum in 1997 and 1998, mainly reflecting weak international commodity prices. Barring unforeseeable economic and market events, agricultural trade is expected to recover to growth rates of about 6 percent yearly over 1999-2002. Nevertheless, agricultural trade growth would continue to lag, by two to three percentage points, behind that of merchandise trade as a whole.

After a temporary slump in 1998, agricultural output in the developing countries is expected to regain dynamism in the coming years.

- Prospects for agricultural export growth over 1999-2002 appear particularly favourable for Latin America and the Caribbean, although Asia and the Pacific – especially China – and to a lesser extent Africa would also share in the improved outlook. With agricultural exports and imports following similar trends, no major changes are expected in developing countries' agricultural trade balances overall. Notably, however, sub-Saharan Africa is expected to strengthen its surplus position somewhat, continuing a trend initiated in 1993 (in 1992 the subregion had actually become a net agricultural importer).

- According to IMF forecasts, developing countries' total terms of trade may be expected to deteriorate by a cumulative *c.* 2 percent over 1997 and 1998 and improve somewhat in 1999. LINK forecasts suggest a similar pattern for agricultural terms of trade, which would deteriorate markedly in 1998 and broadly stabilize in the following years up to 2002.

LIFDCs with the lowest capacity to finance food imports[14]

Economic estimates for the LIFDCs with the lowest capacity to finance food imports indicate a major improvement in their economic situation in recent years which is expected to continue in the short term.

The economic situation and prospects of this group of poor countries, for which food imports represent a particularly high share of total export earnings and total imports, is periodically reviewed in *The State of Food and Agriculture.* Economic estimates and short-term (1998-99) forecasts for these countries, as prepared for FAO by IMF, indicate a major improvement in their economic situation in recent years which is expected to continue in the short term at least. Taking as a reference the periods 1991-95 and 1998-99, the forecasts point in particular to the following developments:

- An acceleration in GDP growth, from an annual average 3.2 percent in 1991-95 to about 5.5 percent in 1998 and 1999. Such an acceleration would be sustained by a significant increase in gross capital formation, from an equivalent of 17.8 percent of GDP to more than 20 percent during the same period.

- A two-thirds reduction in inflation rates, from 18 to 6 percent.

- Major progress in fiscal stabilization, with deficits in central governments' fiscal balances falling from an equivalent of 6 percent of GDP to slightly above 3 percent.

- A reduced debt burden, with debt-service payments as a share of total goods and services exports falling from around 29 to 13 percent. This would result both from improvements in export purchasing capacity and from the extension of special debt-relief initiatives, such as that agreed in May 1998 by the Group of Eight (G8) industrialized economies in favour of the world's poorest countries – several of which are in this group.

However, the picture appears less bright with regard to external balances. These countries are expected to face increasingly large trade deficits (from $20 billion to $30 billion), which would be only partially compensated by increased aggregate net transfers (largely in the form of net official development finance in favour of African countries in the group). The overall current account balances, which are in chronic deficit in these countries as a whole, would see such deficits rise from an average $6 billion to nearly $13 billion. Nevertheless, they would see their terms of trade stabilize after a long period of unfavourable trends (from 1987 to 1993), while the purchasing power of their exports would continue to expand significantly, thanks to larger export volumes, after the large gains recorded in 1995 and 1997.

After a long period of depressed performances, the improved economic situation and outlook – and therefore food security – of these countries in recent years is most encouraging. That such improvement was achieved, despite the depressing effects of the Asian economic crisis worldwide and less than favourable movements in external accounts, suggests that domestic factors had a strong offsetting impact.[15] These included determined efforts aimed at macroeconomic stabilization and reform – namely in Egypt and the seven CFA countries in the group, where the initial shock of currency devaluation and accompanying measures gave way to a period of rapid growth – and the end of wars and civil strife in countries such as Mozambique, Nicaragua and Rwanda – although the recent armed confrontation between Ethiopia and Eritrea was a warning that conflict may lie latent in countries of this group, which is still afflicted by political tensions, unresolved collective and ethnic identities and economic and social frustration.

Measures aimed at macroeconomic stabilization and reform in some countries and the end of war and civil strife in others have contributed to the improved outlook for these LIFDCs.

The weakening of commodity prices in the wake of the Asian crisis and expectations of continued depressed prices for some commodities will have asymmetric effects on these economies. On the one hand, lower food prices in international markets will have an immediate positive effect on economies heavily dependent on food imports. On the other hand, somewhat paradoxically, the export sector in these countries is also agriculture-based in many cases. For instance, for countries such as Ethiopia, Rwanda and Sierra Leone, where coffee is a major export item, depressed prices of this commodity mean significant losses in export earnings and uncertainties over growth prospects in the short term.

WORLD REVIEW

IV. SELECTED ISSUES

Feeding the cities

INTRODUCTION

People by the millions move to cities in order to improve their lives, find better jobs and have access to goods and services that are not available in rural areas. As they attract more people, cities assemble and provide the goods and amenities that these people need and want. Foremost among these is food. A common sight throughout cities of the developing world are carts piled high with food – maize cobs, heads of lettuce, crates of potatoes, baskets of fruit, etc. – which has been brought in from the countryside or periphery to keep the urban population fed.

It is a huge task to feed a city of several million people, or even of several hundred thousand, who require many tonnes of food each day. For instance, a city of 10 million people – for example Manila, Cairo or Rio de Janeiro – may need to import at least 6 000 tonnes of food per day. This requires much coordination among producers, transporters, market managers and retailers in stores, on the street and in open-air markets. City officials and private operators must act together to achieve that coordination and provision cities adequately.

A city of 10 million people may need to import at least 6 000 tonnes of food per day.

As cities grow in population and space, they require more extensive and more developed transportation and distribution systems for bringing food to consumers, including roads, vehicles and marketplaces that are accessible to all segments of the population. Similarly, as cities grow, the task of planning and managing the land area and infrastructure becomes more complicated and expensive. Frequently, city administrators in the developing world find themselves struggling to cope with burgeoning populations in a physical environment that is really only adequate for a fraction of the inhabitants. A shared understanding among city officials of common problems and potential solutions for feeding the cities, along with appropriate technical assistance and resource support from national and international agencies, can help pave the road towards sustainable cities in the twenty-first century.

Map 4

CITIES WITH POPULATIONS OF MORE THAN 10 MILLION (MEGACITIES)

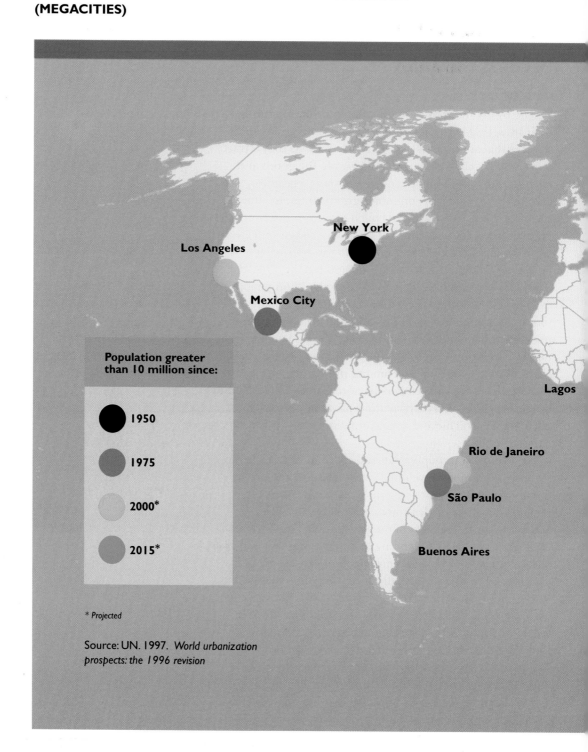

Population greater than 10 million since:

1950

1975

2000*

2015*

Los Angeles

New York

Mexico City

Lagos

Rio de Janeiro

São Paulo

Buenos Aires

* Projected

Source: UN. 1997. *World urbanization prospects: the 1996 revision*

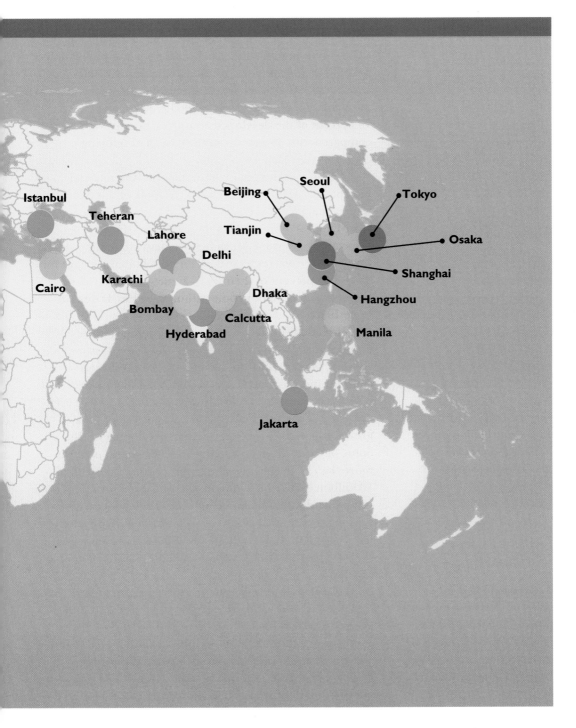

CITIES AND FOOD
Urban demographic trends

At one stage in history, the world's entire population was "rural", living a nomadic or pastoral life and providing for their own food needs. Over time, this way of life gave way to trade-oriented, specialized economic and social patterns in which people gain certain benefits from gathering together to live in towns and cities. The world's current population of 5.9 billion[16] is split more or less equally between cities and rural areas, with urban areas expected to surpass rural areas in population around the year 2005.[17] At present, 75 percent of the developed countries' population is urban compared with 38 percent in the case of developing countries (see Map 4).[18]

A majority of the population in North America and Europe has lived in cities since the middle of this century, while a majority of the population in Latin America and the Near East has done so since the 1960s and since 1980, respectively. Asia and Africa have remained predominantly rural: today their respective urban populations account for 35 and 36 percent of their total. Figure 17 shows the rural-urban distribution of people within countries, by region since 1950.

It is more difficult to make projections on a more reduced scale, such as that of a city, than for an entire country. Many factors can change the trends that are causing cities to grow. However, the general tendencies will remain the same, as it is only the rates of change that are uncertain. Over the next 20 years, 93 percent of urban growth will occur in the cities of the developing world. Some of these cities are already huge: the world now has more than 20 megacities with a population of more than 10 million each, while 50 years ago only New York City could claim that distinction. Some of the largest cities are also growing very quickly. For example, Dhaka in Bangladesh has a population of 9 million and is growing at an annual rate of 5 percent, which means an additional 1 300 people per day.[19]

As the world's population grows, the less urbanized regions, Asia and Africa, are growing the fastest, and the fastest-growing areas both in these regions and within their countries are the cities and peripheral zones. Asian cities are currently growing at a rate of 3 percent per year compared with an overall growth rate in Asia of 1.4 percent per year, while African cities are growing at a rate of

Over the next 20 years, 93 percent of urban growth will occur in the cities of the developing world.

As the world's population grows, the less urbanized regions, Asia and Africa, are growing the fastest, and their fastest-growing areas are the cities and peripheral zones.

Figure 17

RURAL / URBAN DISTRIBUTION OF POPULATION,
1950, 1975, 2000*

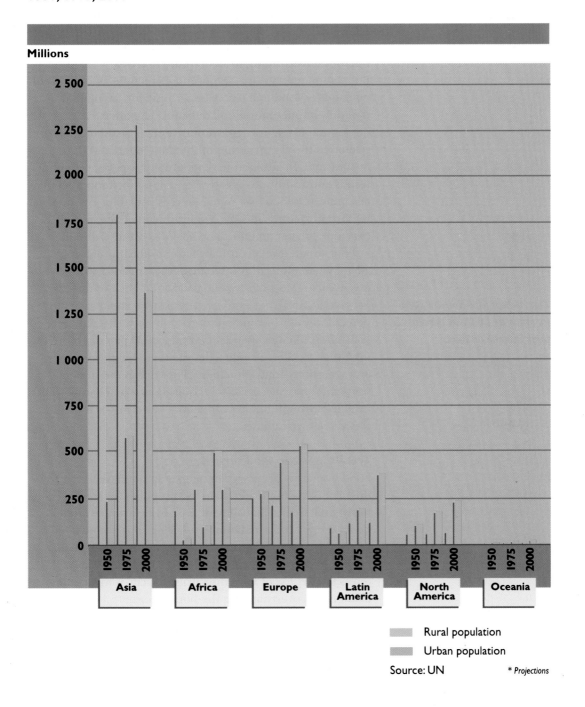

Rural population

Urban population

Source: UN   * Projections

4 percent per year compared with an overall growth of 2.6 percent per year. At the same time, smaller cities and towns are also expanding relatively rapidly – in some countries faster than the largest urban centres. Figure 18 shows regional population projections to 2020 for urban and rural population.

Factors determining food demand in cities

Population growth is an important element in the growth of demand for food in a city. A larger resident population naturally implies more food demand. The other demographic factors determining food demand in a city are related to the age structure of the population and the fertility rate. In addition to demographic aspects, economic trends and conditions greatly affect how much food people consume as well as how much there is available. The most important factor is income level: as incomes rise, people consume greater amounts and a greater variety of food.

Poor urban families can spend as much as 60 to 80 percent of their income on food.

Poor urban dwellers usually have trouble purchasing adequate amounts of food to meet their needs and preferences. Most of the food consumed in cities must be purchased, and poor families can spend as much as 60 to 80 percent of their income on food. One study showed that consumers in cities spend an average of 30 percent more for food than rural consumers, despite there being a lower average caloric intake in cities.[20] Poor urban consumers sometimes have access to food outside market channels, for instance through home production, bartering or food assistance programmes.

Trends in urban food security

Food insecurity occurs when people do not have access to or the means to obtain adequate food supplies for their nutritional needs. Statistics on food insecurity are often sketchy, even at the national level. Thus, it is not possible to tell clearly where urban food insecurity is most severe or how it compares with rural food insecurity. One way to assess the degree of food insecurity in a city is to examine changes in poverty among the population.

As Africa and parts of Asia become increasingly urbanized, food insecurity will become more of an urban problem.

In some cases, the proportion of poor living in urban areas has surpassed that in the rural areas and, in the countries that are already highly urbanized, an increasing absolute number of poor live in cities. The World Bank has estimated that the number of urban poor will rise from 400 million to 1 billion during the 1990s.[21] A study of eight Asian

Figure 18

PROJECTED POPULATION, 2000, 2010, 2020

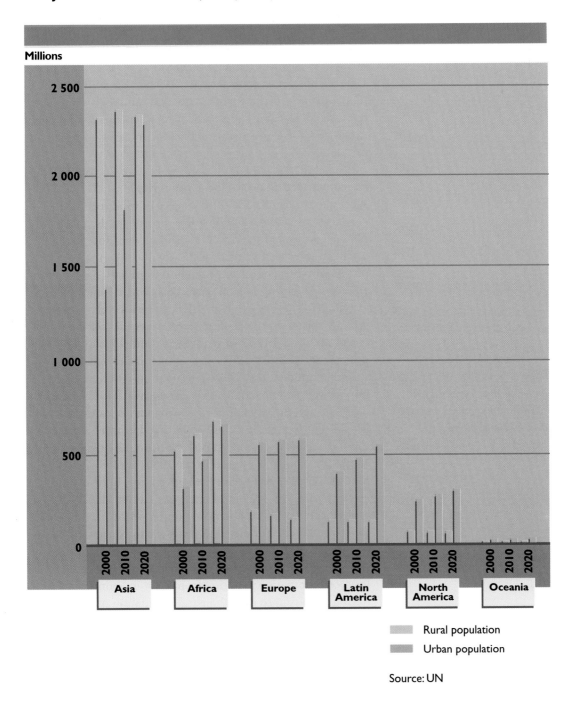

Millions

Source: UN

and four Latin American countries also shows that a rising proportion of the poor are living in cities. For instance, 18 percent of the Republic of Korea's poor lived in cities in 1970, while 80 percent did so in 1990. At the same time, the country's urban population share rose from 54 to 60 percent. In Brazil, while the urban population share rose from 55 to 75 percent, the proportion of the country's poor living in cities rose from 39 percent in 1970 to 54 percent in 1990.[22] Thus, cities at present may be home to more or less than a proportionate share of the total number of poor in a country, but as Africa and parts of Asia become increasingly urbanized, food insecurity will become more of an urban problem.

Factors affecting urban food insecurity

A number of factors affect the degree of food security in countries and cities, including low income levels, a lack of physical access to food, high relative prices of food and unfavourable weather patterns that reduce the food production in a country or region for a period. Such factors affect people living in rural areas as well as in cities.

Structural adjustment policies have reduced job opportunities, removed food subsidies and led to currency devaluations, making imported food more expensive.

Other factors affect city dwellers more severely or are directly related to the economic and physical conditions of urban life itself. In recent years, structural adjustment policies have reduced job opportunities, removed food subsidies and led to currency devaluations (which cause imported food to become more expensive). These changes have harmed the urban poor in particular. Because most of the food consumed in cities is purchased, household access to food is highly sensitive to prices. During the period of economic change witnessed in the 1980s and 1990s, urban food prices rose more than the general cost of living and more than incomes in a wide range of case studies.[23]

Physical conditions also pose unique problems for urban food consumers. For instance, poor urban consumers can be disadvantaged by: a lack of transport and/or having to travel long distances to and from markets; poor hygiene and food contamination resulting from crowded conditions; and having to rely more than the rural population on purchased food and supplies. Food supplies entering a city do not always reach the consumer. Food losses between the production and retail stages are estimated to range from 10 to 30 percent and are caused by a combination of on-farm, transport, distribution and spoilage problems which are greater in urban than rural areas.

The built-up urban areas in developing countries are expected to double in size over the next 10 to 15 years, with major implications for the environment, social relationships and commercial activity.[24] The physical expansion of cities is driven by economic growth and greater numbers of residents, which in most developing countries nowadays arise more from internal increases than from rural-urban migration. In many locations, the physical availability of urban land is relatively constrained, but good planning and appropriate policies can mitigate conflicts and congestion in most circumstances.

It may seem paradoxical that the dismal urban conditions apparent in many developing countries have not stemmed the flow of migrants from rural areas, but urban consumers do benefit from city life in various ways. One of the main attractions is the expectation of an improved life compared with the opportunities offered in rural areas. While the improvement may not come immediately, perhaps not even for a generation or more, it is a strong motivator of rural-urban migration. In addition, throughout the developing world, urban dwellers have greater access to such necessities as piped water, sanitation and health care services than people living in rural areas.

In city planning and design, attention must be paid to essentials such as the location of wholesale and retail markets; modes and efficiency of transport, both for goods and people; parking space for trucks and cars around markets; access to utilities and waste disposal services; and accurate information – destined for buyers and sellers alike – on the prices, quantities and quality of food. Planners will also have to recognize where and how much urban food insecurity exists and address the problem with specifically formulated programmes. These are some of the issues faced by local and national authorities today as their cities head towards the twenty-first century.

FOOD SUPPLY AND DISTRIBUTION CONDITIONS IN URBAN AREAS

In order to reach urban consumers, food passes through a variety of marketing, negotiation and organizational systems. A useful distinction can be made between the traditional steps involved in bringing food to consumers and the delivery systems developed more recently. The two differ both in the level of technological and financial capital required and in who has access to it.

The built-up urban areas in developing countries are expected to double in size over the next 10 to 15 years, with major implications for the environment, social relationships and commercial activity.

Box 2

BUYING FOOD IN CITIES
Fictional story of a poor urban consumer – issues at stake

Now that I am living in town, I have to buy my food. With my small income, I have little choice but to buy the cheapest food I can find – once a day. Meat? The only chance I get to eat meat is when it has been used to make a sauce, which is once a week at the most.

Consumption limited by low incomes

At times, I have so little money that I simply cannot feed my family. They have to fend for themselves, while I buy street foods or visit my cousin who has a job and who can go home for dinner. He will not deny me food.

Street foods as a low-cost food source – extended family obligations leading to high-cost individual consumption

I hear from many people that my children should eat salad and vegetables, but I cannot afford them.

Poor access to micronutrients, especially for children

If I had enough cash to buy a refrigerator, I could buy larger quantities of food and save money by making bulk purchases and storing fresh or cooked food – plus we would not have to eat everything immediately. The problem is that all my relatives and friends who visit me frequently would help themselves to my food stores.

Poor people forced to buy food at higher prices – economies of scale are out of reach

When I want to buy fish, meat, vegetables or fruit, I must go to the market very early in the morning before the heat ruins the food and thousands of flies land on it.

Markets as a source of consumer health problems

WHAT THE PROBLEM IS:

I don't mind going to the central market because I meet people there and the food is often cheaper. But the market looks like a mud puddle, there are flies everywhere and the vegetables and fruit are sometimes rotten. I wish I could buy food for my family from a cleaner place, but there is no other.

Inadequate market maintenance

I nearly had a fight recently with a market trader who tried to cheat me on the weight of the rice I was buying. I know they will try, but this time it was really too much. Only the other day, I bought a packet of biscuits but I felt sick as soon as I put one in my mouth. Checking the expiry date, I saw that it was two years ago! The problem is that consumers can do nothing against these frauds: no one listens.

Commercial frauds and little consumer power

The market is always full of people. When they need to go to the toilet, they hide behind a wall or a heap of boxes. I have to do the same as well because there are no toilets to be found, and I very much doubt that people wash their hands before touching the food again.

Poor hygienic conditions

When I want better quality or more choice, I go to the abattoir or fish market and to the special vegetable stall near the market gardens. If I had a market or a shop with cold storage next to my house, I could save on the cost of transport.

Inadequate retail-level availability leading to higher consumer prices

Our local market burnt down last week and I now have to walk to another one on the other side of town. Not only has this market put its prices up since the fire at ours, but just getting there also means more money and time spent.

Poor market operating practices leading to accidents – poor consumers particularly affected

WHAT THE PROBLEM IS:

There used to be an old lady at the market who was very knowledgeable about ways of preserving and cooking foods that do not keep long. She also knew when foods were good and safe to eat. As one of her many customers, I learned to experiment with new dishes and vary my children's diet, while also saving a lot of money. Unfortunately, she is no longer there.

Private traders offering a useful service and advice to consumers

On certain occasions we like to prepare the dishes we used to eat in our village. It is important for us not to lose this part of our tradition but, because these dishes require specific ingredients that are not easily found in the city, I have to visit several markets in the town.

Limited food availability impeding traditional, often healthier, consumption patterns

WHAT THE PROBLEM IS:

Source: Programme on Food Supply and Distribution to Cities, FAO Marketing and Rural Finance Service.

E. BONITATIBUS/FAO/15517

The traditional sector comprises wholesale merchants (wholesalers, transporters, dealers) and retail operators (small shopkeepers, market retailers, street sellers). The modern sector consists of large, vertically integrated distributors and agro-industrial supply networks (which deal especially with animal products) and national or international trading companies.

Most of those involved in transporting, marketing and distributing food in cities are private businesses and individuals. They bring food supplies into cities, conduct wholesale to retail transactions, negotiate prices and assure adequate quantities to meet demand. The role of the public sector in supply and distribution operations varies from country to country, but is generally declining across regions of the world because of privatization. The involvement of the public sector tends to be the provision of infrastructure: roads, storage facilities and public markets – both wholesale and retail. Sometimes the public sector provides credit for specific activities.

Shortages of food occur in a city for many reasons, the most common being agricultural supply shocks and emergency conditions of civil unrest or war which interrupt food production and/or disrupt the channels for getting food to market. Under normal conditions, the

Transporting food to urban markets

A Sri Lankan man transports coconuts by bicycle to sell in the city. Farmers use many methods to take food to urban wholesale and retail markets.

Most operators in the marketing and distribution of food in cities are private businesses and individuals. The role of the public sector is generally declining because of privatization.

R. FAIDUTTI/FAO/15574

Contamination creates health risks

A lack of clean water and washing facilities creates unsanitary conditions for streetfood vendors in urban areas.

marketing and distribution system in a city can supply food in a timely and regular manner to meet the needs of the population. However, inefficiencies and service breakdowns do occur with great frequency in many cities of the developing world. When they occur, even though the effects may be localized or temporary, it is the poor who suffer as they must spend more time or money to acquire the food they need.

Problems of food distribution at the wholesale level

The problems affecting urban food supply were identified years ago.[25] Much of the food bought by urban consumers passes through wholesalers, who purchase food from producers and traders and deliver it to retailers. In many cities in developing countries, wholesale markets are not well maintained or managed, and are often too old and too small to meet the needs of the growing community. The problems range from lack of coordination among wholesale traders, to prices that vary widely across the city with little systematic information available, to very congested – and sometimes unsanitary – locations for conducting business.

The situation is particularly alarming in cities where there is inadequate infrastructure, as is the case for many

African cities.[26] Wholesale markets in this region are often spontaneously formed groups of wholesalers dispersed across the city and lacking physical facilities. One can find concentrations of wholesalers close to, or even within, large central retail markets, at the discharge points of roads entering the urban fringe, or grouped within urban open spaces used as storage areas. In Dakar, the two main "wholesale markets" for fruits, vegetables and roots and tubers – Thiaroye Gare and Syndicat markets – are located in places where retail products of various kinds are being sold. About 400 000 tonnes of food are handled annually in these areas, mostly directly on the roads around the markets. Similar situations are found in Abidjan, Lagos and Accra.

In many Asian and Latin American countries, the creation and expansion of wholesale markets has lagged behind the growth in urban populations and merchandise flows, resulting in overuse of the existing markets. As a result, the storage facilities are not large enough to handle all the food brought in, the refrigeration systems are overtaxed and food cannot be conserved properly, there are far too many vehicles for the parking and loading spaces, and hygiene and safety problems ensue. The combination of all these conditions causes high food losses, the costs of which are imposed on consumers. The wholesale markets are still often located at the very centre of cities where they originated when the city was smaller. The heavy vehicle and foot traffic around them causes traffic jams, while the waste production and water use lead to environmental damage.

Following marketing liberalization in a number of countries, notably in Africa, former single-channel grain marketing outlets have been replaced by a multitude of small traders at both the wholesale and the retail level. Markets, which were already overcrowded handling only horticultural products, are now handling increasing quantities of grains without having the necessary space or facilities to handle them effectively, with the result that losses caused by exposure to the elements are at unacceptable levels.

New wholesale markets were constructed in many growing cities during the 1980s in response to the problems described above. In Mexico City and Buenos Aires improvements were made in food marketing (better physical conditions and quality of products, more

Wholesale markets in Africa are often spontaneously formed groups of wholesalers who lack physical facilities and are dispersed across the city.

New markets sometimes fail owing to inadequate consideration of the wholesalers' needs and a lack of coordination between the public sector and wholesale operators.

accurate information on prices, etc.) and in the traffic flow. However, new markets, at both the wholesale and the retail level, sometimes fail owing to inadequate consideration of wholesalers' needs, and lack of coordination between the public sector and wholesale operators. Curiously, they may remain empty as merchants refuse to move to them. One reason is that they may be located in areas of town which are out of the mainstream. In Buenos Aires, for example, a new wholesale market for fruits and vegetables located far from the urban centre has created a new layer of transport intermediaries between wholesalers and traditional small shops. The retailers can ill afford the transport costs to the market, nor do they have the finances to buy in bulk to save on the number of trips needed.

In addition, the larger wholesalers may resist moving because they fear losing their dominant position established over years in the existing market configuration; and the rents charged in the new markets can be set too high for the smaller operators.

Even well-planned and well-located new markets do not resolve all the existing problems of wholesale food markets in cities. It is not uncommon for a few large wholesalers to have oligopolistic power in pricing food to retailers. Since the wholesalers often act as creditors to their retail customers who lack sufficient working capital, they can make different deals with each. The result is lack of transparency in transactions, often exploitative relationships and inefficiencies.

The management of wholesale markets, generally the domain of local authorities and public organizations, can be a particular problem. The market authorities lack professional training and may not have good communication with counterparts in other areas of the city, nor with supply channels from the peri-urban and rural areas. They generally fail to achieve the standards of efficiency obtained in the modern commercial sector.

Problems of food distribution at the retail level

Retail food distribution is highly adapted to serving the needs of different customers. The primary activity involves providing a convenient location where customers can go and select food with a variety of choices, where they have confidence in the availability and quality of food, and where

It is not uncommon for a few large wholesalers to have oligopolistic power in pricing food to retailers.

they have the means of purchasing their food either through cash or credit. The poor generally purchase their food at local shops or marketplaces near their homes. Such shops consist of small family enterprises with very limited capital (generally self-financing) whose owners and managers have little qualification and training. Middle- and high-income consumers are shopping increasingly at modern supermarket facilities, identical to any that would be found in North American or large European cities, employing modern technology and having access to credit from banks and suppliers.

The dichotomy between small shops and large supermarkets is most obvious in Latin America, where food distribution evolved during the 1970s in response to the urbanization that occurred during the 1960s. By the early 1990s, large supermarkets accounted for about 30 percent of the retail sales of food in most Latin American cities. Because of their location in the central and residential areas, as well as the extensive variety of products offered, these stores offer high levels of service to middle- and high-income groups. The traditional retail sale systems have remained in the poorer zones and have responded to their constantly expanding needs. This polarization is typical of

The dichotomy between small shops and large supermarkets is most obvious in Latin America, where food distribution evolved during the 1970s in response to the urbanization of the 1960s.

Urban retail food market
Organized, well-functioning retail food markets provide good jobs for urban dwellers and access to food at reasonable prices.

G. DIANA/FAO/17622

Latin American cities, but is found much less in other parts of the developing world.

In many cities, new retail markets have not been built fast enough to meet the needs of growing urban populations, nor has the capacity of existing markets kept pace with the increase in the number of vendors. These two factors together account for significant congestion, disorganization and unhealthy situations in the existing facilities. As a result, both new and existing markets are not often well equipped with basic infrastructure (water, electricity, drainage) and, when present, such facilities work inefficiently. Storage and refrigerated rental areas are rare. As with the wholesale markets, retail market management is often poor, and it is not uncommon for shopowners to face illegal taxation and collusion between market authorities and the larger businesses.

The strong reliance on street foods is driven by changes in the urban way of life as well as urban poverty.

One recourse of market vendors to compensate for lack of space has been to create "spontaneous markets" wherever possible near consumers. In Dakar, three-quarters of the retail markets are spontaneous markets, while in New Delhi this type of market accounts for 60 percent of all fruit and vegetable markets. In Lima, out of 306 markets surveyed, only 72 operate in established municipal market facilities, while the rest have arisen spontaneously, often near slums where there are scarce public facilities.

A strong reliance on street foods is another characteristic of urban food distribution systems, driven by changes in the urban way of life (the need to commute to a distant working place, the development of women's work outside the home) as well as urban poverty. Thus, the importance of street foods varies according to social and economic patterns in the cities. For instance, street foods represent 20 to 25 percent of household food expenditure in Bogota and Caracas, but only 6 percent in Buenos Aires.[27] In Africa, where there are fewer large restaurants or public facilities for eating, consumption of street foods is widespread and growing.

Higher costs and inefficiencies increase consumer prices
Several factors which add to the costs of delivering food commonly exist in developing country cities, thus raising consumer prices. These include market failures that can be corrected and actual increases in costs owing to the difficult conditions of urban food systems. Among the causes of additional costs are:

- an absence of market transparency combined with an oligopolistic control by a small number of wholesalers;
- a lack of scale economies along the distribution system, in particular limited financial capacity;
- higher transport costs compared with locally produced food in rural areas;
- high physical losses at all levels of distribution;
- the common occurrence of corruption and bribes imposed on market sellers;
- compensation for the risks incurred by wholesalers as creditors to many retail operations.

The general economic conditions within a city also affect the efficient functioning of wholesale and retail markets. Public authorities often claim that the multiplicity of intermediaries in urban food distribution is the main reason for the high prices of products. Yet, authorities are often reluctant to promote modernization of the distribution channels, since traditional systems are important sources of employment. As cities develop, modernization of this sector brings greater specialization among the market intermediaries, as well as the introduction of new technologies (refrigerated transportation and storage, information systems that track inventories, etc.). This evolution is most apparent in Latin America, where food marketing is often done by a more limited number of commercial enterprises.

As cities develop, modernized food distribution channels introduce new technologies and bring greater specialization among market intermediaries.

IMPROVING FOOD SUPPLY AND DISTRIBUTION EFFICIENCY IN THE CITIES

General improvement of the supply and distribution systems has rarely been seen as a policy priority in most developing countries. Policies have focused instead on subsidizing basic foodstuffs, and on direct food distribution programmes for poor populations. Specific steps can be taken to address the efficiency and equity of food distribution in the cities. They include:

General improvement of food supply and distribution systems has rarely been seen as a policy priority in most developing countries.

- building facilities and physical infrastructure;
- establishing partnerships between the public and the private sector;
- improving credit availability and access;
- strengthening relationships with producers;
- improving the institutional environment;
- changing perceptions in the public sector.

Creating facilities for wholesale and retail markets

Improving food supply and distribution systems requires infrastructure for both retail and wholesale markets. New markets should be carefully planned to determine the location preferred, the products and operators involved, the types of installation and services required, etc. These aspects must take into account the financial capacity of the users in order to arrive at a realistic level of charges that will enable repayment and maintenance of the market facilities. Other key issues are the organizational rules, the management of the market and the criteria for allocating spaces. At the central level, urban planners must examine food supply flows. This information is crucial for assessing the amount and allocation of the financial resources required for building or improving large infrastructures (slaughterhouses, wholesale markets, truck stations, trunk roads, etc.).

Local food traders and their organizations have their own role to play in planning for growing urban areas. They must establish new retail markets especially in poorly served zones, modernize those already existing, increase their capacity, improve structures and services, reformulate the management rules, and reserve areas for the different commercial and transport activities involved in urban food distribution. Planning and organizational efforts are ineffective when their implementation is hindered by a lack of training and information, as well as the uncertainty of acquiring space for a specific function such as a commercial activity. Consumers and their representatives should be involved in developing imaginative solutions to distribution and access problems.

Involving the private sector and developing new partnerships

In most developing country cities, local traders' organizations have assumed the role of building facilities and organizing markets which had formerly been performed by the public sector. However, large infrastructures such as wholesale markets or slaughterhouses can rarely be financed by private funds, given the very limited resources and conflicting priorities for the market. Therefore, other private sector actors and public agencies must be encouraged to participate in the financing and management of the facilities. Such support is often available to create facilities for export activities (storage, warehousing, transport equipment), and should similarly be extended to investment in infrastructure and services for urban food supply.

One of the most important aspects is harnessing the cooperation of all the relevant actors, including users, the public sector (authorities responsible for infrastructure and utilities) and the private sector (food collectives, trade associations, banks, traders, etc.).

Government involvement should be well defined. One mistake to be avoided is the former tendency to overbuild elaborate and expensive facilities instead of more usable and appropriate ones. The public sector role should assure the viability of markets (providing for transport networks, water, electric power, drainage) and should encourage participation of users (wholesalers) in the financing of superstructures (outhouses, storage facilities). One way to develop needed support structures might be to finance them with bonds that could be paid off over a long period through moderate charges to users. Similar measures can be applied to retail markets, in cooperation with trader associations.

Improving credit access

Lack of access to credit is a major constraint for all those involved in food supply and distribution. Bank credit is generally limited to the commercial sector involved in import and export activities. Greater liquidity and financial support must be made available for the commercial food sector through private bank participation. This will require giving attention to the special problems of agricultural markets (instability, risk) and adapting normal credit and collateral practices to them.

The food supply systems of urban areas need to adopt modern technology as it becomes available. This can be done while retaining the small shopkeeper orientation of the traditional sector. Sustained action is needed in the areas of credit and technical assistance with the participation of local chambers of commerce and business organizations. Among the potential approaches would be for public authorities to support private sector credit provision by guaranteeing loans for modernization in the sector, or by performing initial screening of loans or offering guidelines for applicants and thereby reducing the administrative costs of processing loan applications.

These experiences must be analysed and implemented through careful understanding of the local context and

Urban food supply systems need to adopt modern technology as it becomes available, and this can be done while retaining the small shopkeeper orientation of the traditional sector.

needs. An example is the new commercial centre opened in Nouakchott, Mauritania, in late 1997 by a women's enterprise. Its creation was supported by a government effort to increase female access to credit for entrepreuneurship.[28]

Reinforcing upstream producer organizations

Competitiveness in the wholesale food trade is an important factor in achieving an efficient pricing system. One way to increase competitiveness is for producers' organizations to use their negotiating capacity effectively in marketing their products to wholesalers. When they maintain a presence in the wholesale markets, they obtain market price and supply information efficiently and reliably.[29] This helps them have some market power in dealing with wholesalers, as well as helping them adjust their planting, harvesting and pricing decisions appropriately to respond to the market requirements.

A favourable institutional environment

While local traders' organizations can play a major role in the organization of food supply in their cities, the action of governments is decisive in creating an institutional environment conducive to the efficient marketing of food products. The sound organization and modernization of supply and distribution channels requires a coherent and transparent legal framework that clearly defines the rights and obligations of the various contractors.

One of the major roles for government in food supply and distribution is monitoring and enforcing food safety and quality requirements.

Regulatory authority for food supply and distribution is often scattered among different agencies which do not coordinate their efforts. These efforts need to be harmonized and reinforced. One of the major roles for government is monitoring and enforcing food safety and quality requirements.

Raising consciousness and changing perceptions in the public sector

Local authorities are still inadequately aware that improving food supply and distribution systems, from the physical, organizational and financial viewpoints, has an impact on the whole functioning of the cities and on the living conditions of their populations. Resources are scarce and the pace of urban growth increases the urgency of the task. Difficult policy choices and considerations confront local authorities: establishing priorities, justifying expenditures that may benefit a group of citizens in the name of the interests of all and assessing the political benefits of a given choice. Priorities are necessarily different from one city to another and one country to another, depending on the general level of development and the existing structures and facilities. Nevertheless, it is widely apparent that both public and private actors need increased awareness of the conditions and problems of food supply and distribution systems in these cities. Thus, they need both the information and the tools for decision-making.

Opportunities for greater coordination exist among national and municipal agencies. Agriculture ministries are not involved in urban activities and are inclined to see farm producers as their primary constituency. Yet, they should be aware that urban demand cannot act as an engine in agricultural transformation without adequate supply and distribution channels. They can play a fundamental part in organizing agricultural supply channels and improving marketing of the products through the provision of information and the assurance of an adequate basic infrastructure. Improved supply lines will also improve returns to farmers. National agricultural marketing services generally ignore the functioning of food markets as they are more interested in the modern import/export and distribution sectors. The converse is true of municipal authorities who are inclined to see food as an economic issue for rural interests and orient their planning efforts towards modernization and upper-class needs.

It is therefore necessary to make these different actors more aware of the importance of what is at stake in feeding the cities, to involve them in a global strategy and to determine the responsibilities of each of them. It is important to install or reinforce institutions for cooperation that involve politicians, administrators, traders, merchants and technicians at different levels (state, region, municipality).

Implementing a global strategy to address urban food supply and distribution problems requires an important public investment in information and reinforcement of technical competences at all levels. Donors and international organizations can assist this effort in several ways. For instance, improving information available to, and the competence of, urban managers can be a major field of intervention in support of decentralized development. Another example is support to improved policy formulation, strategy and programme development to improve urban food supply and distribution systems, such as that provided by the FAO subregional programme Food Supply and Distribution in Francophone Africa and that envisaged under the interregional Food Supply and Distribution to Cities programme.

Integrating fisheries and agriculture to enhance fish production and food security

INTRODUCTION

There are manifold interactions between fisheries and agriculture through the common use of land and water resources and concurrent production activities to support rural village communities and supply urban areas with the needed quantity and variety of food. Such interactions extend to the institutional sphere, as fisheries and agriculture often fall within one government ministry. Improved integration between the two sectors is therefore an important means for enhancing fish production and food security. The term "fisheries" is broadly defined here to include the capture of wild fish stocks from inland and marine waters, the capture of fish stocks that have been enhanced through stocking and other measures and various types of aquaculture. The most direct interactions between agriculture and fisheries occur where these two sectors compete for the same kinds of resource, especially land and water, and where measures aimed at higher agricultural production can alter natural fish habitats.

Improved integration between fisheries and agriculture is an important means for enhancing fish production and food security.

At present, the reported capture fisheries production from freshwater ecosystems, including rivers and lakes, is about 7.5 million tonnes. Actual catches, however, are believed to be significantly higher and could be as much as double the reported statistics.[30] Except for some industrial commercial fisheries in the great lakes of Africa and North America, most inland capture fisheries are small-scale by nature and much of the catch is destined for local consumption. Inland fisheries activities are often undertaken by farmers during the agricultural lean season when they provide needed food and income. Thus, the significance of freshwater catches for food security far exceeds what recorded production figures alone might suggest. The importance of fish, particularly in the diet of rural communities, can be judged by its contribution to total animal protein intake. In many Asian countries, over one-half of animal protein intake comes from fish, while in Africa the proportion is 17.5 percent. Moreover, recreational fisheries in inland waters are gaining more economic importance in Asia, Europe and North and South America, where they serve as valued tourist attractions.

In many Asian countries, over one-half of animal protein intake comes from fish. In Africa the proportion is 17.5 percent.

In spite of their nutritional and economic importance and their significant future development potential, inland fisheries landings relative to outputs from other fishery production systems have been waning over the past few decades.[31] The diminished role of inland fisheries has to some extent resulted from physical and chemical changes in the aquatic environment, brought about by agricultural practices such as damming, wetland reclamation, drainage and water abstraction and transfer for irrigation. Recent experience has shown that these environmental changes are often reversible, in which case fisheries habitats can be restored without compromising agricultural production. In other cases, changes can be anticipated and planned for in a way that enhances fisheries potential beyond natural productivity. The full range of fisheries enhancement techniques – including stocking, the modification of water bodies, fertilization and the introduction of genetically improved species – can only be realized when human-induced changes are planned and implemented in an integrated manner that prevents harmful effects on fisheries resources and their habitats.

Aquaculture is one of the world's fastest-growing food production sectors, providing an important substitute for stagnating yields from wild fish stocks.

Aquaculture is one of the world's fastest-growing food-producing sectors, providing an important supplement to and substitute for stagnating yields from wild fish stocks. The importance of aquaculture for future food security was acknowledged by the 1996 World Food Summit, which agreed "to promote the development of environmentally sound and sustainable aquaculture well integrated into rural, agricultural and coastal development". Over the last decade, aquaculture production increased at an average compounded growth rate of nearly 11 percent per annum. By 1996, total annual production of cultured fish, molluscs, crustaceans and aquatic plants reached a record 34.12 million tonnes, valued at $46.5 billion. Of special importance is the fact that more than 85 percent of total aquaculture food production came from developing countries, and in particular from LIFDCs. Production within this group is concentrated in Asian countries, with China being by far the largest producer.

Annual aquaculture production is projected to exceed 40 million tonnes by 2010. Much of this increase is expected to come from the farming of fish and crustaceans in ponds, enhanced production in small and medium-sized water bodies and integrated fish and crustacean farming, primarily with rice but also with vegetables and other crops as well as livestock. Efficiency in the use of water (particularly freshwater) and land resources is becoming a crucial factor in sustaining high growth rates. In many areas where aquaculture has rapidly expanded over the last decade, there is growing pressure on limited land and water resources, and planning for integrated fisheries and agricultural development is therefore of the utmost importance.

THE BENEFITS OF INTEGRATION

The overall objective of integrating fisheries and agriculture is to maximize the synergistic and minimize the antagonistic interactions between the two sectors. The former are mainly derived from the recycling of nutrients arising in the course of agricultural, livestock and fish production processes, from integrated pest management IPM and from the optimal use of water resources.

Antagonistic interactions arise from: the application of pesticides and herbicides that harm aquatic living organisms; the eutrophication of inland water bodies and near-shore coastal waters caused by nutrient runoff (after excessive or inappropriate chemical fertilizer application); soil erosion, which increases the sediment load of natural watercourses; alterations to the hydrological regimes of rivers, lakes and other natural water bodies; drainage of wetlands and swamps; and the obstruction of fish migration routes.

The benefits to be gained from maximizing and minimizing synergistic and antagonistic interactions, respectively, are examined in the next section. Following this is a discussion on how institutional constraints can be overcome at various levels to achieve a better integration of the two sectors.

Optimal nutrient use through by-product recycling

Agricultural by-products, such as manure from livestock and crop residues, can serve as fertilizer and feed inputs for small-scale and commercial aquaculture. After availability of freshwater, the existence of livestock and agricultural crop production systems is the principal factor influencing aquaculture potential in countries and regions.[32]

Resource scarcity is commonly the overriding incentive directing technical and institutional change towards higher levels of efficiency. Sophisticated techniques and institutional arrangements for managing resource use can

The efficient use of water and land resources is a crucial factor in sustaining high growth rates in production.

Synergism between fisheries and agriculture mainly derives from the recycling of nutrients arising during production processes, from IPM and from the optimal use of water.

Integrated fish, livestock and crop farming in China dates back to more than 2 400 years ago.

In India, integrated rice-fish systems combined with vegetable or fruit crops have been reported to improve economic benefits twelvefold over traditional rice farming.

be found in areas of both high and low population densities, depending on the abundance of resources. In arid areas with a low population density, for example, complex systems for the allocation of scarce freshwater resources are known to have existed for centuries.[33]

Integrated farming in China dates back to more than 2 400 years ago, when it involved a complex complementary system combining fish polyculture with poultry, livestock and crop production and the integrated use of manure, grass and other crops as feed and fertilizer.[34] While the scientific foundations of these systems, as well as their regional diversity, have yet to be fully understood, there is no doubt about their high level of efficiency, particularly regarding the use of natural resources.

Rotational farming of rice and shrimps has a long history in the intertidal zones of Bangladesh, India, Indonesia, Thailand, Viet Nam and other Asian countries.[35] In the traditional system, natural stocking occurs as tidal water is let into the fields. Over the past 15 years, shrimp culture yields have been increased through stocking, the control of predatory species and limited feeding and fertilization. In well-managed systems, the rotational cultivation of rice prevents the accumulation of excess nutrients in pond soils while also increasing yields and reducing fertilizer costs. The simultaneous culture of fish and crustaceans with rice often increases rice yields, particularly on poorer soils and in unfertilized crops, probably because the fertilization effect of fish is greatest under these conditions.

Globally, integrated farming systems are receiving increasing attention. In Argentina, Brazil, Haiti, Panama and Peru, the technical feasibility of rice-fish farming is being studied. Concurrent and rotational cultivation of fish and crustaceans with rice are also attracting interest in economically advanced countries: in Louisiana in the United States, about 50 000 tonnes of high-value crayfish are produced concurrently with rice; in Spain, current crayfish production in rice-fields is in the order of 5 000 tonnes and the potential of tilapia-rice cultivation is being explored; and in Italy, the University of Bologna is examining the revival of fish-rice cultivation for ecological and economic reasons after it had been discontinued during the Second World War.

The extent of potential efficiency gains from integrated farming systems may be gauged by a report of the Indian

Figure 19

RICE-FISH AREA AND FISH PRODUCTION IN CHINA

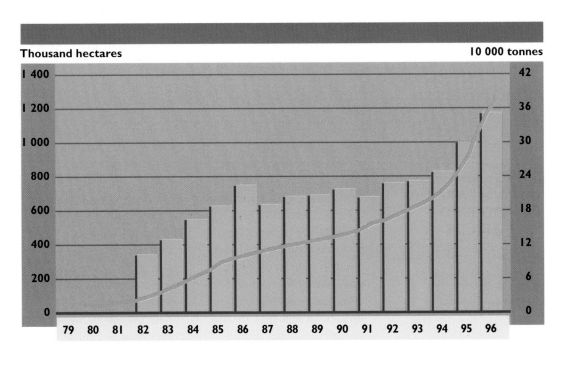

Thousand hectares   **10 000 tonnes**

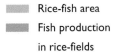

Rice-fish area

Fish production
in rice-fields

Source: FAO

Council of Agricultural Research citing a twelve-fold increase in economic benefits from integrated rice-fish systems combined with vegetable or fruit crops grown on the bunds, as compared with traditional rice farming.[36]

Globally, the area of irrigated rice-fields is estimated to be 81 million ha, 90 percent of which are in Asia. At present, only a fraction of this area is being utilized for rice-fish and rice-crustacean farming, especially in China (1.2 million ha), Egypt (173 000 ha), Indonesia (138 000 ha), Madagascar (13 400 ha), Thailand (25 000 ha) and Viet Nam (40 000 ha in the Mekong delta only). Particularly noteworthy is the case of China, where rice-fish area and fish production have moved from very low levels in the early 1980s to over 1.2 million ha in recent years (Figure 19). Precise area data are not available for a number of other countries where rice-fish/crustacean farming is known to be practised, such as Bangladesh, Cambodia, India and the Lao People's Democratic Republic (see Box 3). In addition to the stocking of hatchery-reared seed, the capture of wild species is common in many countries where seed is supplied naturally with water intake. In Thailand, for example, wild fish capture is carried out on nearly 3 million ha of rice-fields.[37]

Integrated pest management

Generally, integrated pest management (IPM) practices are recommended for rice-fish farming. The use of pest- and

---

Box 3

BANGLADESH: PRAWN FARMING IN MODIFIED RICE-FIELDS

The cultivation of freshwater prawns in modified rice-fields, referred to as *ghers*, is a recent development in Bangladesh and one which was genuinely originated by farmers. *Ghers* are often constructed in *beels*, the local term for seasonal, open water bodies which often encompass low-lying agricultural land. They are also formed by adapting existing rice-fields. The fields are stocked around May with post-larval prawns, and these are usually harvested from November to January. Rice is generally cultivated in the central plateaus of the *ghers* during the dry season from February until May. Fish are usually farmed with the prawns but are harvested throughout the year.

Prawns are a highly valued product on the international market and their production therefore has the potential to increase subsistence farmers' incomes considerably. However, there are certain constraints that need to be

overcome, including a lack of basic knowledge regarding prawn and fish cultivation methods in *gher* environments; an insufficient knowledge of IPM and rice cultivation techniques compatible with prawn and fish cultivation; the need for the development of lower-cost prawn feed to reduce the current, heavy dependence on natural, decreasing supplies of snails which have been the standard feed since the inception of prawn cultivation in *gher* systems; access to lower-cost and high-quality post larvae from prawn hatcheries to reduce what is almost a total reliance on wild post larvae at present; the development of methods to maximize use and income from dykes; and improved financial planning and management skills.

These and other issues will be explored by a CARE-funded project entitled Greater Options for Local Development from Aquaculture (GOLDA).

disease-resistant rice varieties is encouraged to minimize the use of pesticide. In rice monoculture, the chance of pests reaching a population level that economically justifies definite control action is usually low, and the potential income to be gained by integrating fish production shifts the economic threshold to a level that is even less likely to justify pest control. From the point of view of IPM, fish

Box 4

THE LAO PEOPLE'S DEMOCRATIC REPUBLIC: RICE-FISH FARMING

The Lao People's Democratic Republic has extensive water resources in the form of rivers, lakes and wetlands. Fisheries and the collection of aquatic animals during the rainy season are major activities and fish is an important part of the national diet. Rice cultivation is widespread in rainfed, irrigated and terraced fields. Usually one crop is cultivated per year although, in irrigated areas, two crops are possible.

In upland rainfed fields, bunds are often raised to increase water depth for fish culture. In some cases, a small channel is constructed to facilitate capture. In the Mekong River plain, rice-fish farming is practised in rainfed rice-fields where soils are relatively impermeable and in irrigated rice-fields that offer ideal conditions for fish culture. As is the case elsewhere, there are few reliable data available concerning production levels from rice-fish farming but annual production volumes of 125 to 240 kg per ha have been reported for upland rice-fish systems. Carp, tilapia and other species cultured in this system are mainly produced for home consumption.

While rice-fish farming is popular with farmers, certain constraints need to be addressed: pesticide use needs to be reduced through IPM practices and the availability of fingerlings should be improved, as must farmers' access to credit.

From the point of view of IPM, fish culture and rice farming are complementary activities because fish reduce pest populations.

culture and rice farming are complementary activities because it has been shown that fish reduce pest populations. In Indonesia, evidence from the Inter-country Programme for Integrated Pest Control in Rice in South and Southeast Asia shows that the number of pesticide applications in rice-fields can be drastically reduced through IPM. Such a reduction not only lowers costs but also eliminates an important constraint to the adoption of fish farming. With savings on pesticides and additional earnings from fish sales, increases in net income on rice-fish farms are reported to be significantly higher than on rice monoculture farms – by widely varying margins of 7 to 65 percent.[38]

In Viet Nam, recent experiments have demonstrated the effectiveness of carp as a means of biological control of snails, both in rice-fields and communal water reservoirs. In the Republic of Korea, researchers are focusing on the impact that indigenous fish species have on malaria vectors in rice-fields.[39]

Efficient use of water resources

In economic terms, water use efficiency may be measured by the net economic benefits attained per unit of water. Fish and crustaceans are grown in artificial water bodies such as village tanks, reservoirs and channels whose primary purpose is water abstraction, storage and transport for use in agriculture and/or power generation and as drinking-water. Engineering details of construction as well as seasonal water abstraction and use schedules can influence the potential of these structures for fish production. For example, rapid drawdowns in reservoirs may cause the loss of vital spawning habitat, thereby limiting fish production.

Under irrigated conditions, water losses associated with evaporation and seepage can be minimized by applying drip irrigation and by storing and transporting water in covered or underground structures. Since such measures impede fish production, however, the advantages of preventing water evaporation need to be compared with the economic and nutritional benefits derived from fish. Except for in arid and semi-arid areas, water scarcity and evaporation rates may be too low to justify the cost of installing closed systems and forgoing the opportunities offered by fish production.

Apart from the production of fish, the benefits gained through enhanced fish culture in reservoirs and channels often derive also from the maintenance of water quality and the physical functions of these bodies. Stocking with grass carp, for example, controls aquatic weeds in irrigation channels, thereby facilitating water flow and reducing evaporation rates during water transport. Stocking and fish culture can also reduce human health hazards caused by mosquitoes and other insects. Moreover, fish can be used to harvest certain plankton species and aquatic weeds, and thus indirectly reduce nutrient levels, thereby minimizing the harmful effects of eutrophication.

Use of biocides

The extent to which fish are able to tolerate pesticides and herbicides, including their residues, is an acknowledged indicator of the potential human health hazards associated with the use of these products in agriculture. Significant advancements have been made in recent decades in limiting undesired harmful effects of chemicals applied for pest and weed control. In fact, the negative impact of biocides on fisheries is often caused not so much by their use but rather by their inappropriate application, which may have wide-ranging effects on fish and other aquatic organisms. Mortality is not the only negative effect; equally serious consequences of biocide misuse include changes in an organism's reproduction system, metabolism and growth patterns, in food availability and in population size and numbers, etc. If biocides are applied according to prescription, the risks for fish and fisheries can be minimized. Many governments have established lists of recommended pesticides and herbicides and have laid down regulations on imports and domestic production, while extension programmes and training of farmers in their correct use have expanded. All these measures help to reduce the risks of pest and weed control for fisheries and human health.

The extent to which fish are able to tolerate pesticides and herbicides is an indicator of the potential human health hazards associated with the use of these products.

Eutrophication

Nutrient runoff from fertilized agricultural fields and urban and industrial sewage discharge are the two main causes of nutrient enrichment of inland waters, near-shore marine waters and semi-enclosed water bodies such as the Mediterranean and Black Seas. The fisheries potential of nutrient-poor water bodies may initially increase owing to the enhanced availability of nutrients associated with agricultural runoff and other effluent, as has most likely happened in the Mediterranean Sea, which historically has been a nutrient-poor water body. Overloading or excessive nutrient enrichment, however, can result in eutrophication, which may severely affect the reproduction, growth and survival of fish and other aquatic organisms by creating anaerobic conditions and by causing physical damage and intoxication associated with the occurrence of harmful algal blooms. Increasingly frequent occurrences and larger sizes of harmful, sometimes toxic, algal blooms in coastal marine waters have caused substantial losses to coastal fisheries and aquaculture over the last two decades.

Compared with human and industrial sewage discharges, the contribution of agriculture to nutrient loading may often be relatively small, but it is not insignificant. This seems to be illustrated by the experience with Lake Constance: the introduction of sewage water treatment systems in the Austrian, German and Swiss communities and towns around this lake over the past 20 years has led to a significant reduction in the lake's nutrient loading. Over the same period, no significant reduction in agricultural runoff has occurred.

Alterations in hydrological systems

Many of the world's large and small river basins have undergone major human-induced changes in their hydrological regimes over the past 40 to 50 years. In some European river systems, such as the Rhine, control measures were taken as far back as 100 years ago or more. The construction of dams, reservoirs, embankments, barrages and channels for purposes of water abstraction and storage, flood control, power generation and irrigation have produced large economic benefits. In some cases, these changes have also yielded large gains for fisheries in reservoirs, such as in Lake Kariba in Africa, as well as in irrigated rice-fields whose full fisheries potential still remains to be realized in many parts of the world.

Artificial dams, reservoirs, embankments and channels have generated considerable economic benefits, yet modifications in hydrological systems have also reduced natural fish populations and hence catches and incomes from fishing.

In many other instances, modifications in hydrological systems have caused drastic declines in natural fish populations and dramatically reduced fish catches and incomes from fishing. In some cases where fish migration routes and spawning and nursery areas have been lost, species have become extinct. In many rivers of Europe, for example, wild stocks of salmon, sturgeon and Allis shad no longer exist.

Past experiences have greatly improved scientific knowledge regarding the short-term and long-term consequences of different designs and features of structural alterations to river basin hydrology. This expertise can now bear fruit by preserving the essential ecological features that sustain wild fish stocks and/or create optimal conditions for fish production in new reservoirs and channels. According to current ideas in the field of integrated water resources management (IWRM), agricultural ecosystems such as seasonal floodplains, coastal wetlands and estuaries provide essential permanent or seasonal habitat for fish and serve as repositories of aquatic biodiversity.[40] Wetlands are also important fish nurseries.

Soil and groundwater salination
In general, most culture-based fisheries and aquaculture acitivities have no or few significant negative environmental effects and are highly complementary to agriculture. However, shrimp culture practices have been associated with reduced agricultural yields in certain localities where soil conditions allowed saline water to seep through embankments and pond bottoms into adjacent fields. In addition, excessive abstraction of groundwater for various purposes such as agriculture, domestic water supply, industrial activities and, in some cases, shrimp culture, is

Agricultural ecosystems such as seasonal floodplains and coastal wetlands provide essential habitat for fish and serve as repositories of aquatic biodiversity.

Local children fishing from a rice-field in Madagascar

In Madagascar, 13 000 ha of irrigated rice-fields are used for integrated rice and fish production.

D. MAROTIANA/FAO/20540

Shrimp culture has been associated with reduced agricultural yields where soil conditions allow saline water to seep into adjacent fields, although there have been numerous experiences of the beneficial coexistence of coastal aquaculture and agriculture, including rice-shrimp systems.

causing seawater intrusion into coastal aquifers. Appropriate planning and allocation of land and water resources in coastal areas can help minimize the degradation of groundwater and soil quality resulting from salination. Furthermore, there have been numerous experiences of the beneficial coexistence of coastal aquaculture and agriculture; for example, the rotational systems of rice-fish or rice-shrimp culture, where advantage is taken of saltwater-resistant paddy, an abundant freshwater influx in the rainy season and the opportunity to cultivate brackishwater aquaculture species.

APPROACHES TO BETTER INTEGRATION

Human resource development and institutional strengthening are widely held to be the principal requirements for improving integration at the level of individual farms and communities, in river basin and coastal area management and at the level of sectoral and macroeconomic policies. At the farm level, attention needs to focus first on resource use efficiency and the economic incentives that influence farmers when they decide on cropping patterns and the use of water, fertilizer, pesticides and herbicides and other inputs. Next, the emphasis should be on farmers' knowledge of available production and pest management options as well as on their ability to apply these. Agriculture and aquaculture offer a large variety of cropping patterns under different climatic and soil conditions. If they have the right skills, together with access to the necessary inputs, farmers will adopt the farming or aquaculture system that is most suitable and economically advantageous for their specific situation. Extension and training are crucial for informed decision-making, and physical infrastructure, efficient input markets and credit facilities are indispensable for the optimal development and integration of farming and aquaculture systems.

Extension and training are crucial for informed decision-making; if farmers have the right skills and access to the necessary inputs, they will adopt the farming and aquaculture system that is most suitable and advantageous for their specific case.

Markets for certain important natural resource inputs, such as water, and the environment's capacity to assimilate effluent are often entirely non-existent or distorted because of their common property or open-access nature. The levying of use fees and/or the introduction of tradable rights have been suggested to achieve a higher level of efficiency in the use of water and other natural resources such as wild fish stocks. Resource management through such market-based instruments can entail high administrative costs because of the need to monitor individual farmers' resource use and to institute well-defined and enforceable individual user rights. Where tradable rights are applicable, they may reinforce an inequitable distribution of incomes and assets, especially where other services (e.g. for credit) are inefficient.

The alternative approaches of comanagement and community-based management of common property resources have received increasing attention in recent years because of their assumed greater efficiency and prevention of undesired distributional implications. Factors that users themselves have identified as being important for successful resource management include: small group size, which facilitates the formulation, observance and monitoring of a collective agreement; social cohesion; resource characteristics that facilitate the exclusion of outsiders; and visible signs of successful collective management.[41] These factors could well apply to a number of fisheries in reservoirs and other small water bodies, where the potential for self-management, however, is not utilized because responsibility is not delegated to the local level and collective rights are not sufficiently protected. Similar favourable conditions exist in many other situations, for example for resources such as water and mangrove forests where, again, the potential for effective management has yet to be realized. In addition to the recognition of common rights, community-based and joint management need support through extension and training services and scientific assessments of resource abundance.

At the level of river basins and coastal areas, integration is aimed at managing sectoral components as parts of a functional whole, explicitly recognizing that management needs to focus on human behaviour, not physical stocks of natural resources such as fish, land or water. Integrated river basin and coastal area management employs a multisectoral strategic approach to the efficient allocation of scarce resources among competing uses and the minimization of unintended natural resource and environmental effects.[42] Land use planning and zoning, together with environmental impact assessment procedures, are vital tools for preventing the occurrence of antagonistic intersectoral interactions and for fostering synergistic and harmonious development while preserving ecosystem functionalities. The involvement of fisheries agencies in these activities therefore is absolutely essential.

At the level of river basins and coastal areas, management needs to focus on human behaviour, not physical stocks of natural resources such as fish, land or water.

97

The participation of all resource users and other stakeholders at an early stage of land use planning is indispensable, not least because of their knowledge of local socio-economic conditions and natural resources.

The participation of all resource users and other stakeholders at an early stage is indispensable for effective land use planning and zoning, not least because of their intimate knowledge of local socio-economic conditions and the state of natural resources. At the government level, the functions of the various agencies with regulatory and development mandates need to be well coordinated. Two broad distinctions can be made in the wide range of possible institutional arrangements for integrated river basin and coastal area management:

- *Multisectoral integration.* This involves coordinating the various agencies responsible for river basin and coastal management on the basis of a common policy and bringing together the various government agencies concerned as well as other stakeholders so that they can work towards common goals by following mutually agreed strategies.
- *Structural integration.* Here, an entirely new, integrated institutional structure is created by placing management, development and policy initiatives within a single institution.

Multisectoral coordination tends to be preferred, since line ministries are typically highly protective of their core responsibilities which relate directly to their power base and funding. The establishment of an organization with broad administrative responsibilities overlapping the traditional jurisdictions of line ministries – as would be the case if management, policy and development functions were integrated within a single institution – is often likely to meet with resistance rather than cooperation. Integration and coordination should be thought of as being separate but mutually supportive.[43]

However, a caveat has arisen from experiences to date. Integrated planning and institutional coordination are often difficult to achieve and can entail significant costs. The difficulties and costs relate to the often cumbersome bureaucratic structures and procedures of government agencies; the complexity of the scientific, technical and economic issues involved; and the potentially large number of informed decisions that need to be taken. In addition to high administrative costs, the decision-making process could be protracted and may slow down economic development.

Many river basin and coastal management issues can be addressed through sound sectoral management, but taking into full account the impacts of and interdependencies with other sectors and ecosystem processes;[44] the provision and enforcement of environmental legislation; the need for a transparent and consultative process of land use planning and siting; and the design of major infrastructure projects such as dams. The costs of a formal process for the preparation of a river basin or coastal area management plan are always likely to be justified in areas where intense multisectoral resource utilization either exists or is planned.

At the macrolevel, economic policies such as subsidies for production inputs and import and export duties can have profound impacts on the characteristics and level of resource use as well as on the occurrence of undesirable environmental effects. The advantages of subsidizing chemical inputs such as fertilizer and pesticides need to be weighted against the potential harm they can do to aquatic environments and to fishery resources, which provide food for fishers and fish consumers alike.

The advantages of subsidizing chemical inputs need to be weighed against the harm they can do to aquatic environments and to fishery resources, which provide food for fishers and fish consumers alike.

CONCLUSION

Modern advances in information and data processing technologies have dramatically increased the capacity of humans to analyse complex multiple resource-use options and to link up large numbers of people into integrated decision-making structures. At the same time, new research findings have greatly broadened the understanding of local communities' ability to coordinate common property resource use while maintaining their essential social and cultural attributes. Finally, governments have become more aware of sectoral and environmental interdependencies. Such all-round progress has created conditions favourable to the full realization of benefits resulting from the enhanced integration of fisheries and agriculture as well as their integration with the rest of the economy.

NOTES

1 The term "undernourishment" is used throughout this section to define a situation of inadequate food availability. It should not be equated with "undernutrition" which is the result not only of an inadequate food intake but also of the insufficient utilization of food by the body, particulary as a result of health disorders.

2 For the period 1990-92, the new estimate of undernourished people worldwide is 822 million. This differs from the earlier estimate of 840 million reported for the same period at the World Food Summit and in *The State of Food and Agriculture 1997*, mainly because of retrospective downward revisions in the UN estimates of total population figures for some critical countries. These revisions also made it necessary to revise estimates of the number of undernourished for past periods, leading to slight adjustments for a number of countries. It should be noted that the changes shown for the early 1990s are based on the assumption that the coefficient of variation of intracountry food distribution remained constant between 1990-92 and 1994-96.

3 For certain indicators, data are not available for all 98 countries.

4 Increasing numbers of people in rural areas are involved in economic activities outside agriculture, as discussed in Part III of this issue, entitled *Rural non-farm income in developing countries*.

5 This report is based on information available as of May 1998. Current information on the global cereal supply and demand situation can be found in FAO's bimonthly *Food Outlook*.

6 The broad definition of agriculture includes agriculture, forestry, fisheries, land and water management, agro-industries, environment, manufacturing of agricultural inputs and machinery, regional and river development and rural development.

7 The narrow definition of agriculture includes only agriculture (crops and animal husbandry), forestry, fisheries and development of land and water resources.

8 Based on information available from the World Food Programme (WFP) as of May 1998.

9 While cereal shipments are monitored on a July/June basis, shipments of non-cereals are monitored on a calendar year basis.

10 This report is based on information available as of May 1998. Current information on cereal prices can be found in FAO's bimonthly *Food Outlook*.

11 Unless otherwise specified, economic estimates and forecasts in this section are from IMF. 1998. World Economic Outlook. Washington, DC.

12 Such a positive overall view of global economic prospects is shared by most major specialized centres and agencies, which had forecast the current economic slowdown to be less pronounced than those of the mid-1970s, early 1980s and early 1990s. However, the highly tentative nature of any economic forecast in the current fluid situation must again be emphasized. The same caveat holds with regard to agricultural market assumptions, which are notoriously subject to uncertainty.

13 These agricultural forecasts were prepared for FAO by the Institute for Policy Analysis, University of Toronto, Canada, associated with the Project LINK economic forecast model.

14 Food imports account for 25 percent or more of total export earnings for each of these 31 countries, which are a subgroup of the traditional FAO-defined group of LIFDCs. The subgroup includes: Afghanistan, Bangladesh, Cambodia, Benin, Burkina Faso, Cape Verde, Comoros, Djibouti, Dominican Republic, Egypt, Ethiopia, the Gambia, Guinea-Bissau, Haiti, The Lao People's Democratic Republic, Lesotho, Maldives, Mali, Mauritania, Mozambique, Nepal, Nicaragua, Rwanda, Samoa, Senegal, Sierra Leone, Somalia, Sri Lanka, the Sudan, Togo and Yemen.

15 The limited impact of the crisis on these economies reflects their lack of integration with the world economy and, in particular, the small role played by private capital flows in many of them (Egypt, where high growth rates in recent years were fuelled by private investment, being an exception). In sub-Saharan Africa, where a majority (17 out of 31 countries) of this group are located, private investment only accounts for about two-thirds of total investment. This region only attracts 2 to 3 percent of total world foreign direct investment.

16 US Bureau of the Census. (April)1998. International Programs Center.

17 UN. 1997. *World urbanization prospects: the 1996 revision.* New York, UN Secretariat Population Division.

18 Strictly speaking, "city" is not the same as "urban". An urban area is defined differently from one country to the next, but usually by the number of its inhabitants. In Senegal, an urban area must have 10 000 inhabitants, while in Peru an urban area is an agglomeration of at least a few hundred people. A city is an urban area, usually defined by the size of its population, but it is also a complex of economic, social and other activities implying a different mode of living than that typical of the countryside.

19 All population and urbanization projections have been drawn from UN, op. cit., note 17.

20 Asaduzzaman. 1989. Cited in D. Drakakis-Smith. 1992. Food production and under-nutrition in the Third World. *Hunger Notes,* 18(2): 5-6.

21 World Bank. 1991. *Urban policy and economic development.* Washington, DC.

22 IFPRI. 1996. Urban challenges to nutrition security: a review of food security, health and care in the cities (unpublished manuscript). Washington, DC.

23 Tabatabai (1993), Gebre (1993), Maxwell (1995) et al. Cited in IFPRI, op. cit., note 22.

24 UN. 1995. *The challenge of urbanization.* New York.

25 According to IFPRI, op. cit., note 22, urban food distribution problems have been identified in Mittendorf and Abbott (1979) and Lourenco-Lindell (1995), but most research on urban food systems has been location-specific and viewed from the narrow perspective of certain actors. FAO's Programme on Food Supply and Distribution to Cities is contributing to a deeper understanding of the issues through case studies (in progress).

26 Exceptions are the wholesale market of Bouaké, a city of about 300 000 inhabitants in Côte d'Ivoire, and the wholesale fresh fish market of Dakar, Senegal.

27 FAO. *Analysis of food marketing in the large cities of the developing world* (forthcoming).

28 *National Report on Implementation of the World Food Summit Plan of Action.* Mauritania, January 1998.

29 See, for example, a review of Indonesia's interesting price information system, by A. Sheperd and A.J.F. Schalke in FAO. 1995. *An assessment of the Indonesian Horticultural Market Information Service.* Rome.

30 A household food consumption survey undertaken in northeastern Thailand, for example, has revealed that fish consumption was five to six times higher than reported fish catches from the Mekong River. See *Mekong Fisheries Network Newsletter,* August 1996, 2(1).

31 FAO. 1997. *Technical guidelines for responsible fisheries. No. 6. Inland Fisheries.* Rome.

32 The development of agriculture implies that at least a minimum amount of physical and institutional infrastructure has already been developed, Kapetsky and Nath conclude that, in general, the conditions encouraging agriculture favour aquaculture development and vice versa. This fact has been used by these authors and by Aguilar-Manjarrez and Nath in their estimates of aquaculture potential in Africa and Latin America. See J.M. Kapetsky and S.S. Nath in FAO. 1997. *A strategic assessment of the potential for freshwater fish farming in Latin America.* COPESCAL Technical Paper No. 10. Rome; and J. Aguilar-Manjarrez and S.S. Nath in FAO. 1998. *A strategic reassessment of fish farming potential in Africa.* CIFA Technical Paper No. 32. Rome.

33 Many examples of traditional management of water resources and other common property or common pool resources can be found in National Academy Press. 1986. *Proceedings of the Conference on Common Property Resource Management.* Washington, DC.

34 Network of Aquaculture Centres in Asia and the Pacific (NACA). 1989. *Integrated fish farming in China.* Technical Manual No. 7.

35 A recent review of the trends in rice-fish farming is provided by M. Halwart. 1998. Trends in rice-fish farming. In *FAO Aquaculture Newsletter*, 18: 3-11.

36 K.C. Mathur. 1996. Rainfed lowlands become remunerative through rice-fish systems. *Indian Council of Agricultural Research News*, 2(1): 1-3.

37 Halwart, op. cit., note 35.

38 Ibid.

39 Ibid.

40 A comprehensive discussion on this issue took place during the Expert Group Meeting on Strategic Approaches to Freshwater Management, organized by the UN Department of Economic and Social Affairs and held in Harare, Zimbabwe, 27-30 January 1998.

41 See E. Ostrom. 1990. *Governing the commons. The evolution of institutions for collective action.* Cambridge, UK, Cambridge University Press; and J.-M. Baland and J.-P. Platteau. 1996. *Halting degradation of natural resources. Is there a role for local communities?* Published for FAO by Oxford University Press (Clarendon academic imprint), UK.

42 Scura Fallon. 1994. *Typological framework and strategy elements for integrated coastal fisheries management.* FAO/UNOP Project INT/91/007. Field document 2. Rome.

43 For this and other aspects of integration, such as conflict management and economic valuation of natural resources, see the detailed discussion in FAO. 1998. *Integrated coastal area management and agriculture, forestry and fisheries.* Edited by N. Scialabba. Rome.

44 This has been named "enhanced sectoral management" in a recent survey of coastal management programmes. See S. Olsen, K. Lowry, J. Tobey, P. Burbridge and S. Humphrey. 1997. *Survey of current purposes and methods for evaluating coastal management projects and programs funded by international donors.* Coastal Management Report No. 2200. Coastal Resources Center, University of Rhode Island, USA. A detailed discussion of integration aspects with respect to inland fisheries is provided in U. Barg, I.G. Dunn, T. Petr and R.L. Welcomme. 1996. Inland fisheries. In A.K. Biswas, ed. *Water Resources - Environmental planning, management and development.* New York, McGraw-Hill.

PART II

REGIONAL REVIEW

REGIONAL REVIEW

Africa

REGIONAL OVERVIEW
General economic performance

After four consecutive years of accelerating GDP growth, reaching 5.5 percent in 1996[1], the growth rate of Africa[2] declined in 1997 to a more modest 3.2 percent. The International Monetary Fund (IMF) attributes the decline mainly to the adverse weather conditions affecting a number of countries as well as to a downturn in commodity prices and, in a few cases, to armed conflicts. The sharpness of the decline in economic expansion is to a large extent the consequence of a slowdown in economic activity in North Africa, which is particularly strong in Morocco but is also affecting Algeria and Tunisia.[3] In sub-Saharan Africa, the slowdown in GDP growth was somewhat more contained, falling from 4.9 percent in 1996 to a still relatively encouraging 4 percent in 1997. This was accompanied by a reduction in inflation rates in the majority of the countries in the subregion as well as a further narrowing of government fiscal deficits.

In spite of the slowdown in economic growth in the subregion as a whole in 1997, the trend still shows a significant improvement in economic performance since the early 1990s. The three years from 1995 to 1997 have indeed brought increases in per caput GDP for the first time in the 1990s. For the same period, the average annual per caput growth rate estimated by IMF corresponds to 1.8 percent, which compares with a rate of -1.2 percent over the 1990-94 period and -0.5 percent for 1981-89.

The years 1995 to 1997 brought increases in per caput GDP for the first time in the 1990s.

In countries south of the Sahara, a large portion of the recorded decline in the rate of expansion of economic activity in 1997 was the result of a slowdown in South Africa, by far the largest economy in the subregion, where real GDP growth in 1997 fell to 1.7 percent from the 3.2 percent of the previous year, reflecting weakness in both domestic and external demand. According to IMF, South Africa is the only African country that has so far recorded any significant impact of the Southeast Asian crisis, as pressure on the currency led to a 4 percent depreciation of the rand in October 1997. In Nigeria, the other economic giant of the subregion, economic activity in 1997 accelerated for the third consecutive year, reaching a GDP growth rate of 5.1 percent. IMF, however, points to the hampering of economic activity by power and fuel shortages as well as the still unfavourable investment climate, and it projects a sharp slowdown in GDP growth in 1998.

Excluding the two major economies, South Africa and Nigeria, sub-Saharan Africa recorded a certain slowdown in growth in 1997 relative to the previous year as the rate of expansion of GDP slipped to 4.5 percent compared with 5.6 percent in 1996, although the momentum of the preceding years' positive performances was maintained. In particular, the CFA franc-zone countries as a whole continued to show positive growth performances in 1997, with most of them recording growth rates above the average for the subregion and maintaining the momentum gained following the 1994 devaluation of the CFA franc. At the same time, consumer price inflation continued a downward trend, the sole exceptions being Côte d'Ivoire and Togo. Inflation rates in all but one of the CFA countries are now well below the subregional average, indicating that inflation has been brought firmly under control since devaluation. Double-digit rates of inflation have only been recorded in Guinea-Bissau, which has just recently become a member of the West African Economic and Monetary Union (UEMOA)[4] and adopted the CFA franc.

In sub-Saharan Africa, IMF records accelerating rates of GDP growth in 1997 for 24 of the 45 countries for which estimates exist,[5] decelerating rates in 17 countries and stable rates in three, while an actual decline in GDP is reported only for the Democratic Republic of the Congo. Rates of GDP growth, however, slowed in a number of the major countries of the subregion in 1997. This was the case for the two countries, among others, that had shown the most impressive growth performance of recent years – Ethiopia and Uganda. In Ethiopia, as growth in agricultural output slowed significantly because of unfavourable weather, GDP growth fell back to an estimated 5.3 percent following an expansion of 10.6 percent in 1996. In Uganda, GDP growth slowed to 5 percent compared with the rates of 8.1 percent in 1996 and 10.5 percent in 1995. Two other major countries of the sub-Saharan subregion, Ghana and Kenya, also

Since devaluation of the CFA franc, inflation has been brought firmly under control in the CFA countries.

recorded lower rates of GDP growth in 1997. On the other hand, in the Democratic Republic of the Congo, affected by civil conflict, the economic decline of the preceding years was not halted and GDP contracted by an estimated 5.7 percent. The United Republic of Tanzania maintained the estimated growth rate of 4.1 percent reached in 1996, while a particularly positive performance in 1997 was posted by the Sudan which, according to IMF estimates, managed to accelerate economic growth further to 5.5 percent from the 4.7 percent of 1996.

From its economic projections, IMF expects sub-Saharan Africa's improved economic performance and prospects – chiefly attributed to improved macroeconomic policies and structural reforms – to continue in the coming years, thereby bringing further gains in per caput GDP. This outcome is, however, considered conditional on the continuation of rigorous macroeconomic policies and structural reforms. So far, with the exception of South Africa, the Asian crisis has not significantly affected African financial markets and IMF expects less of an impact than for other developing country regions because of the limited private capital flows. However, it does expect an impact on some African countries owing to the role of East Asian countries, and in particular Malaysia, as sources of foreign direct investment (FDI) and because of the higher cost of foreign borrowing.

Specifically, for 1998 IMF projects economic activity in the subregion to expand at a rate of 4.1 percent, roughly that of 1997. Nigeria will, however, contribute significantly to pulling down the overall growth rate in 1998, as IMF forecasts a slowdown in GDP growth from 5.1 percent in 1997 to only 2.7 percent in 1998. In South Africa, also, GDP growth will remain below the average for the subregion, although accelerating to 2.2 percent, from 1.7 percent in 1997. Excluding the two major economies, for the remaining part of the sub-Saharan subregion GDP projections for 1998 appear to be more encouraging, as economic growth should accelerate to 5.2 percent from the 4.5 percent estimated for 1997. Again, the countries of the CFA zone appear set to record particularly promising growth performances, as the average GDP growth rate for this group in 1998 is projected at 6 percent, up from an estimated 5.5 percent in 1997. For 1999, IMF expects a further strengthening of

Sub-Saharan Africa's improved economic performance and prospects are expected to continue.

economic growth, with the GDP growth rate rising to 4.8 percent for the sub-Saharan subregion and to 5.7 percent if Nigeria and South Africa are excluded.

Among the major uncertainties in IMF's economic growth projections for sub-Saharan Africa are particularly important factors affecting agriculture. Possible adverse effects of the El Niño phenomenon on agricultural production as well as the possibility of declines in commodity prices could indeed lead to lower growth rates than those currently projected for the subregion.

Agricultural performance

Poor agricultural performance, largely related to unfavourable weather conditions, was a major factor contributing to a certain slowdown in economic growth in sub-Saharan Africa in 1997, in spite of the still significant overall improvement in economic performance. Indeed, according to FAO's current estimates of overall crop and livestock production (production index numbers), output in 1997 declined by 1 percent in the sub-Saharan subregion,[6] constituting the first estimated decline in overall agricultural production since 1987. The drop represents a 3 to 4 percent contraction of per caput production, which follows four years of gradual expansion in per caput agricultural production. The percentage variation for food production is comparable, with production in 1997 having declined by an estimated 1.2 percent, corresponding to a 3.9 percent decline in per caput terms, while production of non-food agricultural products is estimated to have increased by 0.8 percent. If developed South Africa is included, the decline in crop and livestock production rises slightly to 1.4 percent as South African output is estimated to have declined by some 4 to 5 percent in 1997.

The contraction recorded in agricultural production in 1997 is accounted for by an estimated reduction in crop production of 1.8 percent, with cereal production falling by as much as 3 percent. For livestock, although production is estimated to have increased by about 1 percent, this is nevertheless a slowdown relative to the previous four years.

The pattern of production performances in 1997 differs widely across the continent with the negative performances largely linked to unfavourable weather conditions. The most siginificant declines were in southern Africa, where crop production was down sharply in a number of countries (Botswana, Lesotho, Malawi, South Africa, Swaziland and Zambia) owing to unfavourable weather. In East Africa, a severe drought at the beginning of the year substantially reduced second-season food production in Kenya, the United Republic of Tanzania, Uganda, Somalia and large parts of southern Ethiopia, while late or erratic rainfall later in the year led to reduced main season harvests in some countries, particularly in the United Republic of Tanzania and Uganda. In the Great Lakes region, dry weather in parts of Rwanda and Burundi, coupled with insecurity in conflict-affected areas, contributed to a slow recovery in food production. In West Africa, and particularly in Mauritania, crop production was severely affected by a prolonged mid-season dry spell.

When seen in a longer-term perspective, and even considering 1997 as a particularly negative crop year, agricultural production performances over the last five years indicate that, although expansion in production is now roughly keeping pace with the high rate of population growth in the subregion (see Figure 20), the agricultural sector can still not claim to have moved towards the level of expanding per caput output required in order to enhance the sector's contribution to economic development and food security. Indeed, although FAO's per caput agricultural production index for the subregion (excluding South Africa) stood at 100 at the beginning of the 1990s (average for the period 1989-91), by 1996 it had not moved beyond 101.7, after which it fell back to 97.6 in 1997.

Agriculture has not yet reached the level of per caput output required to enhance the sector's contribution to economic development and food security.

Similarly, for 1998, production prospects appear generally unfavourable owing to the unpredictable El Niño-related weather conditions. In East Africa, excessive and heavy rains starting in October 1997 resulted in extensive flooding, causing loss of human life as well as substantial crop and livestock losses, and inflicted severe damage on the subregion's road and rail networks. In southern Africa, although the widespread threat of El Niño-related drought has receded, erratic and excessive rains in part caused localized crop losses.

Developments in policies
In its assessment of the factors behind the improved overall economic performance in sub-Saharan Africa

Figure 20

SUB-SAHARAN AFRICA

Agricultural export and import values and share in total merchandise trade

Agricultural exports ($)

Agricultural imports ($)

Ag. exports as share of total (%)

Ag. imports as share of total (%)

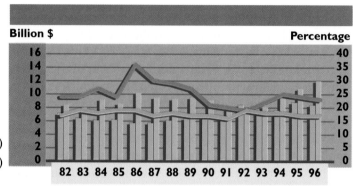

Agricultural exports
(Index 1989-91=100)

Value

Unit value

Quantity

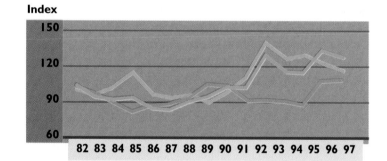

Agricultural imports
(Index 1989-91=100)

Value

Unit Value

Quantity

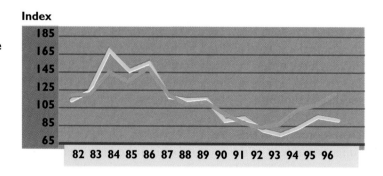

Net barter and income agricultural terms of trade
(Index 1989-91=100)

Net barter

Income

SUB-SAHARAN AFRICA

Percentage

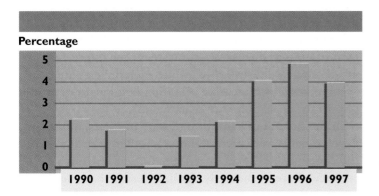

Real GDP*

(Percentage change over previous year)

* *Including South Africa*

kcal

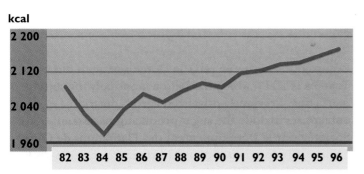

Dietary energy supplies

(kcal per caput per day)

Index

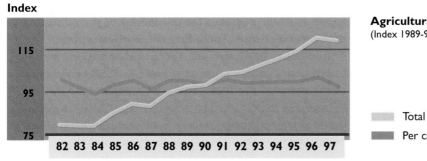

Agricultural production

(Index 1989-91=100)

Total

Per caput

Source: FAO and IMF

There have been numerous developments in the privatization of state interests in a number of countries.

during recent years, IMF clearly gives greatest importance to the economic reforms that have been undertaken, and in which the agricultural sector has also participated. During 1997 and early 1998 the main thrust of policy developments in the subregion has continued to be towards increased market orientation of policies with privatization or dismantling of state-owned interests in production and distribution, while such policies are accompanied by increasing attention being paid to issues of poverty alleviation and social needs.

In the field of privatization of state interests, numerous developments were recorded in a number of countries in the course of 1997 and early 1998. Côte d'Ivoire is a country where particularly significant steps have been taken in the direction of privatization. In 1997, the privatization of the parastatal vegetable oil producer, Palmindustrie, was completed in June while privatization was scheduled to begin of the national cotton industry, Compagnie Ivoirienne pour le Développement des Textiles (CIDT), which has held a monopoly for cotton marketing. Previously privatized agro-industrial enterprises include the sugar-producing parastatal, Société pour le Développement des Plantations de Canne à Sucre, l'Industrialisation et la Commercialisation du Sucre (SODESUCRE). Important developments can also be cited for other countries. In Botswana, a task force was set up to draft proposals for modalities of privatization of state-owned entities, including the Botswana Meat Commission. In Cameroon, recent privatizations include the national rubber company, while in 1998 privatization of the palm oil producer, Société Camerounaise de Palmeraies (SOCAPALM), is under way. Other companies slated for privatization before 2000 include three other major agro-industrial companies: Cameroon Sugar Company, Inc. (CAMSUCO), Société de Développment du Coton au Cameroun (SODECOTON) and the Cameroon Development Corporation, which has activities in the production of bananas, rubber, tea and oil palm and, with 13 000 employees, is the country's largest employer (after the state). The Ethiopian Government is continuing its privatization programme with recent moves to sell off a textile enterprise as well as a number of state-owned tanneries. In Guinea-Bissau the government is implementing a privatization programme which will also affect parastatals in both the timber and the food processing industries. In Kenya, privatization through flotation of stock is planned of the largest national sugar producer, Mumias Sugar. Scheduled for privatization as part of the Lesotho Government's privatization programme are the state-owned Lesotho Flour Mills, which had been set up as part of the previous government's efforts to enhance food self-reliance. The previous monopoly position of the company, resulting from market and price controls, had already been eroded by policy reforms introduced in 1995 which had removed prior controls. In Malawi, recent privatization efforts include the listing of the national sugar-producing companies on the Malawi Stock Exchange. The Government of the Niger is reportedly committed to accelerating the privatization of a number of publicly owned companies, including the national textile company and agro-industrial companies operating in rice, meat and milk processing. Likewise, in Rwanda, privatization has gained momentum, affecting, *inter alia,* state-owned dairies and tea factories. In Senegal, the government is moving ahead with its efforts to sell off a 51 percent stake in the national groundnut processing company, Société Nationale de Commercialisation des Oléogineux du Sénégal (SONACOS). In the United Republic of Tanzania, the main object of the government's privatization efforts in 1997 has been the tea industry – the sale the Tanzanian Tea Authority's tea factories is to be accompanied by efforts to develop the smallholder sector. In Zimbabwe, 1997 saw the flotation of the former Dairy Marketing Board, now Dairyboard Zimbabwe Limited. The next targets in the implementation of the government's policy of privatizing the agricultural marketing parastatals were expected to be the former Cotton Marketing Board and the former Cold Storage Commission.

Liberalization of markets and trade is a field where significant reforms have already been undertaken by numerous African countries but where 1997 and early 1998 saw some further developments in a number of countries. In Côte d'Ivoire, after having liberalized rice imports in January in 1997 (and revised import tariffs so as to provide protection of domestic production), in June the government freed the domestic prices of sugar and locally produced tobacco products. The government reportedly plans to liberalize exports of coffee from 1998/99 and

1997 and early 1998 saw further developments in the field of market and trade liberalization in a number of countries.

subsequently those of cocoa. In general, the government is moving towards reducing its intervention in agricultural production and marketing while at the same time promoting the creation of professional farmers' associations with a view to representing farmers in the negotiation of producer prices and ensuring input supplies and technical assistance to farmers. In Madagascar, the gradual liberalization of agricultural trade culminated in May 1997 with the abolition of the vanilla export tax. Mozambique, in 1997, abolished administratively set minimum prices for food crops, while those for most cash crops are to be abolished in 1998. The country is also making efforts to eliminate administrative obstacles to foreign investors. The procedures for registration and the granting of trading licences to companies were to be simplified in 1997, a development that would also affect agricultural marketing. The Government of Nigeria decided to deregulate the fertilizer trade and remove the subsidy on fertilizers following several years of severe scarcity. In spite of the undoubtedly favourable impact on availability, concern was nevertheless expressed in the country about the cost of fertilizers to small-scale farmers. In South Africa, 1997 saw the gradual implementation of the Marketing of Agricultural Products Act, which was approved in September 1996 and entered into force in November the same year. The Act had set a 13-month timetable for the dismantling of state control over single-channel marketing boards which had previously controlled the marketing of a range of agricultural products. Among the last to abandon its monopoly position (towards the end of 1997) was the Wheat Board. The marketing activities of the boards are to be taken over by the private sector while efforts are being made to transform some of them into non-profit companies to ensure the continuation of some of the services previously provided by the boards, such as information dissemination. As a consequence of the liberalization of agricultural marketing, the only restrictions remaining on imports of agricultural products are import tariffs.

Poverty alleviation and improved social welfare are being specifically incorporated in African governments' policy and the programmes they negotiate with IMF.

Poverty alleviation and improved social welfare are two objectives that are being specifically incorporated in African governments' policy and are also explicitly included in programmes negotiated by African governments with IMF. Examples are Botswana, where 1997 saw the publication of a government study on the impact and alleviation of poverty in the country, and Burkina Faso, one of the lowest-ranking countries in UNDP's human development index, where the government has set precise quantitative targets in the education and health sectors aimed at increasing primary school enrolment and the number of health centres. Similarly, for Mozambique, the economic programme for 1997/98 supported by IMF targets an increase in social expenditure to reduce poverty and emphasizes smallholder agricultural development to raise rural income levels. In the Niger, another country ranking very low on the human development index, in accordance with the IMF-supported programme the government is committed to undertaking family planning initiatives and programmes aimed at improving the quality of life for women. It is setting precise targets for increased school enrolment from 1996 to 1999 as well as increased budgetary expenditures for health and education from 1997 to 2000.

Land tenure is another issue of priority concern for at least some of the African governments. In Eritrea, a new land law came into force in 1997. The law allows for Eritrean nationals and foreigners to lease land, while the responsibility for the allocation of land is moved from the municipalities to a new Ministry of Land, Water and Environment. Reportedly, in Malawi the government is considering major land reform with a view to improving the conditions of smallholders. Also in the pipeline in Senegal is a major land reform designed to give farmers ownership of their land, thus replacing the traditional tenure system. In South Africa, the government's programme of land redistribution and assistance to small farmers is proceeding slowly. The objective of redistributing farmland to black farmers is not to be attained through expropriation but by using state-owned land and land repossessed from indebted white farmers.

African governments are increasingly concerned about the need to protect and regenerate national forest resources. In Burkina Faso, a major reforestation campaign was launched in July 1997. The campaign, which foresees the planting of 7 million trees in some of the more arid parts of the country, follows a similar three-year campaign from 1994 to 1997 during which 15 million trees were planted in areas threatened by desertification. The new campaign focuses on varieties that can also produce marketable products with a view to enhancing rural

The need to protect and regenerate national forest resources is receiving increasing attention from African governments.

Box 5

STRONG COMMITMENT TO DECENTRALIZATION IN GHANA

Ghana is one of the African countries that is pursuing decentralization with most determination. The decentralization of legislative and executive bodies was initiated by the Decentralization Law (PNDC Law No. 207) which was passed in 1988. This law transfers public-sector tasks from the national and regional levels to districts and municipalities, aiming to ease the pressure on the central government, increase productive efficiency and increase the share of costs assumed by the beneficiaries.

The constitution stipulates that at least 5 percent of national tax revenue (i.e. a common fund) be redistributed to the districts. Relevant implementing laws were passed in 1994, adequately specifying the framework conditions for decentralized development processes. However, the district authorities lack the required knowledge and expertise.

The Ministry of Local Government and Rural Development is responsible for the promotion of the decentralization process. It also assumes responsibility for rural development. Its tasks focus on adapting relevant laws and implementing regulations, on training and upgrading personnel at the district level and on strengthening capacities required to this end. It has supervisory control over the district administrations, but no authority over the district assemblies, provided they keep within the legal framework. The planning unit, with a staff of about a dozen experts, provides support and advisory services for the decentralization process.

Despite the progress achieved in creating the institutional basis for decentralization, a number of problems, varying in intensity from district to district, remain to be solved. Local self-help capacities are not yet sufficiently mobilized and individual initiative at the district level is not used to its potential. In addition, members of the assembly are not fully aware of their responsibility to their constituencies or of their decision-making powers as members of the legislative body. Officials of the district administration often still consider themselves to represent the central government and make decisions without the district assembly's mandate. Staff in sector departments continue to follow standards set by their ministries and measures are implemented without the approval of the district assembly. There are as yet no comprehensive district development plans.

Source: A. Engel. 1997. Decentralization, local capacity and regional rural development: experiences from GTZ-supported initiatives in Africa. Paper presented at the Technical Consultation on Decentralization, 16-18 December 1997, FAO, Rome.

incomes. The Government of Côte d'Ivoire, in 1996, banned all log exports with the exception of teak in an effort to put a brake on overexploitation of the forest resources and to promote domestic processing. The authorities are also reported to be facing difficulties in controlling illegal farming in protected forest areas. In Gabon, the government aims to process 50 percent of logged timber locally, and is reported to be considering fiscal reforms to stimulate investment in the sector. Madagascar's native forests have already shrunk considerably, and concerns from the international community have led to debt-for-nature swaps. In Namibia, also, forest resources are threatened by illegal felling and export regulations were tightened in 1997 to help control the problem.

Experiences in institutional decentralization

Even prior to the current policy reforms undertaken in Africa, many governments had attempted to transfer decisional and operational functions to provincial or communal levels of public services, local and regional institutions and communities or civil society organizations. As in other continents, however, past experiences in this domain have not been universally successful. Unsolved problems that hindered better results have frequently been the absence or weakness of institutions necessary to support management capacity at the local level. Other difficulties include weak links between local and central administrations.[7]

Decentralization, however, appears to have gained momentum again, also owing to the changing political and economic environment. Indeed, advancement in democracy, increased market orientation of economic policies and the generalized adoption of stabilization and structural adjustment policies have contributed to creating an environment which is more conducive to institutional decentralization.

In a country such as Ghana (see Box 5), institutional decentralization has indeed been a major element of structural reform policies, also involving institutions with responsibilities over rural development. In spite of some shortcomings that can be overcome, this example points to the positive contribution to rural development that can be expected from a strong commitment to participatory and decentralized rural development approaches.

Stabilization and structural adjustment policies have helped to create an environment that is more conducive to institutional decentralization.

119

Map 5

UGANDA

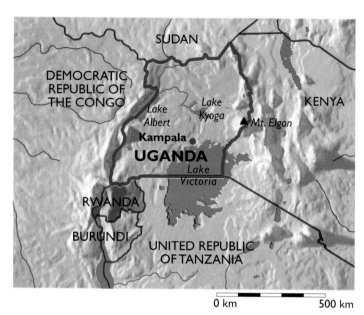

0 km   500 km

UGANDA
Overview

After a long period of economic disaster, since 1986 Uganda has undergone a steady process of rehabilitation that has borne fruit. The fundamental economic indicators are greatly improved and social progress is a government priority. For the past ten years, real GDP growth has far surpassed the average rate of sub-Saharan African countries (6.4 percent per year in Uganda compared with an average of 1.6 percent in the remainder of sub-Saharan Africa) and per caput income has grown by almost 50 percent.

Uganda is an extremely poor country with a population of 20 million people of diverse ethnic backgrounds. It is listed among the world's poorest countries with a per caput GDP in 1996/97 of $301 (or $1 480 per year on a purchasing power basis). The population is growing at an annual rate of about 3.1 percent and, at 6.7 children per woman of child-bearing age, fertility rates are among the highest in the world. At 42 years, life expectancy is among the lowest in the world, and the disease of AIDS is widespread. In sum, the low level of income, high fertility rate and ominous health outlook create a daunting agenda for Uganda's leaders.

Uganda is located in the Great Lakes region of Africa, adjacent to Lake Victoria. It is a landlocked country containing 197 000 ha of rich land resources that are very favourable for agriculture. Uganda has few mineral resources, but has abundant savannah grassland, woodlands and bush. Compared with its neighbours, Uganda has a high population density, but is still 89 percent rural. The country is heavily dependent on agriculture as its economic mainstay, with the main products being subsistence food crops. The primary export is coffee.

Uganda's economy has demonstrated a steady improvement after being completely shattered during the 1970s, but is still largely producing food crops, as many people provide for their needs through subsistence farming. Current economic problems stem from heavy rains in 1997 which cut back agricultural production and export earnings and are causing domestic food price hikes.

Economic history

In its 35 years of independence, Uganda has weathered some of the worst tragedies and strife that can befall a country. Tribal and territorial conflicts have been a constant factor as factions struggle for control over Uganda and its productive resources. The country suffered severely during Idi Amin's military regime between 1971 and 1980, and then experienced repeated coup attempts over the next five years which culminated in civil war in 1986. An estimated 500 000 Ugandans died during the course of the terrorism and civil war, and up to another one million people were forced to flee their homes.

From 1971 to 1980, a number of economic policy decisions were taken with the aim of enriching élite supporters of the regime. This was done at great economic cost, as most of the policies introduced were protectionist and expropriative, very few economic activities were left untouched by the intrusion of the public sector and virtually no industry was able to operate efficiently or competitively. By the end of the civil war in 1986, Uganda faced border struggles with Kenya, a collapsed economy, a history of rampant corruption and more than 100 000 refugees within its borders. The decade since then has seen steady progress in social and economic spheres.

Uganda's macroeconomic and industrial indicators are just now approaching the levels recorded in 1970 when savings rates and private investments were 15 percent of GDP; per caput GDP had peaked at $331; exports of coffee, tobacco, tea and cotton were sufficient to produce a consistent current account surplus; and the multifaceted

Uganda's economy has steadily improved after being completely shattered during the 1970s, and the country's macroeconomic and industrial indicators are just now approaching the levels recorded in 1970.

Figure 21

CHANGE IN REAL GDP GROWTH IN UGANDA, 1965-70 to 1997-98

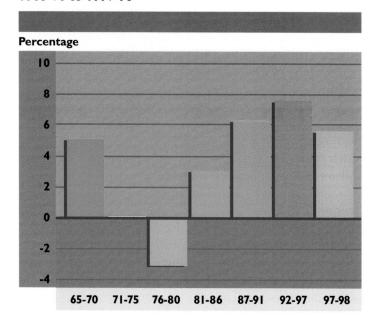

Percentage

Source: Statistical Abstract,
Government of Uganda, 1997

transport system, a legacy of British colonial times, allowed the smooth functioning of trade and market operations. Social conditions were relatively good, with a 70 percent child immunization rate, good-quality education services and a broad-based health care network, even in rural areas.

In the 30 years from 1965 to 1995, Uganda's average annual growth in real GDP was a moderate 2.8 percent, but this average hides a decade-long decline from the beginning of the Idi Amin regime to its eventual overthrow in the early 1980s. The country's economy had been growing at almost 5 percent per year in the first years of national independence (see Figure 21). Between 1971 and 1981, however, real GDP dropped by 20 percent and real per caput GDP by 60 percent, to less than U$_{sh}$ 100 000 per year ($100). Exports also plummeted by 60 percent. By 1981, government spending on education and health in real terms was 27 and 9 percent of 1970 levels, respectively.

The economy showed some improvement in the early to mid-1980s with positive real growth returning, but many of the more modern sectors had been damaged, manufacturing was operating at 5 percent of capacity and the composition of output was heavily agricultural and domestically oriented. In general, poor performance was due to inappropriate price and trade incentives, poor government decisions, badly functioning credit markets and high levels of economic risk.

The slow economic recovery that had begun in 1981 gained momentum subsequently. Average economic growth accelerated from 3 percent in 1981-86, to 6.5 percent in 1987-97. Annual per caput income has risen to slightly above 1965 levels ($301 in 1997) and structural reform has occurred throughout the economy. Greater confidence in the economy and improved political conditions have encouraged savings and investment as well as increased use of the monetary system. In 1986, more than one-third of the entire economy and one-half of the agricultural economy involved barter and other non-monetary transactions, but those figures have lessened with the better functioning of the financial system. Currently, about 24 percent of the economy operates outside monetary channels.

Greater confidence in the economy and improved political conditions have encouraged savings and investments as well as increased use of the monetary system.

Substantial amounts of international loans and assistance have been channelled to support Uganda's economy. In the ten years of economic recovery since 1988, the country has received concessionary loans from IMF and the World Bank totalling more than $4 billion. These credits have been made through extended credit and structural adjustment facilities in IMF and the World Bank, and have been used to support the rebuilding and reorientation of the macroeconomy. In some years, external assistance has represented as much as one-fifth of GDP. In November 1997, an IMF loan of $140 million was approved for the 1997-2000 period. In addition to multilateral donors, Uganda has received substantial support from individual members of the European Union as well as Japan.

In some years, external assistance has represented as much as one-fifth of GDP but, as a result of this support, Uganda today is undergoing a recovery.

As a result, Uganda today is in a fragile recovery from a long period of self-destruction. The investment rate is up, inflation has been kept relatively low for four years, the government has reduced its expenditures and created improved conditions for private investment, and the current account deficit has been cut. The country's progress in structural and sectoral policy reform earned forgiveness of 20 percent of its foreign debt in early 1998. Under the

Figure 22

SECTORAL DISTRIBUTION OF GDP IN UGANDA

Percentage

- Government and social services
- Mining and manufacturing
- Utilities
- Wholesale and retail
- Construction
- Hotels and restaurants
- Transport and communication
- Agriculture

Source: Statistical Abstract, Government of Uganda, 1997

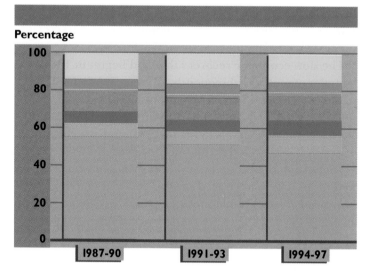

heavily indebted poor countries (HIPCs) initiative, the World Bank and IMF have forgiven $650 million of Uganda's $3.25 billion total external debt. This move will reduce even further Uganda's debt-to-GDP ratio, which was 80 percent as recently as 1993/94 and is expected to decline to 50 percent in 1998.

Macroeconomic conditions

Uganda could be considered a success story for structural adjustment programmes. In ten years Uganda's economic reforms have reduced the current account deficit from 50 to about 10 percent of GDP, reduced its debt service from over 125 to 21 percent of GDP and lowered inflation from 237 to 11 percent. Achieving these levels has not been easy, but Uganda has moved relatively rapidly towards the ambitious goals it set in its Economic Recovery Programme in 1987.

In 1997, GDP was $6.3 billion, of which 88 percent was accounted for by private consumption, 9 percent by government expenditures and 20 percent by investment spending (both private and public). The real growth rate in 1996/97 (the fiscal year runs from July to June) was 5 percent, with 5.5 percent forecast for 1997/98 and 7 percent for 1998/99. With the population increasing at about 3 percent per year, those growth rates imply significant gains in per caput income. The economy is largely agricultural, although this sector is gradually declining in importance as manufacturing and the wholesale and retail trade recover some of their former capacity (see Figure 22).

Uganda's economic programme of reform consisted of an ambitious and wide-ranging agenda, encompassing physical and economic rebuilding, as well as a shift from a war-oriented to a production-oriented society. On the list of critical changes were: the liberalization of producer and consumer prices; the stabilization of inflation; decontrol of the overvalued exchange rate; a 60 percent reduction of the military forces; a decrease in government ownership of industry; the rebuilding of infrastructure; and restoration of the financial system and credit relationships.

The immediate steps taken in 1987/88 set the tone for a determined move towards a restructured economy. In the first in a series of devaluations, the shilling was replaced by the new Ugandan shilling in 1987 and devalued by 60 percent, increasing exports and lowering imports. Producer prices for agricultural exports were allowed to rise in response to the devaluation and production followed suit. Within the next few years, government expenditures declined substantially, although priority sectors of primary health care, road maintenance and education were protected from cuts. While not meeting the original targets for reductions, 20 000 soldiers were discharged from military service and civil service employment was reduced. In order to improve the savings rate and develop a functioning credit system, the government liberalized interest rates and initiated a market in treasury bills to finance its operations.

All of these moves contributed to a more stable macroeconomic environment. Markets of all types began to function more smoothly, consumers and producers became willing to operate within the monetary system and importers and exporters faced world prices. Payment for critical imports was guaranteed by donor agencies, thus heading off bottlenecks and credit problems that would keep out needed capital products.

Current conditions
The government is projecting GDP growth for 1997/98 at a rate of 7.5 percent but, owing to excess seasonal rainfall,

The weather problems of 1996 and 1997 slowed growth in agricultural production, the economic mainstay, but the economy is expected to recover quickly if government spending is kept in check.

outside observers are anticipating only about 5.5 percent. The weather problems of 1996 and 1997 slowed growth in agricultural production particularly, the economic mainstay, to only 1.1 percent in 1996/97, which resulted in some shrinkage of the non-monetary sector of the economy. Expectations are that the economy will recover relatively quickly if government spending is kept in check, preventing inflation from rising again and restoring GDP growth to near the levels of 7 to 8 percent. The current account deficit for 1996/97 was 6.5 percent of GDP, while it is projected to be slightly lower in 1997/98 at 5.8 percent. Excluding official grants, the current account deficit would have been 6.1 percent of GDP in the past year. Foreign exchange reserves have gradually risen to 4.6 months' worth of imports in 1996/97.

Public revenue shortfalls continue to be a problem. The government has been under strong pressure from international lenders to improve revenue flows and create systems that will eliminate smuggling and corruption. Some improvement was seen between 1991 and 1995/96 with government revenues doubling to 11 percent of GDP and the introduction of a value-added tax. A change in the governance of the revenue service was carried out in late 1997 to stem apparent corruption. This was one of the conditions of the $140 million IMF loan approved in November 1997. Nonetheless, tax revenues continue to fall short of government goals and the high level of non-monetized activity is part of the problem. Another problem is in implementing completely the new value-added tax.

The government's recent policy orientation and priorities continue to emphasize broad growth and diversification, monetary and fiscal stringency and protection of the poor during continued economic adjustment. These policies are described in the Policy Framework Paper developed in cooperation with the major multilateral creditors and disseminated in October 1997. Financial sector reforms and privatization of some further manufacturing facilities and government-owned utilities are going ahead. These changes are expected to increase government revenues, reduce the civil service and spawn substantial private investment in Uganda. The government's goal is to see an increase in investment from 20 to 23 percent of GDP during the three-year planning period.

FDI has picked up in recent years since the liberalization of foreign ownership in 1991. FDI was only $3 million in

1993 but had grown to $160 million in 1996/97. Combined with large inflows of capital in the form of concessionary loans and aid, Uganda has incurred a balance-of-payments surplus in the past few years. This has put some upward pressure on the Ugandan shilling at times, and the government has had to work hard to avoid exchange rate fluctuations. Some exchange rate intervention was performed in 1996/97 and again in 1997/98 to maintain a stable currency. This has been made difficult by the increasing use of the Ugandan shilling for business transactions in the eastern part of the Democratic Republic of the Congo. Remittances from that region have jumped by 70 percent from normal flows, and some observers estimate that up to one-third of Ugandan currency is in use in the Democratic Republic of the Congo. Liquidity problems may ensue.

Uganda's balance-of-payments surplus has sometimes put upward pressure on the Ugandan shilling.

Privatization has been carried out rather slowly. The IMF credit granted in November 1997 is designed in part to hasten the process. There have been efficiency-enhancing investments and privatizations in many sectors, but telecommunications, banking and electricity are all still in need of rehabilitation. The current schedule agreed on with external donor support is to complete the privatization process by 1999 through the sale of more than 70 public mining and manufacturing enterprises. However, in early 1998, a controversy erupted in the parliament over the privatization programme amid concerns that companies were being sold too cheaply to foreign investors, and that credit would be unavailable to the rural population after the sale of the Uganda Commercial Bank. Similar issues have held up the sale of the Uganda Post and Telecommunications enterprise.

Trade

Trade is important to Uganda, but is not highly diversified. As a share of GDP, trade in goods and services comprises 25 percent, with imports accounting for the bulk of that total – nearly 20 percent of GDP. Uganda is a member of the Common Market for Eastern and Southern Africa (COMESA) and as such has low and preferential tariff treatment with the other 12 member states. Uganda also participates as a member of the International Coffee Organization, the International Sugar Agreement and the International Cotton Council.

Trade in goods and services comprises 25 percent of GDP, with imports accounting for the bulk of that total.

Figure 23A

UGANDA: MAJOR IMPORTS, 1996

Road vehicles
Machinery
Petroleum and products
Medical products
Iron and steel
Mineral products
Cereals
Textile yarn
Textile fibres
Chemicals
Vegetable fats

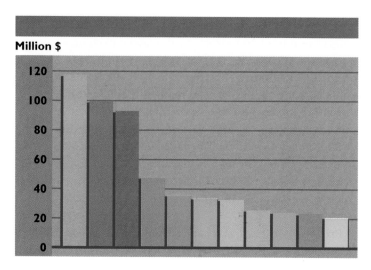

Figure 23B

UGANDA: MAJOR EXPORTS, 1996

Coffee
Cotton
Tea
Tobacco
Maize
Beans
Fish
Gold and compounds

Source: Statistical Abstract,
Government of Uganda, 1997

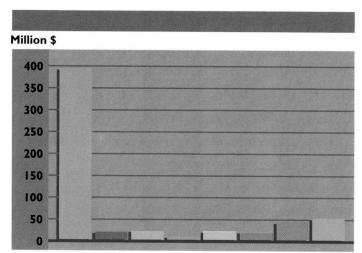

Figure 24A

UGANDA: PRODUCTION OF MAJOR EXPORT CROPS, 1987-1997

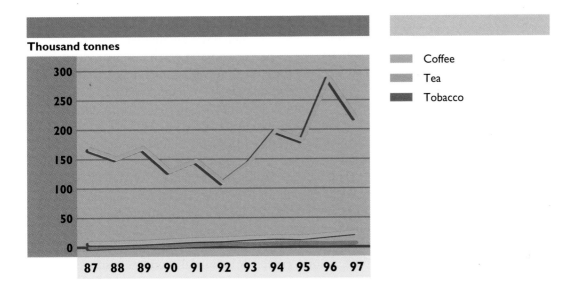

Thousand tonnes

Coffee
Tea
Tobacco

Figure 24B

UGANDA: PRODUCTION OF PRIMARY FOOD CROPS, 1987-1997

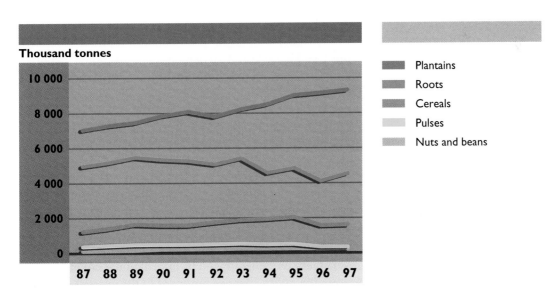

Thousand tonnes

Plantains
Roots
Cereals
Pulses
Nuts and beans

Despite COMESA, Uganda's major trading partners for imports are in Europe and Asia, and import duties have contributed the largest share of government revenues until very recently (40 percent in 1994/95). An export tax on coffee alone contributed 50 percent of the government's revenue in 1992/93 when it was eliminated. The average tariff rate was 17 percent in 1994/95, but some reduction has occurred since then, including the replacement of the 145 percent tariff on petroleum imports with a 215 percent excise tax. Similar switching of an excise tax for import duties was applied to luxury goods in 1993/94, although they still face relatively high tariffs. Agricultural inputs enter duty-free.

Uganda runs a substantial deficit on its current account, owing to its imports of vehicles, machinery and equipment and petroleum which together currently account for about one-half of total imports. These are largely funded by foreign assistance credits. Imports have increased faster than exports, especially industrial products to support economic restructuring (see Figure 23). While the country produces some of its energy needs through hydropower, it lacks petroleum resources and must import petroleum for a major part of its manufacturing and transportation operations.

Exports of traditional agricultural products have increased in value but not as a proportion of GDP or total trade.

Exports of traditional agricultural products (coffee, tea and cotton) have increased in value in recent years, although not as a proportion of GDP or total trade as economic growth outpaces production of traditional export crops (see Figure 24). A 70 percent jump in "other" exports, mainly gold, served to bolster the overall merchandise balance and prevent a larger increase in the current account deficit in 1997.

Total exports increased by 7 percent in 1997 over the previous year, despite a 13 percent decrease in the value of coffee exports that dampened the expected performance. This was caused by a drop in international coffee prices. Export revenues from coffee worsened in 1997/98 with the 24 percent drop in coffee production caused by poor weather.

Further trade liberalization has been promised by the government and encouraged by international creditors. Among the policy changes proposed in the current budget are the reduction of import duties on goods from non-COMESA countries from 30 to 20 percent and the elimination of import bans on all products.

Agricultural conditions

The Ugandan economy is heavily oriented towards
agriculture. Accounting for 44 percent of total output and
80 percent of employment, the agricultural sector is
concentrated in the southern part of the country where
weather patterns provide for two growing seasons. Table 4
shows the output of various agricultural products in
Uganda. The most important export crops are coffee,
cotton, tea and maize. The main food crops are tubers and
roots, maize, beans, sesame and sorghum. Almost half of
agricultural production (19 percent of GDP) is traded or
bartered for subsistence consumption outside the market
system. Most agriculture is performed on farms of less than
2 ha, using family labour and non-mechanized methods.
Subsistence production of agriculture still accounts for
about two-fifths of agricultural output, and one-fifth of total
economic output.

*Almost half of agricultural
production is traded or
bartered for subsistence
consumption outside the
market system.*

Table 4

AGRICULTURAL PRODUCTION IN UGANDA, 1996/97

Commodity	Volume ('000 tonnes)	Percentage of total
Coffee	287 925	88
Tea	16 939	5
Plantains	9 144	3
Tobacco	6 349	2
Root crops	4 111	1
Cereals	1 588	0.5
Pulses	356	0.11
Nuts	285	0.09
Total	**326 697**	**100**

It was Uganda's subsistence agricultural sector that
enabled the population to survive the devastation and
collapse of the modern economy under the Idi Amin
regime, and many people still rely on small plots of land
or gardens to provide a steady supply of food. Even in the
urban areas of Kampala and smaller towns, a farming
tradition, coupled with an uncertain food supply from the
rural areas, leads to urban agricultural production.
Various estimates indicate that between 30 and 50 percent
of families in Kampala engage in some form of
agriculture.[8]

R. FAIDUTTI/FAO/19294

Family members gathering coffee berries

Coffee represents about 60 percent of Uganda's exports.

Prior to the economic collapse, Uganda had been self-sufficient in food, thanks to its good soil fertility and favourable climate.

Prior to the economic collapse, Uganda had been self-sufficient in food, thanks to its good soil fertility and favourable climate. Currently, 6 percent of Uganda's total imports are food products (sugar, vegetable oil and cereals). Agriculture had also been a large earner of foreign exchange and was the main reason for successive current account surpluses. There is a strong possibility that this position can be regained, according to the positive trends of the economic reforms under way.

Only about one-third of the land available for cultivation is currently in use, and almost none is irrigated. The largest area of cultivated land is planted with bananas (30 percent of cultivated area, concentrated in the mountain systems in the west and east); cereal planting takes up 23 percent of cultivated land, largely in the north and northwest of the country, followed by, in declining order of land utilization, roots, pulses, oilseeds, coffee and cotton.

Despite the dominance of Uganda's agricultural sector in GDP and employment and its growth in absolute terms, it has actually receded substantially over the past decade in relative terms. Following the breakdown in the economy in the 1970s and early 1980s, agriculture was practically the sole productive activity for Ugandans, and was critically important to the country's survival. However, both export

Figure 25

COMPOSITION OF UGANDAN EXPORTS, 1990-1996

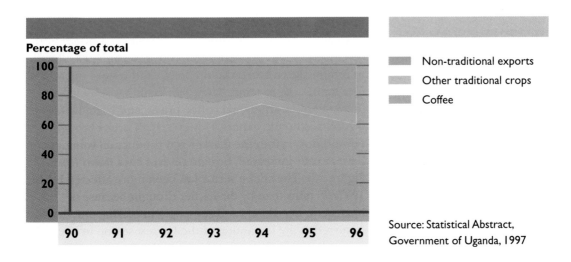

Percentage of total

Non-traditional exports
Other traditional crops
Coffee

Source: Statistical Abstract,
Government of Uganda, 1997

agriculture and agricultural processing were greatly damaged, leaving subsistence agriculture as the primary economic activity.

As recently as 1990, agriculture accounted for 57 percent of GDP in Uganda, and coffee accounted for 80 percent of exports. The Economic Recovery Plan successfully diversified the economy so that manufacturing now accounts for 12 percent of output, up from only 5 percent in 1987. The agricultural sector has also become more diversified. Coffee has dropped to about 60 percent of all exports, but export revenues from coffee have fluctuated very widely since the 1989 breakup of the quotas established by the International Coffee Organization (see Figure 25).

Food crops account for 71 percent of agricultural output, and take up 92 percent of planted land. This subsector was seriously damaged in late 1996 and early 1997 by drought conditions, and again in late 1997 and early 1998 by extremely heavy rainfall and then flooding. Because of the drought, total agricultural production grew by only 3.9 percent from 1996 to 1997, compared with 8.6 percent the previous year. The combined effect was a drop of 25 percent in crop production between early 1997 and early 1998, which caused IMF to adjust its forecast for GDP growth from 8 to 5.5 percent for 1997/98. Food-crop production fell

Uganda is Africa's leading coffee producer.

substantially short of the population's needs in 1997. Severe food shortages declared in 21 out of 39 government districts, especially in some of the most vulnerable areas of the north, northwest and southwest which have large refugee settlements.

Uganda is Africa's leading coffee producer. Coffee revenues have been a mainstay of the government's efforts to reduce the current account deficit and restore the foreign reserve position. The early 1990s saw substantial increases in international coffee prices, and Uganda was in a good position to export. However, high prices brought new producers into the market and production volumes have already increased, bringing prices back down (see Figure 26). The coffee sector has been more affected by the 1997/98 rains than by the earlier drought because of harvest timing. Delays and stoppages in picking and drying occurred at the beginning of the harvest season in late 1997 and processing plants were underutilized because of a lack of coffee crop. Export volumes were cut by almost two-thirds from the previous year in the initial stages of the harvest, but recovered substantially by the end of the export season in April 1998.

Nonetheless, price weaknesses continue to reduce export earnings from coffee. Average prices for Uganda's main variety of coffee, robusta, are forecast to fall by 9 percent between 1997 and 1998. Furthermore, the new suppliers and a new quality control system implemented by a major international coffee trading company based in London may permanently harm the market for Ugandan coffee beans. There have been reports recently of excessive moisture in Uganda's coffee shipments, and there is serious concern that negative publicity may cause buyers to try other coffee producers now that new production is available.

Tea and cotton are also important traditional export crops for Uganda. Tea production rose again in 1997/98, compared with 1996, and export earnings should rise as well. Cotton production was damaged by the drought in the early part of 1997, which curtailed planting, and then the late-season rains interfered with the transport of cotton to the ginning plants late in the year. Thus, at 110 000 bales in 1996/97, cotton production is little more than half the volume of the previous year; however, cotton output is still greatly increased since the early 1990s. A substantial amount of multilateral assistance has been

Figure 26

UGANDA: EXPORT EARNINGS AND WORLD COFFEE PRICES, 1985-1996

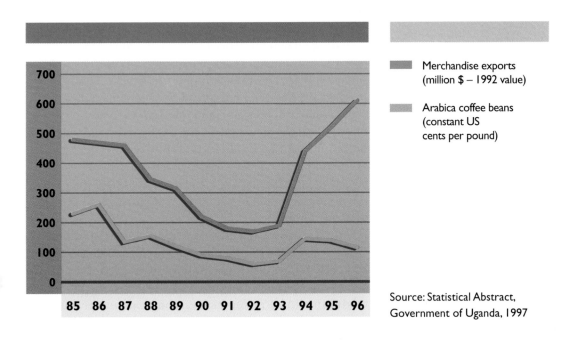

Merchandise exports
(million $ – 1992 value)

Arabica coffee beans
(constant US
cents per pound)

Source: Statistical Abstract,
Government of Uganda, 1997

directed at modernizing the cotton processing facilities in order to return cotton to being a major foreign exchange earner for Uganda.

Among other important crops grown in Uganda are sugar, grazing livestock and forestry. Each of these sectors has shown substantial recovery since the collapse of the 1970s and 1980s, but has yet to become an important economic contributor. Fishing, which is concentrated in the major lakes that dot Uganda's borders and interior, is an important source of protein for Uganda's population as well as producing significant exports.

The past two years of weather-related problems illustrate the fragility of Uganda's economic dependence on agriculture. Flooding and landslides caused by the torrential rains wiped out bridges and roads, swept away fields of planted crops and disrupted harvesting, delivery and marketing of food crops. Food prices jumped quite precipitously in some regions, especially where roads became totally impassable and crops could not be delivered to processing plants. The decline in food production and lower growth in agricultural production

The past two years of weather-related problems illustrate the fragility of Uganda's economic dependence on agriculture.

overall in 1997/98 both contributed to slower overall growth.

Agricultural issues and policies

Lack of modern farming methods. The rural areas of Uganda, including farming practices, have changed relatively little over the last three decades. Ninety percent of the rural population are subsistence farmers or fishers. Their productivity has been hampered by lack of machines or even animal traction; pre- and post-harvest pest infestations; the vicissitudes of drought and flood; inadequate storage facilities; and the destruction of much of the excellent transportation infrastructure that existed 30 years ago. Electricity is available to about 5 percent of the population, half of whom are in Kampala and the rest in major towns.

The government intends to improve the productivity of subsistence farmers who are the backbone of the economy.

With its recently released agricultural modernization plan to the year 2002, Uganda is exiting the rehabilitation phase and entering the development phase of economic growth. Uganda will put more emphasis on regional trade in local foodstuffs and on newer, high-value agricultural products destined for international markets. The government wants to improve the productivity of subsistence farmers who are the backbone of the economy, and expand by 6 percent annually the area under crops, particularly for large-scale commercial farmers.

The underutilization of cultivable land has been a key weakness in Uganda's efforts to reduce poverty in rural areas. It stems from the historical neglect of the smallholder farmers and inability to extend mechanization to large numbers of farmers beyond the northeastern area where it was adopted early on. Among the agricultural policy changes encouraged since 1990 has been acceptance of the reliance on small farmers for food production, reduction of transaction costs and market failures in land and credit markets and the expansion of agricultural services.

It is estimated that the cost of implementing the modernization plan, published in January 1998, will be U sh 367 billion (roughly $305.8 million). The four key areas for intervention are: improving research, extension and farmer linkages; targeting production in certain agricultural zones; improving credit access in rural areas; and promoting the development of agro-based rural industries. Success is dependent on continued investment in the country's transport network, particularly rural feeder roads.

The modernization plan tackles head-on the fact that Uganda, a country with the potential to feed much of East Africa, has extremely low crop yields owing to subsistence farming practices. Fertilizer use is very low as there is no systematic market and prices vary widely throughout the country. The plan calls for the expenditure of $120 million on improved and decentralized research and extension services. However, even though most farmers are women, the extension programme gives little emphasis to gender issues and the number of extensionists remains minimal.

Uganda has the potential to feed much of East Africa, but current subsistence farming practices result in extremely low crop yields.

Given the volatility of international markets for coffee and for the country's other traditional exports – cotton, tea, sugar and tobacco – the government is eager to diversify its economic base. One way in which it intends to do so is by increasing the sales of non-traditional agricultural exports. In 1996, non-traditional agricultural exports accounted for 34.5 percent of export earnings, compared with 14 percent in 1990. The two types of non-traditional exports are:

- Low-value traditional foods that are not traditionally exported, particularly maize, rice, beans, oilseeds and dairy products. These are sold to Uganda's neighbouring countries.
- New, high-value agricultural products destined for wealthy markets: spices, fancy vegetables, fruits, nuts, livestock products including hides and live goats for the Near East, fish, silk, pyrethrum and citronella oil.

Uganda's storage and transportation infrastructure is weak so producers have difficulty meeting the developed world's complex requirements for highly perishable produce, be it for crisp dwarf vegetables or just-budding hothouse flowers. "The export markets are limited, competitive and volatile," the modernization plan states. "Requirements are also demanding in terms of produce type, size, quality, packaging, delivery schedule and frequency." As a landlocked country, Uganda is at a disadvantage in competing with coastal neighbours such as Kenya for sales of these high-value crops.

Regional markets for lower-value produce are more accessible to Uganda. The modernization plan identifies

137

two types of regional client: other East African countries such as Kenya, the United Republic of Tanzania and Ethiopia which suffer regularly from food shortages owing to drought and flooding; and international agencies serving refugees and displaced persons in the region. The modernization plan calls for a 20 percent expansion in the production of maize, rice, beans, oilseeds and dairy products for sale regionally.

The Achilles' heel of this regional approach is the persistence of trade barriers between countries of the region. COMESA has achieved some success in breaking down regional trade barriers with a mandate to promote trade, investment and payments among the signatories. Another issue is whether neighbouring governments and relief agencies will be in a position to buy Uganda's foodstuffs. Money is not the only problem. The World Food Programme (WFP) has been discouraged from buying foodstuffs in Uganda because local trading houses have not always adhered to their contractual obligations with WFP, and the food quality does not always meet WFP's standards.

One of the greatest hindrances to growth in Uganda is the poor transport infrastructure.

One of the greatest hindrances to growth in Uganda is the poor transport infrastructure. A lack of institutional capacity combined with natural disasters has held back the roads rehabilitation programme. While principal and trunk highways have been restored, it is estimated that one-quarter of feeder roads are impassable during the rainy season. In 1996, the World Bank and Uganda signed a ten-year programme of $1.5 billion for roads. In 1997, the World Bank invested $30 million to build institutional capacity for road construction and maintenance, and another $30 million for emergency road repairs necessitated by damage inflicted by the torrential rains and flooding.

Unavailability of farm credit. If agriculture is to be Uganda's economic engine of growth, as it must be, investment must focus on the sector. But peasant farmers have almost no access to credit to improve their productivity or to begin micro-enterprises. Formal banks do not have adequate branch networks in rural areas and tend to view rural lending as too risky and expensive. Efforts have been made to increase access to credit for small farmers. These include the Rural Farmers' Credit Scheme which was funded by external aid donors and aimed specifically at small food growers. Farmer cooperative organizations exist in many villages and have been an important source of interim financing and other support for individual farmers.

The modernization plan seeks $37.27 million to improve access and availability of credit in rural areas. The three-stage plan would begin with small-scale microcredit groups encouraging peasants to save as well as offering them access to small sums of credit from external sources. Those would develop into fully fledged village banks linked to the formal banking system. Later, the village banks would coalesce to form district or regional banks, competing with the established banks. Village-level producer cooperatives and non-governmental organizations (NGOs) are expected to be key players in development of this model.

Uganda faces economic instability but has resources for development. In general, the Ugandan economy is still vulnerable to several sources of instability. The main one is weather, which can create boom times such as the 1992/93 period of 8.4 percent GDP growth, but can also create a severe production crisis in agriculture, such as in 1996 and 1997, thus slowing overall growth. There is little resilience in the agricultural sector to these supply shocks because of the lack of irrigation, the relatively underdeveloped mechanization, and poor storage, transportation and distribution mechanisms.

Border military activities and refugee populations are another source of instability. The country currently shelters an estimated 265 000 refugees from the Sudan, the Democratic Republic of the Congo and Rwanda who live in rural settlement camps and temporary transit points. These people are generally subsistence farmers who have faced displacement and insecurity in northern Uganda from insurgencies and attacks on their camps. In 1997, a large number of Sudanese refugees returned to areas in southern Sudan, while others voluntarily left the refugee camps and are living along the northern border of Uganda.

The other source of instability for the Ugandan economy is also a source of stability: foreign assistance. Uganda has performed well in its macroeconomic restructuring, so is favoured in the lending programmes of multilateral and bilateral donors. However, many of the government's continued reforms are almost entirely dependent on support from outside sources. Imports of equipment and machinery, which are urgently needed to continue strengthening the manufacturing sector, are generally financed by foreign funds, so there is no threat of those imports not being paid for. This process of financing physical capital imports also maintains the current account deficit that could not be maintained without aid. Nonetheless, the long-term benefits of increasing manufacturing capacity justify the trade imbalance.

Asia and the Pacific

REGIONAL OVERVIEW
Economic developments

Despite the financial crisis in East and Southeast Asia and the effects of the El Niño phenomenon, economic growth in developing Asia and the Pacific in 1997 again exceeded that of any other region and contributed to a rising per caput income in most countries. However, the regional growth rate of 6.1 percent was lower than the 7.5 percent recorded in 1996 (in turn lower than the 8.2 percent of 1995), and all subregions of Asia (except for the central Asian republics) shared in the slowdown. There was a substantial variation across countries, with Southeast Asia and the Republic of Korea being particularly affected by currency and financial turmoil in the second half of the year. In Southeast Asia as a whole, economic growth declined by almost half. Economic growth in Thailand and a number of Pacific Island countries was actually negative. Average growth across the newly industrialized economies of Hong Kong, the Republic of Korea, Singapore and Taiwan Province of China slowed but remained substantial at 6 percent. Economic activity in China continued to cool down but still expanded at an impressive 8.8 percent. In India, GDP growth slowed from 7.5 to 5 percent. As the full impacts of the currency and financial crisis take hold, real economic growth in developing Asia is expected to decline to about 4 percent in 1998 before making a slight recovery to a little more than 5 percent in 1999.[9]

Economic growth in developing Asia and the Pacific in 1997 exceeded that of any other region.

The most striking aspect of Asian economic performance in 1997 was the combined effect of two negative events in Southeast Asia: the countries in this subregion suffered from El Niño-related climatic disturbances, with implications for agricultural performance, food security and public health, at the same time as suffering from severe financial disturbances created by currency depreciations, reversals of net capital flows and strains on banking systems and capital markets as well as on corporate liquidity and credit availability. By the end of the year, these financial disturbances had spread to the Republic of Korea and precipitated IMF-led rescue packages for Indonesia, the Republic of Korea and Thailand, totalling more than $100 billion.

A stylized account of the regional currency and financial crisis can be explained as follows. While rapid globalization

Figure 27

ASIA AND THE PACIFIC

Agricultural export and import values and share in total merchandise trade

Agricultural exports ($)

Agricultural imports ($)

Ag. exports as share of total (%)

Ag. imports as share of total (%)

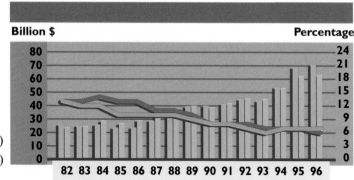

Agricultural exports
(Index 1989-91=100)

Value

Unit value

Quantity

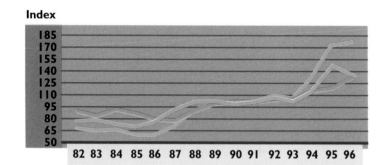

Agricultural imports
(Index 1989-91=100)

Value

Unit value

Quantity

Net barter and income agricultural terms of trade
(Index 1989-91=100)

Net barter

Income

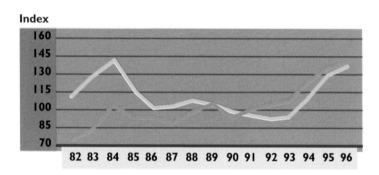

ASIA AND THE PACIFIC

Percentage

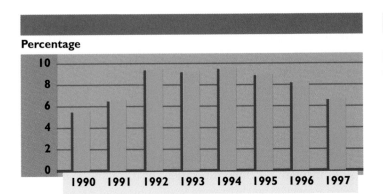

Real GDP
(Percentage change over previous year)

kcal

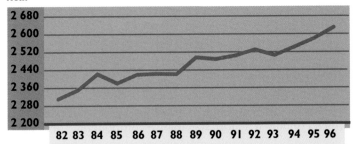

Dietary energy supplies
(kcal per caput per day)

Index

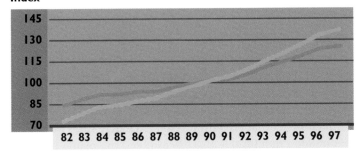

Agricultural production
(Index 1989-91=100)

Total
Per caput

Source: FAO and IMF

143

had brought substantial benefits to developing Asia, it also heightened risks associated with the failure to address policy mistakes, weaknesses in financial sector institutions and problems in corporate and public governance. As trade grew rapidly and nominal exchange rates remained effectively pegged to a rising US dollar, substantial current account deficits arose. These were partly in response to structural changes in the "real" side of the affected economies and partly due to an appreciation of their real exchange rates. The combination of increased current account deficits and rising real exchange rates was sustained by private capital flows from abroad. Only a small fraction of this flow came in the form of FDI; the remainder came either through portfolio investment or through the banking sector, especially as short-term loans. Once the surge of private capital inflows started, a rampant increase in domestic asset prices ensued, in turn inducing further capital inflows.

The surge of private foreign capital brought about imbalances in the banking sector of the countries most affected, as foreign liabilities of commercial banks increased more rapidly than foreign assets and much of the collateral for loans consisted of real estate and equities, the prices of which contained a large speculative component. There was also an imbalance in the maturity structure of banks' assets and liabilities. Financial institutions were often subject to non-transparent and lax regulatory enforcement. In addition, the behaviour of some financial institutions reflected an implicit belief that their financial liabilities were guaranteed by their respective governments. In a context of surging capital inflows, implicit government guarantees to creditors encouraged excessive risks to be taken and allowed loan portfolio quality to deteriorate. An implicit belief that effectively fixed exchange rates would be maintained indefinitely also discouraged the prudent hedging of foreign liabilities.

While saving was generally high, it was often not invested most productively. As falling returns began to disappoint investors, particularly following the 1996 export slowdown, their exuberance faded rapidly. The five economies most adversely affected by the crisis (Indonesia, Malaysia, the Philippines, the Republic of Korea and Thailand) recorded an aggregate net foreign capital outflow of $12 billion in 1997, compared with an inflow of $93 billion in 1996. The values of currencies began to fall and interest rates to climb in these countries. High, unhedged debt-to-equity ratios, which had offered easy financial assistance for growth in better times, began to imperil company finances as well as those of the financial institutions that lent to them.

The social consequences of the economic crisis are likely to be serious, although they are becoming apparent more gradually. Unemployment and inflation are rising, while company closures and the resultant redundancies are leading to massive migration flows out of the countries affected. Social safety nets, which were already weak or poorly developed in many places, are coming under increasing pressure. These problems vary in gravity, in some cases giving cause for concern. For instance, in the Republic of Korea, the wholesale and retail trade index fell in the second half of 1997 for the first time in 18 years, and it is expected to fall again by record amounts during the first half of 1998. Such a slowdown in consumption is indicative of both low income growth and loss of consumer confidence. Indonesia was particularly hard-hit by the financial crisis, the impact of which was compounded by internal political problems and extensive forest fires in areas affected by El Niño-induced drought. The population has suffered from food shortages and price increases; despite very weak private consumption, the inflation rate is expected to rise from the 11 percent recorded in 1996 to 16 percent in 1998; and the country's already high unemployment numbers are expected to increase significantly (reaching 8 or 9 million in 1998). The Philippines weathered the financial crisis with a satisfactory economic performance featuring a 5.8 percent growth in GNP, a level supported by substantial remittances of hard currency from overseas contract workers. Thus, the Philippines is expected to emerge from the crisis ahead of most other countries in the region, although it will still face lower growth and higher unemployment rates, the latter being expected to increase from 8.7 percent in 1997 to more than 9 percent in 1998.

For the countries of the region, and indeed for the rest of the world, economic prospects greatly depend on the pace and extent of the recovery in Japan. Domestic economic problems in Japan, including those in the financial sector, are very serious and likely to remain so for some time. Consequently, at least in the short term, Asian economies can expect little in the way of stimulation from Japan's

After an inflow of $93 billion in 1996, five economies most affected by the crisis recorded a net foreign capital outflow of $12 billion in 1997.

Economic prospects, for Asia and the world, greatly depend on the pace and extent of the recovery in Japan.

Provided policy corrections and institutional reforms are carried through, the foundations that propelled rapid growth in the past should do so once again.

import demand. Furthermore, Japanese investments in the region are also depressed. If Japan enters into a protracted recession, this can only mean gloomier economic prospects for the region as a whole, and especially for closer trading partners.

In any case, it will take some time before countries in the region resume rates of growth comparable to those of the recent past. For some economies the road back may be longer than for others but, provided policy corrections are made and institutional reforms carried through, the foundations that propelled rapid growth in the past should do so once again.

Economic growth in China has been steadily decelerating since 1992, as efforts to avoid economic overheating through fiscal, monetary, price and credit policies have taken effect. For 1997, economic growth was 8.8 percent. While the 1997 financial crisis in Asia did not have an immediate impact on China, it may have medium-term effects by weakening demand for the country's exports, increasing competition for their markets from countries with sharply depreciated currencies and, possibly, reducing foreign investment. Meanwhile, redoubled efforts to address weaknesses in the banking and state-owned enterprise sectors may help to reduce China's vulnerability to similar crises in the future.

Weather effects, more moderate demand for manufacturing output and infrastructure bottlenecks contributed to a reduction in economic growth in India in 1997, as real GDP growth slowed from 7.5 to 5 percent. The country's current account deficit rose by more than $2 billion as imports, facilitated by trade liberalization, increased to meet a shortfall in domestic production of basic necessities, including food. The Indian economy is expected to expand by between 6.5 and 7 percent in both 1998 and 1999, with stronger growth limited by infrastructure constraints. A depreciation of the rupee may be required to maintain external competitiveness in the face of the massive depreciations in Southeast Asian currencies.

Growth in real GDP of the newly industrialized economies (Hong Kong, the Republic of Korea, Singapore and Taiwan Province of China) slipped to 6 percent in 1997, largely because of weaker export performances as world demand for electronics, semiconductors, steel and petrochemicals moderated.

Inflation remained subdued at 3.5 percent. The transfer of Hong Kong's sovereignty to China occurred smoothly in mid-1997. The new Hong Kong Special Administrative Region continues to develop as a financial and business services centre, although the region's economic crisis and higher interest rates have reduced the pace of economic activity. In late 1997, the currency and financial turmoil in Southeast Asia spread to the Republic of Korea, which eventually resorted to an IMF-led rescue package of more than $50 billion, conditional on substantial policy reforms. The restrictive policy measures required imply that the economy will contract, and expectations are that full recovery to the country's potential growth path will take at least two years. Singapore emerged from the region's financial crisis in a better economic condition than its immediate neighbours, although it suffered some currency depreciation and a substantial fall in its stock market index. Spillover effects, especially from Indonesia, are likely to keep Singapore's economic growth subdued in the near future, however. The financial crisis left Taiwan Province of China relatively unscathed, but reforms in the banking and financial sectors and the policy of encouraging high-technology activities in the country are continuing.

Southeast Asia suffered both from the physical effects of El Niño and the economic consequences of the financial crisis in 1997 and early 1998. Economic growth declined from more than 7 to less than 4 percent. Cambodia's economic performance was lacklustre, with a real GDP growth rate of just 2 percent, an inflation rate of more than 9 percent and budget revenues of less than 10 percent of GDP. However, agriculture is the largest sector in Cambodia's economy and its growth rate in 1997 picked up to 4.9 percent, compared with just 1.8 percent in 1996. Despite favourable macroeconomic fundamentals, Indonesia was hit particularly hard by the regional crisis in late 1997, as mentioned above. The country is now undergoing comprehensive economic reforms in the context of an international rescue package of roughly $40 billion. In 1997, the Lao People's Democratic Republic continued its steady growth, but its trade and currency suffered from the crisis in neighbouring Thailand, its largest trading partner. In Malaysia, economic growth slowed to 7.5 percent in 1997 as the financial crisis took its toll through a massive

The new Hong Kong Special Administrative Region continues to develop as a financial and business services centre.

depreciation of the ringgit and a steep decline in stock market values. Fiscal and monetary measures introduced in response to the crisis in the later part of the year also restrained growth. Myanmar continued the slow process of implementing a market economy, and its entry into the Association of Southeast Asian Nations (ASEAN) should improve its integration into the regional and global economies. Thailand's extended period of high growth ended sharply and growth turned slightly negative in 1997 as the collapse of the baht precipitated the regional currency and financial crisis. Reforms under an international assistance package have proceeded well and, after further negative growth in 1998, the economy is expected to return to positive, if slight, growth in 1999. Viet Nam registered strong economic growth of 9.2 percent in 1997, supported by vigorous growth in both agriculture and industry. Growth is likely to be more moderate in 1998, as Viet Nam is affected by the events elsewhere in the region.

In South Asia, economic growth slipped below 5 percent in 1997, after averaging 6.8 percent from 1994 to 1996. Differences in investment and growth rates in agriculture and manufacturing accounted for wide disparities in growth among the subregion's economies. Bangladesh's economy grew rapidly in agriculture but lagged in manufacturing, posting a 5.7 percent overall growth rate. Low increases in food prices helped the country maintain its inflation rate at about 4 percent. GDP growth in Nepal declined to 4.3 percent in 1997, primarily owing to a slowdown in the non-agricultural sectors that was brought about by infrastructure and human-capacity constraints. Pakistan's growth rate dipped to 3.1 percent in 1997 and the country experienced increasing macroeconomic imbalances as its fiscal and current account deficits increased to about 6 percent of GDP. Sri Lanka experienced rapid growth in both agriculture and manufacturing, which helped increase its overall growth rate to a substantial 6.3 percent while bringing inflation down into single digits.

For agriculture, 1997 was an unfavourable year for Asia and the Pacific – despite the general economic growth registered in the region.

Agricultural performance and issues

Overall, 1997 was an unfavourable agricultural year for the region. Indeed, the rate of expansion of agricultural production fell to only 2.6 percent,[10] the lowest rate recorded in the 1990s and only the second time in the same period that agricultural production expanded by less than 4 percent. This reflects declines in the rate of agricultural production growth in most of the major countries of the region, including Bangladesh, Cambodia, China, India, Malaysia, Myanmar, the Philippines and Viet Nam. Agricultural production actually declined, by an estimated 2 to 3 percent, in Indonesia. The rate of expansion of agricultural production rose in Nepal, Pakistan, the Republic of Korea and Sri Lanka, although for this last country most of the increase represented a recovery from the sharp decline experienced in 1996.

In China, a third consecutive year of bumper grain harvests contributed to strong, if more moderate, economic growth and reduced inflation in 1997. Measures introduced since 1995 under the Grain Bag Policy, such as greater public investment in agriculture and higher procurement prices, have kept agriculture growing at 4 percent, following two years at about 7 percent. At 441 million tonnes, total cereal production was lower than in 1996, but still the second highest ever. Grain-sown area has expanded by several million hectares since 1994, most notably in the coastal provinces.

Agriculture accounts for slightly more than one-quarter of India's GDP, but production grew by little more than 1 percent in 1997, as monsoons arrived late in some areas and unseasonable and heavy rainfall occurred in others. In the first major trade liberalization of agricultural products since the current reforms began, the Government of India partially or completely liberalized imports of 150 food items and reduced maximum tariff rates from 50 to 40 percent. Meanwhile, India remains a substantial net exporter of agricultural products and is usually self-sufficient in foodgrains. The government has also begun to consider the rising cost of subsidies, including agricultural subsidies such as those on foodgrains, fertilizers and water and power – these last two being substantial. A reduction of these subsidies would promote more efficient input use and grain distribution, but could have significant equity impacts and be politically difficult to implement.

In Bangladesh, the agricultural sector registered a 1 percent expansion in production following two years of a strong, 4.5 percent growth, helped by greater input availability and expanded rural credit. Agriculture still accounts for about one-third of GDP and more than two-thirds of employment. However, food and agricultural production has barely kept up with population growth in the course of the 1990s, more than half of the population is below the food-based poverty line and child and maternal malnutrition are widespread. There is a further risk that the country may experience reduced competitiveness in labour-intensive exports such as garments and frozen foods because of the large depreciations of Southeast Asian currencies.

In Indonesia, agricultural production was reduced by drought brought about by the El Niño phenomenon, compounded by forest fires and the resulting haze. This, together with the sharp depreciation of the rupiah, caused food prices to rise. The Government of Indonesia responded to the drought with cloud-seeding activities, the provision of free seeds to farmers whose food crop (especially rice) production failed and the distribution of hand tractors to accelerate planting in the main rice-producing areas. Nevertheless, this year's paddy production is forecast to be significantly smaller than the already reduced one of 1997. Large-scale international assistance is required to meet the shortage of rice. The government plans to import approximately 1.5 million tonnes, leaving an uncovered deficit estimated to be 2 million tonnes.

Three years of natural disasters in the Democratic People's Republic of Korea have aggravated the severe structural problems in the country's economy.

In the Democratic People's Republic of Korea, a severe drought in the summer of 1997 as well as a destructive typhoon, both occurring after two consecutive years of floods, resulted in a desperate food situation that was characterized by severe hardship for the population and rapidly declining nutritional standards. Total cereal production in the country in 1997 was down to an estimated 3.7 million tonnes from the 4.5 million tonnes of 1996 and the 5 million tonnes recorded as late as 1994. The effects of the three consecutive years of natural disasters have, however, only aggravated the severe structural problems in the economy, including the agricultural sector. Cereal production has indeed followed a consistently downward trend since peaking at 7.1 million tonnes in 1986.

In the Lao People's Democratic Republic, in 1997, despite floods affecting some areas, improved climatic conditions overall and increased incentives for agricultural production led to higher growth levels in the agricultural sector, which continues to account for more than one-half of the country's GDP. The important sector of subsistence agriculture helped to buffer the real economy from the regional crisis to some extent, but the events in Thailand combined with the effects of flooding to push up agricultural prices.

In mid-1997, serious flooding in Myanmar destroyed about 1.2 million ha of paddy, driving up food prices and general inflation. By early September, the government was forced to request emergency food relief from the United Nations. To increase paddy production and possibly exports, in November the government replaced its system of procuring paddy directly from farmers under a quota system with a system of purchases through a sealed tender bidding process.

Agriculture's share in Nepal's GDP has fallen to about 41 percent, but still about 80 percent of the total labour force depend on agriculture for their livelihood. Therefore, the 3 percent growth in agricultural production in 1997 helped a large share of the population. Implementation of the Agriculture Perspective Plan is expected in part to offset the effects of unfavourable weather in early 1998, but agricultural growth is still likely to decline.

In Pakistan, agricultural production growth in 1997 was 2 percent, as unseasonable rainfall and cotton pests and viruses compounded the effects of low productivity. The production of major crops such as cotton, sugar cane and wheat declined, while reduced cotton production also contributed to a drop in exports. To improve performance in the agricultural sector and reduce agricultural imports, the government announced a comprehensive package of incentives, including higher product support prices, lower input prices, an expansion of agricultural credit and improved irrigation and drainage facilities.

In the Philippines, 1997 agricultural growth was just 0.4 percent, as it was hampered by severe droughts brought on by the El Niño phenomenon and the fall in the peso. Agricultural employment, at about 40 percent of the labour force, is likely to fall in 1998 when the full impact of El Niño finally hits.

Aided by favourable weather, Sri Lanka's agricultural sector recovered in 1997, with a 7 to 8 percent growth in production. Agricultural exports rose in value terms as a result of higher tea and coconut prices, and expanded slightly in volume as well.

Agricultural production in Thailand was also hit by El Niño-related drought, and only rose marginally in 1997, with cereal output actually declining by an estimated 3 percent. The country's strong economic performance in recent years until mid-1997 has increased and diversified consumer demand for agricultural products. At the same time, agricultural exports, particularly rice, sugar, fisheries products, rubber and poultry meat have contributed to the rapid economic growth. The current financial crisis is threatening this synergistic growth, however, by crimping domestic demand and raising the prices of imported agricultural inputs. On the other hand, the depreciation of the baht may increase Thailand's export competitiveness, particularly for commodities with a low import content.

The production of rice in Viet Nam, where it is the staple food, dominant agricultural activity and an important export, was spared the worst effects of the El Niño phenomenon, and agricultural output increased by 1.5 percent. The prices of rice and other foodstuffs declined in the first half of 1997, contributing to a decline in inflation.

Issues and prospects for regional agriculture
As noted above, the unexpected Asian financial crisis is taking a heavy toll on the region, and particularly on Indonesia, Malaysia, the Philippines, the Republic of Korea and Thailand. The impacts will be felt throughout these economies, including their agricultural sectors. Currency depreciations and income contraction are reducing import demand, for instance, although the currency depreciations and greater availability of exportable surplus resulting from reduced consumption should boost export competitiveness. At the global level, these effects are likely to be seen in the markets for maize, bovine meat, soybean meal, temperate fruits, cotton and hides and skins, where Asia's imports are likely to be reduced, and in the region's exports of tropical fruits and rubber. Attempts to predict the quantitative changes likely in the future are complicated by the fact that the crisis has reduced the availability of trade financing in the countries most affected, although donor countries and multilateral financial institutions have been trying to ease the burden

Currency depreciations and the greater availability of exportable surplus resulting from reduced consumption should boost the region's agricultural export competitiveness.

with export credits and loans to the region's export-import banks.

Among cereals, the impact of the crisis is expected to fall mainly on coarse grains, and particularly maize, as the contraction in meat demand will lower import demand by an estimated 2 to 3 million tonnes. Imports of wheat, a staple food in the region, are expected to contract by not more than 1 million tonnes, with a minimal impact at the global level. Likewise, the global rice market is not expected to be affected much by the financial crisis, although El Niño-induced droughts may increase imports by Indonesia, Malaysia and the Philippines in 1998. This may work to the benefit of Thailand and possibly Viet Nam, although pressure on the US dollar price of rice will be moderated by the depreciation of the Thai baht. Exports of cassava and its products are unlikely to increase significantly, as poor weather has reduced the exportable surplus.

The financial crisis is expected to have the largest impact on the region's demand for meat, particularly bovine meat, which has high price and income elasticities of demand. The reduced demand for bovine meat in the region may be sufficient to weaken world prices in 1998 and even more so in 1999 if the crisis appears to be prolonged. The regional demand for pig and poultry meat is largely satisfied by domestic production, so little effect on these global markets is expected although there may be some trade diversion owing both to changes in demand and to changes in competitiveness, such as the recent inroads made by Thailand in Brazil's poultry sector. Regional trade in sheep meat also represents just a small share of global trade and is unlikely to influence world markets except perhaps through substitution effects as relative prices of other meats change.

Vegetable oils are staple foods in the region and their consumption is therefore unlikely to be significantly influenced by the region's income and price changes. But with reduced demand for meat, there will also be reduced demand for oilmeals and oil cakes, which are important feedstuffs. Soybean meal from China and India may be in greater demand in the region than relatively more expensive meal from Brazil or the United States. Cheaper or domestically produced palm kernel and copra meals could also be substituted for soybean meal. At the global level, the impacts on oilmeal trade are likely to be

The reduced demand for bovine meat in the Asia and Pacific region may weaken world prices in 1998 and 1999.

153

primarily in terms of trade diversion, since Southeast Asia's enhanced competitiveness will have little effect until exportable surpluses resume.

Reduced demand for dairy products in the region will primarily affect milk powder exports from Australia and New Zealand. The region's reduced demand for tropical beverages is expected to have little impact on world markets since the five most affected countries together account for only 1 to 3 percent of world imports. Tea, with low price and income elasticities of demand, will probably be affected the least, while demand for coffee is expected to fall sharply in the region but only slightly at the global level. The 1998 Indonesian coffee harvest is reported to be reduced by 30 percent owing to El Niño-induced drought but, when more favourable weather returns, the country's increased competitiveness can be expected to boost exports, assuming trade financing is available by then. The region's demand for cocoa beans for processing is expected to remain strong, given its increased export competitiveness and large installed processing capacity.

Although household consumption of sugar is relatively insensitive to price and income fluctuations, industrial sugar demand is expected to be more affected, exerting downward pressure on prices. Sugar production in Thailand was sharply reduced in 1997 and is unlikely to recover completely in 1998, thus limiting the competitiveness advantages of the baht's depreciation for this commodity.

Imports of fruits and vegetables, which have high price and income elasticities, can be expected to decline significantly, particularly those of temperate fruits and vegetables from outside the region. On the other hand, exports of tropical fruits are expected to increase, possibly displacing some African and Latin American exports in European and North American markets.

In terms of agricultural raw materials, imports of cotton by the affected countries can be expected to decline, with some impact on world prices. Demand for natural rubber has fallen with the drop in demand for automobiles, while the greater availability of rural labour is expected to increase supply, thereby depressing world rubber prices. Global demand for hides and skins will be negatively affected, particularly in the world's second largest importer, the Republic of Korea, where reduced access to working capital and foreign exchange should more than offset enhanced export competitiveness for final products.

Whether or not the numerous small (and the few greater) effects of the regional crisis on world markets become more substantial will depend on a number of factors. Chief among these are the breadth and depth of the crisis, which is not yet fully apparent, the future evolution of exchange rates and trade policies and the ease with which credit flows may be resumed, particularly for companies of processed products. The speed and extent of recovery will vary from country to country, but should nevertheless help to place future economic growth on a more solid institutional foundation.

Experiences in fiscal decentralization

As in other regions, several Asian countries have endeavoured to take advantage of decentralization as a means of fostering regional and rural development. A

Box 6

FISCAL DECENTRALIZATION IN PAKISTAN

In the last ten years, of Pakistan's total revenue generated, on average 89 percent accrued to the federal government while the share of provincial and municipal governments was 5 and 6 percent, respectively. The federal government incurs 74 percent of total recurring expenditure, followed by provincial governments with 23 percent and local governments with 4 percent. The intergovernmental fiscal transfers are made, in order of importance, from the federal government to the provincial governments, from the provincial governments to the local governments, from the federal government to the local governments and, finally, between local governments.

One of the most significant forms of fiscal transfer from the federal to the provincial governments is the sharing of revenues from taxes collected by the federal government. Provincial shares in the divisible pool are historically based on two parameters, population and collection. Development expenditure by the provincial governments is also, by and large, financed by the Annual Development Programme (ADP) of the federal government. Of overall ADP funding, 90 percent is distributed among the provinces on the basis of population while the remaining 10 percent is given to the two least-developed provinces, North-West Frontier and Baluchistan.

Local governments share revenues on the basis of origin, i.e. according to their contribution to the total tax collection. There is no revenue-sharing arrangement at present between the provincial and the rural local governments. The second fundamental difference in the fiscal transfers carried out at the various levels is the lack of access by local governments to revenue-deficit grants, which is not the case for the provincial governments. Grants-in-aid received from the provincial governments are specific in nature and generally used to finance recurring expenditures on education, health, etc., while local governments must finance any recurring deficits themselves.

During the last 15 years, therefore, provincial governments' dependence on the federal government would appear to have increased, for both a

recurring and development accounts, whereas local governments (urban and rural) have had to rely more on their own resources to discharge their obligations. The lack of increase in financial support from provincial governments is attributable to the deterioration that has taken place in their financial position over time.

Although revenue sharing has benefited all four provincial governments in Pakistan, the extent of benefit varies significantly across provinces, with some of the anomalies perhaps resulting from the lack of innovation in revenue-sharing arrangements and the exclusion of important considerations such as level of development and urbanization, land area, etc.

On top of this, it can be argued that the process of decentralization and devolution of functions will be incomplete unless the relationship between the provincial and local governments is also reformed at the same time. The strengthening of local governments is the last remaining step in the process of decentralization. Without

this, the goal of involving people in the management of matters of concern to them will remain largely unfulfilled.

Source: Q. Masood. 1997. Design of intergovernmental fiscal relations and international finance institutions. Allocations for rural development. Paper presented at the Technical Consultation on Decentralization, 16-18 December 1997, FAO, Rome.

Box 7

FISCAL DECENTRALIZATION IN CHINA

An empirical study of the impact of fiscal decentralization on rural development in China was carried out using two panel data sets. The first was a province-level panel, covering 28 provinces for the period 1970-1993, and the second a county-level panel, including ten counties each from three provinces for the period 1970-1995. The major findings were:

- *Fiscal decentralization reduced real budget revenues of county governments but increased those of provincial governments. This was despite the observation that political decentralization and adoption of the household responsibility system had impeded the ability of both the provincial and the county governments to collect taxes.*
- *Fiscal decentralization contributed to economic growth at the county level but not at the provincial level. At the county level, fiscal decentralization was found*

to have a positive, but not a significant, correlation with total income, while its correlation with agricultural income was both positive and significant. This suggests that, to have a positive effect on economic growth, fiscal resources and decision-making powers should be decentralized to the county government rather than to the provincial government level. Indeed, many provinces in China are much larger than most countries, and provincial governments may therefore not be particularly knowledgeable about or responsive to local-level conditions and needs. Moreover, because of price distortions and the government's role as investor in the Chinese economy, more autonomy may encourage provincial governments to invest in industries that duplicate others, protect provincial industries and underinvest in agricultural projects.

- *Political decentralization and the household responsibility system positively affect economic growth at the county level. Both political decentralization and the household responsibility system provide private actors with more scope for initiative, which stimulates economic growth.*
- *Except for senior high school enrolment at the provincial level, fiscal decentralization has insignificant effects on various indicators of development – including rural development – at the provincial and county levels.*
- *The household responsibility system was positively correlated with the number of doctors and nurses at the provincial level. No other decentralization measures had positive and significant effects on development indicators at the provincial or county levels.*

These results suggest that, while decentralization had a positive effect on economic growth, overall this did not extend to other dimensions of development.

The study concluded with lessons to be learned from China's experience with decentralization. For instance, to ensure that decentralization has desirable effects on rural development in China, the government's role in the economy needs to be reformed. The government's owning and operating profit-oriented economic activities runs counter to decentralization, unlike state provision of public goods which benefits the process. Finally, to be truly effective, decentralization should be extended to the lowest level of government feasible – the county in China.

Source: Lin Justin, Zhiqiang Liu and Funing Zhong. 1997. Fiscal decentralization and rural development in China. Paper presented at the Technical Consultation on Decentralization, 16-18 December 1997, FAO, Rome.

frequent reason – reported worldwide – as to why such efforts give unsatisfactory results is a lack of financial decentralization, which is needed to back up the devolution of responsibilities to levels below central government. In this respect it is interesting to note the different experiences of Pakistan and China in implementing fiscal decentralization (see Boxes 6 and 7).

Major reforms aimed at decentralization have been undertaken in China since 1979, and fiscal decentralization has been a part of these moves, involving financial arrangements between government and state enterprises and between central and local governments. In China's case, there is also evidence of the specific impact of fiscal decentralization on rural development. This, together with the impact of other reform measures on rural development, is the subject of an empirical study reviewed in Box 7.

MALAYSIA
General characteristics
Malaysia is a diverse country, in both its geography and its people. Its land area of 32 million ha is divided between the southern peninsula of Southeast Asia (West Malaysia) and the states of Sarawak and Sabah (East Malaysia), which are parts of the island of Borneo in the South China Sea. Almost 70 percent of the land area is forested, much of it is mountainous and a very small

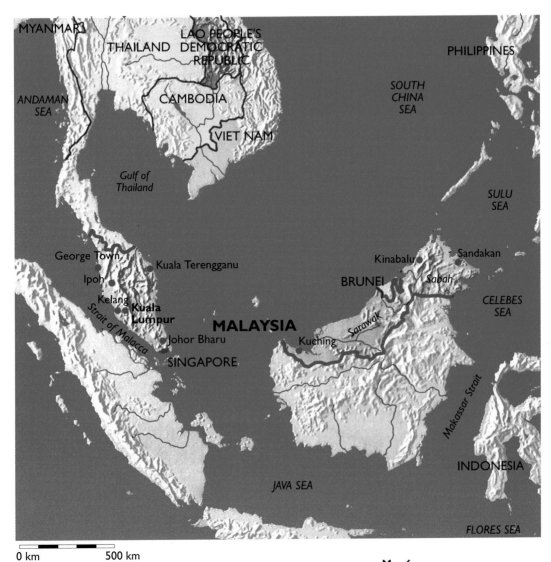

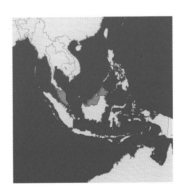

Map 6

MALAYSIA

portion consists of irrigated cropland. Malaysia has an equatorial climate with a high rainfall during the two monsoon seasons.

Malaysia's neighbours are Thailand, which is to the north of West Malaysia; Singapore, which lies just across the narrow straits below the southern tip of West Malaysia; and Borneo, an Indonesian state. Thanks to this location, Malaysia is a country of ethnic, religious and cultural diversity. In mid-1996,[11] it had a population of 21.2 million people, of whom 12 million were Malay, 5.3 million Chinese and 1.5 million Indian. Also included are about 1.3 million migrant workers, originating mainly from neighbouring Southeast Asian countries.

Historical perspective on economic development

Malaysia has been one of the world's economic success stories for the last three decades: in 1970, it had a GDP per caput of only 1 049 Malaysian ringgit ($M) ($342); by 1997, per caput income had risen to an estimated $M 11 303 ($4 316).[12] This phenomenal economic growth was accompanied by a sharp drop in the poverty rate which fell from 38 percent of the population in 1970 to 15 percent by 1995.[13] Hard-core poverty (as defined by the World Bank's lower poverty line) represented only 2.1 percent of the total population, while about 88 percent of all urban households and 72 percent of rural households had access to electricity. Moreover, at least two-thirds of rural households and 96 percent of urban households had access to such necessities as safe drinking-water, health care and education facilities.

This record of economic achievement owes much to a series of economic policy decisions, beginning with the New Economic Policy (NEP) initiated in 1971. The broad aim of the NEP was to eradicate poverty across all population groups and to ease ethnic tensions by reducing occupational barriers based on ethnicity. Other policy objectives were to increase the productivity of the rural sector by ensuring the adoption of modern techniques and the provision of better facilities; facilitate intersectoral labour mobility through education and training; and provide subsidized social services to low-income families.[14] Finally, Malaysia shifted its trade policy from import substitution towards increased exports of existing export commodities – rubber, petroleum, tin, palm oil, cocoa, forestry products and pepper. Tax incentives were created to encourage investment in basic export industries and to develop downstream processing capacity which would lead to greater exports of higher-value products.

The result of these policy moves has been the achievement of major macroeconomic goals since 1971. Malaysia has seen increased incomes and wages, stable prices, high savings and investment rates, an economy increasingly oriented towards manufactures and services, and increasing trade and diversification of exports. Rapid economic growth, which averaged 6.7 percent annually from 1970 to 1990 and more than 8 percent annually from 1990 to 1996, has occurred without igniting inflation. Prices have increased by about 3 percent per

Since 1971, Malaysia has seen increased incomes and wages, stable prices, high savings and investment rates, growing manufactures and services sectors, expanding trade and diversification of exports.

year since 1980, well below the rates of many other fast-growing economies. The financial crisis in 1997 has put greater pressure on prices, as imports have become more costly. Even so, private sources project an increase in consumer prices of 7.5 percent in 1998 and just under 5 percent in 1999.[15]

Table 5 shows the structural changes in the Malaysian economy from 1970 to 1995, during which time agriculture declined in importance from 29.9 percent of GDP to 13.6 percent. Although agriculture achieved an annual growth rate of more than 4 percent during the two decades up to 1990 and a rate of 2 percent in the 1990s, other sectors grew much faster. Manufacturing, finance, transport and communications and government services all grew faster than the agricultural sector, and hence accounted for a greater proportion of GDP in 1995.

Two decades of strong growth have led to some pressure on productive resources in Malaysia, principally caused by a tightness in labour markets, leading to rising real costs of skilled and unskilled labour and a shift of some manufacturing to neighbouring countries with lower labour costs. Labour turnover has been high, as workers have moved from one to another higher-paying job, and average pay was rising faster than productivity rates before the financial crisis.

Agriculture, construction and domestic services were most affected by the shortage of unskilled workers relative to the growing demands. The response was an influx of a foreign labour force, mostly drawn from Bangladesh, Indonesia and the Philippines. In 1995, Malaysia issued a

Table 5

GDP BY INDUSTRY OF ORIGIN[1]

Sector	1970 (million $M)	(%)	1980 (million $M)	(%)	1990 (million $M)	(%)
Agriculture, forestry, livestock, fisheries	5 949	29.9	14 829	18.7	16 406	13.6
Industry	6 423	32.2	33 368	42.2	83 289	69.2
Services	7 507	37.7	31 954	40.4	50 358	41.9
GDP at factor cost	19 929		79 103		120 316	

[1] In 1978 prices.

High wages led to the erosion of Malaysia's price competitiveness in international markets.

total of 650 000 work permits[16] but there was estimated to be an equal number of illegal foreign workers in the country.[17]

Higher wages in some sectors spilled over into others, and Malaysia saw its price competitiveness eroded in international markets. Labour shortages and higher costs eventually forced some industries to shift manufacturing activities to neighbouring countries such as Indonesia and the Philippines where there is a greater abundance of low-wage labour. The recent currency devaluation has, for the moment, relieved some of the cost pressure in some of these industries. Nevertheless, among the low-wage countries, the ringgit has depreciated only against China's renmingbi; it has maintained its value against the Thai baht and the Philippine peso and appreciated sharply against the Indonesian rupiah.

Malaysia's position has shifted from that of a low-cost supplier of labour-intensive, basic manufactured products to a country in the process of developing the human capital and technical capacity to produce goods and services with a higher value-added component.

Structure of Malaysian agriculture

Malaysian agriculture, broadly defined, includes perennial and food crops as well as livestock, fisheries and forestry. Table 6 shows the value added by each of the major sectors during the first half of the 1990s. The perennial commodities account for the largest share of Malaysia's agricultural output with 57 percent of the total value added for agriculture in 1995. Within this group are three major export commodities, rubber, palm oil and cocoa. Palm oil is the largest by far and was the only one of the three to have a positive growth rate for the period shown.

The food commodity group accounted for 21 percent of value added in agriculture in 1995, with fisheries being the most important, followed by livestock and paddy. Each experienced positive growth in the period. Forestry products, as measured by the output of sawlogs, experienced a 4 percent average annual decline. Miscellaneous crops, including tobacco, pineapple, other fruits and vegetables, sago, etc., accounted for roughly 10 percent of agricultural value added and, as a group, grew faster than any other major grouping over the period.

Table 6

AGRICULTURAL VALUE ADDED, 1990-1995[1]

	1990	1995	1995 share	Average
	(million $M)		(%)	annual growth (%)
Perennial commodities	8 585	9 365	57.1	1.7
Rubber	2 043	1 745	10.6	-3.1
Palm oil	5 312	6 801	41.4	5.1
Cocoa	1 230	819	5.0	-7.8
Food commodities	2 738	3 502	21.3	4.9
Paddy	600	666	4.1	2.1
Livestock	604	838	5.1	6.8
Fisheries	1 534	1 998	12.2	3.7
Forestry (sawlogs)	2 315	1 876	11.4	-4.1
Miscellaneous	1 189	1 663	10.1	6.7
Total	14 827	16 406	100.0	2.0

[1] In 1978 prices.
Source: Government of Malaysia, Economic Planning Unit. 1991 and 1996. Sixth Malaysia Plan, 1991-1995 and Seventh Malaysia Plan, 1996-2000. Kuala Lumpur, Percetakan Nasional Malaysia Berhad.

Perennial crops: palm oil, rubber and cocoa[18]

Figure 28 shows the change in area planted to the three major perennial crops in Malaysia since 1980. (Data are divided between estate and smallholder production regimes, which are discussed under the section Land allocation policies, p.165.) The total area planted in perennial crops grew from 3 million to 4.3 million ha between 1980 and 1990, but expansion slowed during the 1990s as limits on land availability were reached. By 1995, total area planted to the three crops was only 4.5 million ha. Oil palm area doubled during the 1980s and has maintained that pace of expansion during the first half of the 1990s. The overall slowdown is due to an absolute decline in area planted to the other two crops.

Oil palm covers about one-third of Malaysia's cultivated area, with 1.9 million ha on the peninsula and 600 000 ha in Sabah and Sarawak. Most of the new land for oil palm is coming from eastern Malaysia because very little land for agricultural development is available on the peninsula. Production of crude palm oil reached 7.8 million tonnes in 1995, accounting for 51 percent of world palm oil production and 8.3 percent of world oils and fats output. Malaysia is the world's largest producer and exporter of

Expansion of the total area planted to perennial crops in Malaysia slowed during the 1990s as land availability was exhausted.

Malaysia is the world's largest producer and exporter of palm oil.

palm oil; the country's exports account for about 65 percent of world palm oil trade and, in 1995, its earnings from exports of palm oil and derived products amounted to almost $M 13 billion.

The rapid development of the palm oil industry may be attributed to good growing conditions and increasing prices relative to other export commodities. Favourable climatic conditions in Malaysia have made the crop easily adaptable from its origin of West Africa and the tropical regions of the American continent (its natural habitat). This, combined with a strong global demand for fats and oils over the last two decades, has provided a tremendous economic incentive to expand production.

The success of oil palm stands in sharp contrast to the other two major perennial crops, rubber and cocoa. The production of natural rubber in 1995 was only 1.1 million tonnes – down from a peak of 1.6 million tonnes in 1976. Rising labour costs have hit the estates especially hard, and some have moved into oil palm because of its higher returns. Figure 28 shows the decline in land area planted to rubber among the estates. There has been less change in smallholder area planted to rubber as the crop is well suited to smallholders who can devote part of their household labour to tapping and maintenance of the rubber trees while working full time in other enterprises. Thus, smallholders are less affected by the tight labour markets. Rubber is and will remain an important crop in Malaysia, however. Exports still accounted for more than $M 4 billion in sales in 1995 and, although conversion of land out of rubber will continue, there are large areas where other crops cannot be planted economically and where rubber is likely to be the most profitable choice.

Although land is being converted out of rubber, there are large areas where other crops are not economically viable and so rubber remains the most profitable choice.

Cocoa (and its products) is Malaysia's third most important export crop with total sales in 1996 of $M 594 million. Cocoa was one of the crops identified in a diversification strategy of the 1970s when falling rubber and palm oil prices led the government to seek ways of increasing the earnings of agricultural producers, especially smallholders. Throughout the early 1990s, a combination of falling world prices for cocoa, rising labour costs, and a decline in yields associated with the cocoa borer pest led to a decline in area planted to cocoa. By 1996, production had fallen to 120 000 tonnes (dry bean basis) from a peak of 247 000 tonnes in 1990.[19] Seventy percent of Malaysia's cocoa production originates in Sabah.

Figure 28

AREA PLANTED TO PERENNIAL CROPS IN MALAYSIA

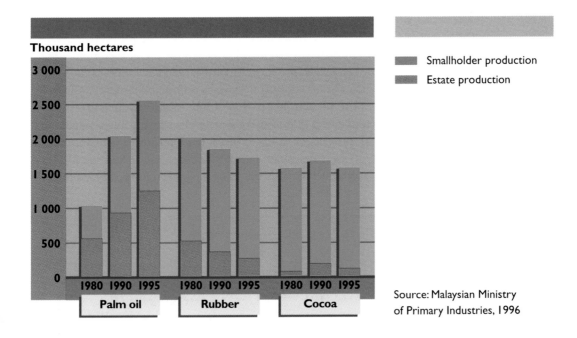

Thousand hectares

■ Smallholder production
■ Estate production

Source: Malaysian Ministry of Primary Industries, 1996

Perennial crops: policy environment

Three sets of policies have influenced the growth of the perennial crops – land allocation policies, trade policies and, recently, immigration policies (which is mentioned in the section on Labour issues, p.170).

Land allocation policies. Malaysia's three major perennial crops – palm oil, rubber and cocoa – are produced by the estate and smallholder subsectors. The latter includes independent producers on private holdings as well as participants in government land development schemes. The estate subsector largely comprises privately owned farms using hired (often foreign) labour and modern technology and usually owning some of the necessary processing and/or refining facilities. Many of these estates are under publicly traded corporate ownership.

Smallholders often farm part time to supplement other income sources and, when prices are low, reduce or temporarily abandon farming activities so as to increase

Smallholders often farm part time to supplement other income sources and reduce or temporarily abandon farming activities when prices are low.

their work effort in other areas. Hence, yields in the smallholder subsector tend to fluctuate more with economic conditions.

However, even when prices are strong for the perennial crops, smallholder yields are much lower than those in the estate sector. Smallholder yields are 60 percent of estate yields for rubber and 70 percent of those for oil palm. This yield disparity is a major concern for the government whose assistance in the form of land settlement schemes (see Box 8) and extension services is directed almost exclusively at the smallholder sector. Other assistance, such as replanting grants and government loans, while available to all producers, tends to be more generous for smallholders.

The issue of the disparity between estate and smallholder productivity continues to be a concern for policy-makers,

Box 8

MALAYSIA'S LAND ALLOCATION PROGRAMMES

Since attaining independence in 1957, Malaysia has used its relatively abundant undeveloped land resources as a means of redistributing income and improving the welfare of its rural poor. The purpose of the land allocation programmes is to provide income opportunities for poor farmers by growing cash crops for export – rubber, oil palm and, later, cocoa – rather than subsistence crops.[1]

There are three major allocation programmes: the Federal Land Development Authority (FELDA), the Rubber Industry Smallholders' Development Authority (RISDA) and the Federal Land Consolidation and Rehabilitation Authority (FELCRA). The aims of each are basically to encourage the production of export crops, settle unused land with poor rural households and form efficient production units by uniting smallholders.

FELDA is the largest and oldest resettlement scheme. Initiated in 1956, its projects now cover 883 000 ha and support 109 000 households. Oil palm is planted on 76 percent of the land, rubber on 18 percent and sugar cane, cocoa and other minor crops on the remainder.

The basic approach is to identify a suitable site of approximately 2 000 ha for the settlement of 400 families. At this size, the site qualifies for the provision of essential rural services, including a clinic, a school and a police station, and the development of rural roads, electricity and piped water can be justified. Settler selection requirements are that applicants be between 21 and 45 years of age, particularly since a large portion of the smallholders are on government land schemes.

The lost potential production from the failure to increase yields in the smallholder farm subsector is more costly to the economy now that the country is facing an economic contraction. However, although many smallholders had reduced their farming effort in response to better income opportunities elsewhere, they may now reverse their initial shift away from farming, since a diversification of income sources could be their best protection against the aftershocks of the economic decline.

Estates were quicker than smallholders in shifting area out of rubber and cocoa and into oil palm in the early 1990s. This may also be an indication of the rigidities in

married – preferably with children – and physically fit. Prospective settlers must be landless, but have an agricultural background. FELDA hires a contractor to clear the land and plant the trees, often stipulating that the contractor must hire settlers to do part of the work. Settlers receive a subsistence allowance until the trees mature – usually after three to four years – at which time each settler is given a 4 ha plot.

Settlers normally work in teams to maintain and harvest the product from a group of holdings. Thus, settler's earnings are a function of both their team's efforts and the productivity of their own plot. Settlers are obligated to use a portion of their earnings to pay back a 15-year loan covering the cost of establishing the project. When the loan is paid off, they are given title to the land.

Land allocation efforts are affected by three current issues:

• With a lack of available land on peninsular Malaysia, new land development projects are focused on Sabah and, to a lesser extent, Sarawak.
• Agencies have very high administrative costs, as the number of settler families per FELDA officer has been estimated to be 12 to 1.

• Land schemes are no longer attracting settlers because of the availability of alternative employment.

[1] T.S. Bahrin. 1988. Land settlement in Malaysia: a case study of the Federal Land Development Authority Projects. In A.S. Oberai, ed. *Land settlement policies and population redistribution in developing countries.* New York, Praeger.

the federal land schemes which prevent individual smallholders from acting without the consensus of others within a project. Whatever the differences in incentives, the smallholder share of rubber and cocoa area has nevertheless become more dominant in the last 15 years. In addition, a growing proportion of estate owners have shifted completely out of agricultural production and into other economic activities altogether, such as manufacturing and tourism. Larger landowners have more choices than smallholders when investing in alternative activities.

A final difference between the two production regimes is that the difficulty of attracting hired labour to the estates seems to have resulted in about 1 million ha (5 percent of cultivable land) remaining idle.

Trade policies. Palm oil is Malaysia's second largest export after machinery products, accounting for 7 percent of export earnings. Palm oil has been subject to export taxes throughout its 50-year commercial history in Malaysia. In the 1950s and 1960s, the tax was a flat 5 to 7.5 percent of the value of the export, but in the 1970s the government changed the tax structure to favour the development of downstream processing. It put a high tax on exports of crude palm oil (CPO) while reducing the tax levied at each level of processing. Virtually none of the palm oil that Malaysia exported in 1997 was CPO. Initially, the industry overreacted to the processing incentives and developed a huge overcapacity in processing and refining facilities in the mid-1980s which depressed processing margins. The closure of some plants, coupled with a gradual increase in production as the area under oil palm expanded, has alleviated the problem.

The government also supported the production of palm oil by allowing the use of rubber replanting grants for planting oil palm. The grants for replanting oil palm amounted to $M 4 447 ($1 710) per hectare for holdings of less than 4.05 ha and $M 3 459 ($1 330) per hectare for larger holdings.

Many of the trade policies for palm oil have also been applied to rubber, which is Malaysia's oldest commercial export crop and consequently has a policy history dating back to the British colonial administration at the turn of the twentieth century. An export tax on rubber was introduced in 1907 and remained in place until it was abolished in 1991 in order to lighten the tax burden on an already contracting industry.

Rubber trees have an economic life of 25 years, after which their latex production begins to decline. The government's policy is designed to encourage the replacement of older trees with newer varieties by providing replanting grants. These grants are available to both smallholders and estates and are intended to cover the cost of replacing trees as well as some of the income forgone by farmers while waiting for the new trees to mature (four to seven years). In 1995, grants were $M 6 177 ($2 375) per hectare for holdings of less than 4.05 ha and $M 4 200 ($1 615) for larger holdings. Payments were reduced if rubber was planted with other crops.

Both replanting and research grants for rubber are funded by a duty levied on each kilogram of rubber exported – this duty was maintained after the export tax was abolished. The management and utilization of the proceeds are under the control of the Rubber Industry Smallholders' Development Authority (RISDA).

Until 1994, the trade policy for cocoa had been one of protection against competition from foreign imports. The rapid increase in cocoa production in the 1980s was partly due to policies providing support to the industry through subsidies to smallholders and a 15 percent import tariff. The tariff was abolished in 1994 so as to facilitate the entry of Ghanaian cocoa bean imports, as these are blended with Malaysian beans to improve the chocolate flavour. This policy change was to facilitate downstream processing activities of cocoa beans into cocoa products.

The government has also implemented regulatory

Tending trees on a palm plantation

Palm trees produce many exportable products, e.g. palm oil, of which Malaysia is the world's largest exporter.

G. BIZZARRI/FAO/19676

measures, including compulsory grading to ensure standardization and quality in Malaysian cocoa beans. These measures will contribute towards the creation of a market "niche" for Malaysian cocoa beans. Cocoa butter made from Malaysian cocoa beans has a higher melting temperature than cocoa butter from other countries, an advantage that is expected to help the industry remain competitive in the international market.

A continual decline in the size of the agricultural workforce has resulted in a sectoral labour shortage in Malaysia.

Labour issues. Labour has been a limiting factor to the expansion of perennial crops in Malaysia, as a continual decline in the size of the agricultural workforce – reflecting a natural progression of the development process – has resulted in a sectoral labour shortage. The share of agricultural employment in Malaysia's total workforce declined from 26 percent in 1990 to 18 percent in 1995.

Between 1980 and 1995, 20 percent of the country's rural population migrated to the cities and, by 1995, 55 percent of the country's population was classified as urban. Most of the shift was driven by the availability of higher-paying employment opportunities outside agriculture. During most of this 15-year period, real wages in agriculture were stagnant. Eventually, in 1995 workers on rubber and oil palm estates obtained a 30 percent increase in wage settlements, but this may be considered "too little, too late" for drawing young members of the workforce back to agriculture.[20] In addition to raising wages, the sector has increased mechanization and land consolidation in an effort to reduce the need for labour.

Malaysia's immigration policy is of crucial importance to the estate subsector, as agriculture employs at least 250 000 foreign workers (with permits), which is roughly one-third of the legal foreign workers present in the country. There is also likely to be a large number of illegal workers employed in the sector but the size of this group is not known. A change in immigration rules or a tightening of enforcement could reduce the foreign labour available to the sector and put further upward pressure on wages.

As already mentioned, the labour issue is one of the most intransigent problems facing the perennial crop subsector in Malaysian agriculture. Rubber, palm oil and cocoa are labour-intensive crops: labour accounts for 40 to 60 percent of perennial crop production costs and is also significant in annual crop production. Low-cost foreign workers hold down wage increases and allow plantations to remain competitive while still using their current production practices. At the same time, however, low wages are a disincentive to the development and adoption of labour-saving techniques and equipment. This is the dilemma faced by sectoral and macro policy-makers. As the scope for improving labour productivity is limited, especially in the short term, what both the industry and the government fear is that tighter restrictions on the use of foreign labour will simply force production to move to other countries.

The labour dilemma is slightly different for the smallholder sector, much of which is on government land schemes. The major success of these land schemes, which were established as part of a social policy to alleviate rural poverty, has been the opening up of new land, the redistribution of income and the delivery of government services to the rural poor. With the exodus of workers in search of better-paying employment outside agriculture, the government land schemes have been left with an ageing population of workers. In 1990, one-third of farm household heads were more than 55 years old and two-thirds were more than 46 years old.

The two largest land settlement schemes, the Federal Land Development Authority (FELDA) and RISDA, are already under pressure to reform because the size of the administrative bureaucracy is too large for the number of settlers. Their original mandate is less relevant in an economy with a labour shortage and a lack of suitable land for expansion. The current conditions suggest that these programmes may have accomplished their original goals. Reforms are being considered, but the economic crisis will make it difficult for the government to take any steps that might reduce the sizeable administrative staff of such programmes until the economy improves.

The economic crisis has complicated the labour issue because the government, concerned with the growing number of redundancies, has become more intent on reducing the number of foreign workers in Malaysia. At the same time, as a result of strong export demand, oil palm producers are struggling to increase output to take advantage of the high prices on the world market. The impact of the financial crisis on the non-agricultural sector may mitigate, at least temporarily, the labour shortage in agriculture.

The increase in the price of palm oil may help to retain labour in the smallholder sector if relative wages also continue to rise, especially since the opportunity cost of leaving agriculture has recently increased, farm prices have risen and job opportunities outside the sector have diminished. However, many of those who remain are part of an ageing farm population and, even with higher agricultural prices, agriculture is not likely to persuade many outside the sector to return to farming. Even if the financial crisis continues for two or three years, it will at best bring only a temporary slowing of the long-term decline in the agricultural workforce.

Forestry

Forestry has traditionally been one of the major sources of income, export earnings and employment in the Malaysian agricultural sector. Taxes and royalties on forestry products have been, and continue to be, a major source of revenue for state governments, particularly those with large forested areas such as Sarawak. In 1990, sawlogs accounted for a value added of $M 2.3 billion (in 1978 prices) or 15.6 percent of the valued added to agriculture, meaning it was second only to palm oil. Forestry's annual contribution to value added followed a downward trend until 1997, when a 3.4 percent rise in production was expected because of a partial lifting of the export ban on raw logs and also because of an increased processing capacity.

Malaysia is the world's leading producer of tropical sawlogs. Forested areas in Malaysia totalled 18.5 million ha in 1992, the last year for which complete data are available. Of this, the peninsula had 5.5 million ha, Sabah 4.2 million ha and Sarawak had 8.8 million ha. Although Sarawak has the largest forested area, the infrastructure for accessing that area is undeveloped and the costs of exploiting the forest resources are much higher than on the peninsula. Nonetheless, 55 percent of the recent increases in production have come from Sarawak, and the government has expressed concern about concession holders not replanting harvested areas.

There are three classifications of forested area – state lands, permanent forest estate (PFE) and parks and reserves. Logging is not permitted on the 1.4 million ha of park land, as this area is restricted to recreational and conservation uses. The difference between state and PFE lands is in how they are administered. State lands are under the administration of the individual states, whereas the logging on PFE lands is administered by the Forestry Department and must follow stricter guidelines established at the federal level. State lands account for only 0.2 million ha in the peninsula and 0.6 million ha in Sabah, where virtually all the areas for logging are in PFEs. Sarawak, on the other hand, has 3.9 million ha (or 45 percent) in state lands.

Very little of Malaysia's forest area is virgin forest. The largest proportion is in Sarawak where about one-quarter of the area is undisturbed. Because they have not previously been logged, virgin forests have a higher yield of higher-quality trees than other forested areas and they are also richer in biodiversity. Logging in Malaysia is done on a selected basis (as opposed to the clear-cutting carried out in some temperate climates). The Forestry Department monitors harvesting and, once an area is harvested, prohibits its use for further production until a sufficient number of trees have grown to the minimum size required to permit a second harvest.

Forestry policy environment. Forestry policy has been designed to meet three objectives which are not entirely compatible: employment, government revenues and conservation. Logging provides employment and income as well as the principal raw material required by the country's expanding wood manufacturing industry. In states where logging is a major activity, revenues collected from the licensing of logging activities provide a significant share of the state's operating revenue. At the same time, there is greater recognition of the fact that current exploitation of forest resources exceeds levels that can be sustained over the long term.

Key forestry policies fall into two areas: logging and export. A sustainable annual cutting area for PFE land is set at the federal level and then allocated by state. The states then follow federal guidelines in issuing licences. Logging companies must pay two fees: a royalty based on the volume of logs cut and a premium based on the area

Employment, government revenue and conservation are the three objectives of Malaysia's forestry policy.

173

licensed for cutting. Both federal and state authorities face difficulties in enforcing the log harvesting regulations. Eventually, the goal is to reach a sustainable level of cutting, balancing reforestation with harvest rates; however, logging is usually conducted in remote areas and there are large financial incentives to circumvent taxes and regulations.

Export policies differ between the peninsula and Sabah and Sarawak, with differential taxation of raw logs and processed wood products. The peninsula has banned the export of logs since 1992, while Sabah instituted the ban two years later with the dual objectives of preserving its biologically valuable rain forest and encouraging value-added wood manufacturing. However, Sabah partially lifted its ban in 1997. Sarawak allows log exports but imposes an export tax, while the peninsula imposes export duties on timber products, including sawntimber, plywood and veneer.

Fisheries

Fish contributes about two-thirds of all animal protein consumed by Malaysians and the industry employs about 1.6 percent of the economically active population. Production totalled 1.3 million tonnes in 1995, of which 1.2 million tonnes were marine catch and the remaining 0.1 million tonnes were from aquaculture. Production expanded by 30 percent between 1990 and 1995, with one-quarter of the increase coming from aquaculture, which had previously been negligible. The increase in the production of marine fisheries is attributed to an increase in the deep-sea catch as inshore fish resources continued to decline.

Fish imports are mainly from Thailand, the bulk of which are low-grade fish species. Imports help bridge the gap between supply and demand for low-grade species and, to some extent, stabilize domestic fish prices. Exports are mainly to Singapore and are confined to high-quality fish species and prawns.

Fisheries policy. Government intervention in the fishery sector is extensive. The Fisheries Act of 1985 was enacted to curb overexploitation of fishery resources, minimize conflict and promote equality between coastal and trawl fishermen. The act defines a zoning policy which allocates fishing grounds by types of fishing gear, size of vessel and ownership status of vessel. The act bans all trawling activities in waters that are five miles or less from the coast. The government has also sought to promote an increase in fish catch, primarily by encouraging deep sea fishing and aquaculture development. It has made low-cost loans available for the purchase of deep sea fishing equipment and invested in deep sea landing facilities.

Food commodities

Malaysia is dependent on imports for all major food items except vegetable oils. Although it is self-sufficient (or a small net exporter) in fruit, poultry, eggs and pork, it is heavily dependent on imported feedstuffs. Before examining the details of how Malaysia meets its food needs, some information is provided on the Malaysian food budget.

In 1993/94, Malaysians spent 23 percent of their average monthly household income on food for home consumption and an additional 12 percent on purchases of food and beverages away from home. Figure 29 shows how consumers allocated their at-home food expenditures.[21]

Fish is clearly the largest expenditure, accounting for almost 20 percent of the food budget. A number of other items – rice, other cereals, poultry, fruits, vegetables and other foods – each account for 10 to 12 percent of expenditures. Pork, beef, lamb, eggs, milk and fats are of less importance.

Table 7 shows Malaysia's balance of supply and use for major food groups. Poultry and pork are almost totally dependent on imported feedgrains as well as imported protein meal, which is either imported directly or produced from imported soybeans. Although Malaysia is technically self-sufficient in marine fish, it is still heavily involved in the fish trade, exporting high-value fish and importing lower-value fish for the domestic market. Fruits and vegetables have a similar pattern of supply and use, with Malaysia exporting tropical products (the largest share going to Singapore) and importing temperate products. For beef and mutton, Malaysia is almost entirely dependent on imports. High-quality beef is produced domestically and imported from Australia, New Zealand and the United States, while the greatest volume of imports is of frozen, lower-quality beef from India. Mutton and lamb imports come primarily from New Zealand.

Malaysia is dependent on imports for all major food items except vegetable oils.

Food policies. Except for rice, food commodities are largely free of government intervention, although at the retail level, the government does control prices of a set of basic staples, including rice, wheat flour and cooking oil. With the recent devaluation of the ringgit, this has put wheat millers in a difficult position. After buying the raw product on the world market in US dollars, they then have to sell their product in the Malaysian market according to ringgit prices controlled by the government. The government realizes the need to allow these companies to raise retail prices but would like to limit the rise in order to minimize the effects of the financial crisis on low-income consumers. Cooking oil and rice do not present the same problem because they are supplied primarily from domestic production.

Rice policy. Since rice is an important staple in the Malaysian diet, the government has taken measures to ensure that the country maintains at least a 65 percent level of self-sufficiency in rice. The government supports rice farmers by several means, including input subsidies and output incentives. Furthermore, it has assisted paddy farmers in the application of pest control methods, farm management and the consolidation of small farms. Each rice producer is eligible for a fertilizer grant and for loans from the Bank Pertanian Malaysia at a virtually interest-free

Table 7

MALAYSIA'S BALANCE OF SUPPLY AND USE FOR MAJOR FOOD ITEMS, 1995

	Production ('000 tonnes)	Imports ('000 tonnes)	Exports ('000 tonnes)	Domestic use ('000 tonnes)	Per caput use (kg per caput)	Self-sufficiency (ratio)
Fish	1 065	261	248	1 078	52.1	.99
Poultry	687	6	8	684	33.0	1.00
Pork	283	—	—	283	13.7	1.00
Beef	19	68	1	86	4.2	.22
Mutton	1	10	—	11	0.5	.06
Fruit	2 200	259	242	2 217	107	.99
Vegetables	844	411	250	1 005	48.6	.84
Rice	1 372	428	2	1 797	86.9	.76
Feedgrains	45	2 343	—	2 436	n.a.	.02
Protein meal[1]	1 839	548	1 340	1 064	n.a.	n.a.
of which:						
– PKC	1 360		1 332	40	n.a.	n.a.
– Soymeal	432	500	5	932	n.a.	

[1] Palm kernel cake (PKC) is not used in domestic feed rations; soymeal production is entirely from imported soybeans.

Figure 29

MALAYSIA: CONSUMER FOOD EXPENDITURES

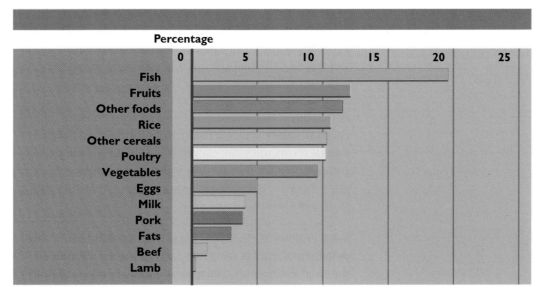

Source: Department of Statistics,
Malaysia, 1995

rate. When the crop is produced, the government guarantees producers a price of $M 496 (1995 value) per tonne of paddy. In addition, each producer is eligible to receive a government "income" supplement.

All these support policies have served only to slow the long-term decline in rice output, which has been relatively stagnant at about 2 million tonnes per year since 1996. The trend is the result of land conversion from rice paddies to more lucrative uses. Malaysia imports about one-fifth of its domestic needs from Thailand and Viet Nam, which produce surpluses in rice and have lower production costs than Malaysia.

Malaysia's long-term decline in rice output is the result of land conversion from rice paddies to more lucrative uses.

The financial crisis and agricultural policy
Malaysian agriculture already faced challenges before the onset of the financial and economic crisis in the second half of 1997. A reduction in available labour, the disparity in estate and smallholder yields and reconsideration of the land allocation programmes were issues confronting the sector. The economic crisis has added a level of complexity to these "old" problems while contributing new pressures and opportunities for agriculture.

177

With its slow growth and shrinking relative role in the Malaysian economy, agriculture had often been referred to as a "sunset industry". The financial crisis, however, has changed that perspective. Agriculture's enhanced export performance can play a significant role in reducing the impact of the economic downturn and it will certainly have a major part in the country's economic recovery. Compared with manufactured goods, agricultural exports rely less on imported inputs. Therefore, the sector's comparative advantage should benefit from the currency devaluation. Considering also the increase in palm oil and cocoa prices in dollar terms since mid-1997 (and even in ringgit terms since the currency devaluation), the export component of the sector can be seen as a bright spot in an economy plagued with a growing number of layoffs and company closures.

There is a danger that policy imperatives at the national level could introduce new pressures that will have severe detrimental effects on other parts of the sector, namely the food economy. Government measures taken to hold down food price increases have already put import-based domestic food industries in a bind. Caught between the rising cost of imported raw material prices (e.g. animal feedstuffs, wheat, milk powder) and an inability to raise product prices, many processors for the domestic market are facing severe losses. If the crisis persists and the government does not allow food prices to reflect the increase in the cost of imported raw materials, Malaysia's domestic food-processing industries will face a long and severe contraction. Malaysia-based companies without extensive international operations will be the least capable of surviving.

Conclusions

Malaysia has undergone a major transformation from being an economy based on the production and export of primary products to a growing, industrial and financial centre. Over the past three decades, Malaysia has continued to invest in and develop its agricultural base, even as it pursued policies to foster the growth of the industrial sector. This balanced development approach has put Malaysia in a much stronger position to weather economic storms. The period has also seen a significant improvement in the nutritional status of Malaysia's population, only 7 percent of which is estimated to be undernourished today. This achievement has been

A balanced development approach has put Malaysia in a comparatively strong position to weather economic storms.

Figure 30

MALAYSIA: DOMESTIC SUPPLY AND UTILIZATION OF CEREALS

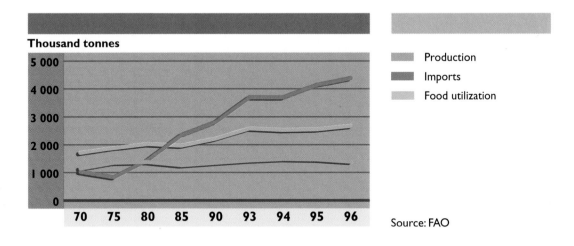

Thousand tonnes

Legend:
- Production
- Imports
- Food utilization

Source: FAO

made possible by the rapid growth in economic activity as well as in real incomes.

Economic growth has also enabled the country to meet the growing food needs of the population through food imports which, while increasing steadily in volume and value, have corresponded to an ever-declining share of total merchandise export revenues (22 percent in the early 1970s, 13 percent in the early 1980s and about 5 percent in recent years). Thus, the issue of a large and growing food import dependence, which was a matter of concern in many other country circumstances, has not constituted a major economic problem or an obstacle to food security in Malaysia.

Nevertheless, the economic environment has changed significantly in the past year. Along with other countries in Asia, Malaysia now faces a potentially severe and protracted economic crisis. This points again to the importance of maintaining a balanced approach to sectoral development, and one in which agriculture plays a proper role. This means, in particular, adequately addressing the problems of disparity in productivity between estates and smallholders and taking full advantage of the new opportunities that may emerge in the agricultural export sector. The importance of labour markets responding properly to economic opportunities has also been underlined. For these endeavours, a key to prudent economic decisions will be to allow price signals unleashed by the crisis to stimulate economic recovery – while also shielding the poorest and vulnerable population groups from the impact of rising food prices.

Latin America and the Caribbean

REGIONAL OVERVIEW

General economic performance

The Latin America and Caribbean region in 1997 achieved its best economic performance in a quarter of a century, despite the destabilizing effects of the financial crisis in Asia.[22] The region as a whole exhibited a growth rate of 5.3 percent, up from an average 3.2 percent during the previous five years, while also achieving an inflation rate of less than 11 percent, down from 18 percent in 1996, 26 percent in 1995 and more than 300 percent in 1994.

Unprecedented capital inflows exceeding $73 billion – two-thirds of which were in the form of FDI – more than compensated for the widening current account deficit, estimated to be $60 billion. Some improvement was recorded in the unemployment situation, which nevertheless remained a serious problem, especially in the Central America and Caribbean subregions and Argentina. Little progress was achieved in the reduction of poverty and inequality, which continued to be dark features of the region's economic and social landscape.

Two main factors explained the robust economic growth of the region: a strong recovery in investment, spurred by the overall favourable macroeconomic environment and general optimism of domestic and foreign investors; and a continued expansion of exports (reflecting increased export volumes, since average prices remained broadly stationary), with particularly dynamic intraregional trade.

The high levels of growth registered in 1997 are not expected to be maintained in 1998. Indeed, the 1997 boom chiefly reflected the recovery of Argentina and Mexico after the 1994-1995 Mexican crisis and, consequently, growth rates were far above the region's long-term potential. Furthermore, while the first impact of the Asian crisis was relatively well absorbed – to a large extent owing to the progress achieved in macroeconomic stabilization and reform – it did have negative effects on trade and financial flows, the latter having slackened somewhat during the last quarter of 1997. It also underscored the risks of an excessive dependence on foreign capital in the face of too low a level of domestic

In 1997, the Latin America and Caribbean region achieved its best economic performances in a quarter of a century.

Figure 31

LATIN AMERICA AND THE CARIBBEAN

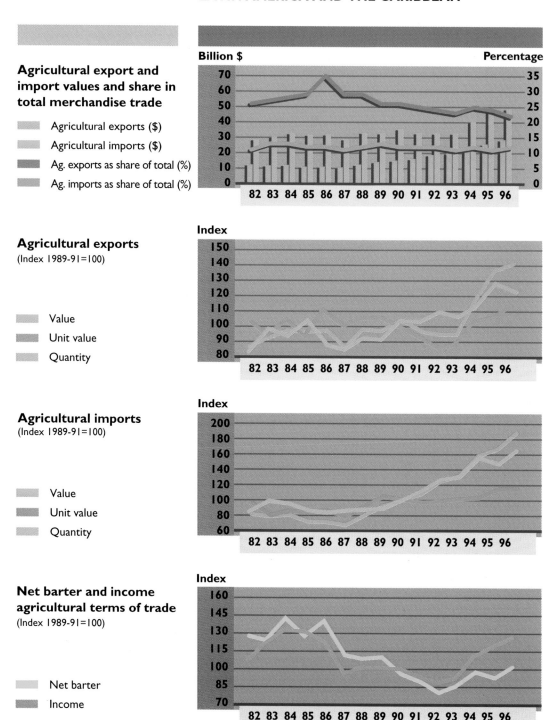

Agricultural export and import values and share in total merchandise trade

- Agricultural exports ($)
- Agricultural imports ($)
- Ag. exports as share of total (%)
- Ag. imports as share of total (%)

Agricultural exports
(Index 1989-91=100)

- Value
- Unit value
- Quantity

Agricultural imports
(Index 1989-91=100)

- Value
- Unit value
- Quantity

Net barter and income agricultural terms of trade
(Index 1989-91=100)

- Net barter
- Income

LATIN AMERICA AND THE CARIBBEAN

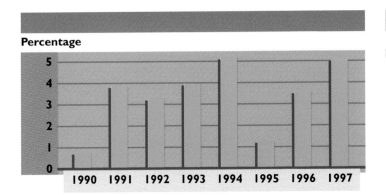

Percentage

Real GDP
(Percentage change over previous year)

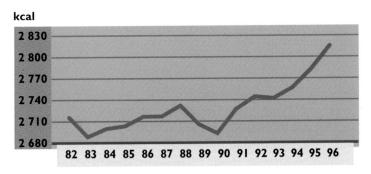

kcal

Dietary energy supplies
(kcal per caput per day)

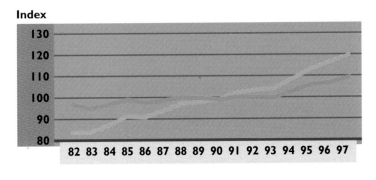

Index

Agricultural production
(Index 1989-91=100)

Total
Per caput

Source: FAO and IMF

savings to generate rapid and sustained growth, as well as underdeveloped domestic capital markets. The outlook will much depend on the course of events in Brazil, which accounts for a large share of the region's output and is a leading trading partner for many of its neighbours. Because of its wide deficits in budget and current accounts, Brazil was particularly exposed to the effects of the financial turmoil in Asia, which resulted in sharp falls in share and bond prices and speculative pressure on its currency. The emergency fiscal and credit measures taken by this country stemmed the immediate crisis but introduced risks of a slowdown in growth, which is expected to decelerate to less than 1 percent in 1998. Although the impact of the crisis varied elsewhere in the region, several countries were facing prospects of lower growth, higher inflation and larger current account deficits in the short term. Overall, expectations for the region as a whole are for a slowdown in economic growth to about 3.3 percent in 1998.

Agricultural performance

Crop and livestock production rose by about 2.9 percent, but this increase was concentrated in a small number of countries.

Contrasting with the generally bright economic performances in 1997, this was on the whole a lacklustre year for agriculture in the region. Crop and livestock production rose by about 2.9 percent, slightly above the average of the previous five years and about 1 percent above population growth. However, the overall increase was concentrated in a relatively small number of countries. Out of 44 countries in the region, only 13 achieved some gain in agricultural production in per caput terms. For a number of these, including Argentina, Barbados, Bolivia, Brazil, Peru and Uruguay, this represented the continuation of an already favourable trend of the previous five years. At the other extreme, several countries in Central America and the Caribbean (Cuba, Dominica, the Dominican Republic, Grenada, Guatemala, Haiti, Panama, St Lucia and St Vincent) as well as Colombia and Paraguay recorded negative growth in per caput agricultural production in 1997, following already poor average performances over the previous five years. The rest of the region had mixed results, with Mexico exhibiting a weak recovery after a disastrous year in 1996 and Chile recording a less than 1 percent increase in agricultural production, its poorest result since 1985.

Crop and livestock shortfalls in 1997 reflected in many cases the early effects of the El Niño phenomenon, the impact of which is to be fully felt in 1998. High temperatures and droughts in large areas of Central America, together with the alternation of droughts and torrential rains and flooding in Caribbean countries, have caused major losses in all farm activities and in some cases severe food supply problems (see World review, Food shortages and emergencies, p. 16). Among the worst affected were Haiti, Guyana and Jamaica but many other countries in the Caribbean area reported heavy losses from droughts. El Niño-related low rainfalls have also caused droughts and extensive forest fires in Central America and Brazil, while several Andean countries have been hit hard by heavy rains and flooding. In Peru, however, despite the severe El Niño effects, agricultural output rose by an estimated 5 percent in 1997. Indeed, some products such as hard maize and rice benefited from the rains, while preventive measures taken by the government limited the extent of the damage.

The overall effect of El Niño-associated calamities on output is hard to assess as yet but is likely to be considerable in several countries. For instance, based on past experiences with El Niño, the Government of Colombia has forecast yield reductions in crop output during 1998 as follows: approximately 4 percent for cocoa, 4 to 5 percent for maize, 5 percent for both rice and milk and 7 percent for both barley and oil palm.

Along with these problem areas, however, the region's agriculture has also recorded success stories. In Argentina, record cereal output levels were achieved, as the area planted was unprecedented, owing to generally favourable prices, the continued adoption of advanced farming technology and favourable markets for Argentinian grains. The longer-term outlook also appears positive in view of reduced export subsidies and agricultural support worldwide. The prospects are also good for meat exports now that the International Epizootics Office has declared the country to be free of foot-and-mouth disease with vaccination. If no outbreak occurs in the next three years the "with vaccination" qualification will be removed, probably opening up new market opportunities for Argentinian beef at premium prices. A decision by the United States authorities in June 1997 to authorize imports of Argentinian beef after

El Niño-associated calamities are likely to have a considerable effect on output in 1998 in several Latin American and Caribbean countries.

almost 70 years of prohibition was significant in this context.

Agricultural performances were also favourable in Uruguay, where agricultural production rose by nearly 8 percent in 1997, with rice posting its fourth consecutive year of record output. Helped by a generally improving macroeconomic situation and a wider use of modern technology and management practices, agriculture is a leading growth sector of the economy. Meanwhile, preferential access to the Brazilian market under the Southern Common Market (MERCOSUR) agreement is creating a strong increase in demand for many products, including rice, wheat, dairy, beef and fruits. Wheat output has also increased considerably in recent years, despite early fears that the entry of Uruguay into MERCOSUR would put the country in a disadvantageous competitive position *vis-à-vis* Argentina. Uruguay's prospects for expanding agricultural markets are also improving thanks to successful efforts by both the public and private sectors to improve the sanitary and phytosanitary status of several of the country's products.

Agricultural policies

The region's agricultural sector has reacted favourably to the market opportunities propitiated by the reformed environment.

Agricultural policies in the region have continued to follow the general objectives of domestic and external market liberalization. The agricultural sector has in many cases reacted favourably to the market opportunities propitiated by the reformed environment, all the more so since the improved economic conditions in recent years also reinforced internal and domestic demand. Several countries in the region that are already well positioned in international markets and others whose policies and programmes helped them gain competitiveness, have also benefited from the general move towards trade liberalization and regional trade agreements.

Nevertheless, the removal of protective mechanisms that formerly shielded agriculture, including the exposure to market forces of farms at widely different levels of efficiency, has also produced crisis situations and new policy challenges. The recent experiences of two neighbouring countries, Ecuador and Colombia, exemplify the often contrasting consequences of liberalization. In the case of Ecuador, which enjoys a comparative advantage for a variety of products, the liberalization of the economy and trade of agricultural products as well as the reduction of import tariff rates over the last five years are seen as important factors explaining the overall robust production performance of the sector. Greater market opportunities prompted increases in agricultural investment and in the use of modern agricultural technology such as artificial insemination and hybrid seeds. Some sectors also benefited from the Andean Free Trade Area and accession to the World Trade Organization (WTO).

In the case of Colombia, however, the policy of *apertura* (opening) is being implemented amid serious difficulties in the sector. With economic opening, Colombia is expected to specialize in production lines where it enjoys a comparative advantage – such as cut flowers, coffee, sugar cane, fruits and vegetables – and away from grains and oilseeds. Indeed, several of the "comparative advantage" crops have registered gains in both production and productivity. However, external competition rendered most grain and oilseed crop cultivation unprofitable, causing a sharp decline in the production of these commodities, an accentuation of unemployment and rural poverty and a loss of dynamism in rural business activity. Moreover, the elimination of subsidized credit aggravated farm debt levels. In order to meet the domestic demand, including for the dynamic mixed feed industry, large volumes of imports were required.

Such conflicting effects of market liberalization pose increasing difficulties for policy-makers in the region. The persistence or aggravation of social problems, causing riots and civil unrest in some countries, have required compensatory and contingency measures in favour of the most underprivileged sectors. Nevertheless, in many cases the scope of these measures has been gradually reduced and their transitory character explicitly underlined.

Within this overall context, there were wide variations in the way economic and social concerns translated into policy action in the region. The following sections review some recent policy developments in four key areas: programmes and measures in favour of agriculture; agricultural credit and financing; food prices and consumer protection; and action towards environmental conservation.

Programmes and measures in favour of agriculture
Although nearly all countries have maintained some form of support to the agricultural sector, such support has tended to diminish and to focus on subsectors considered

to be of strategic importance. The Government of Argentina, strongly committed to market principles and facing severe fiscal limitations from the Convertibility Plan adopted in 1991, does not provide any specific financial support to the sector. Nevertheless, the sector has benefited from the reduction and elimination of export taxes, while export tax rebates have also been reduced. A similar situation is found in Paraguay where, despite the fundamental importance of agriculture to the economy, government direct intervention is modest and is mainly intended to assist small producers in coping with emergency situations such as harsh weather conditions and credit shortages.

Farm support has focused on economically promising producers and crops, in particular those better able to generate foreign exchange.

In many cases, farm support has focused on economically promising producers and crops, in particular those better able to generate foreign exchange. Examples are Honduras, where the policy orientation is beginning to shift towards medium- and large-scale farming rather than focusing on small subsistence farming; and the Dominican Republic, where support has focused particularly on competitive export crops, although some food staples such as rice, beans, potatoes, onions and poultry meat have also received official assistance.

In Mexico several programmes are being implemented to promote production growth while easing the transition to a more market-oriented economy. The comprehensive Alianza para el Campo (Rural Alliance) programme encompasses several other initiatives, including PROCAMPO (which aims at rationalizing crop production by abolishing crop price supports and replacing them with direct government payments that are made on a per hectare basis and do not affect commodity prices); PRODUCE (Direct and Productive Assistance to Agriculture); various programmes to restock the Mexican cattle herd; and technical assistance, including research and education aimed at improving the output of coffee, livestock and crops.

In Peru, the government has continued to purchase small amounts of agricultural products directly from producers. Some of these are milk, rice, cotton and alpaca wool fibre. Although producers complain that the amounts bought by the government are insufficient, the purchases have in some cases helped to support prices.

Nicaragua has set up the National Council for Agricultural Production (CONAGRO), an institution designed to boost productivity. CONAGRO is the state entity that submits proposals on agricultural production policies and implements the policies upon approval by the Ministry of Agriculture.

The Government of Colombia continues to operate commodity-specific absorption agreements, originally designed to induce processing industries to purchase local crops at fair price levels determined by the government and tied to costs of production. Such agreements currently apply to maize, sorghum, malting barley and wheat. Nevertheless, the emphasis is now on using these agreements to foster closer working relationships throughout all elements of the marketing chain and ultimately to shift the responsibility for defining sectoral policies to the private sector. An example of this new approach is the yellow maize absorption agreement, implemented in February 1997, which established a formula for automatically setting the price that the mixed feed industry will pay growers over the next five years. Grower prices will no longer be tied to costs of production, but will be adjusted gradually to reflect international price levels.

The Government of Colombia is also considering expanding the operation of existing price stabilization funds – the most important fund being for cotton – to products that were not covered initially. A palm oil price stabilization fund, established in 1996, initiated operations in 1997. A cocoa fund also exists but is not operational and is being reorganized, and price stabilization funds for dairy products, meat products and bananas are being considered.

In Venezuela, producer prices for most agricultural products are determined by supply and demand, but the government continues to mandate producer prices for raw milk, rice, maize and sorghum. The government tends to set these prices, without reference to world prices, at levels that ensure that even inefficient producers can make a profit. The subsidy resulting from this policy is absorbed entirely by the animal feed- and food-processing sectors and, ultimately, the consumer. Mandated producer prices for white maize and sorghum were increased sharply in 1997 in an attempt to counteract poor performances the previous year. Although such increases did boost production, they also entailed risks of distortions in the animal feed, poultry and swine sectors and of declines in chicken, egg and pork output. Many maize flour and animal feed manufacturers refused to pay the government-set prices – those of

The Government of Colombia aims to shift the responsibility for defining sectoral policies to the private sector.

189

sorghum, for instance, were twice the c.i.f. price of imported maize. In the case of feed maize, this led to the imposition of an import licence system to force feed mills to purchase domestic sorghum.

A comprehensive Support Plan for Basic Grain Production in Honduras, launched in May 1996, was intended to boost grain production from the 1996/97 second crop and during the entire 1997/98 season. The plan provided for a National Complementary Credit Guarantee Fund and other credit components. It also included a $15 million technology transfer programme, increased technical assistance and greater distribution of improved seed use by transferring many government-owned silos to farmers and financing other rural storage projects as well as investing in several irrigation projects.

Privatization

Parastatals, government-assisted agro-industries and cooperatives incur heavy financial costs but also represent important sources of income and employment.

Further progress has been recorded in this difficult area, despite considerable debate and opposition in some countries. While it is acknowledged that parastatals, government- assisted agro-industries and cooperatives incur heavy financial costs, they also represent important sources of income and employment. An example is provided by the sugar industry in Peru. The 12 sugar cooperatives, which involve almost 300 000 employees and their families, together with associated businesses, have been under pressure to alter their management and collective ownership structure, which is seen as an obstacle to necessary outside investment. Heavily indebted, the cooperatives face major financial problems and some are unable to meet payroll obligations, a situation that has led them to sell portions of their capital stock to the private sector. Foreign investors are also interested in entering the sugar industry, but a number of problems have yet to be solved concerning the workers' social benefits, housing, education and health care.

Despite similar difficulties, other countries have advanced in the process of privatization. Moves have been under way for the privatization of Costa Rica's Coffee Institute (ICAFE). In El Salvador, the cooperatives set up during the first phase of the 1980 agrarian reform have since accumulated large debts. The private sector has pressed for their privatization, and legislation allowing the breakup and sale of the cooperatives has been approved. In addition, the privatization of government-controlled sugar mills was initiated, despite strong opposition from mill workers who demand a larger share in the mills. Most sugar mills were privatized in the course of 1996 and 1997. Nicaragua has pursued the privatization of the parastatal Nicaraguan Enterprises of Basic Foods (ENABAS).

Haiti has achieved some progress in its privatization programme, although the ambitious original completion date of March 1998 was not met.

In Jamaica, an emerging issue in the drive to make the banana industry more competitive is the cost of maintaining the three parastatal agencies currently involved in marketing and sales of the banana crop.

Agricultural credit and financing

A lack of affordable credit has remained a central concern of agricultural producers in the region and a key constraint to the modernization and diversification of farm activities. The reduced role of the public sector in agricultural financing and the hard terms and conditions for obtaining private credit have penalized small farmers in particular. Although many governments have maintained special lines of credit in their favour, the amounts involved have remained generally modest.

In the case of Argentina, the government makes some credit available to smaller agricultural producers, but such funds are limited and many farmers can only obtain loans at very high interest rates. So-called investment pools, formed to support crop growing, have gained importance in recent years and have helped to ease financial constraints in certain cases. These pools rent farmland, provide inputs and technical expertise and divide profits (or losses) equally among shareholders. In the absence of affordable credit for small- and medium-scale farmers, these investment groups offer many participants an opportunity to keep their farms and also eliminate a large element of risk.

In Peru, farmers have continued to face financial difficulties, despite the relatively favourable production trends and the somewhat greater availability of short-term credit in recent years. Similarly, in Paraguay credit shortages continue to affect small farmers above all, as they tend to suffer from wide swings in cash availability. Credit support is being provided to subsistence farmers who agree to diversify their output by planting different crops.

Small farms have been penalized by the public sector's reduced role in agricultural financing as well as by the conditions for obtaining private credit.

In August 1997, the Venezuelan Government abolished a preferential interest rate for agricultural loans, which had been 85 percent of the commercial rates offered. However, small farms still have access to preferential rates through the Ministry of Agriculture's Agricultural Credit Fund.

Brazil's 1997/98 crop plan, announced in mid-1997, included a reduction in interest rates from a flat 12 percent (1996/97 crop) to different levels according to the size of the producer (9 percent for small producers). About $1 billion were allocated to this programme, of which 20 percent was to cover production costs and 80 percent to cover investment costs.

New credit lines and guarantees have been introduced through various channels in Honduras in an attempt to stimulate growth in farm activities. Greater liquidity in the financial sector and diminishing inflation in 1997 also had a positive effect on commercial lending rates. However, response has so far been only moderately encouraging. Heavy investments are being made in the banana, palm oil and cultivated shrimp industries, which may serve as a catalyst for the sector.

Guatemala entered the 1997 having signed the Peace Accords that concluded its 36-year internal conflict. In response, the international community pledged almost $2 billion in funds to be paid over the next four years in support of economic and social development. This assistance will help finance, in particular, the large investments required to improve transport and trading facilities and services as well as to enhance the competitiveness of the agro-food sector.

Consumer prices and access to food

Most countries have relaxed the rigid food price controls that were characteristic of past policies in the Latin America and Caribbean region.

Most countries have relaxed or even altogether ceased the rigid food price controls that were typical characteristics of past policies in the region. The benefits of economic reform and growth, added to the general decline in inflation, are expected to give consumers more than adequate compensation for the reduction in price controls. However, as such benefits have not yet trickled down to the majority of the population in many cases, various forms of intervention have been required in favour of needy groups.

A particularly extensive programme of food assistance for poor and vulnerable populations is that implemented by Venezuela. When price controls were eliminated in 1996, the government established the Strategic Food Programme (PROAL), providing for the sale of staple foods in special marked packages at prices 40 percent below the prevailing retail prices. Under a similar programme, the Supply and Agricultural Service Corporation (CASA), certain food products are sold at subsidized prices in special stores located throughout the country, mostly in poor neighbourhoods. Food coupons are also distributed to low-income families under the Family Subsidy Programme which, in 1997, had a target population of 2.9 million (about 13 percent of the total population). Furthermore, about 1 million mothers receive subsidized food under the Mother and Infant Food Programme (PAMI). Finally, about 1 million students in poor neighbourhoods receive free milk, mid-morning snacks and lunches at school.

In January 1997, the Government of Honduras also laid down a programme to protect the consumers' basket of basic goods. This basket is composed of 20 products (including beans, maize, rice, milk, sugar, vegetable oil and shortening, chicken meat and coffee). The plan involves considerable restructuring of the government's chain of small retail stores, BANASUPRO: its distribution channels will be redesigned and it will concentrate on supplying only the 20 products contained in the basket of basic goods. Financial support from the government in 1997 was to amount to about 20 million lempiras ($1.5 million). Upcoming policy developments may include modern consumer protection legislation as well as new weights and measures legislation. The creation of a Consumer Protection Institute to strengthen efforts in this regard is also being considered.

The Government of Guatemala does not directly subsidize consumer food prices or provide for any direct food assistance programmes. Nevertheless, the Ministry of Economy publishes the food prices offered by different retail stores, highlighting the best prices, in local newspapers. The Ministry describes this action as an effort to create competitiveness among retailers and to educate consumers.

In the Dominican Republic, although the inflation rate in 1997 was below 10 percent, food prices rose much faster than others, as drought and major storms caused shortages of basic foodstuffs. Lower-income groups were particularly affected, and a call for a national strike was partially attributed to these price increases. In order to alleviate shortages of staple foodstuffs, the government decided to authorize substantial tariff-free imports of these goods.

Environmental protection: forestry

Authorities in the region have continued to emphasize the need to ensure a sustainable use of natural resources, and legislative measures have been introduced or reinforced to this end. Policy action has focused mainly on strengthening the regulatory framework for forest resource exploitation.

In Guatemala, deforestation destroys an estimated 90 000 ha per year, three-fifths of which is attributable to fuelwood consumption and land-clearing activities and two-fifths to timber production, most of it illegal.

Guatemala exemplifies the difficulties involved in preserving the forest resource base, while maintaining dynamism in the forest and manufactured forest products industry (which represents about 2 percent of the country's GDP and approximately $10 million in foreign exchange annually). Deforestation is officially estimated to destroy a total of 90 000 ha per year, with three-fifths of this attributable to fuelwood consumption and land-clearing activities and two-fifths to timber production, most of it illegal. The deforestation rate is likely to rise in the post-war period, as people encroach on areas that were formerly inaccessible owing to the civil conflict.

In Costa Rica, following charges of widespread infringement of forestry regulations, the authorities ordered the suspension of all lumbering activities in the Peninsula de Osa area. A 90-day suspension of all tree felling was enforced, allowing time for a stock inventory.

In Paraguay, export prohibitions have been extended since 1994 to all unprocessed and semi-processed wood. These restrictions are intended exclusively to address the acute problem of deforestation and to preserve domestic species, yet they may also encourage production by local sawmills. Particular emphasis has been placed on strengthening the regulatory framework governing forest exploitation and reafforestation activities as well as on the control of illegal wood exports. There has been little response, however, and the programme could benefit from financial assistance.

In Nicaragua, concern about overexploitation of forest reserves led the National Assembly to ban further logging concessions. A specific prohibition has been issued against felling West Indies cedar (*Cedrela odorata*) and mahogany trees.

In Honduras, more than 1 million ha of forest area has been estimated to be under some form of management plan, while the public auction system for selling public forest resources has been transparent and competitive.

Experiences in institutional decentralization

The redimensioned role of the state, some aspects of which are illustrated in earlier sections, has also revived interest in decentralization. A recent and significant experience in Latin America is that of decentralization through

Box 9
MUNICIPALIZATION AND PEOPLE'S PARTICIPATION IN BOLIVIA

The 1994 People's Participation Law launched the process of decentralization through the municipalities. The process continued at the departmental level with the promulgation of the Administrative Decentralization Law in 1995. Following are the main aspects of the People's Participation Law:

- The creation of urban-rural municipalities that allow for the incorporation of the rural sector in the municipal context. The municipality constitutes the basic territorial unit of the national planning system for the implementation of policies and public management.
- The proportional allocation of fiscal resources to all municipalities based on their population. The law has led to a radical redistribution of fiscal resources in favour of the most disadvantaged regions and rural areas of Bolivia. Before embarking on the decentralization process, the central government had decision-making power for 75 percent of public investments, while at present it has that power for only 30 percent of the same funds.
- The transfer to the municipalities of numerous responsibilities that were previously the domain of the public administration. Among these are the funding and management of health and education services, small-scale irrigation infrastructure

and local roads. The municipalities have decision-making power regarding the utilization of the public investment funds placed at their disposal.

- Legal recognition of rural communities, indigenous villages and local governing bodies that existed before the promulgation of the law. In addition, it assigns them specific responsibilities and duties in the field of municipal planning and management and defines them as entities of popular participation.
- The establishment of a municipal Supervisory Committee, composed of representatives of the rural communities, indigenous villages and local governing bodies that have legal status and control over management of the municipality.

Despite the progress it represents, the People's Participation Law does have certain limitations. In particular, by defining territorial organizations (local governing bodies, rural communities and indigenous villages) as entities of people's participation, the possibility of including other local actors who are not strictly territorial in the participatory process is limited. This is the case, for example, with associations of producers and other economic agents.

The Bolivian decentralization process reached the departmental level through the promulgation of the Administrative Decentralization Law, whereby the departmental prefecture becomes the focal point for national-level policies and supply of resources, departmental policies and development plans and municipal priorities and requests.

The process in Bolivia was duly prepared with community participation in a series of planning exercises at the provincial level, leading to the establishment of municipal development plans for 150 municipalities. This exercise not only constituted a training process, but was also an important part of an information campaign on cofinancing modalities and motivated communities to request a contribution of resources from their local governments.

The Bolivian experience shows that local governments are able to comprehend the needs of the population and to respond adequately. Furthermore, decentralization has had the implicit role of ensuring the presence of the state in many municipalities where it was previously absent.

Source: I. Cossio. 1997. Bolivia: descentralización, participación popular y desarrollo rural. Paper presented at the Technical Consultation on Decentralization, 16-18 December 1997, FAO, Rome.

Box 10

DECENTRALIZATION AND MUNICIPALIZATION IN COLOMBIA

Colombia's 1991 Constitution was the culmination of a process, initiated in 1986, whereby local autonomy acquired a predominant position in the country's institutional structure. Municipalization was manifest in the election of mayors, for instance, and in the deliberate creation of opportunities for community participation.

The country's municipalization process is explicitly oriented towards rural development. In 1987, the municipalities were assigned the task of administering basic public services and, in the agricultural sector, it was decided that they would provide direct and free technical assistance to small-scale producers. For this purpose the Municipal Units for Technical Assistance in Agriculture were set up. Almost all municipalities have one of these technical units which, according to the First National Census, provided assistance to 435 000 small farmers in 1995 whereas, in 1990, prior to their creation, only 120 000 small farmers had been reached. This implied a

220 percent budget increase for such services. At the same time, the cost per beneficiary of these services went down by 10 percent. In 1993, each unit assisted an average of 167 beneficiaries; in 1994, the number reached 269 and in 1995, 436.

In 1993, the establishment of the Municipal Rural Development Councils was approved by law. These councils were formally open to farmers' representatives and were presided over by the mayor, with the participation of representatives of town councils, farmers, guilds and rural communities. The functions and structure of the Municipal Rural Development Councils are defined by the town council based on a proposal put forward by the mayor, with no allowance made for rural associations and communities to participate in its elaboration, except through previous informal negotiations with the mayor. In those municipalities where civil society is weak, especially where farmers have no organizational framework or participatory experience, it is very difficult for these rural development councils to take on the characteristics stipulated by law, and in many cases their establishment would appear to be merely a formality. Rural development councils have been formed in 925 of the 1 074 existing municipalities but, according to information available from the Ministry of Agriculture, only 128 seem to be functioning.

Several reasons can be cited for the limited impact of this initiative. A lack of consolidation of rural organizations, combined with the insufficient and untimely dissemination of information on the rural development councils, resulted in inadequate participation by such organizations. Contrary to the case of Bolivia, where existing organizations were the driving force behind the strengthening of municipalities, here it was hoped that the municipality would promote organization and participation. Another handicap was the insufficient training of social actors and municipal staff to be able to take advantage of the possibilities offered by the rural development councils.

Source: E. Perez. 1997. Los consejos municipales de desarrollo rural o la reglamentación de la participación campesina. Paper presented at the Technical Consultation on Decentralization, 16-18 December 1997, FAO, Rome.

"municipalization", which has assumed major importance and is of considerable relevance to rural development. The process started in the mid-1980s but has gained momentum in recent years. Taking the municipality as a basic territorial unit for decentralization, it promotes all types of participatory activities and institutions at the local level. Examples of this approach can be found in Brazil, Colombia, Nicaragua and Bolivia – this last being perhaps the most successful recent experience (see Box 9).[23]

An equally informative example of municipalization is seen in Colombia (see Box 10), where major efforts have been made to create technical assistance and rural development councils at the municipal level. However, a number of shortcomings have so far limited the impact of these initiatives.

A number of observations can be made concerning experiences with the process of municipalization. The increased role of municipalities has frequently not been accompanied by the transfer of the necessary resources to fulfil the new tasks assigned, nor by the creation of conditions required to ensure participation of the most disadvantaged groups in grassroots organizations. Bolivia's example is indeed remarkable: first in that its municipalization process successfully incorporated previously existing organizations; and, second, in that it put a special emphasis on people's participation, which in turn led to the strengthening of local governments.

CHILE
General characteristics

A 1992 census put Chile's population at 14.5 million people, of which 15 percent live in rural areas and a similar proportion are engaged in agriculture as their main activity. Of the total population, about 23 percent live below the poverty line, down from 40 percent in 1989. The prevalence of poverty in rural areas is significantly higher, however, reaching more than 30 percent of the rural population. The significant decrease in poverty levels is a result of the economy's high rate of growth in the last eight years as well as the strong emphasis that the last two democratic governments placed on social policies – public social expenditure has increased dramatically, reaching $7.8 billion in 1996.

Agriculture contributes 7 percent of GDP. However, its weight in the overall economy is much greater than this figure suggests. In fact, if industrial products closely linked to agriculture are included, the sector's contribution to GDP would rise to nearly 15 percent and its share in export earnings to more than 30 percent.

Out of a total area of approximately 75 million ha, Chile has about 5 million ha under arable land and permanent crops, while natural and improved pastures cover some 13 million ha. About one-third of the total arable land is irrigated. Forest and woodland cover 16.5 million ha. Some 18 percent of the country's territory is under natural parks or reserves, a high proportion by any standard.

Owing to its geographical span and topography, Chile is made up of diverse agro-ecological zones and has a wide variety of microclimates, although it is the only country in the region without tropical agriculture (except for a few small valleys in the northernmost part of the country).

In the desert conditions of the north, extending from the border with Peru to some 400 km north of Santiago, agriculture is almost absent, except in small oases. Dryland

Map 7

CHILE

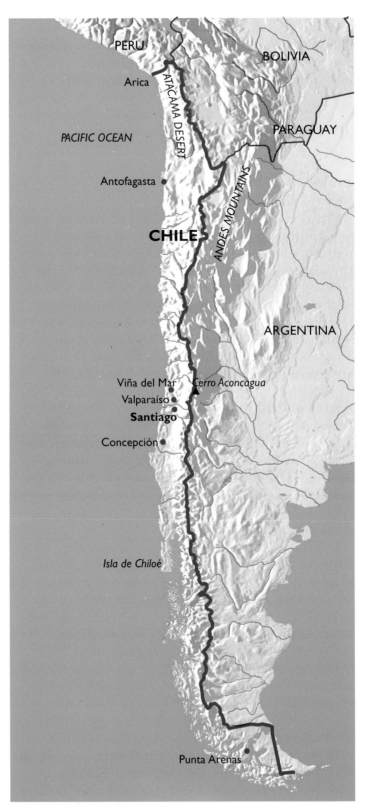

agriculture starts some 400 km north of the capital, where rainfall levels of up to 200 mm allow some very extensive livestock (mainly goat) production. The irrigated areas are similar to the oasis agriculture of the extreme north but are of greater importance, as they are the main producers of early grapes and other fruits for the international market.

Chile's prime agricultural area stretches from 200 km north to 500 km south of the capital. It is here that most of the export fruits and vegetables as well as high-quality wines are produced. This area has a Mediterranean climate with hot dry summers and rains in winter, which steadily increase in level from north to south, reaching 800 mm at the southern point of this macroregion. The topography is mainly an uninterrupted central valley which has been described as "... one of the best tracts of real estate in the world, comparable to the Napa Valley in California ...". It is surrounded by the Andes to the east and the coastal range to the west. On the Andean piedmont and the coastal range, extensive livestock and annual crop (mainly wheat and legumes) production are carried out and, in the last 20 years, forest plantations (mainly of radiata pine and eucalyptus) have been expanding.

Further south and down to the end of continental Chile, about 1 500 km south of Santiago, rainfall, occurring in summer, continues to increase and the terrain becomes hilly and suitable for pasture-based dairy production as well as for cereal crops and natural and plantation forests. Continuing south, the central valley is submerged by the Pacific Ocean, leaving the coastal range, which breaks down into large and small islands, and the Andean range, which peaks at a height of just 1 200 m in this region. This macroregion bears a strong resemblance to New Zealand, which is at the same latitude. In Patagonia, the southernmost part of Chile, sheep and beef cattle production are the main activities, now complemented by some market gardening for regional consumption.

Economic development and policies

The Chilean economy has made a vigorous recovery from the 1982-1983 economic crisis, when GDP plummeted by 14 percent the first year and by a further 0.7 percent the following year. The recovery, led by the agricultural sector followed closely by other tradables such as mining, forestry, fisheries and natural resource processing industries, has seen GDP expand at an annual rate of about 6 percent

The agricultural sector has led a vigorous recovery of the Chilean economy from its 1982-1983 crisis.

since 1984. Such rapid expansion was made possible by the introduction of certain pragmatic measures to strengthen the rigid macroeconomic policies implemented during the first phase of the military government, most of which are still in force today. Paramount among such pragmatic moves was the reintroduction of a managed market for foreign exchange, as compared with the fixed exchange rate policy implemented in 1979 – which, according to many, led to the crisis. This consists of "dirty flotation", whereby the Central Bank fixes a band within which the forces of supply and demand are left to determine the current rate. However, interventions by the Central Bank (buying and selling) can occur at any moment to counter speculative movements, while the floor and ceiling of the band are adjusted monthly according to internal and external inflation. There was also an initial rise in the uniform import tariff from 10 to 35 percent, but it was soon dropped to the current 11 percent.

As the crisis of the early 1980s had resulted from an over indebtedness of the country's private sector, strong pressure from international lenders forced the public sector to assume the payment of private debt in order to renew the flow of foreign resources. This was accompanied by state intervention to correct the asset situation of the main private banks and by more stringent regulations for the country's financial operations. While these measures allowed the economy to set off on a fairly self-sustaining pattern of growth, the enormous cost of the government's paying off private external debt and intervening to consolidate the banking system is still being paid by the nation as a whole and is preventing the Central Bank from taking a more active position in the foreign exchange market. Indeed, the government still owes the Central Bank about $6.6 billion for the bank rescue operations of 1983.

Foreign investment has significantly expanded, reflecting the climate of confidence instilled by the reintroduction of a stable democratic regime and the continuation of proven economic policies.

With democracy reinstated, economic development since 1990 has continued at the same rate, since the economic policy remained basically the same as that of the post-crisis military period. Significant changes have occurred, however, in certain critical areas. For example, foreign investment has significantly expanded, reflecting the climate of confidence instilled by the reintroduction of a stable democratic regime and the continuation of proven economic policies. In fact foreign investment commitments increased by 250 percent between 1990 and 1996, exceeding

$4.5 billion in the last year. This has proved a mixed blessing, however, since capital inflows, combined with the continuing dynamism of the export sector, have led to a significant appreciation – an estimated 26 percent in real terms – of the national currency since 1990.

The centre-left governments since 1990 have placed greater emphasis on addressing the equity problems brought forth by the market-oriented development model. Upon election, the new government launched an expanded taxation programme, with new taxes being periodically introduced as the well-riddled electoral system allows (a new tax reform is currently being discussed). The increased public revenues have been used mainly in social expenditures, especially for health and education, the latter having been designated a priority sector by the current government. In fact, public social expenditure has risen by 50 percent since the early 1990s. Together with rapid economic growth, these efforts account for the drop in absolute poverty mentioned earlier. However, this has not been achieved at the expense of investment, which rose from 18 percent of GDP during the military government, to 24 percent during the first democratic government and is currently nearing 27 percent.

Another high-priority sector, which had been left behind, is infrastructure, where not only has public expenditure expanded significantly, but new legislation has been enacted to allow for massive private investments in road construction, telecommunications, power, etc.

Public expenditure in infrastructure has expanded significantly and new legislation has allowed for massive private investments in this area.

Historical overview of Chilean agricultural development
The post-1930s crisis period. After the crisis of the 1930s, which caused Chile's foreign exchange earnings to fall to one-third of their normal level, the country embarked on an import substitution strategy. Although this move generated an important industrial sector, it severely punished agriculture and fed an increasing inflationary process which peaked in the mid-1950s with annual rates of nearly 100 percent. Agricultural production increased at a sluggish 1.8 percent per year, well below population growth which rose at about 2.5 percent in those years. The mounting import bill that resulted from this gap between production and population growth was a heavy burden to the economy. The major blame was placed on the very skewed land distribution system prevailing in the country at the time, although it was also realized that the "cheap

food prices policy" had some responsibility for the sector's poor performance. It was, however, politically unpalatable to liberalize food prices under the conditions of *latifundia* tenure, since higher prices would primarily have aggravated distortions in wealth and income distribution within the sector (to the detriment of the urban poor) and would have brought only marginal increases in production. This state of affairs set the stage for the land reform process which, prompted by the Alliance for Progress Programme, got off to a slow start in the early 1960s.

The land reform period. In 1964, following the election of the centre-left Christian Democratic candidate, the process of land reform gained momentum. New legislation was approved, facilitating the expropriation of large productive as well as unproductive estates and allowing the unionization of farm workers. As a result, 3.6 million ha (12 percent of the country's agricultural land) were expropriated and organized into new joint exploitation units. At the same time, about 50 percent of the farm workforce was organized into unions, reaching a higher rate of union membership in six years than that of urban workers, who had been allowed to form unions since the beginning of the century.

Chile's comparative advantage in agriculture is mainly in fruit and wine production in the Central Valley and dairy and forest products in the south.

At the same time, a strong production promotion policy was enacted, with increases in the administered prices of basic foodstuffs at the farm level and a series of comprehensive subsectoral promotion programmes. Based on strategic planning studies, the government designed and began implementing a set of programmes to promote what were seen as the main comparative advantages of Chilean agriculture, namely fruit and wine production in the Central Valley and dairy and forestry products in the south. The programmes included the provision of long-term credit, technical assistance, public investment in basic processing infrastructure, improved wine production, milk processing and cellulose plants as well as special incentives for the organization of cooperatives for these products. During this period, the state's strategic planning capacity could be said to have laid the basis for Chile's modern agricultural sector.

As a result, and despite the normally disruptive effect brought about by accelerated social change, growth in the gross value of production jumped from the sluggish 1.8 to 2 percent recorded since the 1930s to a sizeable 5 percent per annum, which is double the population growth rate. This enabled a halt in the persistent increase in the food import bill, despite the boost to internal demand caused by the income distribution policies implemented during this period.

The land reform and unionization processes were greatly accelerated during the Allende period, with little regard paid to their effects on the productive process. Land seizures became widespread, severely undermining the confidence of the remaining large- and medium-scale farmers. In addition, the new units in the reformed sector were either transformed into state enterprises or exploited de facto or *de jure* in a communal system, thereby undermining production incentives also. The result was a collapse in agricultural production, which fell by 4.8 percent per annum between 1970 and 1973. In fact, the deteriorating conditions in rural areas became a determining factor in the coup that took place on 11 September 1973.

The military regime. This period, which lasted from September 1973 to March 1990, can be divided into two subperiods which are separated by the economic crisis of the early 1980s.

1973 to the early 1980s crisis – the orthodox period. Government measures in this period focused on halting the hyperinflation then prevailing (1 000 percent in 1973), and on achieving full and rapid economic liberalization. As the country chose to follow the "shock therapy" proposed by the economist Milton Friedman in 1975, this was a period of profound structural changes and one in which the latest theories of market liberalization were tested in a practically "friction-free social laboratory". Agricultural policies merely reflected the government's objectives for the economy as a whole. In fact, the main objectives for the sector were: the liberalization of agricultural markets; a reduction in the role of the state; and the assurance of full guarantees to private property in the countryside. Perhaps the most significant sectoral policy was the full regularization of agricultural reform, a process that was completed towards 1979. By then, about 30 percent of the land that had been either legally expropriated or seized towards the end of the Allende period was returned to its previous owners;

The period from 1973 until the early 1980s was one of profound structural changes in which the latest theories of market liberalization were tested.

Box 11

FRUIT EXPORT "MIRACLE"

Within 20 years, Chile had become one of the world's leading exporters of off-season temperate fruits. How did this happen so rapidly? As in the case of most "miracle" stories, achievements were based on hard facts. The potential that the country's exceptional climate and geographical location offered for temperate fruit production had first been discovered in the late 1950s and early 1960s as a result of the strategic planning capacity developed by the public sector at the time. Expansion of the fruit subsector was spurred by public sector support in the form of long-term investment credit to finance plantations and processing infrastructure (packing and cold storage plants).

The subsector grew at a moderate rate until the concurrence of two critical developments: i) the liberalization of international trade that occurred during the military period and initially entailed a high real value for foreign exchange; and ii) a shift in tastes in the developed country markets, especially the United States, away from foods rich in carbohydrates and fat towards vitamin- and fibre-rich foods. Combined, these factors caused the fruit trade to expand dramatically during the 1970s and early 1980s, when only Chile and South Africa were in a position to meet such a demand and the latter faced more stringent political difficulties than Chile. Another determining factor was the deregulation and dismantling of the farm workers' union, which resulted in low real salaries and production costs and extraordinarily high rates of return in fruit production (rates of 30 to 50 percent were quite common for some varieties).

another third – mostly Andean piedmont, coastal dryland and potential livestock farmland in the south – was difficult to divide and was auctioned off to the highest bidder; and the rest was allotted in private plots to the former estate farm workers.

In the meantime, however, the reduced support from the state and the high interest rates of the recently liberalized market (in some years reaching 60 percent in real terms) meant that these new owners did not have the means to farm their land properly and were forced to sell at very low prices. By the mid-1980s, it was estimated that

J.-M. MICAUD/FAO/14376

Apples are inspected, packed and stored for off-season export

Fruit exporting is an important and growing subsector in Chile.

nearly 50 percent had sold their activities, despite efforts by the growing NGO movements (led by the Catholic Church and other religious denominations) to replace the dwindling state support services. The sector's response was erratic, especially in the face of policies that kept changing according to macro directives. The value of production between 1974 and 1984 returned to the sluggish 2 percent per annum of the 1930-1960 period, but showing considerable differences within subsectors and regions. Thus, while fruit-tree plantations took off at yearly rates of about 8 to 10 percent during this period, livestock production was severely affected by the drop in domestic demand that resulted from macroeconomic adjustment and high unemployment rates. Annual crops expanded strongly in the early years of the period (probably responding to the improved environment for private property). However, when the exchange rate was fixed in 1979 as part of a new macroeconomic experiment – the "monetary approach to a balance of payments", production began to fall in response to the appreciation of the national currency. Another subsector that began growing strongly in this period was plantation forest. In this case, expansion was a response to enhanced

Box 12

PRICE BAND SYSTEM

The price band system sets a minimum and a maximum import entry price for a particular merchandise. If the entry price is below the minimum, a variable levy is applied to increase the entry price until it reaches the floor of the band. If the entry price is above the ceiling of the band, then existing tariffs are reduced until the two coincide. If such tariff reductions were not enough to bring the entry price in line with the ceiling, an import subsidy would have to be applied (this has never happened). Between these levels, the market operates freely.

The floor and ceiling are calculated by sorting the last 60 monthly international prices of a commodity in descending order and then crossing out the 15 highest to leave the 16th price as the ceiling of the band. At the other extreme, a similar procedure is followed to determine the floor, the lowest 15 prices are crossed out and the 44th price is taken as the floor of the band. Each year, the first year of the series is dropped and the last comes into the calculation.

The severe balance-of-payments crisis starting in the early 1980s forced a return to more pragmatic macroeconomic policies.

incentives brought about by a scheme that subsidized 75 percent of plantation costs and exempted forested lands from property taxes.

1983-1989: Return to pragmatism. The severe balance-of-payments crisis starting in the early 1980s forced a return to more pragmatic macroeconomic policies, i.e. a managed market approach. This involved, in particular, a substantial currency devaluation, with the real value of the dollar practically doubling between 1981 and 1987. This allowed agricultural and all tradables to recover their profitability. In addition, the government implemented a proactive agricultural policy, comprising the following components:

- *Price band.* A price band was established for the major import-substituting products, initially including wheat, oilseeds, sugarbeet, maize and rice, although the last two were later dropped. This system allowed internal prices to follow, with a lag, the trend of international prices, but prevented day-to-day fluctuations from creating havoc in internal markets (see Box 12, Price band system).

- *Special credit.* The government resumed special credit grants to the sector, after having abolished them as part of its "macropolarization" of agriculture. This was done through the still unprivatized state bank and the national Institute of Agricultural Development (INDAP), which provides support to small farmers. Funds were lent at positive, but reasonably low, real interest rates (7 percent per annum) and with repayment periods in accordance with the agriculture production cycle. This included investment credit refinanced by the multilateral financial institutions, the Inter-American Development Bank (IDB) and the International Bank for Reconstruction and Development (IBRD).

- *Technical assistance.* As part of the policy package to recover agricultural dynamism, a strong state-backed technological transfer programme was implemented in favour of both the national agricultural research institute (INIA) and INDAP, assisting small farmers.

- *Other measures.* Other significant measures included the relaunching of the state-owned sugarbeet-processing industry, which resumed its contract farming scheme and became a significant force in the revitalization of agricultural production in the central and southern regions of the country. Also worth mentioning was the establishment of a special fund to subsidize small-scale private water control schemes.

As a result of this package, the agricultural sector was in a position to lead the country's economic recovery, with production expanding by 7 percent per annum between 1983 and 1989. Yields increased substantially: those of wheat, traditionally lingering around 1.5 to 1.7 tonnes/ha, jumped to 3.3 tonnes by 1989; maize yields practically doubled in the same period, from 3.5 to 7.3 tonnes/ha. The revitalization of the sector enabled a fall in agricultural imports from a peak of $900 million in 1981 to $270 million in 1989. Furthermore, because of depressed demand (per caput consumption of most staples was still below 1971 levels), self-sufficiency was reached in traditionally deficit products such as wheat, maize, rice and dairy and meat products. Employment in the sector rose by 30 percent overall between 1982 and 1989.

Chilean agriculture in the early 1990s
The new democratic government sought to maintain those elements of the economic policy followed by the military government that had shown effectiveness, while also introducing changes aimed at enhancing an equitable distribution of the benefits achieved through development. In line with this general approach, three major objectives were laid down for agriculture:

- maintain and improve the dynamism of agricultural production;
- protect natural resources and revert the deterioration that had followed the unchecked expansion of economic activities;
- actively promote the participation of small farmers in the modernized agricultural sector and combat rural poverty.

Of these three objectives, the third had priority but was the most difficult to achieve. Chilean agriculture shares a strongly segmented, dual agrarian structure with the rest of Latin America. The small farm subsector accounts for 25 to 30 percent of total agricultural production but represents about 70 percent of all agricultural producers and owns about one-third of all agricultural land. However, the subsector has a larger share in the traditional annual crops (wheat, pulses, tubers) and livestock and a much lower share in the more dynamic fruit and high-quality wine subsectors. Moreover, small farmers tend to be more concentrated in the marginal lands of the coastal range, Andean piedmont and southern Chile; thus, in addition to their traditional social marginalization, they start with a scarcer and lower-quality resource base than the commercial sector.

The three objectives listed above provided the framework for the following major policies and programmes of the new government.

Production dynamism. When the new government arrived it was clear that the sources of expansion of agricultural production were reaching a limit. Traditional crops and livestock products were reaching the limits of internal demand and fruit exports were also facing stiffer competition from other sources, having lost profitability compared with the high levels of the 1970s and 1980s. The strategy in this respect was to expand the demand for these products while improving the capacity for a flexible response on the supply side.

Domestic demand for agricultural products increased steadily throughout the period as a result of the various distribution policies of the government as well as the strong growth in economic activity and real wages. However, the most significant actions in this area concerned the improvement of internal marketing conditions. These were achieved through the active involvement of the parastatal grain agency, COTRISA (see Box 13, p.212), which prevented the oligopsonistic practices of the milling sector, causes of havoc in the past.

On the external front, cashing in on improved political conditions, the government signed free trade agreements with several Latin American countries, the most significant being those with Argentina and Mexico. At the same time, an offensive to persuade Asian markets to open up to Chile's products, on the grounds of the country's exceptional health standards, began to bear fruit.

On the supply side, the government embarked on a major effort to relaunch irrigation development. Chile's main advantage in agriculture is its Mediterranean climate but, to exploit this asset fully, irrigation is indispensable. Whereas no irrigation development had been carried out by the previous administration, with an investment of $500 million, the new government has reinstated large state irrigation works; assisted private farmers in rehabilitating and expanding existing schemes; promoted new medium-scale projects; and given special impetus to the existing subsidy scheme for small works, opening it up to the small farm sector. The overall plan is expected to be completed towards the year 2000, by which time Chile's current irrigated area of 1.3 million ha should have increased by 30 percent.

With the aim of improving the supply response, the government has also implemented an ambitious IDB-supported programme to improve INIA's research capacity. The programme gave priority to adaptive research on small

Chilean agriculture benefits greatly from the country's Mediterranean climate; however, to exploit this asset fully, irrigation is indispensable.

Box 13

ARE ALL PARASTATALS BAD?

During the privatization drive of the late 1970s, the existing state marketing agency was abolished, yet part of its storage facilities were kept as state property. When the price band system was established after the 1982 crisis, inherent imperfections of the internal cereal markets (e.g. oligopsonistic practices on the part of the millers and small local buyers – usually truck drivers) led to the realization that a buying agency needed to be established in order to make the landed price of the band operative in the internal market. Given the military government's mistrust of any form of direct state action, this function was entrusted to the Confederation of Commercial Grain Producers' Cooperatives (COPAGRO), which operated for the government by way of an open credit line from the state bank and the state-owned storage facilities. After a few seasons under this scheme, COPAGRO went bankrupt and the government was forced to establish a new incorporated company in which the state held the majority share but the millers and producers had a minority share. Thus, the abolished

parastatal grain agency was reborn under a new name, Comercializadora de trigo SA (COTRISA), with a token private sector participation but with a transitory horizon in the view of the military government.

With the advent of the democratic government, which had fewer ideological complexes about state intervention in agricultural markets, COTRISA's role was enhanced and defined as a permanent state function to ensure that the wheat market operates smoothly at the farm level. COTRISA had to be prepared to buy all the wheat that farmers were willing to sell to it at the landed floor price of the band (the full cost of importing wheat at the floor price), less the storage and financial costs of holding the national harvest until it was fully consumed. The credibility of the agency's commitment to buy all the wheat offered was crucial for the stabilization and establishment of a competitive buyers' market. To prove its credibility, COTRISA had to set the correct buying price; if the price was too high, it would be quickly detected by the buyers who would then refrain from buying, thereby causing the agency to be flooded with wheat until it was forced either to modify the price or to stop buying. This was precisely what happened when the new democratic government came into power in March 1990 towards the end of the wheat marketing season. As the previous government had fixed too high a buying price, COTRISA was obliged to ration its buying. The new government lowered the price and, within 15 days, the market was stabilized and the run on COTRISA stopped. That same year, the agency had to buy about 8 percent of the country's total wheat production; since then, it has bought between 0.2 and 3 percent of total production but the wheat markets have operated smoothly in all seasons. Since the beginning of the democratic period, COTRISA's policy has changed from setting up buying outlets in the central valley to opening outlets mainly in the remoter areas of the drylands of the Andean and coastal ranges, where most of the small farmers are located but there are fewer buyers. It has also shifted from a policy of operating the outlets directly to one of contracting them to small farmers' cooperatives and NGOs. In fact, COTRISA outlets increased from five directly operated concerns in 1990 to 27 in 1994/95, of which only seven were directly operated by the agency itself. The opening up of a new outlet in remote areas immediately raises the prices paid by traditional buyers to the level offered by COTRISA, and such increases have ranged from a low 2 percent in a fairly connected and hence competitive locality to 22 percent in remote localities and in the first years of the scheme's operation. As COTRISA has gained credibility the differentials have decreased, as have purchases.

Today COTRISA is a major player in Chile's wheat market, although it intervenes very little, as witnessed by its actual purchases. In some seasons, COTRISA's successful catalytic operations have been extended to the rice and maize markets (the latter is not covered by the price band system), where the agency has had a similar hand in effecting market transparency. As in the case of grain, after a few weeks, the agency has managed to stabilize markets and has all but stopped having to buy supplies, despite oligopsonistic buyers' attempts to test its ability to handle an unknown market.

farm systems, on dryland agriculture and on more ecologically sustainable research, while also reinforcing the capacities of the health control agency, SAG.

Natural resource conservation. Since very little had been done in this area in the past, efforts were mainly oriented towards the establishment of new norms and legislation on maximum air and water pollution levels. Consequently, major conflicts arose with the mining sector, the main air pollutant in rural areas. Legislation to regulate natural forest exploitation and transfer of land from agriculture to urban uses was also elaborated and discussed. In these two areas, where private commercial interests are extremely powerful and strongly opposed to any regulation, little progress could be made despite their importance for the country's population. In the case of natural forests, however, a cadastre indicated a total of 13.3 million ha, far more than the area that was thought to have been left after the exploitation of these resources for wood chip exports.

Promoting the small farm subsector. The new government's action in support of small farmers was aimed at expanding and improving the coverage of existing technical assistance and credit programmes as well as creating new mechanisms to help this subsector compete with the commercial sector.

Regarding technical assistance, opportunities were created for participation by NGOs, including farmers' organizations, and closer links were set up with INIA. Beneficiaries were also involved in periodical evaluations of the programme, and the modality was changed from individual to group assistance. In four years, the programme doubled its coverage from 26 000 to 51 000, which still represents only 20 percent of the country's small farmers.

On the credit side, a major effort was made to increase the coverage of the various schemes, expanding them to benefit the smaller and poorer farmers who were not previously covered, as well as farmers' organizations. A series of new programmes were implemented in order to improve their insertion into the more modernized agricultural sector. These included a major land titling programme which involved some 50 000 farmers during the period; the incorporation of small farmers into the forest plantation subsidy scheme, covering 27 000 ha; and the establishment of various marketing assistance schemes. An interesting programme in this respect was the linking of agro-industrial

Government action in support of small farmers included expanded technical assistance and credit programmes as well as new mechanisms to help them compete with the commercial sector.

plants to the activities of small farmers following the
outgrower scheme. In this programme, INDAP channelled
the technical assistance and credit programme through
cooperating agro-industries that agreed to provide secure
contracts at sowing time and fair pre-established prices.

Perhaps the most successful new programme was the
inclusion of small farmers in the existing small-scale irrigation
subsidy scheme. This programme had formerly been
monopolized by commercial farmers, since its funds were
allocated under an auction system whereby special points were
assigned according to a beneficiary's proposed contribution.
The new government's innovations were to separate small
farmers' auctions from those designed for commercial
concerns and to provide special financing to conduct related
studies. This led to an explosive demand from small farmers,
and about 130 000 ha benefited as a result.

All these programmes had a definite organizational bias
which enabled small farmers' cooperatives to double in
number since 1989 and to achieve a rapid expansion in
their activities. However, there is still a long way to go before
the small farm sector will be strong enough to compete with
the burgeoning commercial sector.

Special development programmes were formulated, in
coordination with the municipalities, for areas with the
highest concentration of rural poverty. Under these
programmes, special funds were allocated to finance
productive activities identified and implemented by the
beneficiaries themselves. They are now serving as a testing
ground for new approaches to combating rural poverty.
Nevertheless, the main efforts in this area focused on
expanding state social services for the poor which, until
1990, had scarcely reached rural areas. In particular, action
was taken to improve the coverage and quality of education
and health services. At the same time, subsidized housing
more than doubled its coverage and a similar increment was
achieved with investment in rural roads and rural water
supplies. The outcome was a decrease in the incidence of
rural poverty of 200 000 people. The proportion of rural
population living under the poverty line fell to 34 percent in
1992, down from 52 percent in 1987, but still above the 28
percent estimated in 1970.

The proportion of rural population living under the poverty line fell from 52 percent in 1987 to 34 percent in 1992.

Chilean agriculture since 1994
In this period, the government followed a similar
programme, aimed at reinforcing the revitalization and

diversification of agricultural production and modernizing the small farm sector. New instruments were created and others were modified: INDAP was decentralized and a comprehensive project approach was followed at the local level. Special assistance mechanisms were implemented to help small farmers' organizations enhance their capitalization and managerial capacities.

In line with the ongoing process of opening up the national economy, agricultural policies have been strongly influenced by the various trade negotiations in which the sector has also been a major player. Of special significance has been Chile's entry into the Asian Pacific Economic Cooperation Council (APEC), which has helped open up Asian markets to Chilean agricultural, forestry and fisheries exports. Another important event has been the negotiation of associate status with MERCOSUR, the trade bloc comprising Argentina, Brazil, Paraguay and Uruguay. While in the case of APEC, the sector's main interest has been in opening up new markets, the emphasis with MERCOSUR has been on establishing gradual tariff-reduction rules and internal programmes to help in the necessary reconversion of traditional crops (cereals, oilseeds, livestock). Such reconversion is needed in view of the strong competition expected from low-cost producers of these commodities, mainly in Argentina and Uruguay. Free trade agreements have also been negotiated with Canada and Mexico as a first step towards possible membership in the North American Free Trade Agreement (NAFTA), as well as with the EU.

Chile has negotiated free trade agreements with Canada and Mexico as a first step towards possible membership of NAFTA.

These new agreements have been the object of intense debate within the sector and in the political sphere. The government has committed significant additional resources to the required modernization of the sector, including special assistance for the groups and areas most likely to be affected by these agreements. The Ministry of Agriculture has the lead role in promoting the transformation of the sector's production systems. The elimination of rural poverty, a priority task, is considered the responsibility of the public sector as a whole, but of the social ministries in particular (education, health, housing, etc.) and also of local governments. Two core commitments have been established by the government:

- the Commitment for the Development of Rural Areas, which focuses on emerging non-agricultural economic

activities in rural areas and on activities that are strictly
social in nature;

- the Commitment for Agriculture, designed to help the
  sector confront economic internationalization and
  increase its competitiveness by allocating supplementary
  budgetary resources.

A six-point agricultural action plan was defined with the
aim of increasing producers' capacities and assets and
improving the trade environment:

i)   Expand agricultural land under irrigation and improve
     efficiency in water resource management.
ii) Rehabilitate degraded soil, improve the quality of
     producers' land and recover the natural heritage.
iii) Improve the sector's health standards with a view to
     enhancing exports of agricultural products.
iv) Encourage technological innovation and improve
     managerial capacity so as to enhance competitiveness of
     the sector.
v)   Improve marketing facilities and systems, increase
     transparency in domestic markets and promote the
     sector's entry into international markets.
vi) Strengthen the development of forestry, enhancing its
     dynamism and involving small and medium-scale farmers
     in the process; promote the sustainable management of
     native forests and strengthen public institutions in the
     sector.

Sectoral performance. Agricultural production increased at an
annual rate of about 4 percent during the 1990-1996 period,
thus slowing down from the 6 percent per annum achieved
after the 1982 crisis. This resulted from the combination of
three negative exogenous factors. First, the inflow of foreign
capital caused a marked appreciation of the national
currency, impairing the competitiveness of agriculture
which, in Chile, is almost fully tradable. Second, the steady
growth of the economy, combined with the government's
determination to improve income distribution, led to
significant real wage increases, thereby affecting the
profitability of labour-intensive activities such as agriculture.
Finally, international prices of basic foodstuffs (mainly
wheat, rice, maize) experienced a pronounced downturn in
1992 and 1993 and, after a temporary recovery, resumed a
downward trend. Under the country's trade regime, these

price declines were immediately transmitted to domestic markets – the price index of annual crops decreased by 16 percent in real terms between 1990 and 1993. Also of note was the severe effect of at least four years of drought during the 1990-1997 period.

These trends conceal wide variations within the sector, reflecting the strong structural changes in Chilean agriculture. Some subsectors showed substantial growth, for example wine, forestry products, vegetables and dairy products, while others (fruits) expanded at a steady, although more moderate rate and others recorded significant reductions in growth (wheat and oilseeds). This occurred, however, amid a generally steady increase in productivity. Census data indicate average national yield levels of 3.8 tonnes/ha for wheat, 9.1 tonnes/ha for maize and more than 50 tonnes/ha for sugarbeet. Exports continued to grow strongly at nearly 12 percent per annum throughout the period. Total agricultural and forestry exports reached $4 750 million in 1997. About 35 percent of these exports were forest products, which continued to expand at an annual rate of nearly 30 percent. Agro-industrial exports, especially wine, have shown an accelerated rate of expansion (42 percent per annum) which shows no sign of abating. The value of total wine exports is currently $434 million, up from $150 million in 1993. A strong modernization of the wine industry took place during this period, together with a diversification of brands and types of wine caused by shifts in international market demand and foreign investments. Agricultural imports also expanded sharply, on the one hand reflecting increased domestic demand brought forth in particular by improved incomes among the poorer segments of the population; and, on the other hand, reflecting the reduced production of import-substituting crops. Nevertheless, the sector's balance of trade has continued to be strongly positive, reaching about $3 000 million in 1997, up from $1 500 million in 1989 .

Forest products account for about 35 percent of total agricultural exports and are expanding at an annual rate of nearly 30 percent.

Concluding remarks

Chile's agricultural development, having evolved through the widely changing political and economic circumstances experienced over the past decades, provides a number of lessons that are relevant to many other country situations.

One obvious lesson to be drawn from the Chilean experience is the need to establish close cooperation between the public and private sectors. Attempts at

Figure 32

CHILE: DOMESTIC SUPPLY
AND UTILIZATION OF SELECTED PRODUCTS

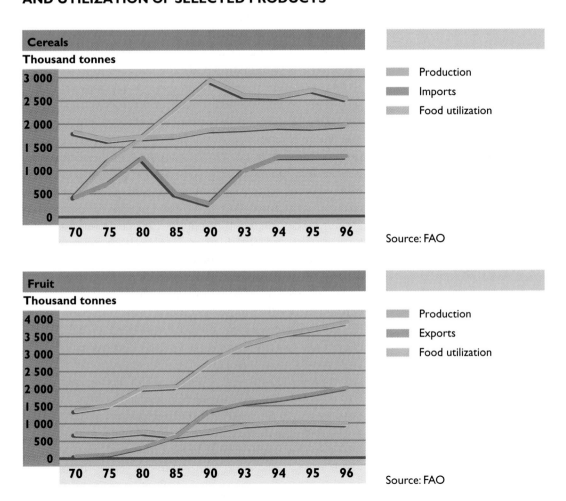

Source: FAO

Source: FAO

substituting state control for private sector initiatives in agricultural production and marketing during the 1970-1973 period resulted in major production failures. Vice versa, a short-sighted absence of state intervention during the early period of the military government also resulted in an erratic response from the sector.

The government played a major role in providing guidance and support in the launching and development of what are, today, the three main pillars of the country's modern agriculture: fruits, forestry and dairy products. Government intervention has also proved essential in the promotion of a competitive marketing system throughout the country as well as in the more traditional areas of health control, research and extension. Chile's experience also suggests that the state cannot forfeit its role in the definition and implementation of sectoral policies. In the case of Chile, adjusting macro policies alone has proved not to be enough.

The above does not mean that sectoral policy can be designed in a vacuum or against the macroeconomic setting, as unfortunately is often done. In fact, few economic sectors are so sensitive to even minor macroeconomic variations. Movements in the rate of exchange, the interest rate and minimum wage levels have a direct impact on the profitability and, hence, the development of the sector. Policies that subordinate the allocational functions of the exchange rate to anti-inflationary objectives can be very costly to agriculture. Widely different macroeconomic circumstances, such as those of the 1982 crisis and, to a lesser extent, the "Dutch disease" of the 1990s – a result of the country's ability to attract foreign investment – have had similarly negative effects on the sector's performance.

The advantages of economic pragmatism can be considered another important lesson, which probably holds for any sector, country or period. However, the Chilean experience in agriculture is particularly illustrative. The large reduction in distortive state interventions has undoubtedly left the sector very lean and flexible, allowing it to respond to market signals. Chilean agriculture today is possibly one of the least distorted agricultural sectors in the world. At the same time, however, the implementation of measures that might appear to be distortions (namely price bands and parastatal intervention in marketing) has been crucial in ensuring the stable growth of agricultural production, yet without isolating the sector or specific crops concerned from market forces. This is shown by the sharp drop in area under wheat and oilseeds, which has nevertheless been accompanied by significant productivity increases. The experience with price bands has added evidence to Peter Timmer's[24] contention that, stabilizing the market of one major staple commodity, even at the cost of temporary protection, can be a critical element for agricultural development and food security. Periods in which ideological development models have prevailed over social, political and sound economic evidence (1939-1952, 1970-1973 and 1974-1982) have witnessed a deterioration in agricultural performance.

Chilean agriculture today is probably one of the least distorted agricultural sectors in the world, and the large reduction of state intervention has left the sector very lean and flexible.

Near East and North Africa

REGIONAL OVERVIEW
General economic performance
Economic growth in the Near East and North Africa region as a whole decelerated, from 4.8 percent in 1996 to 3.5 percent in 1997.[25] The overall slowdown was mainly a reflection of poorer performances in the largest economies of the region, with Egypt being a major exception.

Thus, GDP growth in Turkey slowed from 7.1 percent in 1996 to an estimated 5.7 percent in 1997, and a further slowdown is projected for 1998 as the government attempts to restrain an overheated economy, reduce the rate of inflation (which in 1997 remained in the range of 80 to 90 percent per annum), and bring fiscal balances under control. In the Islamic Republic of Iran, the rate of real GDP expansion slowed from 5.1 percent in 1996 to 3.2 percent in 1997, mainly as a result of weak revenues from oil and gas exports. The poor economic performances in 1997 of two of the major North African economies, Algeria and Morocco, were largely the result of poor weather conditions negatively affecting agricultural production. In Algeria drought severely curtailed agricultural production, contributing to the slowdown in economic growth to only 1.3 percent in 1997, from 3.8 percent the previous year. The economic impact was even more pronounced in Morocco, where a sharp decline in agricultural output in 1997 translated into an estimated 2.2 percent contraction in GDP. Generally, the performance of the Moroccan economy in recent years has been persistently marred by sharp weather-induced oscillations in agricultural production. The Egyptian economy, on the other hand, in 1997 witnessed a further strengthening of economic growth which increased for the fifth consecutive year to a rate of 5 percent. The continued economic recovery bears testimony to the success of the economic stabilization and reform policies pursued by the Egyptian Government since 1991, which brought about a reduction in inflation, improved external and fiscal balances and a stabilization of the currency.

Prospects for 1998 are for a further deceleration in GDP growth owing, in particular, to the likelihood of continued weak international oil prices which would restrain economic activity in the oil-exporting economies of the region. IMF projects GDP growth for the region to be about 3.5 percent,

The overall economic slowdown in North Africa and the Near East was mainly a reflection of poorer performances in the largest economies of the region.

221

Figure 33

NEAR EAST AND NORTH AFRICA

Agricultural export and import values and share in total merchandise trade

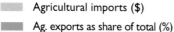 Agricultural exports ($)

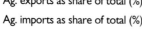 Agricultural imports ($)

Ag. exports as share of total (%)

Ag. imports as share of total (%)

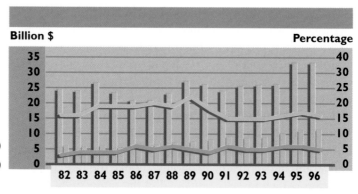

Agricultural exports
(Index 1989-91=100)

 Value

Unit value

Quantity

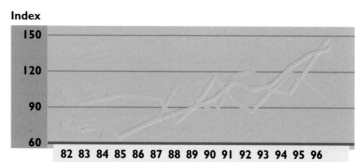

Agricultural imports
(Index 1989-91=100)

 Value

Unit value

Quantity

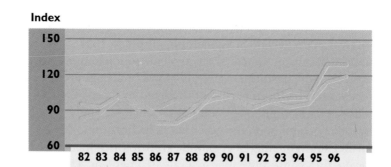

Net barter and income agricultural terms of trade
(Index 1989-91=100)

 Net barter

Income

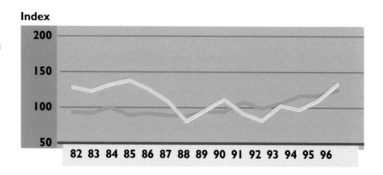

NEAR EAST AND NORTH AFRICA

Percentage

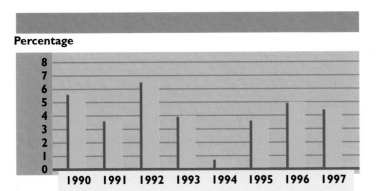

Real GDP
(Percentage change over previous year)

kcal

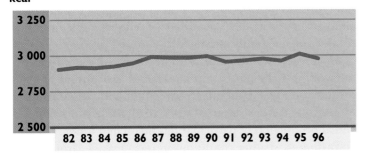

Dietary energy supplies
(kcal per caput per day)

Index

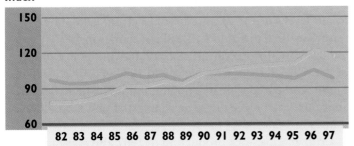

Agricultural production
(Index 1989-91=100)

Total

Per caput

Source: FAO and IMF

which would be the second lowest yearly rate of the 1990s, after the crisis year 1994. Lower rates of growth are expected for Turkey as a result of expected tighter fiscal policies to restrain demand and reduce the budget deficit, and Iran, which will suffer the impact of depressed oil prices, as will the other oil-exporting countries. On the other hand, higher rates of growth are projected in Algeria and Morocco, reflecting to a large extent a recovery from the weather-induced poor performances in 1997. In Egypt, growth is expected to remain vigorous at around 5 percent, the same as in 1997. Prospects for 1999 are for some acceleration in GDP growth, which should reach 4.4 percent in the region as a whole.

Agricultural performance

Agricultural production in the North Africa and Near East region declined by an estimated 4 percent in 1997, after a 10 percent expansion in crop and livestock production the year before.

Following the highly favourable performance of 1996, which saw crop and livestock production in the region expand by almost 10 percent, 1997 recorded a decline in agricultural production, currently estimated at almost 4 percent.

Most severe was the setback in northern Africa, where unfavourable climatic conditions caused agricultural production to fall by about 15 percent in both Algeria and Morocco and 3 percent in Tunisia. In all three countries, cereal production in particular has fluctuated widely according to weather conditions in recent years. Drought caused cereal production to fall in Algeria from 4.9 million tonnes in 1996 to less than 0.9 million tonnes in 1997, the lowest level since 1966; and in Tunisia from 2.9 million tonnes in 1996 to around 1.1 million tonnes in 1997. Similarly, in Morocco insufficient rainfall in the beginning of the year led to a cereal harvest in 1997 of only 4.1 million tonnes compared with 10.1 million tonnes in 1996, but still above the even more disastrous harvest of only 1.8 million tonnes in 1995.

Crop and livestock production in 1997 also contracted in Turkey in spite of a slightly increased cereal harvest, as declines in production were recorded for livestock and a number of other food and non-food crops, including cotton, oilcrops (particularly olives), fruits and vegetables. Agricultural production is also estimated to have declined somewhat in Iran, and more markedly in the Syrian Arab Republic as cereals, and food crops in general, suffered from unfavourable weather conditions. On the other hand, the Syrian cotton crop reached a new record, reflecting a significant increase in planted area. In Iraq, estimated agricultural production declined in 1997, following the increase in 1996, with cereal production down by about 25 percent. Per caput agricultural production in Iraq continues to linger at levels well below those of the 1980s.

In Egypt, agricultural production in 1997 remained at the same level as the preceding year, following two consecutive years of strong expansion at 8 percent per year. Although production in Saudi Arabia expanded for the second consecutive year, it only recovered very partially from the decline of over 20 percent recorded in 1995. In particular cereal production declined sharply from its peak level of 5 million tonnes in 1994, to about 2.4 million tonnes in 1997, following reductions in government producer price support. In terms of value of output, such reduction has been only partially compensated by an expansion of production of fruit and vegetables.

As regards prospects for 1998, improved climatic conditions in Algeria, Morocco and Tunisia are expected to result in a significant increase in cereal crops relative to the disastrous shortfalls of 1997. Crop prospects also appear promising in Turkey and Saudi Arabia, while in Iraq the outlook appears more uncertain owing to inadequate rainfall conditions and persistent shortages of inputs.

In a longer perspective, most countries have recorded sizeable expansions in agricultural production over the past decade, the major exceptions being Iraq, where agriculture has been severely depressed by market, investment and input constraints linked to the economic embargo, and Saudi Arabia, as a consequence of sharp reductions in farm subsidies. For Algeria and Morocco, where agricultural output is subject to wide seasonal fluctuations, a clear trend is not easily discernible.

When translated into per caput terms, agricultural performances in the region over the last decade appear less clearly positive. Among the larger countries, only Iran and Egypt have achieved clear and relatively consistent gains in per caput production, while in Turkey per caput production has been somewhat reduced overall. In the case of the Syrian Arab Republic, per caput agricultural production did tend to increase since 1990, but not enough to compensate for the significant declines recorded throughout the 1980s. Trends are, again, unclear in the widely unstable Maghreb agricultural sectors, but some upward movement in per caput production appears to have taken place in Tunisia.

Severe drought-induced damage in several North African countries in 1997 underscored the crucial importance of water resource management for the region.

Water resource management

The severe damage caused by drought in several countries in northern Africa in 1997 underscored, once again, the crucial importance of water resource management for the countries of the region. In Morocco, where irrigated land accounts for 13 percent of total arable land and land under permanent crops, the drought in 1997 was only the latest of a series of regular similar occurrences. In order to reduce the excessive dependence on rainfed agriculture, the Government of Morocco has established a policy unit specifically charged with addressing this issue. At the same time, the government is pushing ahead with its policy of expanding irrigated areas through an ambitious programme of dam construction. Core objectives of the programme include an expansion of agricultural exports through irrigation and an increase in power supplies. Algeria, where irrigated areas cover only 7 percent of arable land and land under permanent crops, is also pursuing a programme of dam constructions, and works have been resumed on a major dam project which had been abandoned in 1993. In Tunisia, the national water policy foresees the construction of a number of large and smaller dams, but the potential for further expansion of the irrigated area is limited. Other countries where efforts are being made at expanding irrigated areas are Turkey, notably with its South East Anatolia project, and the Syrian Arab Republic.

In Jordan, the Jordan Valley Authority is focusing its efforts on water conservation and improved irrigation efficiency to increase water availability to agriculture. Examples of problems derived from water use can be found in the Syrian Arab Republic, where the unrestricted drilling of wells in the past affected the underground water levels in some areas, and Yemen, where the water table is falling rapidly. In Saudi Arabia, cereal production has been based on non-renewable underground aquifers. In recent years, the government has been deliberately attempting to shift production away from water-intensive cereal production to more water-efficient types of horticultural production.

By far the most ambitious water management scheme in the region is, however, Egypt's South Valley project which was announced in 1997. The scheme aims at expanding both agricultural and populated areas of the country by diverting water from Lake Nasser. When completed, the scheme is planned to be able to settle 6 million people and irrigate about 0.5 million ha. The Egyptian Government announced that the total cost of the scheme up until 2017 would be 300 billion Egyptian pounds (close to $90 billion). The first phase of the project involves the construction of an irrigation canal of the length of 67 km to reclaim an area of 34 000 ha, to be extended subsequently.

Policy developments

Most countries of the region pursued market liberalization and deregulation policies in the course of 1997 and early 1998. However, progress in economic and agricultural reform was uneven and in several cases governments reintroduced or reinforced intervention practices. Recent examples of market-oriented reform in agriculture include the decision in Algeria to transform the national cereal monopoly into a regulatory body for the cereal sector, and the abolition in Jordan of retail price controls for locally produced fruits and vegetables. In Algeria, the government has also indicated its intention to push for a fully privatized agriculture. In Egypt, Law 96, approved by Parliament in 1992, was scheduled to take full effect in 1997. The law liberalized rent of agricultural land, which had remained virtually unchanged since 1952, laying down a five-year grace period for landowners and tenants to arrive at a settlement and providing a compensation package for farmers who accepted a settlement before the expiry of the grace period. The law affected an estimated 700 000 to 800 000 tenant farmers and the share of rented land in 1992 was estimated at 24 percent. In Morocco, in the context of the government's privatization programme, which is among the most advanced in the region, renewed efforts were made to sell off part of the sugar industry. Among companies slated for privatization in 1997 were two of the countries' major wine production and distribution companies. In the Syrian Arab Republic, the government is continuing its efforts of the last few years to encourage private-sector investment in the cotton spinning industry, which had previously been reserved for public sector activity.

In spite of the trend towards liberalization, state intervention in agricultural markets is still widespread in the region and, as mentioned earlier, the recent past has also seen some important cases of reversal of the trend. For example, in November 1997, Lebanon introduced import

Recent progress in economic and agricultural reform has been uneven and several governments have reintroduced or reinforced intervention practices.

Box 14

EU-MEDITERRANEAN PARTNERSHIP

Since 1995, a number of countries in the region have been involved in developing a EU-Mediterranean partnership, leading to the establishment of a free trade area between the EU and the Mediterranean countries. The process was launched at a Conference in Barcelona in November 1995 with participation of the EU and the Mediterranean countries, except the Libyan Arab Jamahiriya, and is planned to lead to the creation of a free trade area by 2010. The first agreements reached between the EU and the Mediterranean countries associated in the process aim at securing a better integration of the countries into the world market through an economic and financial partnership.

The envisaged free trade area would imply:

- free trade in all manufactured goods between the EU and the countries associated in the process;
- reciprocal preferential access for agricultural goods of interest to the partners;
- free trade among the Mediterranean countries themselves.

restrictions on a series of agricultural and processed food products with a view to reducing the food import bill, protecting domestic agriculture and stimulating production. The restrictions include a total ban for a number of products, new import duties for a series of others and a list of products that can only be imported in coordination with the Ministry of Agriculture. In Turkey, there has been a reversal of the policies of the early 1990s towards reduced government intervention in agricultural markets. The reversal, in particular with a return to more generous price support policies, began in the marketing year 1995/96. Thus, after major government cereal procurement in 1996, even larger quantities were procured in 1997. In addition, support prices in the 1997/98 marketing year were increased significantly for a number of crops.

For a number of the countries in the region economic relations with the European countries, and in particular the EU, are of fundamental importance, not least for the agricultural sector. In this context, 1997 saw some further progress with negotiations concluded between Jordan and the EU on an association agreement within the framework of the so-called Barcelona process (see Box 14), making Jordan the fifth country to conclude an agreement after Morocco, Tunisia, Egypt and Israel. For Morocco, relationships with the EU are important also in the area of fisheries. The latest fisheries agreement between Morocco and the EU had been reached in 1996, granting access to Moroccan waters for the EU fisheries fleet for four years, against compensation, but with a gradual scaling down of allowed catch. The Moroccan Government has now indicated its intention not to renew the agreement on its expiry in 1999. Instead the government has announced ambitious plans for the development of the national fisheries industry with, *inter alia*, the expansion of port facilities and reliance on joint ventures with foreign companies.

Relations with Europe are of fundamental importance for a number of countries in the North Africa and Near East region.

ISLAMIC REPUBLIC OF IRAN
Macroeconomic context
Iran's economic situation and policy orientation over the last two decades have been profoundly affected by two major events: the 1979 revolution and the country's adoption of Islamic rules for economic and social policy management; and the eight-year war with Iraq, which entailed severe human and material losses, a critical dislocation of the economy and a protracted period of recovery and reconstruction. Other events that also had a major negative impact on the country's economy over the same period were the 1986 oil price depression, which resulted in a significant fall in the country's revenues at a time when its economy was already in recession, and the trade restrictions imposed by the United States.[26] However, Iran has since then staged a significant economic recovery, as seen below. In addition, with the presidential election and the Islamic Summit held in Teheran in 1997, there are growing signs that the country has entered an era of reduced economic and diplomatic isolation.

Iran is now a lower middle-income country, with a GDP of $82 billion and per caput GDP of $1 300 (1996 figures). Its population is about 61 million, having doubled in 20 years (average population growth was as high as 3.2 percent between 1977 and 1986; with active family planning efforts, it fell to its current level of about 1.6 percent). GDP growth was estimated at 4.2 percent in

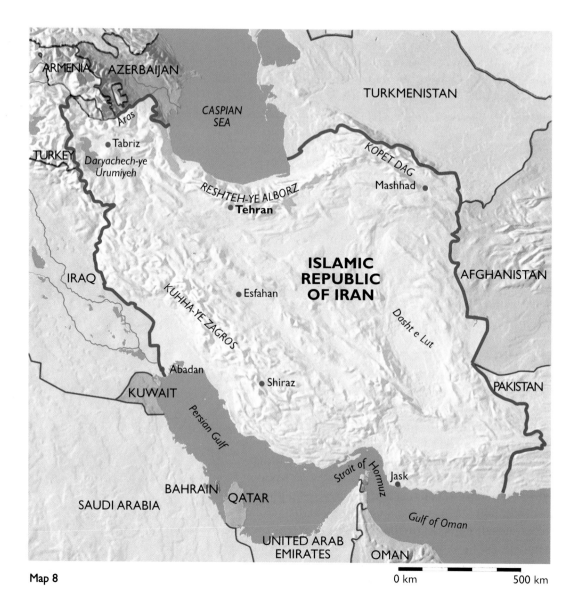

Map 8

0 km   500 km

ISLAMIC REPUBLIC OF IRAN

1995/96, and 5.2 percent in 1996/97,[27] the highest in five years, mainly owing to high crude oil prices in 1996. Subsequent oil price reductions are expected to slow down growth in 1997/98.

Oil production in 1996 was 3.7 million barrels per day, contributing 16 percent of the country's GDP and some 80 percent of its export revenue. New offshore gas fields are being brought on-line and gas is increasing in importance. The government aims at reducing economic dependence on the hydrocarbons sector, and vulnerability to oil price movements, by promoting other sectors, in particular agriculture.

Figure 34

IRAN: DOMESTIC SUPPLY AND UTILIZATION OF CEREALS

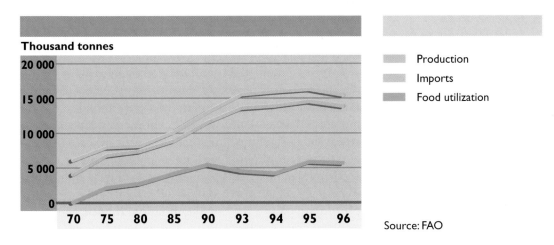

Thousand tonnes

Production
Imports
Food utilization

Source: FAO

After the revolution and the war with Iraq, which had led to emergency policies, the government adopted an economic model combining the objectives of self-reliance with those of liberalization and private sector promotion. A First Five-Year Plan (1989/90 to 1993/94) for reconstruction was launched, which aimed at increasing production and self-sufficiency for all strategic products, raising productivity in key economic sectors and promoting the non-oil export sector. Economic liberalization was pushed forth in the context of a national structural adjustment programme which included correcting price distortions, floating the foreign exchange rate and promoting the private sector. During this period, Iran's economy expanded at strong growth rates, and the Plan's ambitious quantitative objectives were achieved to a large extent.

A Second Plan was introduced for the period 1994/95 to 1999/2000 setting, like its predecessor, ambitious growth objectives. The new Plan confirms the commitment to market liberalization (further privatization and less state involvement in market operations), and the shift of emphasis from oil to non-oil sectors. On the external front, the Plan provides for the adoption of a managed unified floating rate, streamlining of customs procedures and the setting of tariffs at levels that protect domestic producers while maintaining international comparative advantage. In the financial sector, the plan aims

Despite improvements from the critical situation of the early 1990s, external indebtedness and debt servicing remain serious economic problems for Iran.

at keeping monetary growth at non-inflationary rates, with a series of measures regarding incentives for savings and rationalizing bank interest rates, issuing treasury bills, and stimulating private sector participation. Finally, the plan aims at reforming the tax system and its administration, introducing a value-added tax system and eliminating subsidies (while creating safety nets and targeted assistance for vulnerable groups).

External indebtedness and debt servicing remain serious economic problems, despite improvements from the critical situation of the early 1990s. Following important renegotiations in 1993, short-term debts were converted to medium- and long-term obligations. The government committed itself to an ambitious debt-servicing schedule, with payments exceeding $5 billion in some years. This effort led to budgetary austerity and pressure to halt or reverse liberalization. Indeed, the exchange rate was fixed again, and imports heavily regulated, with negative repercussions on the domestic industry. The import bill has been held down to an austerity level of about $13 billon in 1995/96, down from $26 billion in 1991/92.

Iran has made important progress in health, education and population control during the last decade. However, many socio-economic problems remain unsolved. It is estimated that 17 percent of the population live below the poverty line (12.2 and 26 percent in urban and rural areas, respectively, according to a UNDP source). Government statistics indicate that 10 to 14 percent of the workforce is unemployed, a conservative figure that understates the structural labour surplus in the national economy. Despite efforts to reduce subsidies, their weight in the national budget remains considerable.

Iran is not a member of WTO, and its eventual entry into the organization has been the object of debate. Such a move would mean substantial reforms, in particular in the country's protectionist food pricing policy.

Stabilization efforts have considerably reduced consumer price inflation which, however, has remained high. During the First Plan period (1990/91 to 1994/95), inflation averaged 24 percent per year. After peaking at 50 percent in 1995/96, it decelerated to 23 percent in the year ending March 1997. Latest estimates point to an 18 percent inflation rate for the first five months of the 1997/98 Iranian year.

The government was forced to abandon its unified floating rate policy in 1995, owing to difficulties in its implementation, and to reintroduce, on a provisional basis, a double fixed exchange rate.[28] The Central Bank remains a keen advocate of a unified floating exchange rate, a goal whose achievement was hoped for 1999, but which will likely require some more years.

The agricultural sector

Agriculture is a major economic sector in Iran, with great potential for development and, as such, is seen as a key strategic policy area. It contributes more than 25 percent of GDP and one-third of total employment. It also contributes substantial export earnings – $900 million in 1996, i.e. one-third of total non-oil exports.

Iran's population can be considered largely free from food insecurity. Energy supplies are in the range of 2 900 kcal per caput per day.[29] About 80 percent of the national food requirements are covered by national production, and 90 percent of agro-industry needs are covered by domestic supplies.

Agricultural policies over the last two decades have sought to strengthen agricultural activity in order to achieve higher levels of food self-sufficiency and more diversified sources of foreign exchange – thus reducing vulnerability to oil price fluctuations. These general objectives, contained in past development Plans, are also those of the Third Plan and the 25-year strategy under preparation. A central stated goal is to feed 100 million inhabitants with domestically produced food by 2023 (Iranian Islamic Year 1400).

Natural resources for agriculture: a high potential. The total country area is 1.65 million km². Roughly 51 million ha are considered as being potentially arable, of which only 36 percent is cultivated. Iran has a great diversity of climatic conditions, ranging from arid (central plain and southern coast) to semi-arid and Mediterranean (western and northern provinces) and very humid (Caspian Sea). The country's biodiversity is rich, with a total number of plant species estimated to be larger than that of the whole of Europe. Forests cover 11.4 million ha, despite having suffered severe deforestation (more than 5 million ha have been lost since 1960), while rangelands, pasture, mountains and desert occupy 90 million ha (54.6 percent of the national territory).

Iran's population is largely free from food insecurity, with daily energy supplies in the range of 2 900 kcal per caput and about 80 percent of food requirements covered by national production.

Fisheries are a relatively marginal economic area, but have a strong export tradition and potential, based on the combined resources of the Caspian Sea (caviar), the Oman sea and the Persian Gulf.

The 51 million ha of arable land are largely dominated by non-cultivated pasture (32.5 million ha). About 8.8 million ha are irrigated[30] under traditional and modern schemes, while rainfed cultivated areas cover 9.7 million ha. Iranian soils are not considered to be very fertile overall. The soils of the plains and valleys where the major farming areas are located are affected by varying degrees of salinity and/or waterlogging, and those of the plateaus have low organic matter. Only the Caspian basin soils have rather high organic matter contents.

About two-thirds of usable surface water resources are used for agriculture, while groundwater resources are being used at their maximum safe level.

About two-thirds of the total usable surface water resources are used for agricultural irrigation and other uses, while groundwater resources are being used at their maximum safe level, with recent problems of lowering water tables. The efficiency of irrigation water use is low, in the range 30 percent,[31] representing a major bottleneck for the enhancement of production and productivity.

Agricultural policies: ambitious objectives but environmental challenges. Two separate ministries are in charge of the agriculture sector: the Ministry of Agriculture is responsible for the crop subsector (approximately 57 percent of agricultural output); and the Ministry of Jihad-e-Sazandeghi is responsible for livestock (40.8 percent), forestry (1.5 percent) and fisheries (0.5 percent), as well as for rural development and watershed management. The government has actively supported the rural sector and agricultural production since 1979. Two key aspects of this strategy have been ensuring guaranteed prices to the producers for selected crops and products; and a strong effort towards rural development benefiting thousands of villages, as reviewed below.

The growth in food production during the past decade has exceeded that of population, enabling significant gains in domestic consumption per caput and, in general, meeting the objectives of the First Plan. Average yields have also increased considerably during the past decade.

The country has achieved steady increases in self-sufficiency ratios, estimated in 1997 at about 80 percent for wheat, 90 percent for animal protein and 100 percent for poultry products, milk and cheese. Guaranteed, and remunerative, producer prices for major commodities have been the essential policy tool behind such performances.[32]

Table 8

PRODUCTION, IMPORTS AND CONSUMPTION OF SOME MAJOR COMMODITIES, 1985 AND 1995

	Wheat	All cereals	Oilcrops	Vegetables	Fruits
		(million tonnes)			
Production					
1985	6	10.2	0.36	4.2	8.6
1995	11.2	16.3	0.55	6.3	13.4
Imports					
1985	5.2	7.8	-	-	-
1995	3.1	5.8	-	-	-
		(kg/caput/year)			
Consumption					
1989	166	197	-	66.3	130
1995	173	211	-	79.6	164

Despite sizeable reductions in the import component of food consumption, agricultural imports have represented a major, and growing, share of total exports and imports. The agricultural imports share in total merchandise imports was about 15 percent over 1989-91, decreasing in the following years before increasing to reach 27.2 percent in 1995. The value of these agricultural imports absorbed 16.7 percent of the total value of exports in 1989-91, increasing to 18.9 percent in 1995.

Wheat is the core commodity of the food and agriculture system, providing 40 percent of the energy and 45 percent of the total protein supply. In order to boost production of this commodity, in the 1980s, the government launched a comprehensive national wheat programme, which included guaranteed purchase prices, input subsidies, research and extension services, as well as consumers' subsidies on flour and bread. Indirect government support was also provided through subsidized prices for energy, transport and machinery services, and credit. As a result, production almost doubled from 6 million tonnes in 1989 to 11.2 million tonnes in 1996. At the same time, average yields in irrigated areas

Wheat is the core commodity of the Iranian food and agriculture system.

Fruit production has grown by 239 percent over the past decade, with citrus production increasing by 769 percent.

made significant progress, from 2 tonnes to more than 3 tonnes/ha. Similar increases in productivity and production have also been achieved for rice, barley and potato,[33] while the area of perennial crops has continued to expand, reaching now more than 2.7 million ha and consolidating the country's export tradition for pistachio, grapes, dates, apples and citrus.

After a period of moderate growth in the 1970s, production of fruits and vegetables received high attention and increased rapidly. Fruit production growth during the past decade was estimated at 239 percent, including 769 percent for citrus and 294 percent for tree nuts. Horticulture production now covers 1.6 million ha, i.e. 10 percent of cultivated land, of which 1.2 million ha are devoted to fruit trees. Heavy post-harvest losses in fruits and vegetables continue to be a critical issue, linked to a large extent to the poor functioning and management of the marketing systems. Apparent consumption, at about 210 kg per caput, is roughly equivalent to European levels.

As regards livestock products, production of meat and dairy products has increased during the First Plan by 4.1 percent annually. Iran has achieved 90 percent self-sufficiency in protein availability from animal resources and 100 percent self-sufficiency in milk and cheese. Forestry output has increased from 1.9 million m³ in 1990 to 2.2 million m³ in 1997. Production of fisheries has expanded from 315 000 tonnes in 1990 to 389 000 tonnes in 1995, while the number of fishers is estimated to have increased threefold and the number of vessels twofold, since 1986.

Significant rural development achievements. The rural development efforts carried out by the Ministry of Jihad e Sazandegi, in partnership with the rural population, over the last decade have benefited some 15 000 villages, where living conditions have been significantly improved. Over the last ten years, 2.2 million ha of marginal lands have been put under cultivation, and 13 billion m³ of additional irrigation water have been controlled and managed. In addition, 51 000 km of graveled rural roads and 11 600 km of asphalt rural roads were built; electricity was brought into 13 700 villages, 17 500 villages were provided with drinking-water supply systems and 15 000 with full sanitary systems; and rural education and agricultural extension for men and women were actively developed.

The sustainability challenge. Progress in food and agricultural production has been accompanied by increasing pressure on natural resources. Deforestation and erosion have reached alarming proportions. Rangeland has had to support a 50 percent increase in the number of grazing animals over the last 30 years, and because of overgrazing only 16 percent of rangeland is now considered to be in good condition. Millions of hectares were lost both to overgrazing and to ploughing for expansion of rainfed agriculture. Based on estimates for 1986-1992, the pace of deforestation is in the region of 200 000 ha per year. Some 45 percent of arable land is classified as water-eroded and 60 percent as wind-eroded; average soil loss from arable land is estimated at some 20 tonnes per hectare per year. Increasing demand for underground water irrigation has developed through the multiplication of wells and pumping stations, resulting in a critical lowering of the water tables. On the other hand, progress in productivity has been achieved to a large extent through guaranteed prices and massive use of subsidized inputs, a process involving market distortions and heavy treasury costs. Thus, a fundamental issue confronting the government is the economic and environmental sustainability of agricultural performances in the years ahead.

Since the formulation of the Second Plan, efforts have started to reduce the degradation of natural resources, through reforestation, soil protection and fighting desertification projects. Measures for the conservation of biodiversity are being implemented, limited so far to the protected areas (8 million ha, i.e. 5 percent of the territory). Water management enhancement is a major concern and a top priority. Subsidies on pesticides have been removed, pesticide use has been drastically reduced (by about 75 percent) over the last five years, and farmers are increasingly adopting integrated pest management practices. However, much remains to be done to control natural resource degradation effectively.

Current government policies emphasize sustainability of agricultural development and better management of natural resources to be achieved, in particular, by securing the participation of resource users and farmers. The institutional framework for environmental protection is provided by the Third Plan, a National Strategy for the Environment and Sustainable Development, and the Organization for the Preservation of the Environment.

Prices and subsidies. The mechanisms for decision-making regarding subsidies are complex, involving a number of bodies and institutions. The Supreme Council for Economic

Subsidies first gained importance during the war with Iraq.

Affairs, under the President's Office, is the highest authority with regard to economic affairs. Its decisions on guaranteed producer prices and overall subsidies are taken on the basis of proposals prepared by the Planning and Budget Organization and its Bureau for Agricultural Affairs and Rural Development, in coordination with the Office for Protection of Consumers' and Producers' Rights and the Ministry of Agriculture. They are then submitted to Parliament, which rejects, approves or modifies them prior to their incorporation in the annual budget.

Subsidies originally gained importance during the war with Iraq, which required exceptional efforts to secure minimum equitative food supplies and living standards. Subsequently, the government maintained an important subsidy programme in favour of both consumers and producers of agricultural products. Producers benefited from guaranteed prices for their products, based on estimates of average national production costs, which secured significant farm profit margins. In the meantime, consumer food prices were kept broadly constant in real terms. The 1993 budget put the cost of subsidizing basic goods at 2.4 trillion rials, equivalent to 9.4 percent of estimated government revenues and 2.5 percent of projected GDP.[34]

At present, consumer food subsidies are granted for bread, sugar, milk, cheese, meat, tea, vegetable oil and rice; and producer subsidies for improved seeds and a number of farm inputs. Other sectors such as petrol and electricity also benefit from government subsidies.[35]

All food subsidies, including the ones previously earmarked for essential goods and food items, were expected to be eliminated in the first years of the Second

Table 9

GUARANTEED PRODUCER PRICES, 1991/92 TO 1997/98

	1991/92	1992/93	1993/94	1994/95	1995/96	1996/97	1997/98
				(rials/kg)			
Wheat	130	150	225	260	330	410	480
Rice	500	550	715	900	950	1 180	1 400
Barley	115	115	173	210	255	317	387
Sugarbeet	26	27	52	62	78	97	125
Potatoes	78	78	117	135	140	174	210

Source: Government of the Islamic Republic of Iran, Ministry of Agriculture.

Plan so that, in the last two years, no subsidy payment would be effected whatever.[36] However, food subsidies were maintained for a reduced number of key items, and in certain periods some were even reinstated at their high 1992 levels by the Parliament. Some measures towards their reduction have been taken again in recent years. Registered food subsidies represented about 1.8 percent of the 1997 budget.[37] They increased by 22 percent in 1995/96 and by a further 12.7 percent in 1996/97, at current prices.

At the core of the problem is wheat, the marketing of which is almost entirely controlled by the state and which accounts for 70 percent of food subsidies. In 1995/96, the producer was paid 330 rials per kg of wheat, while the wheat flour consumer price was 62 rials per kg.[38] In addition to this price difference, the state was paying all the intermediate additional costs – marketing, transport, processing, storage, losses, administration, etc. For the other main commodities, there are two different markets: the subsidized rations; and the free market.

Measures are gradually being taken to reduce the high producer-consumer price difference on subsidized food products. Consumer prices were allowed to increase significantly in 1996/97: wheat from 62 to 93 rials per kg, rice from 100 to 300 rials per kg, sugar from 27 to 100 rials per kg, edible oils from 60 to 300 rials per kg, red meat from 750 to 1 000 rials per kg and cheese from 450 to 1 000 rials per kg.[39]

Table 10

QUANTITIES AND PRICES OF MAJOR SUBSIDIZED FOOD ITEMS

	Subsidized quantities		Prices	
	1995/96	1996/97	1995/96	1996/97
	('000 tonnes)		(rials/kg)	
Wheat flour	9 300	9 400	62	93
Rice	280	297	100	300
Sugar	340	346	27	100
Edible oils	222	223	60	300
Red meat	53	54	750	1 000
Cheese	15	24	450	1 000
Total	**10 210**	**10 344**		

Source: Organization for the Protection of Consumers and Producers, cited by IMF.

A negative effect of subsidies has been the indiscriminate use of pesticides and fertilizers, which have become major causes of environmental degradation.

One negative effect of subsidies has been the indiscriminate use of cheap pesticides and fertilizers, which have become important causes of environmental degradation.[40] The expansion of cultivated areas stimulated by guaranteed prices has also caused deforestation, rangeland degradation and soil erosion. More recently, the increasing burden on the budget, the administrative dysfunction and the market distortions generated by subsidies (as well as the accumulated delays in the Plan's implementation) have increased the government's concern for their elimination. The equity issue is also at stake; subsidies are not socially targeted, although official figures indicate per caput levels of food subsidy that are more or less equal for rural and urban areas.

Consumer prices remain a highly sensitive issue, especially for the most vulnerable groups. Although the Second Plan's objective was to curtail subsidies drastically, political concern over sharp food price increases has so far slowed down the process; instead of being reduced, food subsidies have tended to stabilize in real terms, growing at a rate parallel to that of inflation. Current plans are to accelerate the process by reducing further the list of items concerned. The policy sequence is first to reduce the subsidies on production inputs, then to proceed with the reduction of the producer-consumer price gap. Most likely, guaranteed prices and consumers' subsidies will be maintained for an unforeseeable period, at least for key products such as wheat. Indeed, a complete elimination of subsidies would mean the abandonment of guaranteed prices and food self-sufficiency objectives.

Land tenure and agrarian reform. Iran has undergone two agrarian reforms, before and after the Islamic revolution, that have deeply transformed land tenure and production systems.

Before the 1962-1972 reform, most land and villages were owned by landlords and worked by tenants. Peasants without landownership, but holding cultivation rights under sharecropping or fixed short-term rental contracts, numbered about 2 million. They were frequently organized in traditional collective groupings called *boneh* (production teams, collective infrastructure maintenance, commons exploitation, etc.). Another 2 million peasants were landless labourers without cultivation rights. By the end of the reform (carried out in three phases covering ten years), some 1.8 million farmers had acquired formal land property. Small peasant family farming had become the dominant production structure in the country, with 83 percent of all farm holdings covering less than 10 ha. The reform also promoted the emergence of new social groups and forms of landownership, including rich peasants and profit-oriented private capitalist farms (13 percent of rural households and 40 percent of land), agro-entrepreneurship with international capital, state agricultural companies based on giant agribusiness schemes, farm corporations and production cooperatives. However, the reform left about 1.9 million landless peasant labourers without access to ownership, as it had focused attention on farmers who already had cultivation rights. As a result, an increased socio-economic stratification occurred within rural areas and urban migration, which the reform was intended to prevent, continued unabated (an estimated 2 million persons left the rural areas between 1962 and 1965).

In March 1980, the Islamic Revolutionary Council passed legislation mandating redistribution of large landholdings. The initial revolutionary Agrarian Reform Law had classified the land that could be considered for confiscation and redistribution under three categories, each with its own specific regulations. Confiscated lands under the first two categories,[41] made up of rangeland and other natural resources and wide *latifundia*, were to be placed under state administration for possible distribution or allocation of cultivation rights. The third category concerned lands covering areas that were more than three times the size of average local subsistence farms (if the average farm size in a given region was 5 ha, properties larger than 15 ha were eligible for confiscation). The implementation of reform for the two first categories did not encounter any major difficulties, but strong reactions and polemics emerged about the third one (falling under Article J of the Agrarian Law). Some religious authorities opposed it on the grounds that it did not conform with Islamic principles. The Islamic concept of "restricted but legitimized land property" was invoked as a principle for preventing excessive confiscation (while accumulation of richness had to be prevented, personal property had to be guaranteed as a legitimate incentive to production). As a result, the implementation of the Law's Article J was suspended. This suspension is still valid and the Council of Guardians, citing the "sanctity of property under Islamic Law", opposed some new and more radical reforms proposed by the Parliament in 1986.

Seven member committees, originally a separate revolutionary body but, since 1984, a part of the Ministry of Agriculture – including representatives from peasants and from the Islamic court – were responsible, *inter alia*, for handling and transferring the land that was eligible for confiscation and distribution. These committees were also in charge of promoting a new cooperative system called *moshaa* and for dealing with rural development affairs related to the Agrarian Reform. Confiscated land was given to landless peasants, but also to small farmers with a land area smaller than the average for their district and to the graduates of agricultural schools. Surface allocations varied from 1 to 15 ha depending on the region. In the period up to 1991, a total of about 1.2 million ha was redistributed among approximately 230 000 farmers' households.[42] The basis for redistribution was the allocation of cultivation rights, rather than true individual ownership of the soil. These rights were not transferable, and land must be returned if not cultivated. Simultaneously, the government promoted and supported among farmers the creation of the new medium-sized cooperatives, or *moshaa.* They averaged from 20 to 60 ha, being made up of five to 15 peasant families, and were based on the principle of collective farming (ownership of the farm was divided among a group of farmers on the basis of equal shares, but boundaries within the farm were not delineated). About 13 000 *moshaa* were established, grouping some 100 000 peasant families. They were conceived as a means for promoting economies of scale and to channel state support services, such as credit, technical assistance, subsidized tractor and machinery services and water pumping facilities. They remain today a significant sector of peasantry, but their collective mode of farming has evolved towards individual farming practices. It is now estimated that about 80 percent of lands formerly under *moshaa* are informally divided among the members for individual farming, or split among two or three households for joint cultivation.

Iran's land tenure panorama is now dominated by small peasant household farms, with 96 percent of all holdings being owner-operated.

Iran's land tenure panorama is now dominated by small individual peasant household farms. Some 96 percent of all holdings are owner-operated. Eighty percent of the farms have less than 10 ha and 66 percent less than 5 ha. Farms that are larger than 10 ha constitute the "modern" sector, contributing an estimated 80 percent of the food commodities sold in markets. Article J land seizures in the post-revolutionary period led to uncertainty among medium or large landowners, preventing them from renting land and from investing in their properties. Another issue is land fragmentation; the average number of plots per farm is 15, with a median size of 2 ha. This situation generates constraints for productivity enhancement and for the provision of support services.

Overall, many complex issues and ambiguities remain. The issue of equity and of access to landownership or cultivation rights for landless peasants has not been clarified from a legal viewpoint. Landownership beyond certain limits is still felt to be somewhat precarious by landlords. Land fragmentation is an obstacle to modernization, but land consolidation and agricultural and rural investment are hindered by uncertainties in the institutional land tenure framework and lack of transparency in land markets. These problems affect negatively the development performances and prospects of the whole agrifood sector.

Water resources and irrigation. Iran's average precipitation does not exceed 250 mm per year, and most of the territory receives less than 100 mm of rain. The use of water resources is dominated by irrigation; agricultural uses, domestic water supply and industrial uses are estimated at 95, 4 and 1 percent of total national water consumption, respectively. However, only 36 percent of arable land is cultivated, water constraints being the main limiting factor to both expanding cultivated areas and improving yields.

The total surface water resources are estimated at 105 billion m³ of which 6.4 billion m³ come from neighbouring countries and *ghanats* (the traditional Iranian underground aqueduct system) and 5.4 billion m³ from springs. Economically and technically usable surface water amounts annually to some 63 billion m³, of which about 40 billion m³ are used.

Total groundwater resources are estimated at about 46.6 billion m³, of which the available net amount for consumption is around 37 billion m³. Excessive exploitation, caused by the multiplication of pumping stations and wells, has led to the lowering of water tables all over the country. This alarming situation has required restrictions and regulations at local levels and recharging the underground resources has become a general concern.

Water resources are unevenly spread; 30 percent of surface water resources are concentrated in one province (Khouzestan), while many other populated provinces fully exploit their scarce available resources. Seasonal and annual river flow regimes are also very irregular and safe yield from surface water requires the building of storage facilities. As of end-1995, 31 large dams had been put into operation and a further 15 are to be completed in the coming years.

Of the total arable land, about one-third (8.8 million ha) is being irrigated under modern or traditional systems. The current overall average irrigation water use efficiency is around 30 percent (the world average is in the region of 45 percent); of the 14 600 m³ of water consumed on average per irrigated hectare, only 4 600 m³ is effectively used by the

About one-third of Iran's total arable land is irrigated under modern or traditional systems.

Fixing sand dunes to prevent erosion

Soil fixation with drought-resistant plants can help protect irrigation systems and waterways from the damaging effects of erosion and siltation.

H. NULL/FAO/6031

cultivated crops. Increasing efficiency of water use is thus a major challenge faced by Iran and is a top priority of the Second Five-Year Plan. The three ministries involved in water management for agriculture (Ministry of Agriculture, Ministry of Jihad-e-Sazandeghi and Ministry of Energy and Water) are coordinating efforts in the formulation of a 20-year programme to reach the objective of 40 to 45 percent efficiency.

Two parallel issues need to be addressed: the technical problem of irrigation efficiency; and that of irrigation management, related to the empowerment of water users' associations and to cropping intensification.

On the technical aspect, important efforts are currently under way to promote the use of pressurized irrigation systems, for which the country has acquired good engineering capacities and self-reliance. Modern pressurized irrigation schemes based on sprinklers, drip and micro-irrigation are being developed (sprinkler irrigation has an efficiency of 70 to 75 percent, while drip and micro-irrigation reaches 90 percent efficiency on average in existing Iranian systems). At present, 250 000 ha are equipped with these systems. The goal is to increase this area by 100 000 ha annually, in order to reach 1 million ha. The national industry, principally within the private sector, is already fully operational in producing the required pressurized irrigation equipment.

As regards improvement of irrigation management, efforts focus in particular on the empowerment of water users' associations, and their involvement in resources management. It is estimated that about 600 000 ha of irrigated land are consolidated with good users' participation and organization. For the 1.2 million ha under modern irrigation schemes, regulations are being prepared for improved water use and lowering water losses. One of the options to improve the performance in modern irrigation systems is to transfer the responsibility for organization and management to water users.

Concluding remarks

Iran has achieved remarkable progress in agricultural and rural development and food security over the past decades. Large sections of the rural and farm sectors have benefited from improved living conditions and remunerative prices for their products. This has enabled important gains in food and agricultural production and progress towards self-sufficiency. However, these positive results have been achieved at high financial and environmental costs.

Iran now faces the difficult challenges of maintaining a dynamic and competitive agricultural sector while ensuring economic and environmental sustainability.

Liberalization, the path chosen for enhancing economic sustainability and efficiency, entails a switch from old protective policies and an elimination of subsidies. The political will for such a switch has been clearly stated, but the reaction of both producers and consumers is a delicate issue to handle, especially in the current austerity context. The issue of maintaining or eliminating farm subsidies is also linked to that of self-sufficiency. The time may come when the opportunity cost and economic soundness of high farm subsidization are examined, along with the concept of self-sufficiency as the best guarantee of food security. But the current policy setting does not consider such options. The country's strategic planning for food and agriculture remains firmly based on the self-sufficiency principle. Underlying such a principle are considerations of food security, in a context of uncertain international political and trading relations and of large oil and gas reserves that provide financial backing for autonomy policies.

Another key challenge is that of agriculture export promotion, an issue closely related to privatization and investment. The process of handing over to the private sector the productive and marketing functions formerly assumed by the state is advancing gradually. However, despite ample scope for developing a large range of agricultural and agro-based industrial products, for which the country possesses actual or potential comparative advantage, investment is not yet forthcoming to any adequate extent. For many investors, the trading environment, infrastructures and services in Iran do not provide adequate guarantees of sure and adequate returns. Complex administratve procedures, deficiencies in marketing systems, uncertain land tenure patterns and the complex currency exchange system are all limiting factors to agro-based export development.

Iran's strategic planning for food and agriculture remains firmly based on the principle of self-sufficiency.

Central and Eastern Europe and the Commonwealth of Independent States

REGIONAL OVERVIEW

Macroeconomic trends and agricultural performance

For the transition countries in Central and Eastern Europe[43] as a whole, 1997 saw a positive rate of GDP growth for the first time since the beginning of the transition process, with a recorded rate of 1.7 percent compared with the -0.1 of 1996.[44] In particular, the Russian Federation experienced its first positive rate of economic growth, although at a very modest rate of only 0.4 percent, while all other countries in the Commonwealth of Independent States (CIS) also recorded positive growth. The exceptions were Ukraine and Turkmenistan, where the contraction of the previous years continued, at a decelerating rate in the case of Ukraine, but very sharply in Turkmenistan.

The countries of Central and Eastern Europe and the Baltic transition countries[45] expanded economic activity overall by 3.1 percent in 1997 compared with 3.6 percent in 1996 and 5.3 percent in 1995.[46] The further deceleration of economic growth concealed uneven trends across countries. Among faster-reforming countries, GDP growth accelerated in Hungary, Poland and Slovenia and slowed down somewhat in Slovakia, while in the Czech Republic economic growth slowed for the second consecutive year, to a mere 1.2 percent. Economic performance continued to improve also in the Baltic republics of Estonia, Latvia and Lithuania, as it did in Croatia. In the other transition countries of southeastern Europe, opposite trends prevailed in economic performance, with a decline of about 7 percent in GDP in Albania, Bulgaria and Romania. In the latter two countries, however, such developments were strongly related to the initial impact of the more comprehensive reform measures finally being undertaken.

Rates of inflation seem to be moving down in many of the transition countries, with improvements recorded in particular in Poland, Hungary, the Baltic republics, the Russian Federation, Ukraine and most of the remaining CIS countries. Inflation on the other hand increased very significantly in Albania, Bulgaria and Romania and slightly, from an already high rate, in Belarus.

For the transition countries in Central and Eastern Europe as a whole, 1997 saw a positive rate of GDP growth for the first time since the beginning of the transition process.

Figure 35

COUNTRIES IN TRANSITION
IN CENTRAL AND EASTERN EUROPE AND CIS

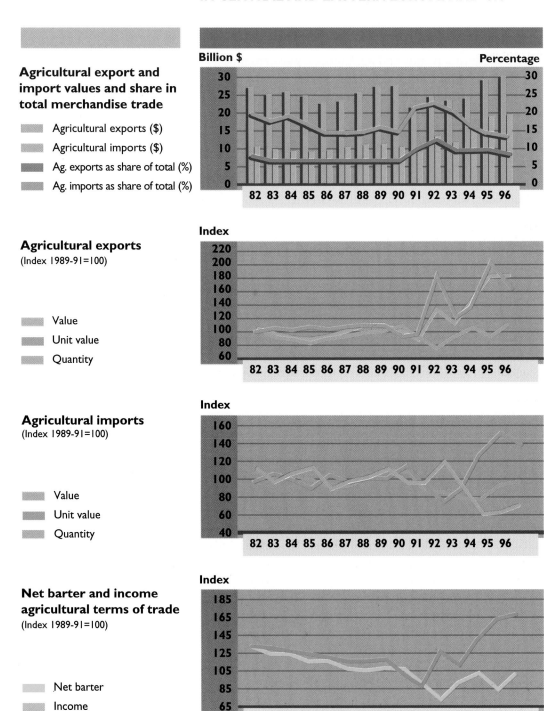

Agricultural export and import values and share in total merchandise trade

- Agricultural exports ($)
- Agricultural imports ($)
- Ag. exports as share of total (%)
- Ag. imports as share of total (%)

Billion $ Percentage

82 83 84 85 86 87 88 89 90 91 92 93 94 95 96

Agricultural exports
(Index 1989-91=100)

- Value
- Unit value
- Quantity

Index

82 83 84 85 86 87 88 89 90 91 92 93 94 95 96

Agricultural imports
(Index 1989-91=100)

- Value
- Unit value
- Quantity

Index

82 83 84 85 86 87 88 89 90 91 92 93 94 95 96

Net barter and income agricultural terms of trade
(Index 1989-91=100)

- Net barter
- Income

Index

82 83 84 85 86 87 88 89 90 91 92 93 94 95 96

COUNTRIES IN TRANSITION
IN CENTRAL AND EASTERN EUROPE AND CIS

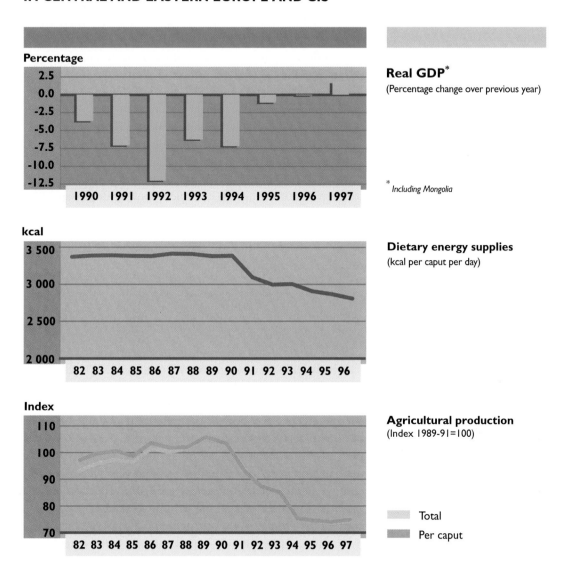

Percentage

Real GDP*
(Percentage change over previous year)

* _Including Mongolia_

kcal

Dietary energy supplies
(kcal per caput per day)

Index

Agricultural production
(Index 1989-91=100)

Total

Per caput

Source: FAO and IMF

249

As for agricultural production, for the first time since 1989, FAO's index of overall crop and livestock production for 1997 indicates a small increase, currently estimated to be 1 percent, in the transition countries as a whole. Behind the overall increase was a major increase of 8 to 9 percent in crop production, with cereal production in particular expanding by as much as 25 percent, while livestock production continued the downward trend that has characterized the entire transition process.

In the CIS countries, agricultural production went up significantly, particularly in Ukraine and somewhat less in the Russian Federation and Kazakhstan, mainly owing to significant increases in cereal production, while livestock production continued to contract. Varying degrees of increase were also recorded in Georgia, the Republic of Moldova, Tajikistan and Turkmenistan, while production declined in the remaining CIS republics. In the Baltic republics, agricultural output was still characterized by a stagnating or moderately declining trend in Estonia and Latvia, but there was a second consecutive year of expansion in Lithuania, largely resulting from a major recovery in cereal production.

In the Central and Eastern European countries, uneven trends also prevailed in agricultural output in 1997. A stagnant, or even slightly declining, net aggregate output was likewise the result of an important upswing in cereal output (by 23 percent in volume terms at the subregional level) and of further declining livestock production (by around 6 percent). Indeed, net agricultural output remained unchanged or declined from the previous year's level in eight countries, with Poland registering a sizeable reduction of around 11 percent (also owing to adverse weather conditions). Romania, in turn, achieved a considerable increase of 10 percent in its cereal output. Higher cereal production was mainly based on better yields, particularly in Bulgaria and Romania (by 50 and 43 percent, respectively). Livestock herd rebuilding was interrupted and pork production in particular was affected by higher grain prices in 1996 and early 1997.

Diverging developments in real disposable incomes determined sometimes contrasting shifts in food consumption patterns. Owing to the precarious macroeconomic situation in southeastern Europe, the share of food in household expenditure further increased to 54,

59 and 75 percent in Bulgaria, Romania and Albania, respectively. This provoked food security problems at the household level for the low-income strata of the population. While in these countries more starchy products were consumed at the expense of animal products, the opposite trend could be observed in the fast-reforming countries. In the latter, the share of livestock products in total food consumption increased and the share of food in the total expenditure of families declined.

Progress in structural reforms in Central and Eastern Europe[47]

A significant positive development of 1997 in Central and Eastern Europe was that comprehensive structural reforms finally embraced the agrifood sector of the entire subregion. Privatization in agriculture was drawing towards its completion in several countries while making major progress in others, including Bulgaria. As a result of this process, land fragmentation has become a problem, with agriculture very often divided into a commercial and a subsistence sector. Key issues for further farm structural development include the speeding up of land registration and land legislation as a prerequisite for developing a leasing and land market, necessary for further structural rationalization. Such measures appear to be of critical importance, particularly in countries that are making efforts to improve their competitiveness and structural maturity in view of future accession to the EU.

With the privatization of agriculture, land fragmentation is becoming a problem, with agriculture often divided into a commercial and a subsistence sector.

Important progress was also made in the privatization of the upstream and downstream sectors in Albania, Bulgaria and Romania. In countries, where privatization was already well advanced in the food-processing and marketing sectors (e.g. in Hungary and Poland), food output patterns became more competitive, featuring a higher share of value-added products. In particular, FDI enhanced the domestic and export competitiveness of processed food items.[48]

Agrifood trade balances deteriorated in most Central and Eastern European countries in 1997 with the exception of Bulgaria and Hungary. In the latter, in spite of record levels of agrifood exports, their share in total exports declined slightly, as even stronger export performances were recorded by the rest of the domestic economy. Similar trends could be observed in some other countries in the subregion. Overall, however, agrifood exports continued to suffer from their underlying structural weakness, above all the high share of bulky primary products and relatively few value-added products.

Trends towards more strongly integrated agrifood sectors through trade further strengthened in 1997, both within Central and Eastern Europe and between this subregion and the EU. Further adjustments to the association agreements with the EU eliminated some earlier weaknesses. Following the Baltic Free Trade Agreement (which came into effect on 1 January 1997), agrifood trade of the three Baltic countries seemed to enter an expansionary phase already in the first year of its operation. The founding member countries of the Central European Free Trade Agreement (CEFTA) – the Czech Republic, Hungary, Poland and Slovakia) – were joined by Slovenia in 1996 and by Romania in 1997, with Bulgaria as the next candidate for membership. However, the original objective of free trade in all agricultural products by 1998 had to be postponed to the year 2000. The reasons may be found in the underlying structural conditions, on the one hand, and in conflicting market policies, on the other. Several CEFTA countries are competing within the same subsectors but apply different levels of market support and export subsidization. Further harmonization of market and trade policies in the direction of less subsidization and more liberalization would appear to be necessary for further progress towards free trade in agricultural and food products in the subregion.

In a number of Central and Eastern European countries, agricultural policy discussions intensified in view of further integration with the EU.

In a number of countries, agricultural policy discussions intensified in view of further future integration with the EU and with accession negotiations with some Central and Eastern European countries scheduled for an early start. Policy efforts were focusing on the harmonization of agrifood legislation in order to take over the EU's policies and regulations, including the very significant veterinary and phytosanitary regulations.

Improving conditions for FDI in the agrifood sector in Central and Eastern Europe

Owing to very low investment activities during the last phase of the period of central planning, the agrifood sector of Central and Eastern Europe entered the new era with rather obsolete production and processing technology. On the other hand, after about eight years of restructuring and privatization in the fast-reforming countries, the first export success of some subsectors has now drawn attention to the importance of capital inflows in general, and FDI in the agrifood sector in particular.

Annual net capital flows into the Central and Eastern European and Baltic countries grew tenfold between 1992 and 1997 to $23.7 billion with an improving composition, both in terms of geographic distribution and types of capital inflow, since 1995. Alongside the fast-reforming countries, the new thrust in economic reforms has now stimulated more substantial net capital flows also towards Bulgaria, Romania, Slovenia and the Baltic states. As a further positive development, the share of FDI was increasing in the total from around 40 to 46 percent between 1994 and 1996.

Up to 1997, the share of the agrifood sector in total FDI ranged from about 8 percent in the Czech Republic to about 25 percent in Bulgaria. The corresponding shares for Poland, Lithuania and Romania were around 14, 16 and 17 percent, respectively. The bulk of FDI has been directed to the processing industries as well as to the marketing sector. On the other hand, restrictive legislation concerning foreign investments in agriculture has so far impeded FDI access to primary agriculture.

Concerning the geographic distribution of agrifood FDI, there are still large discrepancies between countries of the subregion, with Poland and Hungary occupying a leading position and Romania catching up recently. Notably, in Bulgaria the agrifood sector has so far been the main recipient of FDI. These differences are clearly a consequence of both the timing and firmness of market-oriented economic reforms in those countries as well as of the investment climate created for foreign investors. Early timing of reforms may indeed have been a decisive factor for obtaining foreign investment in the agrifood sector of Central and Eastern European countries, while at the same time some countries (e.g. Bulgaria, Hungary, Croatia and Poland) have offered a series of incentives to foreign investors, such as temporary tax exemptions, import tariff reductions and duty-free customs zones.

Still, the main incentive for foreign agrifood companies to invest may be found elsewhere. Indeed, available experience seems to indicate that foreign companies have been interested mainly by the prospect of capturing the

In fast-reforming countries, the first export success of some subsectors has drawn attention to the importance of capital inflows, particularly FDI in the agrifood sector.

domestic Central and Eastern European markets in view of their future expansion resulting from the expected medium-term economic recovery. So far, foreign investors have favoured subsectors with better prospects for increasing value-added production and that had not been adequately developed before. Thus, up to 1996, above all the subsectors of sugar and confectionery, milk and dairy products, beverages and vegetable oils as well as some others (e.g. tobacco industries) received the highest FDI inflows. In several cases, such as Hungary and Poland, processing companies are specializing in the domestic market with their new products.

Another main factor in attracting FDI is obviously the presence of a relatively well-qualified and low-cost labour force. Labour-intensive subsectors can thus be advantageously developed or established. For investors, these conditions also combine well with the prospect for several countries of future EU membership and their resulting access to the large EU market.

The main direct contribution of FDI in the agrifood sector has been to improve food processing and marketing, which is the overriding challenge in Central and Eastern Europe.

The impact of FDI on the subsectors that have benefited from it has been significant. The main direct contribution of FDI in the agrifood sector has been above all to achieve qualitative improvements in food processing and marketing (allowing the output of more value-added products), which was indeed, and remains, the main challenge in the Central and Eastern European countries. Also, foreign investors have been essential in circumventing the problem of domestic capital shortage, while in the export-oriented sector they have helped to create export capacities and facilitated market access.

However, by establishing new quality standards in food supply, Central and Eastern European food industries have also provided new demand impulses to primary agriculture. In several cases, processors have established new vertical structures, both through buying in or by contractual ties. The impact exercised on quality and management aspects of agricultural operations has been considerable, and FDI has thus acted to further structural change in agriculture with a view to responding to actual market demand. In numerous cases, foreign investors have also transferred production expertise, thereby ensuring the introduction of improved techniques in raw material production that would otherwise not be accessible to producers.

In contrast to the positive effects on processing and, indirectly, on primary agriculture in sectors that have been the target of FDI, food-processing subsectors not benefiting from FDI have continued to struggle with technological obsoleteness, scarce finances and marketing difficulties, which has had a depressing impact on their agricultural supply base.

In spite of the obvious positive effect of FDI in terms of restructuring and development of the agrifood sector, there has been some concern about the short-term social impact in some countries. The direct and indirect productivity improvements induced by FDI have led to job losses both within the companies subject to new investment efforts and in other weaker competing ones. Also, owing to imperfect institutional arrangements and still imperfect competition, some investors have acquired *quasi* monopoly positions in some processing subsectors in some transition economies. More recently, such concerns have induced a more cautious policy approach both in privatization practices (e.g. voucher privatization, preferential shares) and in foreign investment policies (the imposition of some restrictions and conditions on FDI in agrifood) in some countries. Such measures, however, do not seem to have contributed to a sustainable solution to the main pressing issues of the agrifood sector as a whole, including the lack of capital, obsolete processing technology and difficult access to export markets.

Productivity improvements induced by FDI have, however, led to job losses both within the companies subject to new investment efforts and in other weaker competitors.

Rural development: a pressing issue in the Central and Eastern European countries

In the course of the ongoing transition process in the Central and Eastern European economies, the current and future role of rural regions as well as their specific problems seem not to have received the attention needed from the point of view of balanced economic and social development, and the issue has rapidly become pressing. Rural regions in most of the countries inherited major structural deficiencies from the prereform era, including an extreme regional specialization of agricultural production, few or no alternative income sources, underdeveloped infrastructure and services, administrative overcentralization, limited access to good-quality education, poor communications and services, ecological damages and destruction of landscapes.

With the advancing transition process, the structural weaknesses were soon aggravated by further stress factors such as declining agricultural incomes, growing rural unemployment and the discontinuation of social services by large-scale farms. In 1996, rural unemployment (affecting above all unskilled labour) ranged from 13 percent in Hungary to 50 percent in Bulgaria. In addition, the rural sector also had to absorb a part of the backflow of unemployed from urban and industrial areas in Albania, Bulgaria, Hungary, Poland and Romania. The situation has given rise to widespread subsistence farming and to an expanding informal economy. The new rural stress factors appeared first in the fast-reforming countries but quickly emerged also in other countries implementing structural reforms. The productivity gap between the agricultural sectors in Central and Eastern Europe and the EU suggests that further reductions in the agricultural labour force will occur in the coming years.

In some Central and Eastern European countries, this situation has brought increased awareness of the need to address the growing economic, social and environmental problems of rural areas with a more coherent package of measures. Nevertheless, the actual policy response to these issues has differed throughout the subregion, but in most countries, the (agricultural) sectoral approach has continued to dominate policy-thinking, implying that financial support for rural areas was still mainly concentrated on agricultural production while support to alternative income-producing activities was non-existent or negligible. There was little recognition of the fact that the complex problems of rural regions required a full-fledged policy approach addressing all important socio-economic, environmental and cultural aspects of regional and local development.

Available statistics on rural structures of Central and Eastern European countries already point to the need for such an integrated approach to rural development. Data from different years between 1990 and 1994 for the Czech Republic, Hungary, Slovenia and Slovakia show that, even in regions where the larger share of the population was living in rural communities (i.e. with fewer than 2 000 inhabitants), agriculture only provided employment for less than one-quarter of the active population. In Poland, the corresponding share was less than one-half in 1993.

In the fast-reforming countries, the rapid downsizing of agriculture in terms of its GDP share and, above all, in total employment urgently calls for a reorientation of development policies away from a sheer agricultural approach towards integrated rural development policies aiming at the rest of the rural economy and population as well. The strong political influence of agricultural production lobbies in some countries supporting the partial interests of restructured large-scale farms did not seem to be helpful in this respect. On the other hand, important lessons from the experience of Western European countries clearly point to the undesired negative consequences of relying exclusively on a narrowly based "traditional" agricultural policy: high costs for taxpayers and consumers, one-sided support effects benefiting areas with the largest farms, overproduction, market distortions and environmental damage. By the mid-1990s, such consequences had already become apparent in some Central and Eastern European countries too.

In some fast-reforming countries, a distinction between rural policies and more narrow agricultural policies was slowly emerging in policy discussions and policy concepts by the mid-1990s (e.g. the programme for a "coherent rural development and renewal of villages" in Slovenia). In some countries (Poland and Slovakia) new central institutions were established for the coordination of rural development. However, in most cases a centralist "top down" approach still dominates, with a deficit in local participation and a lack of cooperating horizontal and vertical partnership linkages (rare exceptions include Slovenia). Reasons for this include inertia in the earlier practice for policy delivery and fund distribution and the relatively low level of economic development resulting in scarcity of local funds. Another major reason was the weakness of democratic and participatory institutions and the lack of entrepreneurship and creative skills at the local level.

In southeastern Europe, the need for adequate rural development policies is becoming especially urgent in the light of a particular situation that is emerging: owing to a rapid decline in industrial output, which is exceeding reductions in agricultural production, agriculture's share in aggregate GDP and in total employment increased between 1989 and 1995. For the share of GDP, the percentage changes were from 32 to 55 in Albania and from 14 to 22 in Romania, while there was no change from the 11 percent recorded formerly in Bulgaria. Relying on the new fragmented structure of landownership, agriculture's buffer role seemed to be very marked: the percentage share of the sector in total employment shot up from 49 to 53 in Albania, from 18 to 22 in Bulgaria and from 28 to 36 in

There is an urgent need to steer away from a purely agricultural approach towards integrated development policies aimed at the entire rural economy and population.

257

Romania. This should not, however, be interpreted as a sign of growing strength of the sector, but rather as the medium-term impact of a sluggish reform process involving these countries' whole economies before 1995/96. The importance of designing integrated rural development policies in southeastern European countries cannot be overemphasized, since the magnitude of the labour force shifts that will occur from future adjustments in agrarian structures is expected to be even greater than in the fast-reforming countries.

The ongoing policy discussions with regard to appropriate rural development strategies in the reforming countries has shown that the specific situation of each of them requires specific policy approaches. Nevertheless, some basic prerequisites for a successful strategy in all Central and Eastern European countries are:

- the collection of basic information (statistical and other) about rural structures to ensure a correct understanding of the complex socio-economic, cultural and ecological problems involved;
- the development of specific strategies and programmes for individual regions;
- the establishment of a flexible form of institutional cooperation (including horizontal and vertical linkages) reflecting the multidisciplinary character of rural problems;
- efforts to achieve a high level of participation by local populations and rural actors who should interact in partnership from the beginning of the policy development process.

POLAND

Overall, the Polish economy has made remarkable progress in the eight years since the beginning of the transition period. GDP growth in the last three years has been about 6 to 7 percent per annum, inflation dropped from triple-digit figures in 1990 to about 15 percent in 1997 and, overall, living standards have improved markedly.

Poland is among the five Central European countries designated as the first to accede to the EU. Consequently, domestic and trade policies are increasingly driven by the need to align with EU policies. Many Poles look forward to EU accession as a means to improve farmers' incomes and to bring in funds for infrastructure improvements. However,

Map 9

POLAND

0 km   500 km

the agricultural sector faces major challenges in meeting EU quality standards and there are also worries about increased competition from EU products.

Overview of the agricultural sector

Agriculture accounted for 7 percent of GDP in 1996 but employed 27 percent of Poland's labour force. Whereas the overall economy began to see significant positive growth in 1992, growth in agriculture has been much slower. Crop yields remain low because of low input use and also owing to unfavourable weather patterns in some recent years. Overall productivity growth is held back by the slow progress in consolidating Poland's small, fragmented private farms.

The most important crop in Poland is wheat, followed by rye and rapeseed. Approximately 8 million to 9 million tonnes of wheat and 5 million to 6 million tonnes of rye are produced each year. The principal livestock product is pork, which accounts for 70 percent of the 2 million to 3 million tonnes of meat produced each year. Other important commodities include potatoes, vegetables and fruits, poultry

In Poland, many people look forward to EU accession as a means to improve farmers' incomes and to bring in funds for infrastructure improvements.

259

and eggs, milk, cattle and sugarbeet. Principal exports are rapeseed, live cattle, processed meat, fruits and vegetables. The main imports are grains, meat, protein meal and cotton.

Even during the period of central planning, Polish agriculture was dominated by more than 2 million private farms, averaging 5 ha in size. The private sector farmed about 80 percent of the agricultural land and produced almost the same percentage share of output. The process of consolidation since 1989 has been quite slow – the average farm size has increased to 8 ha. There is a growing class of commercially viable farms, but at least half the country's farms still produce mainly for self-consumption. Land sales are legal but many landowners are reluctant to sell because of a lack of alternative employment.

Poland is a net agricultural importer, with agricultural products accounting for approximately 11 percent of total imports and 10 percent of total exports. The EU accounts for approximately 65 percent of Polish trade of agricultural and food products, while the independent states of the former Soviet Union account for about 19 percent of Polish trade, and Hungary, the Czech Republic and Slovakia account for about a further 3 percent.

At least half of Poland's farms produce mainly for self-consumption and many landowners are reluctant to sell because of a lack of alternative employment.

Agricultural performance during the transition
Agricultural output has been extremely variable since 1989, but followed a clearly declining trend until 1994, with some moderate recovery in 1995 and 1996. On average, gross output is still below the average for the 1980s. There has been a greater variability in crop yields, as a declining use of inputs has made crops more vulnerable to poor weather. Crop output continues to stagnate, although the livestock sector appears to be rebounding.

Average grain yields for the period 1991-95 were 10 percent below the 1986-90 average. The low yields are in part the result of a declining use of fertilizers and other chemicals, but Poland also suffered some extreme weather conditions, with droughts in 1992 and 1994 and flooding in the summer of 1997. However, despite the fall in real producer prices, area planted to cereals changed very little.

Other principal crops grown in Poland include sugarbeet, potatoes and rapeseed. Of these, sugarbeet production has been on the rise in recent years, with production in 1997 estimated to be 16 million tonnes, up from 12 million in 1994. Production of potato, which

Figure 36

POLAND: DOMESTIC SUPPLY AND UTILIZATION OF CEREALS

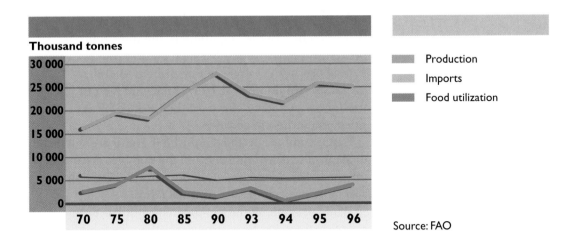

Thousand tonnes

Production
Imports
Food utilization

Source: FAO

continues to be a staple in the Polish diet and an important source of pig feed, is estimated to be 21 million tonnes in 1997. The output of rapeseed, the only major oilseed produced in Poland, has been quite variable since the beginning of the transition. During the second half of the 1980s, output averaged 1.3 million tonnes per year. From 1991 to 1997, output has fluctuated from a low of 450 000 tonnes to a high of 1.4 million tonnes, while area has fluctuated widely in response to changes in relative prices, and yields have been even more variable. With a lower use of inputs, rapeseed has been very vulnerable to extreme weather conditions. Half of the 1997 crop was lost, for example, as a result of winterkill.

As in all the transition economies, inventories of cattle and poultry plummeted immediately after the beginning of the transition. Producers were hit hard by a sudden deterioration in their terms of trade; prices of inputs rose to world market levels, while real output prices fell as a result of plummeting demand. Between 1990 and 1993, both cattle and poultry numbers declined by 24 percent. In contrast, there was not such a clear downward trend in the Polish pig sector; instead the sector has settled into a clearly defined pig cycle, responding rapidly to fluctuations in world grain prices. There is potential for long-term expansion but it is not yet clear by how much.

Poultry production is definitely on the road to recovery, and meat output per bird has risen significantly in the last two years. The sector has been able to respond rapidly to increased consumer demand. In part, this has been due to the shorter production cycle, which makes it easier to increase the numbers rapidly. Another reason is that, even before the beginning of the transition, procedures for contracts between poultry processors and private producers were well established, whereby processors would provide baby chicks and feed to producers and take delivery of the finished birds at a price established in advance.

Cattle numbers declined until 1996. Herds are still mainly dual-purpose dairy and beef, and the numbers are mainly influenced by developments in the dairy market. Cattle are also more difficult to raise on small farms.

While the agricultural production sector has been stagnant, there has been strong growth in the food-processing industry.

While the agricultural production sector has been stagnant, there has been strong growth in the food-processing industry. Overall, output from the food-processing industry rose by 11 percent in 1997 and total growth between 1992 and 1997 was 65 percent. Meat and poultry processing, alcoholic beverage production and sugar and confectionery processing are growing particularly rapidly, and growth is expected to remain strong, fuelled to a large extent by foreign investment.

Trends in food consumption

In contrast to initial fears, the abrupt rise in real food prices and simultaneous drop in income that took place in 1990 did not result in a food security problem. Even though real incomes fell sharply after 1989, total per caput caloric intake, about 3 300 kcal per day, changed relatively little. There was an initial drop in 1990 in per caput consumption of cereal and dairy products. These two products were very heavily subsidized under the system of central planning. Moreover, a considerable amount of bread was wasted or fed to livestock, since bread was cheaper than the original cereal. In the years since 1990, cereal consumption rapidly recovered to levels above those immediately preceding the transition process, while milk consumption continued to decline. Consumption of fruits, vegetables and potatoes did not change much.

Curiously, meat consumption did not fall in the early years of the transition, although it did in later years. There has been a steady decrease in beef consumption and an accompanying rise in poultry consumption, signifying a clear substitution of poultry meat, which is cheaper. Pork consumption has fluctuated considerably in the transition period. Pork is by far the preferred meat, but its prices have fluctuated more than prices of other meats owing to the widely oscillating pig cycle.

Agricultural price and trade policy

The initial years of the transition were characterized by free prices and low border protection. But in 1992 guaranteed minimum prices were introduced for wheat, rye and dairy products, and border tariffs were raised to an average of about 20 percent for agricultural products.

After free prices and low border protection in the initial years of the transition, in 1992 guaranteed minimum prices were introduced for wheat, rye and dairy products, and border tariffs were raised for agricultural products.

The principal government agency in charge of market intervention is the Agency for Agricultural Markets (AMA), which was established in the spring of 1990 with the mission to stabilize prices. Its primary function at that time was to stabilize commodity markets through intervention purchasing – buying up stocks when prices were falling and releasing them back on to the market when supplies were tight. Its role expanded in 1992 when it was given authority to set guaranteed minimum prices for wheat, rye and dairy products, which it supported through intervention purchasing. Since 1992 its role has expanded still further, and it is now involved in the management of the strategic reserve and providing preferential credit to grain producers and warehouses.

Currently, the AMA intervenes in grain markets in the following ways:

- *Direct intervention purchasing*, using funds provided by the state budget.
- *Procurement through a network of authorized warehouses.* The warehouse agrees to purchase wheat at the intervention price and, in return, the AMA provides guarantees for preferential credit to the warehouses. At the end of a three-month period, the AMA will purchase the grain at the intervention price plus storage, interest and handling.
- *Advance payment to selected producers.* Wheat producers who are willing to store wheat can receive an advance payment of 45 percent of the intervention price. Producers are obliged to leave their cereals in storage for three months. At the end of that period, they can either repay the

advance plus interest in cash or forfeit 45 percent of the stored cereals to the agency and take back the remaining 55 percent, which they can either use on-farm or sell on the open market.

The role of the AMA in the Polish cereal market varies from year to year. In the 1997/98 marketing year, its role was quite significant. Total intervention purchases of cereals were 1.1 million tonnes, of which 836 000 tonnes were wheat. The AMA has been under considerable pressure this year because of falling world cereal prices and the generally poor quality of the 1997 crop, which led the agency to lower the quality standards usually imposed for intervention purchasing. Because of the continued softness of the market, the AMA will be forced to take possession of a large portion of the cereals placed in storage, and it therefore anticipates considerable difficulty in clearing out its stocks before the next harvest.

The AMA also sets and administers minimum prices for dairy products, carries out intervention purchasing of pork and sugar, and is periodically engaged in the import and export of these commodities – some exports of which have been subsidized. It does not directly engage in trade, but contracts with commercial companies to carry out the transactions on its behalf. In the early years of its existence, the AMA's share in foreign trade of certain commodities was quite substantial; in recent years its share in foreign trade has been lower but it still has the authority to carry out foreign trade directly.

Intervention in the sugar market takes a different form. Under the 1994 Sugar Industry Act, the Council of Ministers sets separate quotas – quota A for domestic consumption, and quota B for subsidized exports – and distributes these among the 76 processing plants in Poland. A minimum wholesale price is established for sugar produced within these quotas. The AMA carries out intervention purchasing when necessary to support this price and also provides advance payments and credit guarantees to the processors to assist them in procuring beet from producers.

Other support for producers
The period of central planning was characterized by an extensive array of input subsidies. However, most were eliminated in 1989 and, as a result, input prices very quickly

rose to world levels while real output prices fell. In response to pressure from producers, the Agency for Restructuring and Modernizing Agriculture was created in 1992 to reduce input costs for farmers by granting credits at preferential interest rates. The agency seeks to encourage larger producers by limiting its assistance to those who can achieve certain minimum levels of production.

Most input subsidies were eliminated in 1989 and their prices very quickly rose to world levels while real output prices fell.

Enterprise privatization

The privatization of state farms has proven difficult. The Agricultural Property Agency (APA) was created in 1992 to restructure the state farm sector. The agency took over ownership of the state farms with the intention of selling the assets and quickly liquidating the farms. However, the APA has encountered difficulties disposing of former state farm assets. Prior to the land reform initiatives, state farms occupied about 20 percent of agricultural land. Of the 4.1 million ha of farmland taken over by the APA, by 1995 2.7 million ha had been leased to private farmers, 116 000 ha had been sold and 0.8 million ha remained under the agency's management. Formally, state farms do not exist any more and hence do not receive state budget subsidies. The land is administered by the APA and offered for sale or lease at regular open public tenders. While quality of labour of the former state farms was undoubtedly a problem, the lack of demand for farmland in western and northern Poland, where the state farms dominated the agrarian structure, was the principal reason for small sales and low prices of farmland, aggravated by the acute shortage of investment capital among prospective buyers.

The Polish food-processing industry, once dominated by state enterprises, is now more than 90 percent privatized. Thousands of small and medium-sized companies have emerged as a result. However, privatization is lagging in meat processing, which is only 60 percent privatized, and sugar plants, which are still mainly state-owned. Nevertheless, in spite of progress made in privatization, many food-processing enterprises still suffer from outdated technology, insufficient sanitation, high energy and labour costs and poor marketing and managerial skills.

The Polish food-processing industry is now more than 90 percent privatized.

Accession to the EU

Formal negotiations for EU accession began in March 1998 and Polish authorities have expressed the hope that Poland can accede to the EU by 2002. The question in any case is

Rural job creation programmes will be a priority use of EU structural funds when they become available.

no longer whether, but rather when, Poland will join. Potential benefits include higher incomes for farmers and an inflow of funds to support infrastructure development. But the Poles have come increasingly to realize the challenges involved in meeting the requirements of EU membership.

In this regard, agriculture is seen as one of the more problematic areas. Much of Poland's agricultural and food output at present does not meet EU quality standards, and considerable investment will be needed to improve the situation. Moreover, in a single market, Polish products will have to compete on an equal basis with EU products in both the domestic and foreign markets, and recently Poland has suffered large deficits in its agricultural trade with EU countries. There are fears that a large number of Polish producers will not be able to compete.

A major obstacle to increasing the competitiveness of Polish agriculture is its fragmented farm structure and shortage of capital. There are around 2 million farms in Poland, the average size is now about 8 ha, up from 6 ha in 1990. The sector employs 27 percent of the country's labour force but accounts for only 7.6 percent of GDP. Of the 2 million producers in Poland, only about 600 000 to 700 000 can be considered commercial producers and only these producers will be able to survive in a single market. Rural job creation programmes will thus be a priority for use of EU structural funds when they become available.

Accordingly, much of Poland's support to its producers is designed to encourage the development of larger units that will be able to produce according to EU standards. The AMA cereal storage loans mentioned above are only available to those producers who can deliver minimum quantities, for instance. Support to livestock producers is also aimed at more commercially oriented producers. For example, the AMA carries out intervention purchasing of pigs, but plants authorized to purchase on behalf of the AMA must be licensed to export and must meet EU standards. Furthermore, all carcasses that are purchased must meet the top three grades within the EU grading system. Various other measures are being taken to induce producers to grow leaner pigs.

The biggest challenge is in the dairy sector, where quality is a more serious problem. On 1 January 1998, the government passed legislation that is compatible with EU regulations governing sanitary standards in the dairy industry.

Several contentious issues lie ahead in the negotiations. EU officials have taken the position that producers in Poland and other acceding countries should not be eligible for the compensatory payments that are now paid to EU farmers. Such a stand is based on the argument that these payments were intended to compensate producers for the loss of support resulting from recent reform of the Common Agricultural Policy (CAP) and that producers in new member countries should not be compensated for losses they never suffered. Central and Eastern European negotiators, on the other hand, argue that their producers should receive exactly the same support as current EU producers.

Studies have been conducted, both in and outside Poland, in an attempt to estimate the costs and benefits of EU accession on Polish agriculture. Analyses by the Polish Ministry of Agriculture project increases in income for producers of grain, milk and beef, but income declines for poultry and rapeseed producers, and no change for pork. However, other experts disagree, particularly with the pessimistic forecast for poultry. But the outcome depends strongly on the future evolution of the CAP. The unanimous opinion is that an enlarged EU will not be able to afford continuing support at current levels. Thus, some reform of the CAP is inevitable, but the exact form of the future CAP is not known at this stage.

The costs and benefits of EU membership for Poland's agriculture depend strongly on the future evolution of the CAP, some reform of which is inevitable.

On the other hand, there has been little analysis of the welfare implications for consumers. Food prices will certainly rise; however, these rises could be offset by increases in income. The multiplier effect of the structural funds could be significant, yet there are fears that these benefits will be unevenly distributed. There are already significant income disparities between eastern and western Poland – unemployment in the eastern regions is currently as high as 20 percent, and producers in these regions will find it much more difficult to compete in an enlarged EU.

HUNGARY

The economic transformation process has been somewhat smoother for Hungary than for most of the other Central and Eastern European countries, but its economic recovery began later and has been less strong than in the case of Poland. As there had been some liberalization of prices

Map 10

HUNGARY

before 1989, Hungary did not experience the huge jump in prices that occurred in many countries and it also managed to avoid the dramatic changes in farm structures that occurred in Bulgaria and Romania. Although land has been privatized, most continues to be farmed by corporate or restructured cooperative farms and economies of scale have thus been preserved.

Although it slowed down considerably in 1995 and 1996, GDP growth in Hungary again accelerated in 1997. After an acceleration of inflation in 1994, Hungary introduced a stabilization programme in 1995 that was designed to tighten up the money supply. As a result, GDP grew by only 1.5 percent in 1995 and 1.3 percent in 1996, but bounced back to 4 percent in 1997. Real wages fell by 11 percent in 1995 and 5 percent in 1996, but also began to improve in 1997.

Hungary has retained its position as a net agricultural exporter and exports significant amounts of grain and livestock products. It managed more successfully than its neighbours to reorient its trade from the newly independent states to the West, with government intervention and export subsidies playing a major role.

Hungary is among the first five countries expected to join the EU. In general, its agriculture will probably have an easier task adjusting to EU standards than most. However, some experts are concerned that the livestock sector,

particularly pork, will have difficulty in competing in an
enlarged EU.

Agricultural performance during the transition process

Hungary's agriculture accounted for 6 percent of GDP in
1996 and employed 8 percent of the labour force. The
main crops are wheat, maize, sunflowerseed, sugarbeet
and potatoes. Production of wheat and maize in 1997
totalled 5.3 million and 6.8 million tonnes, respectively,
and sunflowerseed production reached about 800 000
tonnes. The principal livestock products are pork and
poultry.

Between 1989 and 1995, overall agricultural output
declined by about 32 percent, with most of that decline
taking place in 1992 and 1993, but has since staged a
partial recovery, with production having risen by 13
percent in 1996 to a level that was maintained in 1997. As
prices of inputs rose to world levels, their use declined
drastically and, as a result, average 1991-95 cereal yields
dropped by 19 percent relative to the previous five-year
period. Total cereal areas changed very little and total
output fell by 20 percent.

At 14.2 million tonnes, in 1997 cereal production
returned to the level of the late 1980s. However, this
bumper crop came as a mixed blessing. Owing to wet
weather during the harvest, the quality of the wheat crop
was low and demand for it has therefore been quite low
also. Maize was of a better quality, but Hungary had
difficulty disposing of its surplus because of a saturated
world market.

As was the case elsewhere in Eastern Europe, Hungary's
livestock sector declined drastically in the early years of the
transition. Inventories of all species declined by 40 to 50
percent between 1990 and 1995. Pig numbers have begun
picking up in 1996 and 1997. Within the poultry sector,
chicken numbers have been flat but there has been an
increase in turkeys.

Even with lower production, Hungary has maintained its
position as a net agricultural exporter, since domestic
demand fell at least as much as production. The largest
exports in terms of value are livestock products, mainly pork
and poultry. Hungary also exports live pigs and cattle and
other exports include grains, fruits, vegetables and
sunflowerseed. The largest category of agricultural imports
is protein meal.

Hungary has managed almost completely to reorient its trade towards the West. It has, however, not given up completely its former Soviet Union markets. Currently 70 percent of Hungary's overall foreign trade is with countries of the Organisation for Economic Cooperation and Development (OECD); 60 percent is with the EU. Before 1990, 60 percent of Hungary's trade was with the Council for Mutual Economic Assistance (CMEA). There has been a particularly marked increase in meat and live animal exports to the EU. With the help of foreign investment and government support, entire subsectors, such as those of beef cattle and turkey, have developed specifically for export.

Differentiating trends in food consumption
The share of food in the average household budget in Hungary is about 28 percent. Within food consumption patterns there is a clear trend for the substitution of poultry for other meats. Consumers still display a pronounced tendency to purchase lower quality meats than they did earlier. Nevertheless, corresponding to the uneven income situation, there is an increasing differentiation in food consumption patterns with a strengthening (but still thin) demand for high-quality processed food items.

Agricultural price and trade policies
Hungary intervenes relatively extensively in its agricultural markets. Guaranteed minimum prices, aimed at covering 85 to 90 percent of production costs, are established for milling wheat, feed maize, pigs and cattle for slaughter and milk. The prices are set by the new Agricultural Intervention Centre in consultation with Product Councils established for each major commodity. These councils include representatives from every level of the production chain: producers, processors, wholesalers, traders, consumers, etc. If the market price falls under the minimum price for a period of two weeks, the Intervention Centre authorizes purchasing up to a certain quota (e.g. 2.4 tonnes of wheat per hectare harvested). Because the minimum price is set so low, intervention purchasing is rarely necessary – it was used for the first time in 1997, when 70 000 tonnes of maize were bought.

The main instrument used to support prices is export subsidies, which are also administered by the Intervention

Figure 37

HUNGARY: DOMESTIC SUPPLY AND UTILIZATION OF CEREALS

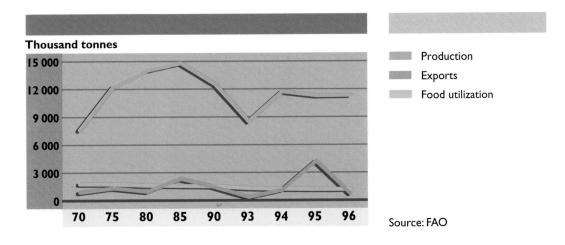

Thousand tonnes

Legend:
- Production
- Exports
- Food utilization

Source: FAO

Centre. The budget for export subsidies has been declining each year in compliance with WTO commitments: the total budget allocated for 1998 is 20 billion forints, for instance, whereas in 1995 export subsidies still totalled 50 billion forints. Since January 1997, these subsidies have been set on a per kilogram basis rather than, as previously, as a percentage of value. A total of 170 products are eligible for export subsidies, including live sheep and cattle, most kinds of meat, various types of processed meats and certain fruits and vegetables, both fresh and processed. Exporters who apply for export subsidies must demonstrate that they have paid the minimum price for the product. Certain products are also subject to export licensing, which is not always automatic. Products subject to export licensing include barley, sugarbeet, milling wheat, feed maize and goose liver. The system is expected to be abolished soon for barley and sugarbeet, but will continue for wheat and maize. Minimum prices must be established before the planting season. Quotas for export subsidies and licences are set at various times in the year and are based on projections of supply and demand.

Other types of market support are also provided. Cereal farmers can choose to store part of their production in a warehouse within the Public Warehouse System. They can receive a loan of 70 percent of the value of the cereal at a reduced interest rate and must leave the grain in storage for three to four months. At the end of that period, if the market is favourable, they can buy back the grain and pay the storage and interest, or they may leave the grain and receive the full price. But the minimum quantity that can be placed in storage under this programme is 500 tonnes. So far there is no system for pooling smaller quantities, so small producers do not benefit from this programme.

For livestock producers, the government introduced a system of target prices in July 1997. If the market price falls below this target by more than 6 forints per kg, a premium ranging from 4 to 12 forints is paid to the producers; if the price rises above the target by more than 6 forints, a premium is paid to the processor. But this support only applies for pigs slaughtered at plants applying EU standards and that meet the top three grades of the EU classification system. In addition, any Hungarian producer who trades in an ordinary sow for a pedigree can receive a subsidy of 30 percent of the value of the new sow. But the producer must be a member of the Breeders' Association and must use boars or semen provided by this association. This subsidy is not attractive for small producers because these high-quality animals must be raised in good conditions, which entails higher production costs.

Additional measures of market support are introduced on an ad hoc basis in response to developments in the market. Recently, for example, following producer concerns over falling cereal and pig prices, the government introduced additional subsidies for these products. These include a 30 forint per kg export subsidy for live pigs, a temporary increase in the subsidies paid under the target price system described above and a special subsidy for producers who sell wheat to feed mills and livestock farms.

Land reform and enterprise privatization
Prior to 1990, Hungarian agriculture was dominated by cooperatives, which farmed 70 percent of the land and covered an average area of 4 200 ha, and state farms, which farmed 12 percent of the land and averaged 7 100 ha in size. Although there was a private sector, only a small portion of that constituted true private farms; most of the private sector consisted of small 0.5 ha plots allotted to cooperative members. Owners of land taken over by the cooperatives had retained title to their land, although they had had no control over its use, nor the right to any profits

from the land. However, as owners died or left the cooperatives, their land had been purchased by the cooperatives at low prices. Thus, by 1990, former owners held title to only one-third of the land farmed by the cooperatives.

Former owners who retained titles were able to get their land back directly, unless it was no longer available as agricultural land, in which case they could receive a comparable parcel. However, the Hungarian Government chose not to return land to those who lost title. Instead these former owners, along with cooperative members and employees who had never owned land, received compensation vouchers with which they could purchase land or other assets of state enterprises. The state and cooperative farms were required to set aside a certain portion of their land to make available through auction to those holding vouchers.

State farms and other state enterprises were converted to shareholding companies, and their shares were offered for sale. Cooperative farms had to restructure either into a shareholding company or into a true cooperative in which members had the right to elect the management and to withdraw their assets at any time.

The agricultural and food sector of Hungary is now nearly 100 percent privatized. The former cooperatives have been restructured in a variety of ways. Some are still cooperatives but are generally smaller than before 1990, as they have sold or liquidated unprofitable lines of production. Others have become shareholding companies; in many of these cases, the majority of shares are held by the managers of the former cooperatives.

Hungary's land restitution process resulted in the development of both very small and very large farms with very few medium-sized units, a situation that has changed little since 1992. Production is divided almost evenly between large-scale corporate and cooperative farms and small private plots. The average plot of land acquired through the auctions was just 3.5 ha, and most new owners simply decided to lease their land back to the cooperatives. But 47 percent of arable land is operated by individual private producers and 29 percent by what the Central Statistical Office lists as "small" producers. In 1996, 56 percent of pigs and 67 percent of poultry were on such farms. In the same year, they produced 53 percent of total cereals, including 38 percent of wheat and 63 percent of maize, and they

Hungary's land restitution process resulted in the development of both very small and very large farms with very few medium-sized units.

accounted for more than 80 percent of fruits and vegetables. Very little of this output enters the market, however, and what does, is sold locally in the peasant markets.

Consolidation of these farms is hampered by the continued lack of a functioning land market. Under current Hungarian law, only individuals may purchase land; commercial companies and cooperatives may only lease land. Furthermore, an individual whose property is in the middle of a tract of land farmed by a cooperative effectively has no choice of how to dispose of the land but to lease it to the cooperative. The situation is even more difficult because a number of landowners still do not have a permanent title.

Foreign investment has played a critical role in the development of Hungary's food-processing sector with 30 percent of overall agribusiness in foreign ownership.

Food processing
The food-processing sector is entirely privatized. This has been achieved through both the sale of shares in the former state-owned companies and the startup of new companies. Foreign investment has played a critical role in the development of Hungary's food-processing sector. Overall, the share of foreign ownership in Hungarian agribusiness is 30 percent, and it is more than 50 percent in the food and beverage industry. Some sectors of Hungary's food-processing industry, such as vegetable oil and tobacco production, are 100 percent foreign-owned. The share of foreign ownership is nearly as high in other sectors: turkey production is 90 percent foreign-owned and meat processing is about 50 percent foreign-owned.

Privatization of the food industry, however, does not necessarily translate into higher incomes for producers. There is concern on the part of producers that, in some sectors, the state monopoly has simply been replaced by a private monopoly. For example the entire vegetable oil industry is controlled by a single firm, while poultry processing is dominated by two large firms which control 90 percent of the market.

Prospects of EU integration
Hungary aims to join the EU by 2002 and has already begun negotiations on the terms of accession. Most Hungarian experts are confident that their food-processing industry will have little difficulty competing in an enlarged EU. The main problems might be in the areas of product quality and marketing techniques. Nevertheless, a good part of the sector is already oriented towards exports to the EU and will

benefit from freer access to that market. It is also believed that the quality of Hungarian cereals is superior to that of the EU.

On the other hand, there are doubts about the livestock sector, particularly pig production. Hungary subsidizes both pork and poultry more than does the EU, which does not subsidize pork at all. The producer price for pork is currently higher in Hungary than in the EU, and it appears that Hungarian production costs are higher. Hungarian pork production lags behind EU production according to all technological indicators: mortality is higher, births per sow are lower and feed consumption per unit of liveweight gain is as much as 1 to 1.3 kg higher than in the EU. Most feed has an inadequate protein content, while protein meal must be imported and high transport costs raise the price.

Ministry experts believe that it is essential to improve these indicators before accession to the EU, since Hungary will have to face lower EU livestock prices. But the real question is whether Hungary's comparative advantage is in livestock production. It could be that Hungary's true comparative advantage lies rather in cereals and that it could well emerge as an important supplier of the enlarged EU.

NOTES

1 Unless otherwise stated, all macroeconomic data in the present section are drawn from IMF. 1998. *World Economic Outlook*. Washington, DC.

2 Excluding Egypt and the Libyan Arab Jamahiriya, which are not included in the IMF regional aggregate.

3 The remaining part of the section focuses on the African countries south of the Sahara, as the North African countries are discussed in more depth in the context of the regional review of the Near East and North Africa.

4 Union Economique et Monétaire Ouest-Africaine.

5 No estimates of GDP growth are provided for Liberia, Sierra Leone and Somalia.

6 Excluding South Africa.

7 For a discussion, see J.-P. Faguet. Decentralization and local government performance. Paper presented at the Technical Consultation on Decentralization, 16-18 December 1997, FAO, Rome.

8 D. Maxwell. 1994. The household logic of urban farming in Kampala. *In* IDRC, ed. *Cities feeding people*. Ottawa, Canada, IDRC.

9 The economic growth rates and projections in this section are based on AsDB. 1998. *Asian Development Outlook*. Manila.

10 Excluding the Democratic People's Republic of Korea, for which an index of total agricultural production is not available.

11 Government of Malaysia, Economic Planning Unit. 1996. *Seventh Malaysia Plan, 1996-2000*. Kuala Lumpur, Percetakan Nasional Malaysia Berhad.

12 Per caput GDP for 1997 is estimated from a 1995 base GDP of $M 202.5 million at current prices using a 1996 growth rate of 8 percent and a 1997 growth rate of 7 percent (see Government of Malaysia, op. cit., note 11). The US dollar value of GDP per caput assumes an average annual exchange rate of $M 2.62 .

13 World Bank. 1995. *Social indicators of development*. Washington, DC.

14 Government of Malaysia, Economic Planning Unit. 1971. *Second Malaysia Plan, 1971-1975*. Kuala Lumpur, Government Press.

15 Emerging market indicators. In *The Economist*, 18 April 1998.

16 Government of Malaysia, op. cit., note 11.

17 P. Waldman. 1998. Malaysia labors to handle crisis as foreign workers lose their jobs. *Asian Wall Street Journal*, 12 January, p.1.

18 Coconut and pepper are also included in Malaysia's perennial crops but neither has much influence on Malaysia's current agricultural development.

19 Malaysian Cocoa Board. 1997. *Malaysian Cocoa Monitor*, June, 6(1).

20 Bank Negara Malaysia. 1995. *Annual Report*. Kuala Lumpur, Percetakan Nasional Malaysia Berhad.

21 Government of Malaysia, Department of Statistics. 1995. *Report on Household Expenditure Survey 1993/94*. Kuala Lumpur, Percetakan Nasional Malaysia Berhad.

22 Unless otherwise specified, economic estimates and forecasts in this section are from the Economic Commission for Latin America and the Caribbean (ECLAC).

23 See FAO. 1994. *New institutional arrangements for agricultural and rural development in the region*; and FAO. 1993. *Municipalidad rural, participación popular e instituciones en servicios de apoyo a pequeños agricultores en Latinoamérica*. Rome.

24 P. Timmer. 1996. Food security strategies: the Asian experience. In IICA/Government of Costa Rica/FAO. *Food policies within the context of Central America*.

25 Excluding Afghanistan. Unless otherwise stated, all macroeconomic data in the present section are drawn from IMF. op. cit., note 1.

26 May 1995, United States President's order prohibiting companies from trading with Iran; and August 1996, the D'Amato law imposing sanctions on non-United States companies investing in the Iranian hydrocarbons industry.

27 Central Bank data. Economist Intelligence Unit estimates state 3.6 percent.

28 1 750 Iranian rials (IR) per $1 for oil export receipts and imports of essential goods and services, debt-service payments and strategic imports for large projects; and IR 3 000 per $1 for non-oil export and service receipt and import payments other than in specified priority areas; the free "bazaar" currency market is tolerated, where the rial has fluctuated between IR 5 000 and 7 000 per $1 over the last two years.

29 Protein supply in the diet was 68 g and increased to 85.6 g over the 1987-1995 period – an annual growth rate of 6 percent. In 1995, the diet was estimated to be made up of 72 percent carbohydrates, 17.6 percent fat and 10.4 percent protein, while the desirable composition is 55 to 75 percent carbohydrates, 15 to 30 percent fat

and 15 to 20 percent proteins. There is therefore a need to have the balance evolve towards about 10 percent fewer carbohydrates and about 10 percent more fats and proteins.

30 7.5 million ha of cultivated area plus 1.3 million ha of fallow land are classified as irrigated area.

31 Of the average 14 600 m^3 consumed per irrigated hectare, only 4 600 m^3 are effectively used by the cultivated crops.

32 Severe drought during 1996/97 affected production and required extraordinary imports of food. Only 10 million tonnes of wheat were produced in 1997 instead of the planned 12 million. In order to satisfy domestic requirements, the 1998/99 budget has allocated $2 billion for importing wheat (5 million tonnes), edible oils (800 000 tonnes), rice (800 000 tonnes), sugar (560 000 tonnes) and red meat.

33 During the First Plan, rice production increased at an annual rate of 4.6 percent, and oilseed production at a rate of 17.5 percent. In ten years, potato production has doubled.

34 These figures exclude producer subsidies on tractor services, credit and water under certain irrigation schemes as well as specific consumer subsidies handled by individual institutions for their staffs. Subsidies on oil and energy are also excluded.

35 The price of petrol for Iranian consumers is only 4 US cents per litre, and electricity is also strongly subsidized. About one-third of Iran's oil production – more than 1 billion barrels per day – is consumed domestically.

36 Paragraph M of Note 19 to the Second Economic, Social and Cultural Development Plan Act.

37 In 1997 there were 5.8 trillion rials of food subsidies out of a budget of 315 trillion rials (source: World Food Summit follow-up, Iran's report, 1998).

38 The average national production cost in the same period was 257 rials per kg for irrigated wheat and 309 rials per kg for rainfed wheat.

39 IMF data.

40 The subsidies regarding pesticides were definitely cut some years ago for environmental reasons, and those regarding fertilizers were reduced by half.

41 Articles A and B of the Agrarian Law.

42 602 000 ha of cultivable, state and pasturelands for 100 000 peasant families, and another 630 000 ha of temporary cultivated lands for 130 000 households.

43 For the purposes of this overview, the Central and Eastern European Countries include: Albania, Bosnia and Herzegovina, Bulgaria, the Czech Republic, Croatia, Hungary, Poland, Romania, Slovakia, Slovenia, The Former Yugoslav Republic of Macedonia and Yugoslavia.

44 All macroeconomic data in the present section are drawn from IMF. op.cit., note 1.

45 Estonia, Latvia and Lithuania.

46 These GDP aggregates from IMF include the Baltic Republics and the Republic of Moldova but exclude Bosnia and Herzegovina and Yugoslavia.

47 The focus in the remaining part of the overview is on the countries of Central and Eastern Europe. Agricultural reforms and issues in the Russian Federation were discussed in *The State of Food and Agriculture 1997*.

48 The role of FDI in developing the agrifood sectors of the Central and Eastern European countries is discussed in more detail in the next section.

PART III

RURAL NON-FARM INCOME IN DEVELOPING COUNTRIES

RURAL NON-FARM INCOME IN DEVELOPING COUNTRIES

INTRODUCTION

The traditional image of farm households in developing countries has been that they focus almost exclusively on farming and undertake little rural non-farm (RNF) activity.[1] This image persists and is widespread even today. Policy debate still tends to equate farm income with rural incomes, and rural/urban relations with farm/non-farm relations. Industry Ministries have thus focused on urban industry and Ministries of Agriculture on farming, and there has been a tendency even among agriculturists and those interested in rural development to neglect the RNF sector.

Nevertheless, there is mounting evidence that RNF income (i.e. income derived in this sector from wage-paying activities and self-employment in commerce, manufacturing and other services) is an important resource for farm and other rural households, including the landless poor as well as rural town residents. Although this source accounts for only part of total off-farm income (which also includes farm wages and migration earnings), this chapter focuses on RNF income so as to enable a closer examination of what can be done within rural areas themselves to increase overall economic activity and employment.

There are several reasons why the promotion of RNF activity can be of great interest to developing country policy-makers. First, the evidence shows that RNF income is an important factor in household economies and therefore also in food security, since it allows greater access to food. This source of income may also prevent rapid or excessive urbanization as well as natural resource degradation through overexploitation.

Second, in the face of credit constraints, RNF activity affects the performance of agriculture by providing farmers with cash to invest in productivity-enhancing inputs. Furthermore, development of RNF activity in the food system (including agroprocessing, distribution and the provision of farm inputs) may increase the profitability of farming by increasing the availability of inputs and

283

improving access to market outlets. In turn, better performance of the food system increases rural incomes and lowers urban food prices.

Third, the nature and performance of agriculture, themselves affected by agricultural policies, can have important effects on the dynamism of the RNF sector to the extent that the latter is linked to agriculture. This sector grows fastest and most equitably where agriculture is dynamic – where farm output is available for processing and distribution, where there are inputs to be sold and equipment repaired and where farm cash incomes are spent on local goods and services.

In the light of these factors, the present review pursues two main purposes: it seeks to sensitize governments, donors and development agencies to the issue of RNF activity and its importance for agricultural and rural development as well as poverty alleviation; and, with a view to furthering the harmonious growth of both the farm and RNF sectors, it cites broad implications that RNF activity may have for agricultural policy and for policy and institutional coordination.

The questions addressed are as follows:

- What are the patterns of RNF income and employment in the different developing country regions? How important is RNF activity, how fast is it growing and what is its nature by region and type of agro-ecological zone?
- What determines patterns of RNF income and employment; in particular, what is the role of agriculture and how is it affected in turn? Also, what is the determining role of rural household characteristics (e.g. education, asset ownership) and how are they affected by those patterns?
- What effects do RNF income and employment have on the levels and distribution of rural household incomes, poverty incidence and food security?
- What policy and programme implications can be drawn from these points?

Serving as background for the rest of this special chapter, the review begins with a conceptual discussion of factors influencing the decision by households to participate in RNF activities and the nature and types of relations and linkages between the farm and non-farm sectors in a rural economy.

REASONS FOR HOUSEHOLD PARTICIPATION IN RNF ACTIVITIES

Decisions made by rural households concerning the form and extent of their involvement in RNF activities (either starting enterprises or entering the wage labour market) generally depend on two main factors:

- the incentives offered, such as the relative profitability and risk of farm and RNF activities;
- the household's capacity (determined by education, income and assets and access to credit, etc.) to undertake such activities.

In the case of enterprises set up by households, the choice of technologies and products will likewise be determined by similar conditions. When opting to undertake RNF activities, farm households[2] may be motivated by:

Households are motivated to undertake RNF activity by either "pull" or "push" factors.

- "pull" factors, such as better returns in the non-farm sector relative to the farm sector; and
- "push" factors,[3] which include in particular:
  - an inadequate farm output, resulting either from temporary events (e.g. a drought) or longer-term problems (e.g. land constraints);
  - an absence of or incomplete crop insurance and consumption credit markets (to use as *ex post* measures for harvest shortfalls);
  - the risks of farming, which induce households to manage income and consumption uncertainties by diversifying and undertaking activities with returns that have a low or negative correlation with those of farming;
  - an absence or failure of farm input markets or input credit markets, compelling households to pay for farm inputs with their own cash resources.

Factors conditioning incentives and capacity for RNF activities

Incentives and capacity for undertaking non-farm activities may diverge. Thus, poor farmers may very well have strong incentives to participate in RNF activities while lacking the capacity to do so because of various constraints.

285

Household wealth and agroclimatic zone.[4] Incentives to participate in RNF activities differ according to households' wealth. Poorer households are less able to tolerate or cope with negative shocks to their income and are thus more averse to this type of risk. They are therefore more likely to diversify in favour of less risky income sources and activities.

Moreover, the agroclimatic characteristics of the zone (favourable or unfavourable, more or less variable) will influence farm households' risk motive for income diversification into non-farm activities. Households in zones with a high-risk agriculture would be more "pushed" to diversify into RNF activities. A larger share of such activity would be undertaken merely to cope (*ex post*) with shocks to farm income (such as from drought), although one would expect diversification of income also in "normal" years (e.g. non-drought years) so as to accumulate resources (wealth) with which to overcome negative shocks. By contrast, households in zones where agriculture is less risky might participate in RNF activities mainly for the higher returns they give or in order to alleviate cash and credit constraints.

Even if the incentives to diversify (for push or pull reasons) are high, whether the household will react to these incentives depends on its capacity to do so. In the absence of well-functioning credit and insurance markets (which is frequent, if not the rule, in rural areas of developing countries), the capacity to invest in a diversified set of activities increases with household wealth. If diversification is costly (i.e. if an activity has high entry barriers – a fact that empirical evidence tends to support) and initially risky, wealthy households are in a more favourable position to diversify into RNF activities since they can use their wealth for self-financing and as a buffer against negative income shocks.

Where households are in the presence of risk are free from credit constraints, it would be reasonable to expect them to diversify less as their wealth increases (because the risk aversion motive for diversification declines as wealth increases). Instead, activities would be more concentrated on (expected) high-profit areas. In this case, poorer households would diversify more. In the presence of liquidity and credit constraints to diversification by the poor, an opposite outcome may occur: the poor may want to diversify for risk reasons but cannot do so because of liquidity constraints, while wealthier households have less of a risk incentive to diversify but are in a better position to self-finance this diversification. Thus, more diversification is observed among the non-poor than among the poor.

Profitability of rural non-farm activities. A number of exogenous factors affect the profitability and risk of farm and rural non-farm activities and thus the mix of the two types of activity undertaken by a household. The profitability of a given RNF activity is determined by the price of the product produced or the wage received in the sector and by the prices of the array of inputs used in the production process or employment.

In general, both product and input prices for RNF activities will be influenced by the transmission of effects of macroeconomic and sectoral policies such as devaluation of the currency, changes in the interest rate and changes in tariffs on imported final and capital goods as well as by factors influencing transport and other transaction costs. Such factors also include the condition of soft infrastructure (e.g. extension, market information and education) and hard infrastructure (e.g. roads and telephone lines). In response to these conditions, private firms can lower transaction costs through contracts and other coordination mechanisms so as to increase interaction among businesses across sectors or subsectors and thus strengthen intersectoral and intrasectoral linkages.

The capacity of local factor markets to provide appropriate productive inputs and financial capital for RNF activities will influence the prevailing input prices. For example, if the local labour market has an insufficient number of skilled workers, the skilled wage rate to be paid by RNF entrepreneurs will be driven up. If the real estate market in a rural town is constrained by building regulations, purchase prices and rental rates for workshop space may also be forced upwards.

Development policies and programmes. Development projects deserve a special mention: as an instrument of development policy, these projects constitute an important set of determinants of incentives and capacity for rural households to participate in RNF activities. In a sense, a development project is a mini-package of public policies and investments that apply to a restricted set of activities in space and time and affect a limited number of participants. A typical example from the RNF sector would be a dairy project, coordinated by an NGO or the government and involving the provision of trainers and equipment to develop a small-scale dairy activity with a selected set of rural households. An immediate aim would be to facilitate milk marketing with project vehicles and donor expertise. This form of support in fact constitutes a (bounded) subsidy policy for inputs (equipment, training services and market facilities) targeted at a given RNF subsector, group of actors and time horizon.

Linkages between farm and non-farm activities

The concept of farm/non-farm linkages is most commonly used to describe the relation between the farm and non-farm sectors. These sectors can be linked directly via *production linkages*, in which case the linkage occurs either "upstream" or "downstream". When growth in the farm sector induces the non-farm sector to increase its activities by investing in productivity or additional capacity for supplying inputs and services to the former, the linkage is upstream. It is downstream (and is often referred to as a value-added activity) in cases where the non-farm sector is induced to invest in capacity to supply agroprocessing and distribution services, using farm products as inputs.

Indirect *expenditure linkages*, on the other hand, occur when incomes generated in one of the two sectors are spent on the output of the other. Finally, there may be *investment linkages* between the two sectors, in which case profits generated in one are invested in the other.

RNF production linkages with local agriculture take place through sale of inputs to and purchase of output from the farm sector, with the agricultural output being used as an input for RNF activities (such as agroprocessing and distribution). Hence, the type of local agriculture will play an important role in determining the incentives for these kinds of RNF activity, as its characteristics will affect the profitability of RNF products and services as well as the market outlets for them. On the side of farm implements, for example, the average farm size determines whether there is a profitable market for tractors in addition to hand-tools. On the farm output side, the composition, timing and quality of output produced by local farms can influence the profitability (and optimal plant size) of agroprocessing industries. The type of technology used in cattle farming affects animal health and milk productivity which, in turn, affects the profitability of non-farm activities such as cheese production and milk pasteurizing.

The farm and non-farm sectors can be linked directly via production linkages, which occur either upstream or downstream.

There are expenditure linkages between RNF and farm activities in that income generated from farm activities is spent on the output of non-farm enterprises and vice versa. Therefore, the profitability and market outlet for these are determined by local incomes (level and distribution) and tastes. Smallholders, the poor, are more likely to spend on local goods and services in the RNF sector, while richer households would tend to spend on items from the modern manufacturing sector located in cities, or on imports. The implication of this is that technical change in agriculture that benefits smallholders will have a greater impact on the local economy via expenditure linkages than would technical change that benefits large landholders.

Where there are constraints on access to credit, investment linkages between RNF activities and the farm sector may also be very important. In such circumstances, non-farm income may be crucial for a farm household's capacity to make farm capital investments and purchase modern inputs. Vice versa, savings generated by farm activities may be at the basis of investments in non-farm activity.

PATTERNS IN RNF ACTIVITY: INTER- AND INTRAREGIONAL DIFFERENCES

This section presents and discusses evidence drawn primarily from household survey results gleaned from the review of some 100 studies focusing mainly on farm households[5] (as opposed to rural town residents) in Africa, Asia and Latin America. It also draws on information from official country-level statistics – where these are available.

The focus on case study data is due to a variety of shortcomings in the availability and quality of official aggregate statistics on RNF income and employment. However, even carefully collected household survey data are not immune from problems; readers should therefore be aware of these and understand that the patterns and results presented here are reliable as indications of broad tendencies but less so as detailed estimates. Despite imperfections, the data are adequate in quality and quantity to allow confidence in the general results shown here (such as the general importance of non-farm income and employment, and its distribution over regions, zones and farm-size levels). Statistical uncertainty increases in the case of disaggregate observations, such as the division of non-farm income share into wage-paying employment and self-employment.

The importance of RNF activity – comparisons across developing country regions

Table 11 summarizes data on the shares of non-farm income and employment in total rural income and employment drawn from studies from the 1970s to the 1990s in the three regions.[6] The sources for the data used are presented country by country in Appendix Tables 1 and 2.[7]

Average non-farm income shares are higher in Africa (42 percent) and Latin America (40 percent) than in Asia (32 percent). Even considering caveats about data quality and coverage, these findings are important and surprising for several reasons.

First, they show the significant importance of non-farm income relative to total income in rural areas, and hence its importance for purchasing power and food security. Second, one would expect the relative importance of non-farm income to be greater in regions with higher levels of GNP per caput. Indeed, richer regions tend to have better

Table 11

SHARE OF NON-FARM INCOME AND EMPLOYMENT IN TOTAL RURAL INCOME AND EMPLOYMENT[1]

Regions and subregions	Non-farm income share		Non-farm employment share		Average per caput GNP,[2] 1995 ($)
	Mean[3] (%)	Coefficient of variation	Mean[3] (%)	Coefficient of variation	
AFRICA	42	0.45	...	...	726
East and southern Africa	45	0.47	...	...	932
West Africa	36	0.36	...	...	313
ASIA	32	0.33	44	0.32	1 847
East Asia	35	0.19	44	0.29	2 889
South Asia	29	0.52	43	0.40	388
LATIN AMERICA	40	0.20	25	0.33	2 499

[1] The data given are regional averages of country cases. The income shares represent the share of non-farm income in the total income of households that are mainly farm households (including the rural landless). The employment shares represent the share of households in the rural population (in both rural areas and small rural towns) for which non-farm activity is the primary occupation.
[2] Average per caput GNP is calculated as the simple average over the countries covered by the case studies. It is based on estimates from World Bank. 1997. *World Development Report 1997*. Washington, DC.
[3] The mean refers to the mean over the case studies considered for each region and subregion.

infrastructure and stronger agricultural sectors, both of which induce RNF development. Hence, the expected ranking would be Latin America, Asia, Africa. However, the fact that Africa is placed first in the ranking suggests that diversification incentives have an important role to play. In other words, although African households are poorer than those in the other regions, the incentive to diversify their incomes is strong (owing to low farm incomes, risks, etc.). This runs counter to conventional wisdom that sees African peasants as being little inclined towards rural income diversification.

Nevertheless, within individual regions, the richer countries and subregions do tend to show higher shares and levels of RNF income (see Figure 38A-D). The two poorest subregions, West Africa and South Asia, nevertheless have fairly different non-farm income shares (36 and 29 percent, respectively). Differences in the nature of RNF activities are discussed in more detail below.

Finally, the variability of non-farm income shares (as measured by the coefficients of variation[8] calculated over country averages) is highest in the poorest areas, i.e. the African subregions and South Asia, reflecting a diversity of conditioning factors (such as degree of agricultural performance, infrastructure, urbanization rates, etc.) even in situations of generalized poverty.

Growth patterns (i.e. changes in non-farm income shares over time) are difficult to discern from available income data, except in some case studies (mainly in Asia). Some approximations may be derived by comparing the data presented here with those emerging from earlier studies. For instance, the range of shares and averages reported here (based mainly on 1980s and 1990s data) exceeds that reported in Haggblade, Hazell and Brown,[9] mainly based on studies conducted in the 1970s. Moreover, some case studies point to a positive growth of non-farm income shares over time in a number of countries (Bangladesh, Burkina Faso, China, parts of India, Java in Indonesia, western Kenya, Malaysia, Mexico, northern Nigeria, the Philippines and Taiwan Province of China).

Data concerning RNF employment (a key indicator) over years and countries show average shares of around 44 percent for Asia and 25 percent for Latin America (relevant data could not be found for Africa). In the case of Asia, this share is higher than the income share, whereas for Latin America it is lower. It should be noted that a direct

Non-farm income is a significant part of total income and, hence, is important for purchasing power and food security.

Figure 38A

NON-FARM SHARE OF RURAL HOUSEHOLD INCOME AND PER CAPUT GNP, SELECTED COUNTRIES IN AFRICA

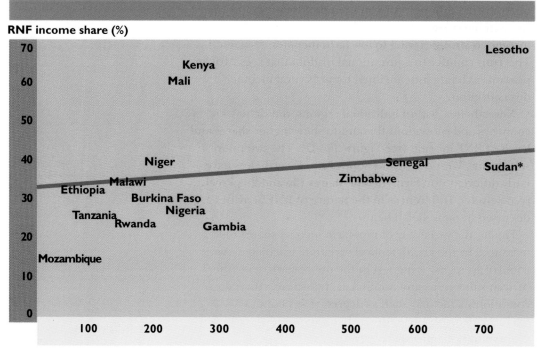

RNF income share (%)

Per caput GNP, 1995, $

Not shown are:
Namibia: Income share = 75%
          Per caput GNP = $2 000
Botswana: Income share = 51%
          Per caput GNP = $3 020

* Sudanese per caput income has been estimated by the World Bank to be less than or equal to $765.

Source: RNF income shares based on rural household income surveys (see Appendix Table 1); per caput GNP from World Bank. 1997. *World Development Report 1997.*

comparison between the employment shares and the income shares above is difficult because the shares may differ as a result of wage rate differences.[10]

The figures for Latin America and Asia show, on average, rapid increases in the share of people employed in RNF activity in the overall rural populations. For Latin America, Figure 39 shows that, in all cases except Peru (showing no difference) and Bolivia (showing negative change), absolute employment in the RNF sector grew much faster than farm employment and hence its share increased. In nearly half of the countries, the farm employment growth rate was negative, while the RNF employment growth rate was positive in all of them. The overall share of rural population with its principal activity in the RNF sector rose from 24 to 29 percent over (roughly) a decade.

Figure 38B

NON-FARM SHARE OF RURAL HOUSEHOLD INCOME AND PER CAPUT GNP, SELECTED COUNTRIES IN ASIA

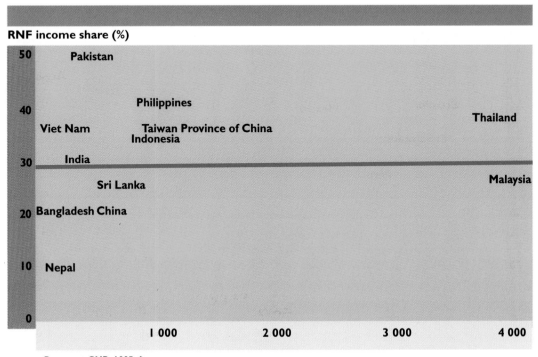

RNF income share (%)

Per caput GNP, 1995, $

The nature of RNF activity and interregional differences

General patterns. The general finding emerging from available data is that the nature of RNF activity differs significantly over regions and subregions. The term "stages of RNF sector transformation" is used here to describe those pattern variations, and some general explanations are offered, based on the nature of RNF employment observed in the different regions. These are only "central tendencies" observed in the various regions, and within a given region there are substantial variety and exceptions.

The patterns in the levels and composition of RNF activity suggest that Africa and South Asia are in what can be considered the first stage of RNF sector transformation. During this stage, RNF activity tends to have a production or expenditure linkage with agriculture while farming directly employs a large share of the rural population and RNF activity tends to be centred on the countryside itself, with little dependence on rural-urban links. Indeed, RNF

Not shown is:
Korea, Rep.: Income share = 32%
   Per caput GNP = $9 700

Source: RNF income shares based on rural household income survey data (see Appendix Table 1); per caput GNP from World Bank. 1997. *World Development Report 1997.*

Figure 38C

NON-FARM SHARE OF RURAL HOUSEHOLD INCOME AND PER CAPUT GNP, SELECTED COUNTRIES IN LATIN AMERICA

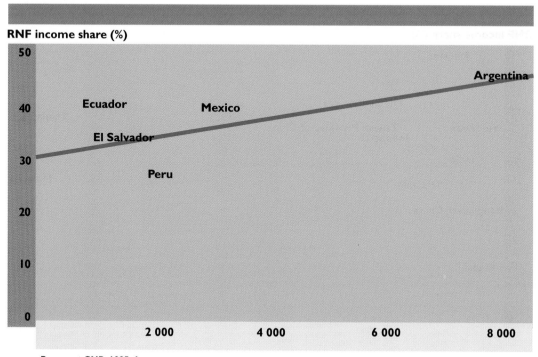

Per caput GNP, 1995, $

Source: RNF income shares based on rural household income survey data (see Appendix Table 1); per caput GNP from World Bank. 1997. *World Development Report 1997.*

activities are mainly home-based and small-scale production of non-tradable goods (goods that are mainly sold locally) produced in the countryside (rather than in rural towns). In terms of farm/non-farm linkages, during this first stage agriculture tends to depend on local supplies of farm inputs and services and on local processing and distribution of farm products, usually carried out by small- to medium-scale firms. Examples of these activities include: the manufacture or mixing of fertilizer; the manufacture, rental and repair of animal traction equipment; cart production; tractor services; crop processing; transport; the construction or maintenance of market facilities; and commerce. For example, Reardon *et al.*[11] show that, in the West African Sahel zones, more than 80 percent of local non-farm activity is in activities that have production linkages with local agriculture.

Latin America is in the second stage of RNF sector transformation, characterized by a tendency towards a

Figure 38D

NON-FARM SHARE OF RURAL HOUSEHOLD INCOME AND PER CAPUT GNP, LOW-INCOME COUNTRIES

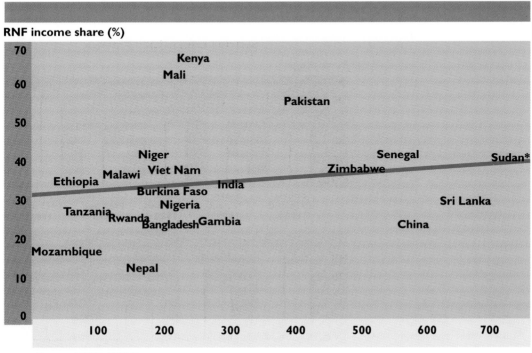

RNF income share (%)

Per caput GNP, 1995, $

* Sudanese per caput income has been estimated by the World Bank to be less than or equal to $765.

Source: RNF income shares based on rural household income survey data (see Appendix Table 1); GNP from World Bank. 1997. *World Development Report 1997*, which defines "low-income countries" as having per caput incomes less than or equal to $765 per year.

greater mix of situations. The range includes activities based on linkages with agriculture as well as on others that are separate – for example tourism, mining and service sector activities, although the latter did grow out of a historical RNF sector transformation based on linkages with agriculture. The share of rural population dependent on farming to a large degree is lower than in Africa and South Asia. There tends to be a greater weight of rural-urban links as the basis for RNF employment than in first-stage RNF sector transformation, with nascent subcontracting of rural companies by urban or foreign businesses (mainly in light durables such as clothing) and a rapid rise in the labour force obliged to commute between the countryside and rural towns and intermediate cities ("rur-urban areas"). There is also a tendency for rapid "agro-industrialization" in commercial agricultural areas, both on a small scale and, particularly, on a medium to large scale. Another characteristic of this phase is the mixed levels of capital

Figure 39

PERCENTAGE SHARES OF RURAL NON-FARM EMPLOYMENT AMONG ECONOMICALLY ACTIVE RURAL POPULATION

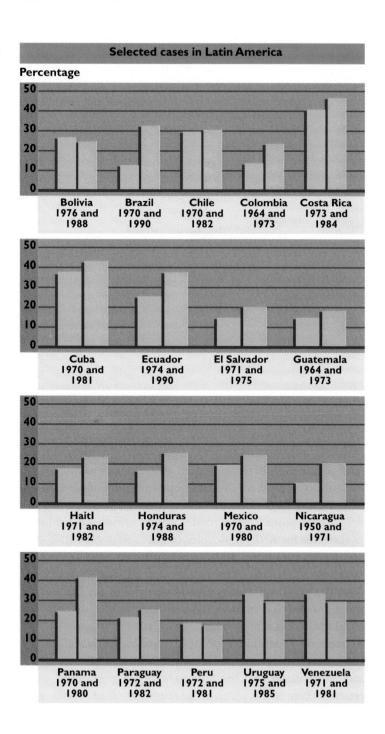

Source: Klein (1992)
and Graziano da Silva (1995),
see Appendix Table
References, p. 346.

intensity, both within and across RNF subsectors. Thus, small-scale labour-intensive production in the countryside is observed alongside relatively capital-intensive enterprises producing the same output in local intermediate cities.

East Asia appears to be in the third stage of RNF sector transformation, identified by an intensification of the characteristics that differentiate the second stage from the first: a greater weight of urban-rural links manifested by the greater importance of more advanced forms of business linkages, such as subcontracting arrangements and labour commuting. A number of other tendencies also characterize this stage of transformation: the expansion of subcontracting beyond light durables to medium durables (such as vehicle parts); substantial RNF employment arising outside linkages with agriculture (even in economies such as Taiwan Province of China which passed through a first-stage RNF sector transformation that was very much linked to agriculture);[12] and rapid agro-industrialization in commercial agriculture.

Sectoral composition, subcontracting and rural-urban links. The sectoral composition of RNF tends to vary over regions. In Africa, most evidence shows that RNF activity is fairly evenly divided over commerce, manufacturing and service sectors, linked directly or indirectly to local agriculture or small towns, and that it is informal rather than formal. In Asia and Latin America, the sector appears to be weighted more towards manufacturing and services.

Drawn from population censuses, information on the overall composition of RNF employment in Latin America indicates that 41 percent of RNF employment is in manufactures, 24 percent in commerce and 35 percent in services. Interestingly enough, the breakdown of urban employment in Latin America is very nearly the same as that of rural employment, contrary to the presumption that the urban economy would have a higher share of services and commerce. This result may vary with city size (with the rur-urban areas perhaps having higher shares of services and commerce) – however, this is a question that needs further research.[13]

Particularly in Latin America and Asia, there appears to have been a long-term increase in commuting by rural residents to non-farm jobs in burgeoning nearby intermediate cities or rural towns and vice versa (town residents commuting to farm labour jobs). Thus, barriers

FAO/17072

Manufacturing cans for food products

Rural agriculture and non-farm employment are closely linked through small-scale processing plants.

between rur-urban areas and the countryside are breaking down and segmentation is disappearing. Klein[14] hypothesizes that, in Latin America, this is leading to a convergence of wage rates and the sectoral mixes in the non-farm sectors of town and countryside.

Subcontracting (between urban and rural enterprises) is another type of link between urban and rural areas that has been growing in importance. There indeed appears to have been an increasing trend towards outsourcing/subcontracting to rural enterprises and households by (larger) manufacturing and trading companies located in rur-urban or metropolitan areas, especially in Latin America and Asia, although the phenomenon appears to be incipient in the more industrial areas of Africa as well (for example in South Africa and Zimbabwe).[15] It may well be that these cases represent a spectrum, with one developing into the other: from light consumer manufactures, organized by traders and undertaken in homes, into consumer and capital goods, subcontracted by urban enterprises and sold in urban markets or used as components in factory-produced goods. In Latin America, most of the current rural subcontracting appears to be focused on light consumer manufactures. Clothing and knitwear are typical activities which employ mainly women in their homes. Subcontracting of this kind allows traders to keep costs low, retain flexibility in volume and labour force and employ a female workforce with a history of skilled artisanal work in clothing. In Asia, it appears that urban-rural subcontracting is more of a spillover of industrial activity from the larger to the smaller cities and towns. It is taking place both in light consumer goods and in consumer and capital durables and has been gathering speed since the 1970s in a number of Asian countries (Indonesia, the Republic of Korea, Malaysia, the Philippines and Taiwan Province of China).[16]

Another trend, supported by evidence in discussions of the Latin American rural situation, is towards an increase in the temporary nature of non-farm work, which probably affects long-term trends in the RNF sector's composition and scale. It is probable that this is driven by outsourcing, agro-industrialization and commuting by the labour force. There are more households precariously working in a set of temporary, part-time jobs as a result of agro-industrial seasonal employment. Women are entering the workforce in great numbers to take up temporary agro-industrial jobs in Latin America and Asia. Moreover, changes in labour laws in parts of Latin America in the 1970s and 1980s made permanent hiring less attractive than the hiring of temporary workers (e.g. see Schaffner[17] for the case of Brazil). But it is not clear whether agro-industrial firms are necessarily moving in the long term towards temporary employees, especially in product lines where there is a need for low turnover of employees and steadily increasing skills; moreover, it depends on the type of agro-industry, as simple processing in large-scale plants tends to use seasonal labour.

In rural Latin America, there is a relatively new trend towards temporary employment in non-farm work.

This relatively new tendency towards temporary employment (with enterprises' labour demand being driven by the need for labour flexibility) should be distinguished from the more common and different phenomenon of pluri-activity, where a rural person or household has several off-farm activities (over the seasons in the year or even over a shorter period), and from income diversification by a rural household. It is becoming more common in Latin America for pluri-activity to include seasonal interrural labour migration for farm work, especially from subsistence to agro-industrial areas, interspersed or overlaid with various non-farm activities. It is probable that the increasing provisional character of non-farm work will tend to magnify the phenomenon of individual pluri-activity.

Owing to the increased integration of rural and urban labour markets (induced by migration and the phenomena of commuting, subcontracting and the location of agro-industrial enterprises in rur-urban areas), forces outside the rural economy (mainly in the cities and in the mining sector) influence the labour use and overall sectoral composition of the RNF economy. Thus, for example, booms in urban construction and mining in a given country or in migration opportunities may have implications for the agricultural sector, since they are associated with the fact that a labour shortage raises local wages in rural economies.

299

This was illustrated in Nigeria during the oil boom in the early 1980s. Such a wage increase can spur investment in labour-saving technology (as observed in Egyptian agriculture[18] or in rural Chilean horticultural zones[19]). Hence, there can be shifts in employment shares induced by these extrarural forces.

Remittances reinvested in local construction and other services may cause rapid growth in those activities, as witnessed in Latin America. Furthermore, returning migrants affect the local non-farm economy through their financial capital and skills acquired in migration. In western Kenya, for example, migrants returning from Nairobi "cornered" the more skilled non-farm jobs.[20] There is also evidence of self-employment (in small enterprises) increasing in rural Zimbabwe with the decline in formal sector employment in Harare after the economic structural adjustment programme.[21]

Farm households, particularly in Africa, earn much more from RNF activitiy than from the farm wage-labour market.

Differences in the nature of RNF employment. The studies reviewed tend to show that farm households earn much more from RNF income than from the farm wage-labour market, particularly in Africa, but also in Asia and Latin America. In the studies from Africa for example, non-farm earnings were on average (with a simple average over study areas) about 20 times as important as farm wage-labour market earnings in the ten study zones where this comparison was possible. Moreover, most of the farm wage labour appeared to be supplied by the poorer households (because local wage employment has lower capital requirements than self-employment and local employment has lower transaction costs than migration employment) or by households hit by early crop failures. On the other hand, one tends to find a larger share of farm wages in the total rural income (but still less than non-farm income) in Asia and Latin America.

The small share of farm wage-labour income in overall rural income emerging from the African studies may reflect the preponderance of semi-subsistence cropping, which tends to use mostly family labour, while hired labour demand is usually a larger but still not an important part of total incomes in cash cropping areas. Other factors contributing to this result may be a relatively equal distribution of land and a low number of landless. Moreover, owing to low farm productivity and the low demand for hired farm labour, the farm wage tends to be lower than the average non-farm wage (and there is abundant evidence to support this).

All things being equal, a higher share of wage income in total RNF income implies a larger firm size. Only a few studies in each of the three continents were identified, however, as distinguishing non-farm wage income and self-employment by rural families. The African studies show (in more than half of the cases) that earnings from non-farm wage labour are more important than self-employment to farm families.[22] The existing evidence for Africa shows that: the majority of enterprises start as one-person concerns and only a minority of microenterprises "graduate" to employing more than five people; and that most of the employment increases in small enterprises are generated by many small companies hiring an additional person rather than a minority of companies increasing employment substantially.[23] The resulting image is one of home-based, individual activities that do not have much capacity to grow or generate employment. By contrast, the evidence from the case studies in East Asia and Latin America points to the opposite image, i.e. one of a preponderance of wage employment (as opposed to self-employment).

The influence of zone type on RNF activity

Agroclimate and agriculture. The differential nature of the RNF economy across agro-ecological zones reflects the diverse nature of agriculture across those zones. There tends to be a negative relationship between the suitability of the agroclimate of the zone (mean and variance of rainfall, quality of soils, crop yields) and the share of income earned in migration by households in the zone. Where the agroclimate is poor, households tend to earn more from migration than from local non-farm activity. Households in the unfavourable agroclimatic zones need to diversify their labour supply beyond the zone to manage crop income risk or to cope with crop income shocks. The reverse holds for favourable agroclimates and more dynamic agriculture – households tend to earn most non-farm income locally, mainly in activities generated by the production or expenditure linkages with the agricultural sector.

The nature and performance of local agriculture can affect the development of the RNF sector in a particular zone in several ways.

First, the local price of the agricultural product affects the profitability of downstream processing (e.g. the price of inputs), while the output price of food also has a more general effect on the RNF sector through its impact on wages.[24] Closely related to these two effects is the influence that a change in the agricultural wage has on the non-farm wage, as demonstrated by situations of rapid change such as that seen in the green revolution areas.[25] Indeed, an increase in the agricultural wage may spread to the non-agricultural sector and cause the unskilled non-farm wage to increase.

The factor bias of agricultural technology (labour-intensive or capital-intensive) and the seasonality of farm labour requirements influence the supply of labour to RNF employment. Crop technology may use labour so intensively that little is left for the family to use in off-farm activities. Such an image of labour-using agriculture constraining off-farm labour availability can be found in Asia's "monsoon economy",[26] with marked seasonality in rice cropping owing to rainfall patterns. Planting and harvesting occupy labour in peak seasons of farm employment. Demand for farm labour is generally low during the rest of the year, hence the need for off-farm sources of income during the slack period. Thus, one should distinguish between absolute underemployment and seasonal unemployment – which can be considered "reserve labour" required to meet high labour demand during the two peak periods within a cropping season. Reserve labour during slack periods is channelled to non-farm activities such as farmers' sideline businesses, cottage industries and small and medium-scale industries that are flexible enough to accommodate the seasonality of the non-farm labour supply.[27]

The composition of agricultural output affects non-farm opportunities. The crop variety and harvest timing affect RNF opportunities through their effects on processing. Certain varieties of a given crop may not be as easily processed as other varieties. The harvest may take place little by little over the production season (as fruit ripens, for example), but having a successful processing operation at an adequate scale would require a much larger amount of fruit to be harvested all at once. There tends to be a correlation between agricultural diversification (away from starchy staples) and income diversification into non-farm activities. As agriculture diversifies into livestock products, fruit and vegetables, opportunities for value added (agroprocessing) increase. Such diversification is generally induced by increasing incomes, which raise demand for foods other than starchy staples.

Yields and harvest volumes affect RNF activity. Yields may be so low that there is insufficient marketable surplus to support downstream processing and distribution businesses. The volume or quality of output may be insufficient or of an inappropriate nature to provide economies of scale for local non-farm activity linked to agriculture or to justify investment in processing plants and local transport capacity.

Agriculture can also affect RNF activity in indirect ways. Thus, constraints on agriculture can "push" farmers to diversify incomes. In areas with poor agroclimates and risky and less dynamic agriculture, off-farm income can be important for coping with this risk (compensating for poor harvests and providing cash to buy food). The off-farm income in those areas tends to be more dependent on income from migration or from towns, i.e. income sources that are not subject to fluctuations similar to those of the local farm economy.

However, while pushing farmers to diversify income sources through RNF activity, constraints on agriculture can at the same time limit their capacity to do so. Land poverty can constrain non-farm activity by limiting the capacity to borrow for such activity and by limiting the cash revenues from farming needed to start non-farm businesses or support migration. There is ample evidence of important informal credit constraints for startup and working capital for small non-farm businesses in rural areas.

There are a significant number of empirical case studies on the magnitude of the impact of agricultural sector performance on the RNF sector through farm/non-farm production and expenditure linkages. In general, the impacts of agricultural output growth on rural non-farm income and employment are strong and tend to be stronger particularly where the production linkages are well developed. The main findings of some of these studies are presented in Box 15.

Box 15

THE MAGNITUDE OF FARM/NON-FARM LINKAGES

On the basis of state- and district-level data for rural areas, rural towns and the combined area in India, Hazell and Haggblade[1] found that on average a 100 rupee (Rs) increase in agricultural income is associated with a Rs 64 increase in RNF income, distributed with Rs 25 in rural areas and Rs 39 in rural towns. Infrastructure, rural population density and farm income levels increase the multiplier. Thus, the figure is as high as 93 in states characterized by high agricultural productivity, high rural population density and rur-urbanization, such as Punjab and Haryana, but only 46 in low productivity states (such as Bihar).

The *IFPRI Annual Report 1985* shows that, in North Arcot district in the Indian State of Tamil Nadu, a 1 percent increase in agricultural output is associated with an additional 0.9 percent growth in non-farm employment. Also from North Arcot district, Hazell, Ramasamy and Rajagopalan[2] found (using 1982/83 data)

that a Rs 1 increase in agricultural value added generated Rs 0.87 of additional value added in the non-farm sector.

Bell, Hazell and Slade[3] found that, in the Muda River region of Malaysia, an increase of agricultural income of 1 percent induced an additional increase in other rural income of 0.83 percent.

Using data from Sierra Leone and Nigeria, Haggblade, Hazell and Brown[4] find multipliers in the order of 1.5; hence a $1 increase in agricultural value added in those African countries generated an additional $0.5 of rural income which is lower than the figures from Asia quoted above.

The African multiplier was generated in a proportion of about 80 percent by expenditure (as opposed to production) linkages, while in the Asian cases the expenditure linkage effect is a lesser share of the total: in the Muda case with which they contrast it, consumption linkages account for only 60

percent of the total multiplier, and in the North Arcot case, only 50 percent.

[1] P. Hazell and S. Haggblade. 1991. Rural-urban growth linkages in India. *India Journal of Agricultural Economics*, 46(4): 515-529.
[2] P. Hazell, C. Ramasamy and V. Rajagopalan. 1991. An analysis of the indirect effects of agricultural growth on the regional economy. In P. Hazell and C. Ramasamy, eds. *The green revolution reconsidered: the impact of high-yielding rice varieties in South India.* Baltimore, USA, The Johns Hopkins University Press.
[3] C. Bell, P. Hazell and R. Slade. 1982. *Project evaluation in regional perspective: a study of an irrigation project in northwest Malaysia.* Baltimore, USA, The Johns Hopkins University Press.
[4] S. Haggblade, P. Hazell and J. Brown. 1989. Farm-nonfarm linkages in rural sub-Saharan Africa. *World Development*, 17(8): 1173-1201.

Infrastructure and rural town density. Regardless of agroclimate, the denser the infrastructure, rural town services and population, the greater the earnings from the RNF sector. This tendency appears more marked in favourable agroclimatic zones. In general, the quality and quantity of hard infrastructure (e.g. roads) and soft infrastructure (e.g. schools) tend to be correlated with population density and the development of rural towns (hence, for example, the difference in infrastructure noted between Asia and Africa[28]). More developed infrastructure and denser population means lower transaction costs for market products (farm or non-farm) and a greater availability of inputs (electricity, tractors, etc.) at a lower cost. Hence, infrastructure quality and quantity have often been identified as key determinants of farm investments and of non-farm business investments (see Box 16, p. 306).

Infrastructure quality and quantity are often identified as key determinants of farm investments and of non-farm business investments.

However, even infrastructure presents some ambiguities in terms of its impact on the RNF economy and employment as well as on sectoral income inequalities. As poorer households tend to be located in the "hinterlands" of the rural zone and thus further from roads and rural towns, depending on how they are undertaken, infrastructure improvements can either increase or decrease sectoral income inequalities. This is illustrated by the opposite cases of Taiwan Province of China and the Republic of Korea. In the former, infrastructure improvements were carried out over regular, cross-country grids, thereby inducing a relatively even rural industrialization. Improvements carried out in the Republic of Korea, on the other hand, brought about concentrated poles of economic development. The agglomeration of capital-intensive firms in rur-urban areas where infrastructure is available can undermine small labour-intensive firms in rural towns and villages, reducing employment per unit of non-farm output even though overall employment may rise.

Furthermore, better roads – and improved infrastructure in general – can be a "double-edged sword" for rural inequality, both overall and sectoral. Poor infrastructure and the consequent high transaction costs provide local protection against outside competition. Opening up the rural economy through commercial deregulation and liberalization as well as by improving infrastructure removes the de facto protection otherwise provided by economic distance and high transaction costs.

Box 16

FOCUS ON THE ROLE OF INFRASTRUCTURE POLICY: COMPARING TAIWAN PROVINCE OF CHINA AND THE REPUBLIC OF KOREA

In Taiwan Province of China, the shift made by rural households to non-farm sources of income began in the late 1960s. Structural reforms in the late 1960s stimulated the spectacular expansion of an outward-oriented export economy. Manufacturing grew by 20 percent per year, leading the way in the sustained double-digit growth of GNP. The consequent pace of labour absorption in the industrial sector took the steam out of the population pressure on the land frontier. The growth of industry is evenly spread across space – a well-known and much lauded feature of the Taiwanese economy. Urban centres are themselves geographically dispersed and infrastructure is also well distributed, making it possible for industrial estates to flourish in the smaller towns.[1] Income diversification trends for the Republic of Korea's farm households diverge radically from those in Taiwan Province of China. The

contraction of farm income in farming households was minimal throughout the rapid growth period of the Republic of Korea in the 1960s and 1970s. The share of wage earnings also remained fairly stable. Several factors contributed to this divergence. First, manufacturing activity was concentrated in just two growth poles: Seoul in the north and Pusan in the south, along with the adjacent provinces. The population in the other provinces remained dependent on agricultural occupations. Second, technological change in Korean agriculture was not characterized by heavy farm mechanization. This kept rural labour tied down to the farms and subjected labour demand to seasonal fluctuations. Third, infrastructure and services were heavily concentrated in the urban centres. The option of commuting from the countryside was constrained by an inadequate rural road network. Instead, there was

considerable migration to the cities.[2] Recently, economic policy in the Republic of Korea has begun to veer away from the urban-based, capital-intensive industrial strategy. With the growing gap in urban and rural average incomes and underemployment of farm labour, emphasis has shifted to promoting RNF activities as well as agricultural development.[3]

[1] S.P.S. Ho. 1986. Off-farm employment and farm households in Taiwan. In R.T. Shand, ed. Off-farm employment in the development of rural Asia. Canberra, National Centre for Development Studies, Australian National University.
[2] F.K. Park. 1986. Off-farm employment in Korea: current status and future prospects. In Shand, op. cit., footnote 1.
[3] J.-S. Choi. 1997. Policies promoting rural non-farm activities in rural development programs in Korea after the Uruguay Round. Paper presented at the 23rd Conference of the International Association of Agricultural Economists, August 1997, Sacramento, California, USA.

The distributional outcome is uncertain and will depend on the involvement of lower-asset households as producers or labourers in activities favoured or harmed by the abolition of de facto protection and the changes that these reduced transaction costs incur in the degree of integration between local and distant labour markets. Increased integration will provide poor or landless households with opportunities for non-farm employment in rural farms and medium-sized cities.

The nature and quantity of infrastructure determine how much a resource-poor area can rely on local RNF activity as opposed to migration. Proximity to cities and mines, together with efficient road and rail links from rural areas to these employment centres, usually increases the share of migration income in overall off-farm income. The studies reviewed in Africa show that, in areas that are not close to major cities or mines, rural households' labour supply to the local non-farm sector is much greater than it is to the migratory labour market. Indeed, in the ten studies reviewed with study areas not near major cities or mines (in Burkina Faso, Ethiopia, Kenya [western], Mozambique, Malawi, the Niger, Senegal, the Sudan, the United Republic of Tanzania and Zimbabwe), local non-farm sector earnings constitute about 80 percent of total non-farm earnings, and migration earnings 20 percent. By contrast, in zones that are close to major cities and to mines or plantations, the migratory labour market appears to be much more important than the local non-farm sector for rural household incomes. In the three studies reviewed that had study areas with such characteristics (in Botswana, Namibia and South Africa), local non-farm earnings constituted about 25 percent, and migration earnings 75 percent, of total non-farm earnings.

The story appears to be different where infrastructure is better and denser and migratory channels are well established, as is seen in certain cases from Asia and Latin America. This is illustrated in the Philippines, where migratory incomes increased after the onset of the green revolution, as families used the capital generated by profitable rice production for investing in education and migration.

Thus, improved hard infrastructure, which can substitute the advantage offered by proximity of rural areas or farms to cities and urban centres, can have two opposite effects on the development of the RNF sector:

The nature and quantity of infrastructure determine how much a resource-poor area can rely on local RNF activity as opposed to migration.

307

- it can favour its growth through increases in overall activity resulting from better access to marketing and lower transaction costs;
- it can create a labour shortage, since the labour force prefers to migrate to urban centres, and thus constrain the sector's growth.

Determinants of RNF activity: interhousehold differences
The motives for rural household income diversification into the RNF sector were explored as a function of related incentives and capacity in the section, Reasons for household participation in RNF activities, p. 285. The present section emphasizes several points related to empirical evidence on incentives and capacity as an introduction to discussing the effects of RNF activity on household welfare.

Responsiveness to relative prices. Field studies show that rural households are responsive to differential returns to activity in the farm and non-farm sectors (although this responsiveness is manifested only where the household has the capacity to participate), given the similar risk profiles of activities in the two sectors. This belies some of the traditional image of peasant households not being market-oriented, especially with respect to labour market opportunities. Households allocate labour to the non-farm sector either because relative returns are better and/or more stable in that sector, or because farm output is inadequate (because of short-term shocks, such as drought, or longer-term constraints, such as lack of land). This allocation can either be a long-term strategy (to manage agricultural risk, compensate for land constraints or take advantage of profitable opportunities off-farm) or a short-term strategy to cope with harvest shortfalls and to smooth incomes over years where there is a failure in or absence of the crop insurance or consumption credit market.

Credit markets. Households can be pushed by underdeveloped or constrained credit markets to earn income off-farm so as to pay for farm inputs and capital. There are ample illustrations of this in recent studies, notably on Africa.[29] A possible pattern emerges in evidence from case studies in Kenya, Mali, Mexico and the Philippines that credit market failure drives farm households to undertake local non-farm and farm investments in two steps: i) rural households migrate to earn cash, returning to rural areas to reinvest the cash in farm capital, cattle, education and housing; ii) with their skills – perhaps learned or honed in migration – and education, they set up local non-farm enterprises (with relatively high capital entry barriers, such as carpentry).

Moreover, given the frequent inadequacy of land to serve as collateral for agricultural loans in informal and formal credit markets, steady pay in the non-farm labour market is used by creditors as substitute collateral for loans. Hence, non-farm earnings allow preferential access to local credit sources, and these non-farm and farm strategies converge to concentrate capital.

Education. The importance of education as a determinant of RNF business success, wage levels and productivity is now widely recognized. Studies of rural industrialization in Asia have emphasized the importance of skill acquisition for a more even distribution of RNF employment, again contrasting Taiwan Province of China and the Republic of Korea in this regard.[30] Given the strong incentive for poor households to diversify their income sources, it is no wonder that one of the first major investments of farmers in cash-cropping zones is education (witness the boom in local investment in rural school buildings in Mali immediately after the devaluation that increased cotton revenues[31]).

Education's importance for a more "egalitarian" income distribution is illustrated by Collier and Lal[32] with reference to central Kenya. More equitable access to education, access to urban wage employment and scale-neutral agricultural innovation (i.e. that could be adopted by both small- and large-scale producers) were what achieved the equal distribution of development. Off-farm income (especially migration income from government employment) was channelled into agriculture. As productivity-increasing innovations were scale-neutral and thus independent of farm size, investment generated with off-farm and migration income (of which education was a strong determinant) caused productivity increases for poor and rich households alike, thereby further enhancing the equalizing effects of access to off-farm employment. Access to off-farm income permitted poorer households to be involved in investments in tree crops (with a long gestation period) and hybrid livestock (sometimes with a high mortality rate). Such investments gave higher returns but also posed greater risks.

Education is a significant determinant of RNF business sector success, wage levels and productivity, and it is therefore important for creating a more "egalitarian" income distribution.

Handmaking terracotta plates, used for cooking tortillas in Mexico

Small rural enterprises produce utensils and crafts which are sold in local villages as well as in city markets.

The other side of the coin is that, where education is poorly distributed, non-farm subsectors or activities within a subsector that require an educated labour force will have highly unequal income distributions. According to their importance in the local economy, therefore, overall inequality may be increased. For example, Adams[33] found that, in Pakistan, although non-farm income had an overall equalizing effect on the income distribution, this was not the case for all specific sources of off-farm income. In fact, the "education-intensive" sources (such as government employment) were found to have an unequalizing effect as they were accessible mainly to wealthier households with more education.

However, there is even ambiguity regarding the relative impact that education has on the sectoral income sources. The little evidence available tends to support the hypothesis that the economic returns from schooling are higher in the non-farm than in the farm sector. In their study of Mexican villages, Taylor and Yunez-Naude[34] document high returns from schooling in both farm and non-farm activities. They also found that education induced households to shift from farm to non-farm activities. These findings are sensitive to schooling type (in this case, family versus farmer education), and results are also likely to differ between

J. SPAULL/FAO/20306

other types of education (e.g. agricultural extension versus general schooling) and location (e.g. in traditional or green revolution farming areas). In any case, provided that access to rural education is not linked to households' ability to pay, rural education can be expected to have a greater effect in reducing inequality in non-farm income than in farm income, but at the same time to equalize the overall size distribution of income.

Such ambiguities might explain situations such as that in Palanpur, India,[35] where non-farm incomes became more equal preceding and during the early stages of the green revolution, but then progressively more unequal (creating a greater source of overall inequality) up to the late green revolution period. In this case, a mix of economic forces had produced a situation where easy-entry off-farm jobs became more plentiful but were relatively low-paying. However, the boom created the conditions for an increase in demand for non-farm products and services and an expansion of relatively better paid non-farm employment opportunities. Such employment opportunities were also attractive to the educated and relatively wealthy households in the village, which in turn were better placed to win in the competition for such jobs. This second effect presumably outweighed the first. Interestingly, this pattern mirrors the common finding of an increase in the demand for farm wage labour (a low-skill, low-barrier employment category) in the early stages of the green revolution, with a levelling off of this demand as the revolution matures and early profits are turned into farm capital accumulation.

A particularly interesting study with regard to the nexus between education, non-farm employment and income inequality is that of central Luzon in the Philippines. The study was undertaken by Estudillo and Otsuka,[36] using non-farm income data spanning several decades for farm households in a green revolution area. They asked whether the observed increase in non-farm income was due to the expansion of human capital (and thus would favour the educated segment of the farm population), or to the expansion of employment opportunities for the rural labour force at large, which would improve the income status of farm households more equally. They found that education has a strong effect on non-farm earnings (but not earnings from green revolution rice farming), both before and after the green revolution, and that educated households generally shift away from farming towards non-farm employment. They noted that a large share of this employment is in urban areas and in migration, both of which require education for entry. They also noted that: "Households who have higher non-farm income were notably the beneficiaries of land reform who invested in their children's education so as to take advantage of increasing returns to education."

Initial household wealth. A household's prior wealth is an important determinant of the degree and nature of its RNF participation. Poor households tend to concentrate on the lower-paying, easy-entry farm labour market as well as on labour-intensive RNF wage employment, and less on RNF self-employment. Given the underdevelopment of credit markets for financing non-farm businesses, own-cash sources (in particular from livestock, cash cropping and migration) are important to start non-farm enterprises and pay the transaction costs to obtain non-farm employment.

The effects of RNF activity on farming

Just as the nature and characteristics of agriculture influence RNF activities, the latter can affect agriculture in a number of ways. To start with, the nature of agro-industrialization[37] can increase the value of land (as it has, for example, in horticultural areas of Chile, Peru and Bolivia) as well as the profitability of the products entering the agro-industrial system (with a relative shift away from subsistence crops). The organizational structure of agro-industry and the type of product produced will affect cropping patterns and the spinoffs to the local economy, depending on the scale and factor bias of the technology used.

Non-farm activities affect the availability of cash for the farm capital investments needed to adopt appropriate technologies.

Income from agro-industrial activities affects farm households' capacity to invest in farm capital and buy modern inputs. Non-farm activities affect the availability of cash to make the farm capital investments (and farm input purchase) needed to adopt appropriate technologies. Thus, non-farm activity by farm households is potentially important for long-term food security because it can increase the use of farm inputs and hence farm productivity and the ability to intensify production. In Africa, non-farm income is usually the main source of cash, or is a "collateral substitute" used to obtain credit. Recent field survey evidence from Burkina Faso, the Niger and Senegal shows that, in most of the Sahel region, formal rural credit is lacking except in cotton and peanut schemes – although for the latter there is less available than previously – and that the informal credit markets are very underdeveloped. Access to non-farm income is crucial for purchasing farm inputs, for example peanut seed, fertilizer and animal traction equipment. This can create a dynamic effect, as cash from the non-farm sector is reinvested in farm equipment, thus creating capital that substitutes for labour and reduces farm labour demand.

The RNF sector also affects the factor and product prices faced by farmers, and hence farm profitability and crop mix. Local cottage manufacturing and services can reduce the price and increase the availability of farm inputs and adapt them to the needs of local farmers, while agroprocessing and distribution can affect the level and stability of output prices.

The converse implication is that RNF constraints "downstream" from the farm sector can block farm sector development by raising processing and distribution costs, thereby undermining farm profits. For example, in northern Senegal, rapid reconnaissance surveys show that the absence of transport and commerce facilities have led to the discontinuance of cowpea cultivation (after its introduction and subsequent production increases). Similarly, survey evidence from Mali shows that a lack of processing services for maize is constraining development of the maize subsector.

Likewise, RNF constraints "upstream" from the farm sector can also hinder development of the farm sector. Agriculture may not spur substantial upstream (input demand) linkages (e.g. for animal traction equipment or tied-ridgers) in a given area if companies in the rural area or local town are producing equipment that is too costly for small farmers or appropriate for only a subset of local soil types and terrains. For example, costly or inappropriate tied-ridger equipment in Burkina Faso hindered development of soil conservation on farms in the cotton zone.

Participation in the RNF economy can lower overall income risk for farm households, increasing the incentive to adopt risky but more profitable farm technologies and to commercialize agriculture. Access to non-farm income may enable a farm household to increase the area of land under cultivation, use more purchased inputs (owing to both increased liquidity and increased security in case of crop failures) and diversify farming into cash crops that raise farm incomes. In general, access to non-farm income may give a household the breathing room to undertake longer-term investments (such as perennial cash crops).

An important point in the analysis of sustainable agricultural systems is that RNF activities can sometimes compete for farmers' resources, and this can affect the factor bias of farm technology. If non-farm labour returns are better than those of farm labour marketing jobs or on-farm labour use then, depending on the integration of the labour market, they will drive up the farm wage, thereby reducing farm labour demand and increasing the capital intensity of farming and/or leading to a shift to less labour-intensive crops. Especially where cropping is most risky, RNF activities can compete for labour and cash for crop technology improvements in the cropping season and for investments in land improvements in the dry season. From the point of view of sustainable agriculture, the implication is that agricultural households might not want to adopt productivity and conservation measures if the payback is not higher or faster than off-farm alternatives: this means that the cost-benefit criterion for resource conservation should include not merely positive profitability but also the level and stability of profitability relative to alternative (non-farm) uses of funds and labour.

A further implication of this last point is that the allure of non-farm opportunities can make labour-intensive agricultural technologies unattractive to farmers, causing technology adoption and extension programmes to fail.

In assessing the sustainability effects of RNF, one should consider that RNF employment can reduce the pressure on land in fragile areas. To the extent that they reduce the incidence of poverty and direct dependence on land resources, non-farm activities can break the vicious cycle of poverty-extensification-degradation-poverty. These activities generate cash that can be used to buy capital inputs to help intensify production on a given piece of land, thus reducing the need for farm households to push on to fragile margins. Non-farm activity can help to smooth income, acting as a crop insurance mechanism and partially displacing the "precautionary motive" for holding livestock and alleviating problems associated with overgrazing. But this effect is ambiguous. In areas without a good rural banking system, farmers often reinvest non-farm income in cattle as an asset accumulation instrument.

EFFECTS OF RNF ACTIVITY ON HOUSEHOLD WELFARE AND INCOME DISTRIBUTION
The RNF sector and food security

There is little controversy about the short-term effects of participation in RNF activity on food access. A given household copes with a drought or other cause of harvest shortfall by, among other things, working off-farm and raising the cash to fill the food deficit. A case study from Burkina Faso before and after the 1984 drought illustrates the typical consequences: households with a greater income diversification were able to buy food and weather the effects of the drought, and also tended to have higher overall incomes than those that were not able to supplement their farm incomes with RNF incomes. Moreover, RNF income is often a major source of savings that farm households in poor areas use to purchase food in difficult times. Finally, as discussed previously, RNF activities influence rural food security through their various linkages with farming.

RNF activity makes a significant contribution to food access and food security.

The controversy begins to emerge when one is dealing with longer-term food security effects. Namely, is it true that working off-farm (or in cash cropping) will reduce household food availability and lead to malnutrition as a result of competition between farm work and food production? The available data do not support this argument. As part of a multicountry study (comprising 13 case studies in Africa, Asia and Latin America) von Braun and Pandya-Lorch[38] sought to determine whether malnourished poor households depended more than non-malnourished households on non-farm income sources, and found that the differences were not significant. Other recent research has produced similar results (e.g. a study in Mexico[39]).

Effects of RNF employment on income inequality: entry barriers

It is often believed that RNF employment, and thus the microenterprise promotion programmes designed to stimulate this sector, will reduce rural income inequality and, as a result, social and political tensions. This position is typically presented as a hypothesis that non-farm activity reduces the inequality of total income in the "village" and hence has an "equalizing" effect.[40] Such an assertion, however, ignores the possibility that the income generated by such activities may be even more unequally distributed in

315

favour of the wealthy and may therefore actually worsen income distribution, even in spite of increasing income levels in all population strata.

Furthermore, in this type of reasoning non-farm income is treated independently of farm income and considered more as an income transfer, i.e. non-farm income compensates for a bad harvest or insufficient land. In other words, for a given household, with a given level of farm income, an increase in non-farm income clearly raises total income by the same amount, enriching the household and "smoothing income" by compensating a drop in agricultural production, for example.

Distribution of non-farm income across landholding classes and overall income strata. The effect of non-farm employment on overall income inequality can be analysed through the relationship between non-farm income, on the one hand, and farm income and/or landholdings, on the other. The implicit view is often that the two move in opposite directions, so that non-farm and farm incomes essentially offset each other. In other words, smaller farms have higher non-farm incomes than large farms, or at least the share of non-farm income in total income declines as total household income increases.

RNF activities do not necessarily improve rural income distribution.

In reality, however, evidence regarding the relationship between the share of non-farm income in total household income and the level of total income and/or the size of landholdings is very mixed. Figure 40A-C presents a selection of different patterns of relationships (from field survey studies – see Appendix Table 3) between non-farm income shares and levels and total household income or landholdings. The selection tends to be representative of the spectrum of patterns found in the different regions.

At one extreme, there is some evidence of a strong negative and linear relationship (following conventional wisdom) between the non-farm share in income and total household income or landholding (Figure 40A). At the other extreme, however, there are cases of a strong positive and linear relationship (contradicting conventional wisdom). This type of relationship is illustrated in Figure 40B. Reardon[41] also found in 18 field studies in Africa that, on average, the share of non-farm income in total income is twice as great in upper-income tercile households as in those of lower terciles. Other cases fall between these two extremes (Figure 40C).

Figure 40A

SELECTED CASES OF A NEGATIVE RELATIONSHIP BETWEEN THE SHARE OF NON-FARM INCOME AND TOTAL INCOME OR LANDHOLDINGS

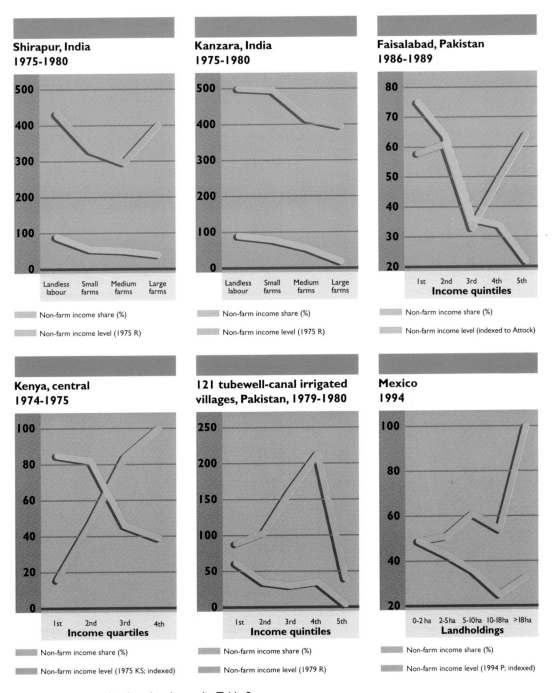

Sources: Survey studies listed in Appendix Table 3

Figure 40B

SELECTED CASES OF A POSITIVE RELATIONSHIP BETWEEN THE SHARE OF NON-FARM INCOME AND TOTAL INCOME OR LANDHOLDINGS

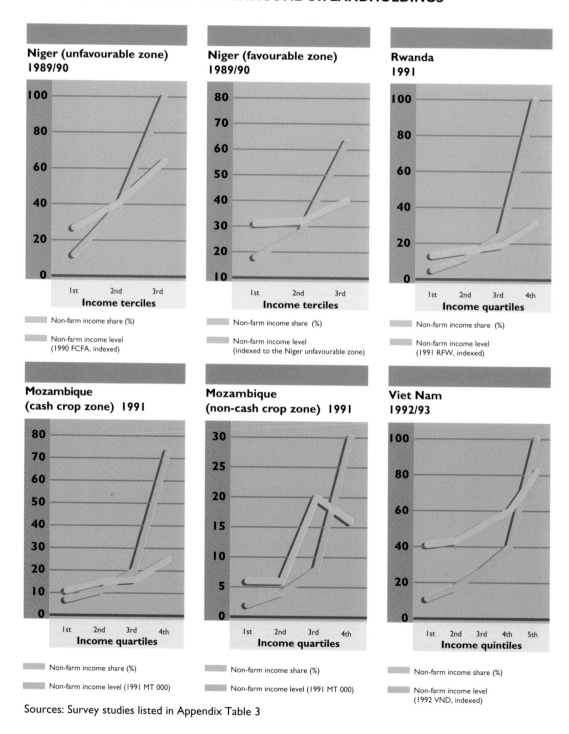

Sources: Survey studies listed in Appendix Table 3

Figure 40C

SELECTED CASES OF OTHER RELATIONSHIPS BETWEEN THE SHARE OF NON-FARM INCOME AND TOTAL INCOME OR LANDHOLDINGS

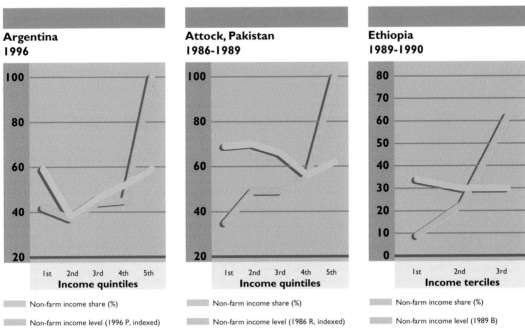

Argentina
1996

Income quintiles

▨ Non-farm income share (%)

▨ Non-farm income level (1996 P, indexed)

Attock, Pakistan
1986-1989

Income quintiles

▨ Non-farm income share (%)

▨ Non-farm income level (1986 R, indexed)

Ethiopia
1989-1990

Income terciles

▨ Non-farm income share (%)

▨ Non-farm income level (1989 B)

Sources: Survey studies listed in Appendix Table 3

These results focus on the share of non-farm income among income and landholding classes. But how do the absolute levels of non-farm income differ among economic classes? Evidence shows that, in many cases, the ratio of the absolute levels of non-farm earnings between the highest and lowest income strata is much higher (i.e. more skewed) than the ratio of shares. Not only that, there are even cases where declining shares of non-farm income for higher-income levels are nevertheless still associated with increasing absolute levels of non-farm incomes.

A key factor behind this is likely to be the existence of substantial entry barriers (e.g. licence fees, equipment purchase or rental, skills acquisition) to activities with high returns to labour. Hence, the low-asset households can spend a large share of their time in non-farm employment, but the wage (hence the level of off-farm income) they will receive is low. On the other hand, higher-income households, may spend the same or a lower share of their resources in non-farm activities but earn much higher returns per unit of resources "invested".

319

It is indeed common in situations with this type of pattern to find large differences in the nature and labour returns of the typical set of non-farm activities undertaken by the poor and rich, or by small- and large-scale farmers. Activities that are intensive in skilled labour and/or physical capital (e.g. cottage manufacturing, transport requiring the use of a vehicle, shop commerce and salaried jobs) have the highest labour returns, as expected, and are undertaken by the wealthiest household strata. The poor (i.e. those with limited assets and/or skills) tend to undertake activities that are intensive in unskilled labour (such as farm wage labour, market porter jobs, wood gathering and unskilled factory jobs).

Case studies also point to the existence of entry barriers to non-farm activity, with evidence of "super profits" in certain non-farm activities and of very high non-farm wages relative to farm wages in several areas. The levels shown in these studies appear well above those justified by intersectoral productivity differences and skill/education levels, suggesting labour market segmentation between farm and non-farm sectors and within the non-farm labour market. It may also be proof of divisions or "lumpiness" in certain subsectors. For example, there is sometimes just enough demand for one full-time blacksmith in a village, and as demand exceeds the smith's capacity, it is rationed through high prices. Furthermore, monopolization of certain activities may occur as a result of caste divisions and other social features that require labour supply to come from specific groups (e.g. blacksmiths and musicians).

Evidence of effects of non-farm income on income distribution. Another methodology that has often been used for analysing the equalizing or "unequalizing" effects of non-farm income is based on a calculation of Gini coefficients,[42] with and without non-farm income, or on a decomposition of the changes in the Gini coefficient as non-farm income changes. The results from such calculations vary widely from case to case.

Again, there is evidence of non-farm income having an unequalizing influence.[43] For instance, by applying the Gini coefficient method to the poor and risky agricultural zone of northern Burkina Faso, Reardon and Taylor[44] found that, from 1983 to 1985, the overall income distribution was more unequal than for farm income alone owing to the unequalizing effect of non-farm income. Thus, the addition of non-farm income "worsened" income distribution. Indeed, a large share of overall income inequality is attributable to non-farm employment. Another example is that of a fast-growing green revolution zone of India (Palanpur in Uttar Pradesh), where Lanjouw and Stern[45] found that non-farm income had a strong unequalizing effect in 1983/84 while, interestingly, it had had an equalizing effect in the same zone two decades earlier.

On the other hand, there are examples of non-farm income exerting an equalizing effect; that is, they lower the overall Gini coefficient. Reardon and Taylor,[46] using the Gini comparison method with cross-section data for the southern zone of Burkina Faso (which has a more favourable agroclimate and thus a dynamic agriculture), found non-farm employment to have an equalizing influence on incomes. Chadha[47] found income distribution in Indian Punjabi villages to be more unequal for total household earnings than for non-farm earnings. In other words, non-farm earnings were more equally distributed. For rural Thailand, income distribution is more unequal for farm income than for income from all sources,[48] which again suggests equalizing effects of non-farm income.

Several cautionary notes are in order, however. It is difficult to tell from data alone how overall income would be distributed in the absence of the non-farm income. Assuming that non-farm income is more unequally distributed than overall income, at face value it would look as though non-farm income increased inequality. However, it is possible that if those currently employed in the non-farm sector were engaged in some alternative employment, such as agricultural labour, agricultural wage rates might be lower and overall income inequality might rise. So rather than raising inequality, the non-farm sector could actually be preventing inequality from rising even further. Moreover, on their own, the Gini coefficients do not indicate what direction and degree of correlation may exist between the two income sources, and hence the two distributions.

Interpreting results on RNF employment and income inequality.
The results cited here can be interpreted as a function of households' incentives and capacities to undertake RNF activity. Inverse (or U-shaped) relationships between non-farm income shares and overall income or wealth imply a relatively high share of non-farm income for the poorest

households and are observed most frequently in Asian and Latin American studies. These relationships are associated with the following:

- The availability of jobs with a high labour-to-capital ratio and low barriers of entry for poor (very low-asset) households. That availability in turn appears to be associated with: relatively good infrastructure, high population and market densities, dynamic agriculture, unequal landholdings and the development of rural towns outside metropolitan areas.
- Possibility for households with average asset holdings to specialize in land-intensive crop production; similarly, this is more common in green revolution areas.
- The ability of high-asset households to diversify into more capital-intensive activities, either self-financing this diversification or using their assets as collateral to obtain credit. Asset holdings enable high-asset households to diversify production for expected income as well as risk motives.

By contrast, in areas that exhibit a positive association between non-farm income shares and total income or wealth levels (as is the case for many of those covered by the African studies), the conditions tend to be very different. There is a scarcity of labour-intensive activities that have low entry barriers; this is so in both non-farm and farm sectors that are characterized by an underdeveloped farm labour market and predominantly traditional production technologies using family inputs. Additional factors include a relatively equal land distribution (and a virtual absence of landless households), a low population and infrastructure density, a relatively low level of rural town development and significant entry barriers for investment in capital-intensive subsectors.

Are income inequalities in the farm and non-farm sectors associated?

Having discussed mixed reports of how the rural non-farm economy affects overall income inequality as well as the conditions for the variation in these outcomes, there still remains a set of relevant questions with important policy implications to be considered. These issues centre around the degree and nature of the association of income inequalities across the farm and non-farm sectors.

Two considerations are whether these inequalities are jointly driven by a common set of external factors that affect households' capacity to generate both farm and non-farm income, and how such factors might be addressed to increase the participation of the poor in the non-farm sector?

Another issue is whether the inequalities in the farm and rural non-farm sectors are directly related, so income generated in one sector, together with the asset accumulation it allows, affects the capacity for income to be earned in the other. More simply, is the asset position of a household a good predictor of its ability to earn non-farm income?

It can thus be hypothesized that sectoral inequalities are mutually dependent (at least partially). The discussion of this hypothesis revolves around productive factors (labour and capital versus land), since it is because of the need for these factors that the different sectors, and hence the inequalities in their income distributions, interact.

First, there may be competition for labour use between the two sectors, and rigidities in the technology of a given sector may block labour availability for development of the other. For example, a traditional labour-using technology can keep smallholder labour "bottled up" on the farm and thus make it unavailable for off-farm activity. The latter corresponds to a situation frequently reported in Asian case studies, i.e. that rural industrialization is constrained until farm mechanization frees labour from farming, at which time seasonal underemployment is reduced because members of farm households are able to specialize in higher-paying non-farm activities. Thus investment in technological change in the farm sector, which may only be accessible to the asset-rich households, is needed to free up labour for the non-farm sector.

There is also evidence of an interrelationship between rural capital and non-farm labour markets, as proof of a steady pay from non-farm employment is frequently used as collateral for loans in the rural sector. This is true in Kenya and Benin, for example. Constraints on earning non-farm income also translate directly into constraints on farm capital accumulation. Where rural credit markets are underdeveloped, non-farm income is the main source of cash for farm investments (migration, livestock and cash crop sales are in second place), and non-farm employment has an important effect on farm investments.[49] As these farm

G. BIZZARRI/FAO/19769

Dressmaking in a small factory

Activities not directly linked to agriculture demonstrate second-stage RNF transformation.

investments determine farm productivity and incomes, which in turn affect cash available for non-farm business starts, this can unleash social differentiation and increase inequality.

Farm households can sometimes use the migratory labour market to break the vicious cycle of poverty of farm assets and inability to earn non-farm income locally. They then use the migration remittances and skills learned through migration to start non-farm businesses, buy farm capital (mainly equipment for cash cropping, cattle and, occasionally, land) and invest in education.

Inequality in access to scarce land also translates into inequality in non-farm employment opportunities because agricultural cash incomes, the use of land as collateral for credit and the political influence that land wealth often implies, can all affect involvement in RNF sector activity. The initial unequal access to land may be even further accentuated, as it appears that inequalities in non-farm earnings result in unequal landholding patterns (e.g. in western Kenya[50]). There is also evidence from Rwanda in a study by André and Platteau,[51] who note that:

"... access to regular off-farm income opportunities tends to accentuate rather than mitigate inequalities in land endowments through the operation of an active (and illegal) land market (which implies that customary restrictions on land sales have largely disappeared) where many land parcels are sold under distress conditions and purchased by people with regular non-agricultural incomes."

However, the effect described here appears to wane as non-farm labour markets develop and human capital supersedes land in driving entry into and returns from non-farm activities. For example, in situations of scale-neutral technological change (such as the green revolution in rice production), over time education takes the place of landholdings as the most important determinant of non-farm income for rural households, as has been the case in the Philippines.[52]

POLICY ISSUES AND IMPLICATIONS
Macropolicies: necessary but not sufficient

Well-designed general macroeconomic policies are necessary, but not sufficient, for the development of RNF activities because they are needed to achieve an efficient use of resources thoughout the economy. If universal economic benefits are to be generated through improved resource allocation, a combination of various policies is needed, including an improvement in the "macro context", a devaluation of the chronic overvaluation of many countries' currencies, liberalization of trade – also involving a reduction of tariff and non-tariff barriers – a reduction of fiscal deficits, the elimination or privatization of parastatals and cuts in subsidies.

The positive effect of these policies in terms of improved resource allocation should extend to the rural areas, particularly to the extent that they eliminate the urban bias frequently found in many developing countries' economic policies. The implication of this last aspect is an improvement in the terms of trade of tradable goods produced in rural areas, which is of particular significance for the agricultural sector but is also relevant to certain goods produced in the RNF sector. Thus, the RNF sector will benefit directly through the improved terms of trade for tradable goods produced within the sector, and indirectly through production, expenditure and investment linkage effects with the agricultural sector.

Macroeconomic reform alone, however, is not sufficient to spur RNF sector development. Two points should be raised in this regard:

- There is often significant ambiguity regarding the effects of reforms on rural areas, particularly in the short term. Indeed, while liberalization may improve the terms of trade and create opportunities for RNF activity, short-term effects can also include the removal of protection previously enjoyed by the RNF sector and the exposure of certain RNF subsectors to competition from urban-based

enterprises and imports. Painful adjustment processes can be forced on the rural economy as a result.
- Depending on the situation, reforms may have a positive effect on the incentives open to rural enterprises and farms, but there are often considerable capacity constraints that limit response to these incentives or prevent their being allocated in an equitable way that includes the asset-poor.

Physical and social infrastructure and institutional reform

Investing in rural infrastructure raises RNF activity and farm productivity.

Rural areas are typically underequipped in terms of infrastructure. Infrastructure investment policies can strengthen linkages between the RNF sector and agriculture and thus create RNF multipliers from the growth of agriculture, as was the case in Taiwan Province of China, Costa Rica and southeastern Burkina Faso, for instance. It is very important to improve both hard infrastructure (e.g. roads, electrification) and soft infrastructure (e.g. banking systems, market information systems) as a means of reducing the transaction costs for business starts and subcontracting in rural areas, and of improving the productivity of RNF entrepreneurs.[53]

Also in terms of education, rural areas are frequently at a disadvantage, and the importance of enhanced rural education for development of the RNF sector is incontrovertible. It was noted earlier that empirical studies reveal education to be a strong determinant of household participation and of the level of wage earned in RNF activities. However, it appears that more specific skills and training are necessary to promote RNF activities in today's environment of competitive, liberalized trade. An example from the non-farm sector is the need to train rural people in skills that allow them to participate in skilled labour markets.

Missing links between agricultural policy and RNF development

The significance of RNF income and employment illustrated in this review should not be taken to mean that RNF development represents an alternative to addressing agricultural development problems; nor should it detract from the importance of agricultural policy and research. On the contrary, in all but the worst agroclimatic zones, the RNF sector is usually closely connected to agriculture, and activities linked to agriculture are predominant forces in first-stage and second-stage RNF sector transformation. This implies that agriculture is often crucial to the success of RNF development strategies, and vice versa. Moreover, sector-specific policies in general, and agriculture policies in particular, tend to be severely neglected in the RNF development debate, which is why they are given special emphasis here.

The general goal of a sector-specific policy orientation should be to identify promising subsectors and then systematically address the constraints to incentives and capacity for development – ranging from the participation of small- and medium-scale farmers, small and medium-sized agro-industrial development and/or linkages with larger agro-industrial companies, and market development and consumer product acceptance. The specific goal should be to provide the incentives and capacity for rural households and RNF enterprises to overcome entry barriers, and to create "linkage friendly" agriculture and RNF activities.

Shifting crop and livestock research from a narrow sectoral to a broad intersectoral perspective

As part of its technology design and product priority strategies, agricultural research may need to consider the weight attached by farmers to the returns to new farm technologies compared with the returns on household resource use off-farm. Following are two important points that emerged earlier concerning the implications of the RNF sector for evaluating policy and project alternatives:

Agricultural research needs to consider the weight farmers attach to the returns on new farm technologies compared with the returns on household resource use off-farm.

- The preference shown by farm households for diversifying into non-farm activities means that, all things being equal, farmers may want to free labour from farming to enable income diversification off-farm. This point has implications for agricultural research which should not necessarily be searching exclusively for labour-using technologies, even in labour-abundant areas.
- One implication is that households might not want to adopt productivity and conservation measures if the payback is not higher or faster than alternatives off-farm: this changes the cost-benefit criteria to include non-farm activities in the alternatives to be considered. Farm households should not be expected to want immediately to adopt natural resource management practices and

FAO/14713

A Gambian woman uses a grinding mill to prepare food for market

This labour-saving technology allows far greater productivity among rural communities than in the past.

conservation investments involving the use of labour and/or capital that could earn higher returns in other sectors.

Another important research implication resulting from the high non-farm share in farm household income and employment relates to the measurement of farm labour productivity. In the simplest labour productivity estimates, the denominator is the number of persons actively engaged in agriculture. Even if non-farm activity is seasonally biased towards the dry season, in most cases some non-farm activity occurs also in the rainy season. Non-farm activity constitutes time in the production season, which should be subtracted from the estimated time spent on agriculture. This will raise the estimate of agricultural productivity per caput, which also adjusts upwards the implicit wage paid for farm labour (farm income per effective workday). Farm management surveys naturally try to measure the actual number of hours dedicated to farm tasks, but these types of survey are costly to conduct.[54]

It is also important for research and extension to put more emphasis on farm/non-farm linkages through agro-industry and agricultural diversification involving small-scale actors. This involves the possibility of developing agricultural technologies that are scale-neutral, and thus benefit small- as well as large-scale farmers, combined with agroprocessing technologies that can be handled by small- and medium-scale agro-industrial firms. Such technologies tend to maximize the rural employment impact of agricultural development to the extent that relatively small-scale concerns have a higher employment-output ratio. Smaller farms and agroprocessing firms will also have a greater tendency to use local farm implement repair services as well as local transport and commercial companies, and will invest profits locally – all leading to further ripple effects in the local economy. Poorer households that would benefit from this employment are also more likely to spend their earnings locally on products and services of RNF firms, leading to greater multipliers through these expenditure linkages. Whether larger agro-industrial companies or farms could generate similar multipliers would need to be assessed on a case-by-case basis and would depend on how labour-intensive they were as well as how much local spinoff activity they could produce.[55]

To help the small players compete, agricultural research and extension should encompass agro-industrial research in its broadest sense, covering implement and input design and marketing; agroprocessing technologies and market strategies; post-harvest storage technologies and marketing; marketing and distribution research; and consumer preference and responsiveness testing (including probing for new market niches). This requires collaboration between local universities, chambers of commerce, farmers' organizations and governments.

Adding a multisectoral perspective to agricultural and rural development policies

A central theme of this review has been the major entry barriers and constraints to competitivity facing the poor in RNF activity. Difficulties may exist even in countries with a good infrastructure, relatively high rates of education and a favourable macroeconomic policy climate. Schejtman[56] points out that, even in Chile, only about 10 to 15 percent of small farmers are participating in the famous recent horticultural boom, and there are apparently relatively few small-scale agro-industrial companies connected with it.

With rising incomes in developing countries, in general potential alternatives for generating farm/non-farm linkages are in processed cereals, tubers and roots and pulses, processed and fresh fruits, vegetables and dairy and other livestock products. Some of these activities, such as

RNF sector development has suffered because it has not belonged to the domain of either Agricultural or Industry Ministries.

those involving fruits, vegetables and dairy products, tend not to be characterized by economies of scale, and the agroprocessing of these products is especially amenable to small- and medium-scale operations.[57] There are a number of serious policy challenges in broadening the participation of rural households in farming and agro-industrial and related enterprises linked to the above products. Addressing these challenges means going beyond increased agricultural productivity to achieve a better coordinated rural policy. Institutional cooperation and coordination is a crucial element in such a policy.

RNF sector development has fallen into an "institutional vacuum", since it has not belonged to the domain of Agricultural Ministries, with their mandate related to farming *per se*, or to that of Industry Ministries, which commonly focus on large-scale, formal-sector companies. The present review, however, has shown that this vacuum may have excluded one-third of the rural economy from the policy debate and related action. Hence, it is very important for policy-makers to establish a system perspective that links the agricultural and RNF sectoral domains. This is not an argument for a simple return to integrated rural development, but rather a call for close cooperation in policy and programme formulation and implementation between Agriculture and other (Industry, Technology, Commerce, etc.) Ministries with respect to the promotion of development in the RNF sector.

To increase the reach of the employment spillover effects of agro-industrialization in rural areas, more small- and medium-scale farmers need to be involved as producers as well. Yet, at present, this participation is limited by constraints on access to inputs, especially after the full or partial dismantling of public input distribution systems. In many countries to date, private sector activity in the areas of input supply and credit has not emerged sufficiently to fill the gap left by government's withdrawal.[58] Farmers are often forced to rely on own-cash sources from off-farm employment and cash cropping to pay for inputs and substitute for credit. There are some striking illustrations of the effect of these changes on farmer participation in agro-industrial contracts (e.g. that of Zamora, Mexico, where many smallholders had to withdraw from strawberry production for the local packing plants[59]), although this situation does not always call for policy action. Often, farmers' need for credit and inputs becomes the driving force for a variety of contractual arrangements with agro-industrial companies, including provision by the latter of inputs and credit for farmers.

One of the most difficult policy challenges will be to facilitate coordination between farms and companies so that scale economies can be created and exploited. That is, agro-industrial firms and spinoff businesses will be reluctant to invest in the critical mass of capacity (to minimum optimal scale) unless they can be reasonably sure that farmers will be forthcoming with sufficient produce of the appropriate (input) type and quality. Similarly, farmers will be reluctant to shift towards the new crops and make the necessary capital and skill investments in the absence of a profitable market among agroprocessors and distributors. The policy solution involves coordination among various institutions of the public and private sectors. The role of the public sector is crucial in facilitating communication, lowering transaction costs and providing technical knowledge that could lead to mutually advantageous solutions generating the requisite investment in both sectors. This would involve legal reforms to sanction contracts, technical training and market information and business-linkage information systems.

Knowing and being able to respect international grades and standards often gives larger urban-based businesses an advantage over local companies, particularly in export markets. Indeed, as well as reducing transaction costs, the establishment of grades and standards can also lead to industrial concentration when smaller players lack access to the means to implement and monitor those standards. Accordingly, an important measure to increase the "linkage friendliness" of farming and to enable small- to medium-scale agro-industrial firms to compete is the creation and wide dissemination of information on grades and standards.

Enabling the poor to participate
Improving the asset base of the poor is crucial. This review has shown that poor farm households often lack the assets (such as liquefiable assets, education, access to credit and security of land use rights) that serve as important capacity variables for participating in RNF activities. In turn, unequal access to more remunerative RNF employment may cause a further concentration of wealth (in the form of land): there is evidence of this, for example, in western Kenya and

Income growth among the rural poor is a crucial engine for rural growth via production and expenditure linkages.

Rwanda. A similar vicious cycle may occur with other farm assets.

In some countries where land is very unequally distributed, the lack of landholding among the poor may constitute a constraint to the growth of RNF activity and employment. Income growth among the rural poor is a crucial engine for rural growth via production and expenditure linkages. On the other hand, increases in the income of wealthier population groups (in this case large landholders) may be associated with leakages to the urban and foreign sectors. For example, Saith[60] showed that land reform was critical to the broad-based rural industrialization in Taiwan Province of China and in mainland China. He notes that this created a broad rural middle class, rising incomes, collateral for loans and demand for outputs and inputs from local agro-industry.

The most far-reaching, but also the most difficult, policy to implement would be land redistribution. Short of that, non-land asset distribution, would still be useful for RNF employment creation and improving access by the poor to RNF activities in the medium term. Prime examples would be the broadening of education and specific training and improved credit access for RNF business starts, such as those undertaken in North Arcot, India, to help the poor start small agro-industrial firms in the context of the green revolution.

Competition between small- to medium-scale RNF firms and large-scale firms

An important issue is whether "the lion can lie down with the lamb". In other words, is a significant increase in RNF activity by small- and medium-sized companies possible in situations where there are large-scale firms competing in the same markets? Trade and foreign investment liberalization and improvement of infrastructure can constitute a threat to small- to medium-sized RNF enterprises. Namely, reductions in economic and "natural" protection of rural companies may create pressures on their competitiveness *vis-à-vis* consumer goods and inputs "imported" from metropolitan areas and/or from abroad. This can be seen in Chile, Mexico, the Philippines and South Africa, or in the context of a dual economy where large retail outlets and large manufacturing companies compete in rural towns and intermediate cities with small- and medium-scale rural enterprises. In globalizing or regionalizing markets, this competition can only become more intense. In such cases, even where small rural firms have the production cost advantage, this will not necessarily translate into a market advantage, as larger urban firms may have better distribution networks, brandname appeal and so on.

The potential competition between small informal sector businesses and large formal sector businesses could take place in terms of production costs, captured markets for farm inputs and processed foods, and distribution channels. The issue is whether the small business sector can face up to the competition with lower costs and prices; more appropriate products in the form of inputs and consumption goods targeted to small-scale farmers and poor rural households; more convenient access to products and services; and niche market strategies. Such competition can, of course, turn out to the benefit of the rural consumer and farmer in terms of lower costs and access to products and services suitable to them.

In a liberal economic policy environment that avoids distorting incentives, and within the political and fiscal constraints faced by governments, the challenge is to help smaller companies identify niche markets and exploit their competitive advantages, promoting various arrangements based on the mutual interest of the small rural companies and larger enterprises or markets.

Links between small rural companies and larger urban enterprises can be promoted through arrangements that are based on their mutual interest.

The most "traditional" arrangement, and what appears to be the conventional image that policy-makers have, is that of a large urban company setting up a factory and hiring local workers, such as in the textile industry in the first half of the 1900s – the foundation stone of Japanese industrialization – or the agro-industrial complexes of northern Mexico or central Chile. Frequently, national or local governments have actively supported such arrangements with tax breaks and installation of infrastructure including electrification and public buses. It has been observed that some employees move on to form their own small companies and use the skills learned from formal sector employment.

A promising type of arrangement, however, is the "business linkage" between big urban companies and small rural businesses in contracted outsourcing and franchising. This is developing rapidly in East Asia and, to a certain degree, in Latin America and a few parts of Africa, such as South Africa and Zimbabwe. Under such arrangements, a small company can serve to enter a niche market for which it is particularly suited and/or to lower labour costs and increase the flexibility of labour arrangements. As labour costs and skills grow in the initial set of companies, there can be a second wave of outsourcing relationships where rural companies subcontract to other rural companies. Infrastructure development that lowers costs constitutes a key ingredient in the success of these arrangements.

This type of subcontracting arrangement appears to have a number of strong advantages, as it teaches skills to small firms, creates access to dynamic markets, in some cases provides credit, etc. The buyer sometimes provides capital to suppliers by providing an advance payment for an order or by supplying raw materials for processing. Business links can help suppliers reduce their capital needs as well as cutting down on search and start-up times by targeting production to an identified market. A small company can also receive marketing advice from a larger partner. An example could be a rural entrepreneur forming a small business to distribute farm inputs or collect and perform the first processing stage of farm outputs on behalf of a large business. This arrangement could be a "strategic alliance" of agro-industrial companies and small-scale farms, or a franchise or outgrower/outsourcing arrangement. Another example could be a franchise arrangement between a big fertilizer company and small mixing stations in rural areas. However, the subcontracting option has the best chance of success where there is a dynamic industrial sector in the urban areas, widespread rural education and good infrastructure and communications.

CONCLUSIONS

The RNF sector is already of great importance to rural economies for its productive and employment effects: it offers services and products upstream and downstream from agriculture in the off-farm components of the food and fibre system, which are critical to the dynamism of agriculture; while the income it provides farm households represents a substantial and growing share of rural incomes, including those of the rural poor. These sectoral contributions will become increasingly significant for food security, poverty alleviation and farm sector competitiveness and productivity in the years to come.

Equitable development of the RNF sector will not be smooth or automatic, however. The conclusion of this review comprises a set of two paradoxes, presented with concomitant policy conclusions and challenges, and a final cautioning about the adjustment costs involved in adapting the RNF sector to open, integrated markets resulting from structural adjustment and liberalization.

First is the "interhousehold paradox", arising from the fact that the poorest households, while facing the greatest need for remunerative RNF employment (because of risk management and the need to cope with income shocks or farm-level limitations), are also the most constrained owing to a lack of key assets (education, skills, startup capital) and opportunities (determined by distance from and access to RNF labour and product markets). Conversely, wealthier households have less "need", but at the same time enjoy a greater capacity to participate in the RNF sector, particularly in its most remunerative activities. The degree and nature of their participation is thus based mainly on considerations of relative returns and profit opportunities. This paradox underlines the inequality in access to RNF employment and draws attention to the entry barriers faced by the poor.

The main conclusion to be drawn is the importance of helping the poor to overcome the constraints and thus enable them to participate in RNF activities. This entails diagnosing the kinds of asset poverty constraining the poor with respect to entrance into the more dynamic and remunerative RNF activities, and using policies and programmes to address those asset constraints. In turn, this will often require investments in general education and specific skill building for RNF activities (such as agroprocessing technologies) and in market and technology information centres in rural areas for the purpose of identifying promising opportunities. It will also mean promoting RNF employment and strengthening agricultural linkages in areas poorly served by infrastructure. This involves public investments aimed at allowing the poorer hinterlands to benefit from and participate in the growth.

Equitable development of the RNF sector will not be smooth or automatic.

335

The second paradox is the "interzone paradox", arising from the fact that the zones or locations with poor agricultural potential (and frequently poor infrastructure) are the ones that have the greatest need for remunerative RNF employment (to offset a poor farm sector) but are the most constrained by a lack of assets for RNF market development (such as good roads, a skilled workforce and economical sources of raw materials). Another aspect of this paradox is that a lack of buying power limits a zone's potential for RNF sector development. The two constraints are linked, since poverty caused by a weak and stagnant farm sector constrains RNF sector development from both the supply and the demand sides. By contrast, more favourable zones that have less "need" for RNF employment (in the sense that the average household has been able to rise from poverty through farming and/or farm wage labour) still have a greater capacity to generate RNF activities, just as there tend to be better-paying RNF jobs in these zones compared with the resource-poor zones. It is indeed most frequently on the basis of RNF "linkage activities" upstream or downstream from the farm, either through production linkages or based on growing farm incomes through consumption linkages, that RNF sector growth and transformations are originally induced.

The main challenge linked to this second paradox is the promotion of private investment in resource-poor zones through well targeted initial public investment. These zones are frequently "written off" on the reasoning that growth of urban economies will simply absorb outmigration from the poor zones, which will consequently depopulate, and that it is therefore a waste of resources to invest in them. However, the congestion of large cities and the secular tendency towards increasing capital/labour ratios in urban economies have shown the limits to migration to cities. Investing in new RNF sector opportunities in resource-poor zones is crucial. Such investments will need to be in the general skill and infrastructure development necessary to establish commerce and small- to medium-scale manufacturing.

A final cautioning is necessary regarding the effects of "opening up" rural areas. Introducing policies aimed at increasing opportunities for the development of RNF activities can also be facilitated by structural adjustment and market liberalization because of the opening and development of internal and external markets and the reduction of the anti-rural bias frequent in developing

R. FAIDUTTI/FAO/19117

countries' economic policies. These effects, which are
strengthened by the development of infrastructure that
bring rural and urban (and even international) markets
closer together, in principle imply more opportunities for
poverty-alleviating RNF development. However, they may at
the same time involve short-term risks and adjustment costs.
Indeed, the openness that creates the opportunities also
deprotects rural areas and brings larger fish into the
backwaters of the RNF economy: large retail stores and big
farm input suppliers that set up branches in rural towns, big
agroprocessors moving into farm areas, etc. This can expose
certain RNF subsectors and activities to new competition
and force painful adjustments on the RNF sector.

Policy-makers are challenged to design policies and
investments that help local economies to adjust and take
advantage of the new situation, rather than putting up
roadblocks to location of large- and medium-scale agro-
industrial or retail firms in rural areas, which would only
serve to maintain the marginalization of those zones from
external and urban markets. An important key to success
lies in helping the poor to participate, through RNF
enterprise starts, contract farming and wage employment.
Again, production sector policies will play a key role in

Basket weaving as a cottage industry
Rural women often work in
their homes to produce
marketable goods.

spurring equitable RNF sector development – which is frequently a missing part in the policy debate. Also important for facilitating such participation are institutional and infrastructure development policies that level the playing field for smaller companies, reduce transaction costs for those in the hinterlands and raise the skills of the poor.

APPENDIX TABLE 1[1]

RURAL NON-FARM INCOME: STUDIES REVIEWED

Region/country	Year	Source[2]
AFRICA		
Botswana	1974/75	Valentine (1993)
	1985/86	
Burkina Faso	1978/79	Barrett et al. (1982)
	1981-85	Reardon et al. (1994)
Ethiopia	1989/90	Webb & Reardon (1992)
Gambia	1985/86	von Braun, Puetz & Wenn (1989)
Kenya	1974/75	Collier and Lal (1984)
	1987/89	Francis and Hoddinot (1993)
	1984	Livingstone (1991)
Lesotho	1976	Low (1986)
Malawi	1990/91	Peters (1992)
Mali	1988/89	Sundberg (1989)
Mozambique	1991	Tschirley & Weber (1994)
Namibia	1992/93	Keyler (1996)
Niger	1989/90	Hopkins & Reardon (1993)
Nigeria	1966/67	Norman (1973)
	1974/75	Matlon (1979)
Rwanda	1991	Reardon & Clay (1998)
Senegal	1988/90	Kelly et al. (1993)
South Africa	1982/86	Nattrass & Natrass (1990)
Sudan	1988	Teklu, von Braun & Zaki (1991)
United Rep. of Tanzania	1980	Collier et al. (1990)
Zimbabwe	1988/89	Chopak (1991)
ASIA		
Bangladesh	1987	Hossain (1994)
	1963	Oshima (1986)
	1973	
	1976	
	1982	Hossain (1987)
China	1988	Lin (1994)
	1979-1986	Jiang & Luo (1987)
	1992	FAO (1992)
India	n.a.	Chadha (1986)
	1987	Ramasamy, Paramasivam & Kandaswamy (1994)
	1975/76-1979/80	Walker, Singh & Binswanger (1983)
	1981	Ahmed (1995/96)
	1957/58	Lanjouw & Stern (1993)
	1962/63	
	1974/75	

Region/country	Year	Source[1]
	1983/84	
	1968/69	Hazell & Haggblade (1991)
	1969/70	
	1970/71	
	1975/76	
Indonesia	1987	Jatileksono (1994)
	n.a.	Hafid (1979)
	1977	Kasryno (1986)
	1983	
Japan	1950	Oshima (1986)
	1955	
	1960	
	1965	
	1970	
	1975	
	1980	
	1978	Saith (1986)
Malaysia	1974	Shand (1986)
	1973	Oshima (1986)
	1979	
	1980	Shand (1986)
	1981	
Nepal	1987	Uphadhyaya & Thapa (1994)
Pakistan	1968	Anderson & Leiserson (1980)
	1986/89	Adams (1994)
	1980/81	Ahmed (1995/96)
	1979/80	Arif, Ahmed & Jannison (1982)
	1986/89	Garcia & Alderman (1993)
Philippines	1985	David, Cordova & Otsuka (1994)
	n.a.	Abedullah (1993)
	1970	Balagot (1974)
	1984/85	Bouis & Haddad (1990)
	1974	Hayami et al. (1990)
	1987	
	1985	Ranis & Stewart (1993)
	1966	Estudillo & Otsuka (1997)
	1986	
	1990	
	1994	
Republic of Korea	1996	Choi (1997)
	1980/81	Ahmed (1995/96)
Sri Lanka	1963	Oshima (1986)
	1978	
Taiwan Province of China	1966	Oshima (1986)
	1970	
	1975	
	1980	

Region/country	Year	Source[1]
Thailand	1973	Oshima (1986)
	1979	
	1987	Isvilinonda & Wattanutchariya (1994)
	1972	Anderson & Leiserson (1980)
Viet Nam	1992/93	Government of Viet Nam (1994)
	1993/94	Wiens (1997)

LATIN AMERICA

Argentina	1996	Wiens (1997)
Ecuador	1995	Lanjouw (1997)
El Salvador	1995	Lopez (1997)
	n.a.	FUSADES (1996)
Mexico	1984	de Janvry et al. (1995)
	1989	
	1994	de Janvry, Gordillo de Anda & Sadoulet (1997)
	1986	IFAD (1991)
	1984	de Janvry et al. (1995)
Peru	1984	Figueroa (1987)

[1] Sources are cited in full in Appendix Table References, p. 346.

Note: n.a. = not applicable.

[2] An expanded version of this table, elaborating on statistical data used in the chapter, is included in the diskette accompanying this publication (see the Excel file directory RNF-DATA).

APPENDIX TABLE 2[1]

RURAL NON-FARM EMPLOYMENT: STUDIES REVIEWED

Region/country	Year	Source[2]
ASIA		
Bangladesh	1979/81	Islam (1984)
	1983/84	Varma & Kuhmar (1996)
	1984/85	
	1990/91	
India	1981	Islam (1984)
Indonesia	1976	Tambunan (1997)
	1980	
	1985	
	1992	
	1980	Kasryno (1986)
	1980/81	Kasryno (1986)
	1980	Islam (1984)
	1971	Kasryno (1986)
	1976	
	1982	
Malaysia	1980	Islam (1984)
Pakistan	1979/81	Islam (1984)
	1979/81	Arif, Ahmed & Jannison (1982)
Philippines	1982	Islam (1984)
Sri Lanka	1979/81	Islam (1984)
Thailand	1979/81	Islam (1984)
LATIN AMERICA		
Bolivia	1976	Klein (1992)
	1988	
Brazil	1970	Graziano da Silva (1995)
	1980	
	1981	
	1990	
	1995	Graziano da Silva & Eduardo del Grossi (1997)
Chile	1970	Klein (1992)
	1982	
Colombia	1964	Klein (1992)
	1973	
Costa Rica	1973	Klein (1992)
	1984	
Cuba	1970	Klein (1992)
	1981	

Region/country	Year	Source[2]
Ecuador	1995	Lanjouw (1997)
	1974	Klein (1992)
	1990	
	1982	de Janvry & Glikman (1991)
El Salvador	1971	Klein (1992)
	1975	
Guatemala	1980	CEPAL (1985)
	1964	Klein (1992)
	1973	
	1989	Weller (1997)
Haiti	1971	Klein (1992)
	1982	
Honduras	1974	Klein (1992)
	1988	
Mexico	1970	Klein (1992)
	1980	
Nicaragua	1950	Klein (1992)
	1971	
Panama	1970	Klein (1992)
	1980	
	1989	Weller (1997)
Paraguay	1972	Klein (1992)
	1982	
Peru	n.a.	Escobal & Valdivia (1997)
	1972	Klein (1992)
	1981	
Uruguay	1975	Klein (1992)
	1985	
Venezuela	1971	Klein (1992)
	1981	
	1992	FUSADES (1996)

[1] An expanded version of this table, elaborating on statistical data used in the chapter, is included in the diskette accompanying this publication (see the Excel file directory RNF-DATA).
[2] Sources are cited in full in Appendix Table References, p. 346.
Note: n.a. = not applicable.

APPENDIX TABLE 3[1]

RURAL NON-FARM HOUSEHOLD INCOME OVER INCOME OR LAND STRATA: STUDIES REVIEWED

Region/country	Year	Source[2]
AFRICA		
Botswana	1985/86	Valentine (1993)
Burkina Faso	1981-85	Reardon et al. (1994)
Ethiopia	1989/90	Webb & Reardon (1992)
Gambia	1985/86	von Braun, Puetz & Webb (1989)
Kenya	1974/75	Collier & Lal (1984)
Lesotho	1976	Low (1986)
Mozambique	1991	Tschirley & Weber (1994)
Niger	1989/90	Hopkins & Reardon (1993)
Rwanda	1991	Reardon & Clay (1998)
Senegal	1988/90	Kelly et al. (1993)
ASIA		
India	n.a.	Chadha (1986)
	1957/58	Lanjouw & Stern (1993)
	1962/63	
	1974/75	
	1983/84	
	1968/69	Hazell & Haggblade (1991)
	1970/71	
	1975/76-1979/80	Walker, Singh & Binswanger (1983)
Indonesia	n.a.	Hafid (1979)
Japan	1978	Saith (1986)
Pakistan	1968	Anderson & Leiserson (1980)
	1986/89	Adams (1994)
	1986/89	Garcia & Alderman (1993)
	1979/80	Arif, Ahmed & Jannison (1982)
Philippines	1984/85	Bouis & Haddad (1990)
	1972	Anderson & Leiserson (1980)
Republic of Korea	1970	Choi (1997)
	1996	
Viet Nam	1992/93	Government of Viet Nam (1994)
LATIN AMERICA		
Argentina	1996	Wiens (1997)
Ecuador	1995	Lanjouw (1997)
El Salvador	1995	Lopez (1996)
Mexico	1984	de Janvry et al. (1995)
	1989	

Region/country	Year	Source[3]
	1994	de Janvry, Gordillo de Anda & Sadoulet (1997)
	1986	Marsh *in* de Janvry *et al.* (1995)
	1984	de Janvry *et al.* (1995)

[1] An expanded version of this table, elaborating on statistical data used in the chapter, is included in the diskette accompanying this publication (see the Excel file directory RNF-DATA).

[2] Sources are cited in full in Appendix Table References, p. 346.

Note: n.a. = not applicable.

APPENDIX TABLE REFERENCES

Abedullah. 1993. The role and nature of risk in alternative cropping patterns in Claveria, northern Mindanao, the Philippines. Los Baños, University of the Philippines. (M.Sc. thesis)

Adams, R.H.J. 1994. Non-farm income and inequality in rural Pakistan: a decomposition analysis. *Journal of Development Studies*, 31(1): 110-133.

Ahmed, M.U. 1995/96. Development of rural non-farm activities: a dynamic approach to poverty alleviation in rural Asia. *Regional Development Studies*, 2(Winter): 1-22.

Anderson, D. & Leiserson, M.W. 1980. Rural nonfarm employment in developing countries. *Economic Development and Cultural Change*, 28(2): 227-248.

Arif, M., Ahmed, B. & Jannison, M. 1982. Demographic employment and wage patterns. In *Expansion of employment and income through local resource mobilisation*. Bangkok, ILO-ARTEP.

Balagot, Q.M. 1974. A Study of Financing Small-Farm Operations in Mindanao, 1969-1970. Los Baños, University of the Philippines. (M.Sc. thesis)

Barrett, V., Lassiter, G., Wilcock, D., Baker, D. & Crawford, E. 1982. *Animal traction in eastern Upper Volta: a technical, economic and institutional analysis*. International Development Paper Report No. 4. East Lansing, USA, Michigan State University.

Bouis, H. & Haddad, L.J. 1990. *Effects of agricultural commercialization on land tenure, household resource allocation and nutrition in the Philippines*. Research Report No. 79. Washington, DC, IFPRI.

Chadha, G.K. 1986. Off-farm economic structure of agriculturally growing regions: a study of Indian Punjab. *In* R.T. Shand, ed. *Off-farm employment in the development of rural Asia*. Canberra, National Centre for Development Studies, Australian National University.

Choi, J.-S. 1997. Policies promoting rural non-farm activities in rural development programs in Korea after the Uruguay Round. Paper presented at the 23rd Conference of the IAAE, August 1997, Sacramento, CA, USA.

Chopak, C.J. 1991. Determinants of rural incomes in communal areas of Zimbabwe: household food security implications. East Lansing, USA, Michigan State University. (Ph.D. Dissertation)

Collier, P. & Lal, D. 1984. Why poor people get rich: Kenya 1960-79. *World Development*, 12(10): 1007-1018.

Collier, P., Radwan, S., Wangwe, S. & Wagner, A. 1990. *Labour and poverty in rural Tanzania: Ujamaa and rural development in the Republic of Tanzania*. Oxford, UK, Clarendon Press.

David, C., Cordova, V. & Otsuka, K. 1994. Technology change, land reform and income distribution in the Philippines. *In* C. David & K. Otsuka, eds. *Modern rice technology and income distribution in Asia*. Los Baños, IRRI.

de Janvry, A., Chiriboga, M., Colmenares, H., Hintermeister, A., Howe, G., Irigoyen, R., Monares, A., Rello, F., Sadoulet, E., Secco, J., van der Pluijm, T. & Varese, S. 1995. *Reformas del sector agrícola y el campesinado en México*. San José, IFAD/IICA.

de Janvry, A. & Glikman, P. 1991. *Encadenamientos de producción en la economía campesina en el Ecuador.* San José, IFAD/IICA.

de Janvry, A., Gordillo de Anda, G. & Sadoulet, E. 1997. *Mexico's second agrarian reform: household and community responses, 1990-1994.* San Diego, USA, La Jolla, Center for US-Mexican Studies, University of California.

ECLAC. 1985. *Inestabilidad y complementariedad de las ocupaciones rurales en Guatemala.* Report No. 269. Santiago de Chile, PREALC.

Escobal, J. & Valdivia, M. 1997. Trabajo en el hogar y trabajo asalariado en las economías rurales del Perú. Los mercados rurales de trabajo en el Perú. Report No. 18-0572. Lima, Grupo de Análisis para el Desarrollo (GRADE).

Estudillo, J.P. & Otsuka, K. 1998. Green revolution, human capital and off-farm employment: changing sources of income among farm households in central Luzon, 1966-94. *Economic Development and Cultural Change* (forthcoming).

FAO. 1992. *Yunnan (Simao) Minority Areas Agricultural Development Project, Socio-economic and Production Systems Diagnostic Study.* FAO/IFAD Cooperative Programme Report Report No. 64/92. Rome.

Figueroa, A. 1987. Introducion. *In* J. Portocarrero Maisch, ed. *Los hogares rurales en el Perú.* Lima, Grupo de Análisis de Política Agrícola Proyecto PADI. Peruvian Ministry of Agriculture and Fundación Friedrich Ebert.

Francis, E. & Hoddinott, J. 1993. Migration and differentiation in western Kenya: a tale of two sub-locations. *Journal of Development Studies,* 30 (October) (1): 115-145.

FUSADES. 1996. Encuesta de desarrollo rural. El Salvador.

Garcia, M. & Alderman, H. 1993. *Poverty, household food security, and nutrition in rural Pakistan.* Research Report No. 96. Washington, DC, IFPRI.

Government of Viet Nam. 1994. *Viet Nam Living Standards Survey.* Hanoi, State Planning Committee, General Statistical Office.

Graziano da Silva, J. 1995. Urbanização e pobreza no campo. In *Agropecuaria e agroindustria no Brasil: Ajuste, Situaço Atual e Perspectivas,* p. 127-170.

Graziano da Silva, J. & Eduardo Del Grossi, M. 1997. A evolução de emprego não agricola no meio rural brasileiro, 1992-1995. *Revista Indicadores Econômicos de Fundação de Economia e Estatística* (Porto Alegre), 25: 105-126.

Hafid, A. 1979. An economic analysis of institutional changes: the case of the rice harvesting system in Java. Los Baños, University of the Philippines. (Ph.D. Dissertation)

Hayami, Y., Kikuchi, M., Bambo, L. & Marciano, E. 1990. *Transformation of a Laguna village in the two decades of the green revolution.* Research Paper Report No. 142. Los Baños, IRRI.

Hazell, P.B.R. & Haggblade, S. 1991. Rural-urban growth linkages in India. *India Journal of Agricultural Economics,* 46(4): 515-529.

Hopkins, J. & Reardon, T. 1993. *Agricultural price policy reform impacts and food aid targeting in Niger.* Washington, DC, IFPRI. (mimeo)

Hossain, M. 1987. *The assault that failed: a profile of absolute poverty in six villages of Bangladesh.* Geneva, UNRISD.

347

Hossain, M. 1994. Production environments, modern variety adoption and income distribution in Bangladesh. *In* C. David & K. Otsuka, eds. *Modern rice technology and income distribution in Asia.* Los Baños, IRRI.

IFAD. 1991. *Proyecto de apoyo a pequeños agricultores de la zona semi-árida de los estados de Falcón y Lara, República de Venezuela. Encuesta socioeconómica, estudio de base.* Rome.

Islam, R. 1984. Rural industrialisation and employment in Asia: issues and evidence. *In* R. Islam, ed. *Strategies for alleviating poverty in rural Asia.* Los Baños, IRRI.

Isvilinonda, S. & Wattanutchariya, S. 1994. Modern variety adoption, factor-price differential and income distribution in Thailand. *In* C. David & K. Otsuka, eds. *Modern rice technology and income distribution in Asia.* Los Baños, IRRI.

Jatileksono, T. 1994. Varietal improvements, productivity change and income distribution: the case of Lampung, Indonesia. *In* C. David & K. Otsuka, eds. *Modern rice technology and income distribution in Asia.* Los Baños, IRRI.

Jiang, J. & Luo, X. 1987. Changes in the income of Chinese peasants since 1978. *In* J. Longworth, ed. *China's rural development miracle: with international comparisons.* Brisbane, Australia, University of Queensland Press.

Kasryno, F. 1986. Structural changes in rural employment and agricultural wage in Indonesia. *In* Y.-B. Choe & F.C. Lo, eds. *Rural industrialization and non-farm activities of Asian farmers.* Seoul, Korea Rural Economics Institute.

Kelly, V., Reardon, T., Diagana, B., Gaye, M. and McNeilly, L. 1993. *Final Report of IFPRI/ISRA Project on Consumption and Supply Impacts of Agricultural Price Policies in Senegal.* Washington, DC, IFPRI. (mimeo)

Keyler, S. 1996. Economics of the Namibian Millet Subsector. East Lansing, USA, Michigan State University. (Ph.D. Dissertation)

Klein, E. 1992. *El empleo rural no agricola en America Latina.* Report No. 364. Santiago de Chile, PREALC.

Lanjouw, P. 1997. Rural non-agricultural employment and poverty in Latin America: evidence from Ecuador and El Salvador. *In* R. Lopez & A. Valdes, eds. *Rural poverty in Latin America: analytics, new empirical evidence and policy.* Washington, DC, World Bank.

Lanjouw, P. & Stern, N. 1993. Markets, opportunities and changes in inequality in Palanpur 1957-1984. *In* A. Braverman, K. Hoff & J. Stiglitz, eds. *The economics of rural organization: theory, practice and policy.* New York, Oxford University Press.

Lin, J.Y. 1994. The nature and impact of hybrid rice in China. *In* C. David & K. Otsuka, eds. *Modern rice technology and income distribution in Asia.* Los Baños, IRRI.

Livingstone, I. 1991. A reassessment of Kenya's rural and urban informal sector. *World Development Report,* 19(6): 651-670.

Lopez, R. 1997. Rural poverty in El Salvador: a quantitative analysis. *In* R. Lopez & A. Valdes, eds. *Rural poverty in Latin America: analytics, new empirical evidence, and policy.* Washington, DC, World Bank.

Low, A. 1986. *Agricultural development in southern Africa: farm household economics and the food crisis.* London, James Curry.

Matlon, P. 1979. *Income distribution among farmers in northern Nigeria.* African Rural Economy Paper Report No. 18. East Lansing, USA, Michigan State University.

Nattrass, N. & Nattrass, J. 1990. The homelands and rural development. *Development Southern Africa,* 7(October): 517-534.

Norman, D. 1973. *Economic analysis of agricultural production and labour utilization among the Hausa in the north of Nigeria.* African Rural Employment Paper Report No. 4. East Lansing, USA, Michigan State University.

Oshima, H. 1986. Levels and trends of farm families' non-agricultural incomes at different stages of monsoon development. *In* Y.-B. Choe & F.C. Lo, eds. *Rural industrialization and non-farm activities of Asian famers.* Seoul, Korea Rural Economics Institute.

Peters, P.E. 1992. *Monitoring the effects of grain market liberalization on the income, food security and nutrition of rural households in Zomba South, Malawi.* Cambridge, Mass., USA, Harvard Institute for International Development (mimeo).

Ramasamy, C., Paramasivam, P. & Kandaswamy, A. 1994. Irrigation quality, modern variety adoption and income distribution: the case of Tamil Nadu in India. *In* C. David & K. Otsuka, eds. *Modern rice technology and income distribution in Asia.* Los Baños, IRRI.

Ranis, G. & Stewart, F. 1993. Rural non-agricultural activities in development. *Journal of Development Economics,* 40: 75-101.

Reardon, T. & Clay, D. 1998. *Income diversification in rural Rwanda.* East Lansing, USA, Department of Agricultural Economics, Michigan State University. (mimeo)

Reardon, T., Fall, A., Kelly, V., Delgado, C., Matlon, P., Hopkins, J. & Badiane, O. 1994. Is income diversification agriculture-led in the West African semi-arid tropics? The nature, causes, effects, distribution and production linkages of off-farm activities. *In* A. Atsain, S. Wangwe & A.G. Drabek, eds. *Economic policy experience in Africa: what have we learned?* Nairobi, African Economic Research Consortium.

Reardon, T. & Taylor, J.E. 1996. Agroclimatic shock, income inequality and poverty: evidence from Burkina Faso. *World Development,* 24(4): 901-914.

Saith, A. 1986. Contrasting experiences in rural industrialisation: are the East Asian successes transferable? *In* R. Islam, ed. *Rural industrialisation and employment in Asia.* New Delhi, ILO-ARTEP.

Shand, R.T. 1986. Agricultural development, non-farm employment and rural income distribution: a case study in Kelantan Malaysia. *In* Y.B. Choe & F.C. Lo, eds. *Rural industrialization and non-farm activities of Asian farmers.* Seoul, Korea Rural Economics Institute.

Sundberg, S. 1989. *OHV Food Consumption and Expenditure Survey: preliminary results on income sources in the OHV.* Research Report. East Lansing, USA, Michigan State University.

Tambunan, M. 1997. Non-agricultural economy in Indonesia. Paper presented at the 23rd Conference of the IAAE, August 1997, Sacramento, CA, USA.

Teklu, T., von Braun, J. & Zaki, E. 1991. *Drought and famine relationships in Sudan: policy implications.* Research Report No. 88. Washington, DC, IFPRI.

Tschirley, D. L. & Weber, M.T. 1994. Food security strategies under extremely adverse conditions: the determinants of household income and consumption in rural Mozambique. *World Development,* 22(2): 159-173.

Uphadhyaya, H. & Thapa, G. 1994. Modern variety adoption, wage differentials and income distribution in Nepal. *In* C. David & K. Otsuka, eds. *Modern rice technology and income distribution in Asia.* Los Baños, IRRI.

Valentine, T.R. 1993. Drought, transfer entitlements and income distribution: the Botswana experience. *World Development,* 21(1): 109-126.

Varma, S. & Kumar, P. 1996. Rural non-farm employment in Bangladesh. Paper presented at the BIDS – World Bank Workshop on Stimulating Growth through Rural Non-Farm Activities in Bangladesh: Review of the Experience and Search for a Policy Agenda, 31 July 1996, Dhaka.

von Braun, J., Puetz, D. & Webb, P. 1989. *Irrigation technology and commercialization of rice in the Gambia: effects on income and nutrition.* Research Report No. 75. Washington, DC, IFPRI.

Walker, T.S., Singh, M. & Binswanger, H.P. 1983. *Fluctuations in income in three villages of India's semi-arid tropics.* ICRISAT.

Webb, P. & Reardon, T. 1992. Drought impact and household response in East and West Africa. *Quarterly Journal of International Agriculture,* 3(July-September): 230-246.

Weller, J. 1997. *El empleo rural no agropecuario en el Istmo Centroamericano.* ECLAC Report No. 62. Santiago de Chile, ECLAC.

Wiens, T.B. 1997. *Rural poverty in Argentina.* Washington, DC, World Bank. (mimeo)

NOTES

1   Throughout this chapter "farm activity" will be used synonymously with "agriculture" and "non-farm activity" synonymously with "non-agricultural activity".

2   Farm households are defined as rural households that carry out some farming activities.

3   The distinction between "push" and "pull" factors is not always precise. Indeed, when considering the relative "merits" of the two sectors, "pull" and "push" factors are interchangeable. In some cases, however (e.g. the risk motive or credit/cash constraints), the distinction is clearer: the risk of farming and lack of insurance and credit markets may "push" farm households to devote some of their productive resources to RNF activities, which produce a more stable income even though the returns expected from the farm activity are higher on average (i.e. when averaged over several periods).

4   Agroclimatic zones are characterized by common rainfall patterns, soil characteristics, sunlight and temperature, and hence by a common potential for agriculture.

5   See note 2.

6   Data on non-farm income shares are based exclusively on survey case studies, while the data on non-farm employment shares are based on a combination of occupation censuses and survey data from Asia and Latin America.

7   A complete documentation of the statistical data used in the analysis can be found in spreadsheet format on the accompanying diskette, which also includes a set of international agricultural time series. The Excel files containing these data are located in the directory RNF-DATA.

8   The coefficient of variation is a statistical indicator of the degree to which the various observations in a sample are dispersed around its mean. The smaller the coefficient of variation, the closer the observations on the whole are to the mean; the larger the coefficient of variation, the more they are dispersed around the mean value of the sample.

9   S. Haggblade, P. Hazell and J. Brown. 1989. Farm-non-farm linkages in rural sub-Saharan Africa. *World Development*, 17(8): 1173-1201.

10 Further reasons why it is difficult to make a comparison between the two sources are: i) the employment shares are derived from official aggregate statistics, while the income shares have been derived from selected case studies; ii) official employment statistics tend to include both rural towns and the countryside while the case study income information mainly refers to the countryside.

11 T. Reardon, A. Fall, V. Kelly, C. Delgado, P. Matlon, J. Hopkins and O. Badiane. 1994. Is income diversification agriculture-led in the West African semi-arid tropics? The nature, causes, effects, distribution and production linkages of off-farm activities. *In* A. Atsain, S. Wangwe and A.G. Drabek, eds. *Economic policy experience in Africa: what have we learned?*, p. 207-230. Nairobi, African Economic Research Consortium.

12 K. Otsuka. 1998. Rural industrialization in East Asia. *In* Y. Hayami and M. Aoki, eds. *The institutional foundation of East Asian economic development.* London, Macmillan.

13 Details on the methodology and findings can be found in A. Klein. 1992. *El empleo rural no agricola en América Latina.* Report No. 364. Santiago, PREALC.

14 Ibid.

15 D. Mead. 1994. The contribution of small enterprises to employment growth in southern and eastern Africa. *World Development*, 22(12): 1881-1894.

16 K. Otsuka, op. cit., note 12.

17 J.A. Schaffner. 1993. Rural labor legislation and permanent agricultural employment in northeastern Brazil. *World Development*, 21(5): 705-719.

18 See R. Adams. 1996. *Remittances, income distribution and rural asset accumulation.* Research Report No. 17. Washington, DC, IFPRI.

19 X. Milicevic and J. Berdegue. 1998. Non-farm employment linked directly and indirectly to the agro-industrial boom: the horticultural belt of central Chile. Paper presented at the III Simposio Latinoamericano de Investigación y Extensión en Sistemas Agropecuarios, 19-21 August 1998, Lima, RIMISP.

20 E. Francis and J. Hoddinott. 1993. Migration and differentiation in western Kenya: a tale of two sub-locations. *Journal of Development Studies*, 30(1): 115-145.

21 L. Daniels. 1995. Entry, exit and growth among small-scale enterprises in Zimbabwe. Michigan State University, East Lansing, USA. (Ph.D. Dissertation)

22 This comparison could be made in the case of household studies reported from Botswana, Ethiopia, Kenya, Malawi, Rwanda, the Sudan and Zimbabwe.

23 C. Liedholm and D. Mead. 1987. *Small-scale industries in developing countries: empirical evidence and policy implications.* Report No. 9. Department of Agricultural Economics. Michigan State University, East Lansing, USA; and D. Mead. 1994. The contribution of small

enterprises to employment growth in southern and eastern Africa.
World Development, 22(12): 1881-1984.

24 The latter argument dates back to the British economist David
Ricardo whose model reflected circumstances in nineteenth-century
United Kingdom but is still widely applicable in developing country
agriculture today. In Ricardo's model, rising food costs (driven by
rising farm production costs from diminishing returns to labour, i.e.
declining factor productivity) drive up the subsistence wage, hence
the market wage, which drives down profits and investment and
growth in the non-farm economy. By contrast, "cheap food" was an
important factor – and agricultural success a preliminary condition –
in the East Asian rural industrialization from the 1950s (A. Saith.
1986. Contrasting experiences in rural industrialization: are the East
Asian successes transferable? *In* R. Islam, ed. *Rural industrialization and
employment in Asia.* New Delhi, ILO). The converse also holds – high
food costs have been a drag on African industrialization, whether
rural or urban (M. Lipton and M. Lipton. 1993. Creating rural
livelihoods: some lessons for South Africa from experience
elsewhere. *World Development*, 21(9): 1515-1548).

25 R. Ahmed and M. Hossain. 1990. *Developmental impact of rural
infrastructure in Bangladesh.* Research Report No. 83. Washington, DC,
IFPRI.

26 H. Oshima. 1986. Levels and trends of farm families' non-agricultural
incomes at different stages of monsoon development. *In* Y.B. Choe
and F.C. Lo, eds. *Rural industrialization and non-farm activities of Asian
farmers.* Seoul, Korea Rural Economics Institute.

27 Y.B. Choe. 1986. M-cycle hypothesis, non-farm activities and rural
industrialization in the Asian monsoon economy. *In* Choe and Lo, op.
cit., note 26.

28 See M.U. Ahmed and N. Rustagi. 1987. Marketing and price incentives
in African and Asian countries: a comparison. *In* E. Elz, ed. *Agricultural
marketing strategy and pricing policy.* Washington, DC, World Bank.

29 Reardon *et al.*, op. cit., note 11.

30 Saith, op. cit., note 24.

31 J. Dione, J.-C. Le Vallée, J. Staatz, J. Tefft, M. Yade, A. Chohin and B.
Kante. 1997. *Lessons from the impact of the devaluation of the CFA franc
on agri-food subsectors in West Africa.* Policy Brief. Department of
Agricultural Economics, Michigan State University, East Lansing, USA.

32 P. Collier and D. Lal. 1984. Why poor people get rich: Kenya 1960-79.
World Development, 12(10): 1007-1018.

33 R. H. J. Adams. 1994. Non-farm income and inequality in rural
Pakistan: a decomposition analysis. *Journal of Development Studies*,
31(1): 110-133.

34 J.E. Taylor and A. Yunez-Naude. 1998. *Selectivity and the returns to schooling in a diversified rural economy.* University of California at Davis, Davis, USA. (mimeo)

35 P. Lanjouw and N. Stern. 1993. Markets, opportunities and changes in inequality in Palanpur, 1957-1984. *In* A. Braverman, K. Hoff and J. Stiglitz, eds. *The economics of rural organization: theory, practice and policy.* New York, Oxford University Press.

36 J.P. Estudillo and K. Otsuka. 1998. Green revolution, human capital and off-farm employment: changing sources of income among farm households in central Luzon, 1966-94. *Economic Development and Cultural Change* (forthcoming).

37 For the purpose of this chapter, agro-industrial activities are defined as the collective set of production linkage activities, i.e. farm input provision and agroprocessing and distribution.

38 J. von Braun and R. Pandya-Lorch. 1991. *Income sources of malnourished people in rural areas: microlevel information and policy implications.* Working Paper No. 5. Washington, DC, IFPRI.

39 A. de Janvry, G. Gordillo de Anda and E. Sadoulet. 1997. *Mexico's second agrarian reform: household and community responses, 1990-1994.* La Jolla, Center for US-Mexican Studies, University of California, San Diego, USA.

40 M.U. Ahmed. 1995/96. Development of rural non-farm activities: a dynamic approach to poverty alleviation in rural Asia. *Regional Development Studies*, 2(winter): 1-22.

41 T. Reardon. 1997. Using evidence of household income diversification to inform study of the rural nonfarm labor market in Africa. *World Development*, 25(5): 735-748.

42 The Gini coefficient is a statistical indicator that measures the extent to which the actual income distribution diverges from a hypothetical perfectly equal distribution. The larger the Gini coefficient is, the more unequal income distribution is.

43 In this case, in a comparison of Gini coefficients, the coefficient for total income is higher when non-farm income is included than when it is not or, if using the Gini decomposition approach, marginal changes in non-farm income – when all other factors are constant – increase the Gini coefficient.

44 T. Reardon and J.E. Taylor. 1996. Agroclimatic shock, income inequality and poverty: evidence from Burkina Faso. *World Development*, 24(4): 901-914.

45 Op. cit., note 35.

46 Op. cit., note 44.

47 G.K. Chadha. 1986. Off-farm economic structure of agriculturally growing regions: a study of Indian Punjab. *In* R.T. Shand, ed. *Off-farm employment in the development of rural Asia.* Canberra, National Centre for Development Studies, Australian National University.

48 A. Narongchai. 1981. *Rural off-farm employment in Thailand.* Bangkok, Industrial Management Company, Ltd.

49 For a report on Mexico, see J.E. Taylor. 1992. Remittances and inequality reconsidered: direct, indirect and intertemporal effects. *Journal of Policy Modeling,* 14(2): 187-208; for a report on Africa, see T. Reardon, E. Crawford and V. Kelly. 1994b. Links between nonfarm income and farm investments in African households: adding the capital market perspective. *American Journal of Agricultural Economics,* 76(5): 1172-1176.

50 Francis and Hoddinott, op. cit., note 20.

51 C. André and J.-P. Platteau. 1998. Land tenure under unbearable stress: Rwanda caught in the Malthusian trap. *Journal of Economic Behavior and Organization,* 34(1).

52 Estudillo and Otsuka, op. cit., note 36.

53 In some countries, an infrastructural instrument that has been used, with mixed results, to effect RNF company starts and the relocation of businesses to rural areas is the establishment of industrial parks or districts (such as in South Africa and the Republic of Korea and in some developed countries, such as Italy).

54 For a further discussion, see V. Kelly, J. Hopkins, T. Reardon and E. Crawford. 1995. *Improving the measurement and analysis of African agricultural productivity: promoting complementarities between micro and macro data.* MSU International Development Paper No. 16. East Lansing, USA, Michigan State University.

55 The assessment of such effects for different agro-industries and products is the subject of a current FAO project on farm/non-farm linkages.

56 A. Schejtman. 1996. *Agroindustria: alcances conceptuales para una política de estimulo a su articulación.* LC/R Report No. 1660. Santiago de Chile, CEPAL.

57 Ibid.

58 For the case of West Africa, see N.N. Dembele and K. Savadogo. 1996. *The need to link soil fertility management to input/output market development in West Africa: key issues.* Paper presented at the

International Fertilizer Development Center Seminar, 19-22 November, Lomé, Togo.

59 FAO. 1996. *Ciudades intermedias y desarrollo rural: el caso de Zamora, Michoacán (Mexico)*. By F. Rello. Santiago de Chile, FAO Regional Office for Latin America and the Caribbean.

60 Op. cit., note 24.

ANNEX

TABLES

COUNTRIES AND TERRITORIES USED FOR STATISTICAL PURPOSES

Developed countries	Countries in transition	Developing countries			
		Sub-Saharan Africa	Asia and the Pacific/ Far East and Oceania	Latin America and the Caribbean	Near East and North Africa
Albania	Albania	Angola	American Samoa	Anguilla	Afghanistan
Andorra		Benin	Bangladesh	Antigua and Barbuda	Algeria
Armenia	Armenia	Botswana	Bhutan	Argentina	Bahrain
Australia		Burkina Faso	British Virgin Islands	Aruba	Cyprus
Austria		Burundi	Brunei Darussalam	Bahamas	Egypt
Azerbaijan	Azerbaijan	Cameroon	Cambodia	Barbados	Gaza Strip
Belarus	Belarus	Cape Verde	China	Belize	Iran, Islamic Rep.
Belgium/ Luxembourg		Central African Rep.	Cocos Islands	Bermuda	Iraq
Bosnia and Herzegovina	Bosnia and Herzegovina	Chad	Cook Islands	Bolivia	Jordan
Bulgaria	Bulgaria	Comoros	East Timor	Brazil	Kuwait
Canada		Congo	Fiji	Cayman Islands	Lebanon
Croatia	Croatia	Côte d'Ivoire	French Polynesia	Chile	Libyan Arab Jamahiriya
Czech Republic	Czech Republic	Democratic Republic of the Congo	Guam	Colombia	Morocco
Denmark		Djibouti	India	Costa Rica	Oman
Estonia	Estonia	Equatorial Guinea	Indonesia	Cuba	Qatar
Faeroe Islands		Eritrea	Kiribati	Dominica	Saudi Arabia
Finland		Ethiopia	Korea, Dem. People's Rep.	Dominican Rep.	Syrian Arab Rep.
France		Gabon	Korea, Rep.	Ecuador	Tunisia
Georgia	Georgia	Gambia	Lao People's Dem. Rep.	El Salvador	Turkey
Germany		Ghana	Macau	Falkland Islands (Malvinas)	United Arab Emirates
Gibraltar		Guinea	Malaysia	French Guiana	West Bank
Greece		Guinea-Bissau	Maldives	Grenada	Yemen
Greenland		Kenya	Marshall Islands	Guadeloupe	
Hungary	Hungary	Lesotho	Micronesia, Fed. States	Guatemala	
Iceland		Liberia	Mongolia	Guyana	
Ireland		Madagascar	Myanmar	Haiti	
Israel		Malawi	Nauru	Honduras	
Italy		Mali	Nepal	Jamaica	
Japan		Mauritania	New Caledonia	Martinique	
Kazakhstan	Kazakhstan	Mauritius	Niue	Mexico	
Kyrgyzstan	Kyrgyzstan	Mozambique	Norfolk Islands	Montserrat	

Developed countries	Countries in transition	Developing countries			
		Sub-Saharan Africa	Asia and the Pacific/ Far East and Oceania	Latin America and the Caribbean	Near East and North Africa
Latvia	Latvia	Namibia	Northern Mariana Islands	Netherlands Antilles	
Liechtenstein		Niger	Pakistan	Nicaragua	
Lithuania	Lithuania	Nigeria	Palau	Panama	
Malta		Réunion	Papua New Guinea	Paraguay	
Monaco		Rwanda	Philippines	Peru	
Netherlands		Saint Helena	Samoa	Puerto Rico	
New Zealand		Sao Tome and Principe	Singapore	Saint Kitts and Nevis	
Norway		Senegal	Solomon Islands	Saint Lucia	
Poland	Poland	Seychelles	Sri Lanka	Saint Vincent and the Grenadines	
Portugal		Sierra Leone	Taiwan Province of China	Suriname	
Republic of Moldova	Republic of Moldova	Somalia	Thailand	Trinidad and Tobago	
Romania	Romania	Sudan	Tokelau	Turks and Caicos Islands	
Russian Federation	Russian Federation	Swaziland	Tonga	United States Virgin Islands	
San Marino		Togo	Vanuatu	Venezuela	
Slovakia	Slovakia	Uganda	Viet Nam	Uruguay	
Slovenia	Slovenia	United Republic of Tanzania	Wallis and Futuna Islands		
Saint Pierre and Miquelon		Zambia	Tuvalu		
South Africa		Zimbabwe			
Spain					
Sweden					
Switzerland					
Tajikistan	Tajikistan				
The Former Yugoslav Republic of Macedonia	The Former Yugoslav Republic of Macedonia				
Turkmenistan	Turkmenistan				
Ukraine	Ukraine				
United Kingdom					
United States					
Uzbekistan	Uzbekistan				
Yugoslavia	Yugoslavia				

Special chapters

In addition to the usual review of the recent world food and agricultural situation, each issue of this report since 1957 has included one or more special studies on problems of longer-term interest. Special chapters in earlier issues have covered the following subjects:

1957   Factors influencing the trend of food consumption
            Postwar changes in some institutional factors affecting agriculture

1958   Food and agricultural developments in Africa south of the Sahara
            The growth of forest industries and their impact on the world's forests

1959   Agricultural incomes and levels of living in countries at different stages of economic development
            Some general problems of agricultural development in less-developed countries in the light of postwar experience

1960   Programming for agricultural development

1961   Land reform and institutional change
            Agricultural extension, education and research in Africa, Asia and Latin America

1962   The role of forest industries in the attack on economic underdevelopment
            The livestock industry in less-developed countries

1963   Basic factors affecting the growth of productivity in agriculture
            Fertilizer use: spearhead of agricultural development

1964   Protein nutrition: needs and prospects
            Synthetics and their effects on agricultural trade

1966   Agriculture and industrialization
            Rice in the world food economy

1967   Incentives and disincentives for farmers in developing countries
            The management of fishery resources

1968   Raising agricultural productivity in developing countries through technological improvement
            Improved storage and its contribution to world food supplies

1969   Agricultural marketing improvement programmes: some lessons from recent experience
            Modernizing institutions to promote forestry development

1970   Agriculture at the threshold of the Second Development Decade
1971   Water pollution and its effects on living aquatic resources and fisheries

FAO Agricultural Policy and Economic Development Series

AGRICULTURE AND ECONOMIC DEVELOPMENT ANALYSIS DIVISION AND POLICY ASSISTANCE DIVISION

1   Searching for common ground – European Union enlargement and agricultural policy (K. Hathaway and D. Hathaway, eds, 1997)
2   Agricultural and rural development policy in Latin America – New directions and new challenges (A. de Janvry, N. Key and E. Sadoulet, 1997)
3   Food security strategies – The Asian experience (P. Timmer, 1997)
4   Guidelines for the integration of sustainable agriculture and rural development into agricultural policies (J.B. Hardaker, 1997)

In preparation

- Farm/non-farm linkages and income diversification in the developing countries: case studies in Africa and Latin America (T. Reardon and K. Stamoulis, eds)
- The role of agriculture in the transition to a market economy (K. Stamoulis and K. Frohberg, eds)

FAO Economic and Social Development Papers

AGRICULTURE AND ECONOMIC DEVELOPMENT ANALYSIS DIVISION*

65   Agricultural stabilization and structural adjustment policies in developing countries (A.H. Sarris, 1987)
66   Agricultural issues in structural adjustment programs (R.D. Norton, 1987)
84   Measures of protection: methodology, economic interpretation and policy relevance (P.L. Scandizzo, 1989)
90   The impact of stabilization and structural adjustment policies on the rural sector – case-studies of Côte d'Ivoire, Senegal, Liberia, Zambia and Morocco (P. Salin and E.-M. Claassen, 1991)
95   Guidelines for monitoring the impact of structural adjustment programmes on the agricultural sector (A.H. Sarris, 1990)
96   The effects of trade and exchange rate policies on production incentives in agriculture (C. Kirkpatrick and D. Diakosavvas, 1990)
98   Institutional changes in agricultural products and input markets and their impact on agricultural performance (A. Thomson, 1991)
99   Agricultural labour markets and structural adjustment in sub-Saharan Africa (L.D. Smith, 1991)
100 Structural adjustment and household welfare in rural areas – a micro-economic perspective (R. Gaiha, 1991)
103 The impact of structural adjustment on smallholders (J.-M. Boussard, 1992)
104 Structural adjustment policy sequencing in sub-Saharan Africa (L.D. Smith and N. Spooner, 1991)
105 The role of public and private agents in the food and agricultural sectors of developing countries (L.D. Smith and A. Thomson, 1991)

107 Land reform and structural adjustment in sub-Saharan Africa: controversies and guidelines (J.-Ph. Platteau, 1992). French version: Réforme agraire et ajustement structurel en Afrique subsaharienne: controverses et orientations

110 Agricultural sustainability: definition and implications for agricultural and trade policy (T. Young, 1992)

115 Design of poverty alleviation strategy in rural areas (R. Gaiha, 1993)

121 Policies for sustainable development: four essays (A. Markandya, 1994)

124 Structural adjustment and agriculture: African and Asian experiences (A. de Janvry and E. Sadoulet, 1994)

125 Transition and price stabilization policies in East European agriculture (E.-M. Claassen, 1994)

128 Agricultural taxation under structural adjustment (A.H. Sarris, 1994)

131 Trade patterns, cooperation and growth (P.L. Scandizzo, 1995)

132 The economics of international agreements for the protection of environmental and agricultural services (S. Barrett, 1996)

133 Implications of regional trade arrangements for agricultural trade (T. Josling, 1997)

134 Rural informal credit markets and the effectiveness of policy reform (A.H. Sarris, 1996)

135 International dynamics of national sugar policies (T.C. Earley and D.W. Westfall, 1996)

136 Growth theories, old and new, and the role of agriculture in economic development (N.S. Stern, 1996)

138 Economic development and environmental policy (S. Barrett, 1997)

139 Population pressure and management of natural resources. An economic analysis of traditional management of small-scale fishing (J.-M. Baland and J.-Ph. Platteau, 1996)

141 Economies in transition – Hungary and Poland (D.G. Johnson, 1997)

142 The political economy of the Common Market in milk and dairy products in the European Union (R.E. Williams, 1997)

• Halting degradation of natural resources. Is there a role for rural communities? (J.-M. Baland and J.-Ph. Platteau, 1996). Published by Oxford University Press

Note: Up to 1996, these papers were published by the former Policy Analysis Division.

In preparation

• Growth, trade and agriculture: an investigative survey (P.L. Scandizzo and M. Spinedi)

• Rural poverty, risk and development (M. Fafchamps)

To obtain the publications listed, please contact:
Sales and Marketing Group, Information Division
Food and Agriculture Organization of the United Nations
Viale delle Terme di Caracalla
00100 Rome, Italy
E-mail: publications-sales@fao.org
Tel.: (39 06) 57051
Fax: (39 06) 5705 3360

TIME SERIES FOR SOFA'98 DISKETTE
Instructions for use

As in the past years, *The State of Food and Agriculture 1998* includes a computer diskette containing time series data for about 150 countries and the necessary software, FAOSTAT TS, to access and display these data.

FAOSTAT TS
FAOSTAT TS software provides quick and easy access to structured annual time series databases. Even inexperienced computer users can use FAOSTAT TS, which does not require spreadsheet, graphics or database programs. FAOSTAT TS is fully menu-driven, so there are no commands to learn. Users can browse through and print graphs and tables, plot multiple-line graphs, fit trend lines and export data for use in other programs. FAOSTAT TS is trilingual (English, French, Spanish) and uses a standard menu format.

FAOSTAT TS software is in the public domain and may be freely distributed. The data files accompanying the software, however, are under FAO copyright, and users must attribute FAO as the source. FAO may provide only very limited support to users of this software and the accompanying data and cannot assist users who modify the software or data files. FAO disclaims all warrants of fitness for the software or data for a particular use.

Technical requirements
FAOSTAT TS software requires an IBM or compatible PC with a hard disk, DOS 3.0 or later version, 300 KB of available RAM and graphics capability. Graphics support is provided for all common graphics adapters (VGA, EGA, MCGA, CGA and Hercules monochrome).

FAOSTAT TS will print graphs on Epson dot matrix, Hewlett-Packard and compatible laser printers. To use FAOSTAT TS with other printers, users can enable their own graphics printing utility before starting the program. One such utility is GRAPHICS.COM in DOS 2.0 or later version.

Because of its use of DOS graphics modes, if FAOSTAT TS is run under MS-Windows or OS/2, it should be set to run in a full screen DOS session.

Installation
Before running FAOSTAT TS you must install the software and data files on your hard disk. Installation is automated through the INSTALL.BAT utility on the diskette.
- To install from drive A: to drive C:
  - Insert the diskette in drive A:
  - Type **A**: and press **ENTER**.
  - Type **INSTALL C**: and press **ENTER**.
  - Press any key.

A C:\SOFA98 directory is created and, after installation, you will already be in this directory.

Entering FAOSTAT TS

- To start the FAOSTAT TS software, if you are not already in the C:\SOFA98 directory (as after installation):
    - Change to this directory by typing **CD\SOFA98** and pressing **ENTER.**
    - From the command prompt in the SOFA98 directory, type **SOFA98** and press **ENTER.**

A graphics title screen will be displayed, followed by the main menu screen.

If FAOSTAT TS does not start, graphs do not display correctly or the menus are difficult to read, your computer may not be compatible with the default functions of FAOSTAT TS. The use of a command-line option may help. You may try to start FAOSTAT TS with the -E parameter (by typing **SOFA98-E**) to disable its use of expanded memory. You may also force the use of a particular graphics or text mode by typing its name as a parameter (e.g. -EGA would force the use of EGA mode graphics).

Language choices

The initial default language for FAOSTAT TS is English. To change the default language to French or Spanish:
- Go to the **FILE** menu.
- Select **LANGUAGE** using the **ARROW** key ($\downarrow$)and pressing ENTER.
- Select your choice of language and press **ENTER.**

The language selected will remain the default language until another is selected.

Navigating the menus

The main menu bar consists of FILE, DATA, GRAPH, TABLE and HELP menus. Most menu options are disabled until you open a data file. Navigate the menus by using the ARROW keys ($\uparrow \downarrow \leftarrow \rightarrow$) and make a selection by highlighting an item and pressing **ENTER.** To back out of a selection, press the **ESC** key.
- If you have a mouse, menu items can be selected with the mouse cursor. The left mouse button selects an item and the right mouse button acts as the **ESC** key.

After you have made a menu selection, the menu will redraw and highlight a possible next choice.
- Several short-cut keys are available throughout the program:

Key	Action
F1	HELP: Displays context-sensitive help text.
ESC	ESCAPE: Backs out of the current menu choice or exits the current graph or table.

ALT+N   NOTES: Displays text notes associated with the current data file, if the text file is available. This text may be edited. Notes will not appear while a graph is displayed.

ALT+X, ALT+Q   EXIT: Exits FAOSTAT TS immediately, without prompting.

Help
- You will see context-sensitive help displayed at the bottom of each screen. Press **F1** for more extensive help on a highlighted option.
- Select **HELP** from the main menu to access the help information. Introductory information on the software, help topics and an "About" summary screen are available from the **HELP** menu.
- The **HELP** menu options call up the same windows obtained by pressing the F1 key at any of the menu screens:
  - FAOSTAT TS displays the top-level help page.
  - TOPICS lists the help contents.
  - ABOUT shows summary program information.

Opening a data file
- To display a list of FAOSTAT TS data files:
  - Go to the **FILE** menu.
  - Select **OPEN.**
All of the FAOSTAT TS data files in the current directory are displayed. Initially, only SOFA98 will be present. Other FAOSTAT PC data files, version 3.0, can be used with FAOSTAT TS.
- Use the **ARROW** keys to highlight the file you wish to view and press **ENTER** to select it. Files are shown with the date of their last revision. You can also highlight your choice by typing the first letters of the file name. The current search string will appear in the lower left corner of the list.
- You can change the default data drive and directory from the file list by selecting the directory or drive of your choice.
If a current data file is open, loading in a new file will return FAOSTAT TS to its defaults (time trend, no trend line, no user-specified units or scalar). Only one file can be loaded at a time.
Once you have made a file selection, all the menu selections are activated.

Selecting a data series
- Use the **DATA** menu to select or modify a data series or to fit a statistical trend.
- Select a data series by choosing the name of a country and a data element from scrolling menus. The first entry displays a list of country names, the second entry displays a list of data item names and the third displays a list of data element names.
If you type the first letters of a name in a list, the menu selection bar will jump to the matching name. For example:

- Type **NEW** to skip to New Zealand.
- Press **ENTER** to select the highlighted name

Displaying graphs and graph options

The **GRAPH** menu allows you to view the data in chart form. You can display time trends and table or column profiles. Options under the **GRAPH** menu change the data series shown as well as its display.

For example, to show a plot of the data selected:
- Go to the **GRAPH** menu.
- Select **DISPLAY.**

Many options to modify, save or print a graph are available only while the graph is on-screen. Remember to use the F1 help key for a reminder of your options.

Graph action keys. You have several options when a graph is displayed:
- Press **ESC** to exit the graph and return to the main menu.
- Press **F1** for help on the graph action keys. The help box lists the choices available while a graph is on-screen. You must exit the help box before making a selection.
- Press the **ARROW** and (↑↓) **PAGEUP, PAGEDOWN** keys to change the series displayed.
- The plus key (+) allows you to add from one to three additional series to the one displayed. Press the **MINUS** key (-) to remove a series. To create a multiline chart:
  - Display an initial series.
  - Press the + key to add subsequent series to the chart.
- Press **A** to display a table of the axis data with statistics. Press **T** to show a table of the fitted trend data, the residuals and fit statistics (if a trend line is selected, see below).
- The **INS** key permits you to insert text directly on the graph. While inserting text, press **F1** for help on your text options. You can type small or large, horizontal or vertical text.
- To print a graph, press **P** and select your choice of printer from the menu. The print output is only a screen dump of the display, so the quality is limited.
- To save a graph for later printing or viewing, press **S**. The graph image will be saved in the common PCX bitmap format. You can use the PRINTPCX program or other software to view or print multiple images later. PRINTPCX also permits you to convert colour PCX images into black and white images suitable for inclusion in a word processing document.

Fitting trend lines

- To fit a statistical function to a data series, select **FIT** from the **DATA** menu. The options under **FIT** allow you to select the type of function, data year limits to include in the fit and a final projection year for a statistical forecast.

- By fitting a trend line (selecting the option under **FIT**) with a projection (selecting **PROJECTION** under **FIT**), a statistical forecast can be plotted. Use the + key to add a new data series to the graph, which can be made with only a few key strokes.

Charting profiles

The options under the **GRAPH** menu allow you to change the year span or style of the graph display (options **LIMITS** and **STYLE,** respectively), or to switch from a time trend to a table or column data profile (**VIEWPOINT**). The **VIEWPOINT** option is an easy means to compare data for a particular year.

Viewpoint

- If you want to change from a time series display to a country or item profile display for a given year, select **VIEWPOINT** from the **GRAPH** menu. Select **DISPLAY** from the **GRAPH** menu, and the profile will be drawn. The initial profile display is for the last year of historical data. To change the year, use the **ARROW** (↑↓) keys. Press **F1** for help.
- For a tables profile (profile of data across countries), you can either choose the tables to be displayed or let FAOSTAT TS select the top members and array them in order.

A limit of 50 items can appear in one profile. By selecting **TOP MEMBERS** instead of **SELECTED MEMBERS**, FAOSTAT TS will sort the values in the file and display a ranking of table or column values.

Viewing tables

- The **TABLE** menu allows you to look at data in a tabular format and to define subset tables that may be saved and imported into other software packages.
  - Go to the **TABLE** menu.
  - Select **BROWSE DATA** to view individual data tables from the current file.
- When viewing tables, a help bar appears at the bottom of the screen. Press **PAGEUP** or **PAGEDOWN** to change the table displayed or press **ALT+1** or **ALT+2** to choose from a list of tables. Use the **ARROW** keys (↑↓←→) to scroll the columns and rows.

Series data

- The **SERIES DATA** option under the **TABLE** menu displays the last data series selected, including summary statistics. This is the series used to plot a graph. To change the series, you must make a new choice from the **DATA** menu.
- The **SERIES DATA** screen can also be displayed while you are in a graph by pressing the letter **A**. If more than one series has been plotted, only the last series is shown. The range of years used for the series and statistics can be adjusted through the **LIMITS** option under the **GRAPH** menu.

- To view country or item profile lists and statistics, select **VIEWPOINT** from the **GRAPH.** You can quickly see a list of the tables with the greatest values (for example, countries with the highest commodity consumption) by choosing a table profile from **VIEWPOINT** and selecting the **TOP MEMBERS** option. Then select **SERIES DATA** from the **TABLE** menu to view the list, or select **DISPLAY** from the **GRAPH** menu to plot a chart.

Trend data

- If the **FIT** option has been selected (from the **DATA** menu) for a time trend, then the values composing the trend can be displayed with the **TREND DATA** option. Summary statistics for the original series and for the trend as well as residual values are included. The list scrolls with the **ARROW** keys, and you can toggle between the axis and trend data with the **A** and **T** keys.

Exporting data

- The **EXPORT** option under the **FILE** menu allows you to export FAOSTAT TS data into other file formats or to create custom tables for viewing or printing. By selecting **EXPORT,** you will jump into another set of menus.
- To select the tables and columns you want to view or save, go to the **DATA** menu. You must mark your choice of options with the + key. To undo all your selections quickly, select **RESET MARKS**.
- To arrange, view, save or print data, go to the options under **EXPORT** (in the **FILE** menu):
  - **FAO TABLE** creates a table with data from the last four available years.
  - **VIEW** displays a temporary text file of the data selected. It is a convenient way to view a subset of the tables and columns in a FAOSTAT TS file and can also be used to see the effects of the **ORIENTATION** or **LAYOUT** selections before using the **SAVE** or **PRINT** option.
  - **SAVE** displays a list of file formats to let you save your data choices in a file. You will be prompted for a file name. If you need to export FAOSTAT TS data for use with other software, use this menu item. The WK1 and DBF file format selections are not affected by the **LAYOUT** options (see below).
  - **PRINT** prints your current table and column selections. Many printers cannot print more than five columns of FAOSTAT TS data. Select **VIEW** to check the table width before printing.
  - **LAYOUT** allows you to display years across rows or down columns. The default direction is down columns.
- To get back to the main FAOSTAT TS menu or to clear your selections and create more tables, go to the **RETURN** option.

Making notes

- To read or edit textual information on the current data file, select **NOTES** from the **FILE** menu. You can also call up the Notes box by pressing **ALT+N** at any of the menus. The option **NOTES** allows you to read or edit text associated with the data file.

DOS shell and exit

The **DOS SHELL** option under the **FILE** menu returns you to the DOS prompt temporarily but keeps FAOSTAT TS in memory. This is not the normal way to exit the program. It is useful if you need to execute a DOS command and would like to return to the same data file. The data file itself is dropped from memory and reloaded on return, so default values will be in effect.

Exiting FAOSTAT TS

- To exit FAOSTAT TS:
    - Go to the **FILE** menu .
    - Select **EXIT.**

The Alt+X or Alt+Q key combinations are short cuts to exit the program from almost any screen.

WHERE TO PURCHASE FAO PUBLICATIONS LOCALLY
POINTS DE VENTE DES PUBLICATIONS DE LA FAO
PUNTOS DE VENTA DE PUBLICACIONES DE LA FAO

• ANGOLA
Empresa Nacional do Disco e de
Publicações, ENDIPU-U.E.E.
Rua Cirilo da Conceição Silva, Nº 7
C.P. Nº 1314-C, Luanda

• ARGENTINA
Librería Agropecuaria
Pasteur 743, 1028 Buenos Aires
Oficina del Libro Internacional
Av. Córdoba 1877, 1120 Buenos Aires
Correo electrónico: olilibro@satlink.com

• AUSTRALIA
Hunter Publications
PO Box 404, Abbotsford, Vic. 3067
Tel.: 61 3 9417 5361
Fax: 61 3 9419 7154
E-mail: jpdavies@ozemail.com.au

• AUSTRIA
Gerold Buch & Co.
Weihburggasse 26, 1010 Vienna

• BANGLADESH
Association of Development
Agencies in Bangladesh
House No. 1/3, Block F
Lalmatia, Dhaka 1207

• BELGIQUE
M.J. De Lannoy
202, avenue du Roi, B-1060 Bruxelles
CCP 000-0808993-13
Mél.: jean.de.lannoy@infoboard.be

• BOLIVIA
Los Amigos del Libro
Av. Heroínas 311, Casilla 450
Cochabamba;
Mercado 1315, La Paz

• BOTSWANA
Botsalo Books (Pty) Ltd
PO Box 1532, Gaborone

• BRAZIL
Fundação Getúlio Vargas
Praia do Botafogo 190, C.P. 9052
Rio de Janeiro
E-mail: valeria@sede.fgvrj.br
Núcleo Editora da Universidade
Federal Fluminense
Rua Miguel de Frias 9
Icaraí-Niterói 24
220-000 Rio de Janeiro
Fundação da Universidade
Federal do Paraná - FUNPAR
Rua Alfredo Bufrem 140, 3º andar
80020-240 Curitiba

• CAMEROUN
CADDES
Centre Africain de Diffusion et
Développement Social
B.P. 7317 Douala Bassa
Tél.: +237 433783
Télécopie: +237 427703

• CANADA
Renouf Publishing
5369 chemin Canotek Road, Unit 1
Ottawa, Ontario K1J 9J3
Tel.: +1 613 745 2665
Fax: +1 613 745 7660
Website: www.renoufbooks.com
E-mail: renouf@fox.nstn.ca

• CHILE
Librería - Oficina Regional, FAO
c/o FAO, Oficina Regional para América
Latina y el Caribe (RLC)
Avda. Dag Hammarskjold, 3241
Vitacura, Santiago
Tel.: +56 2 33 72 314
Correo electrónico:
german.rojas@field.fao.org
Universitaria Textolibros Ltda.
Avda. L. Bernardo O'Higgins 1050
Santiago

• CHINA
China National Publications
Import & Export Corporation
16 Gongti East Road, Beijing 100020
Tel.: +86 10 6506 3070
Fax: +86 10 6506 3101
E-mail: cnpiec@public.3.bta.net.cn

• COLOMBIA
INFOENLACE LTDA
Apartado Aéreo 34270
Santafé de Bogotá
Tel.: +57 1 2851779
Fax: +57 1 288 9882/255 2967
Correo electrónico:
infoenlace@gaitana.interred.net.co

• CONGO
Office national des librairies
populaires
B.P. 577, Brazzaville

• COSTA RICA
Librería Lehmann S.A.
Av. Central, Apartado 10011
1000 San José
CINDE
Coalición Costarricense de Iniciativas
de Desarrollo
Apartado 7170, 1000 San José
Correo electrónico:
rtacinde@sol.rassa.co.cr

• CÔTE D'IVOIRE
CEDA
04 B.P. 541, Abidjan 04
Tél.: +225 22 20 55
Télécopie: +225 21 72 62

• CUBA
Ediciones Cubanas
Empresa de Comercio Exterior
de Publicaciones
Obispo 461, Apartado 605, La Habana

• CZECH REPUBLIC
Artia Pegas Press Ltd
Import of Periodicals
Palác Metro, PO Box 825
Národní 25, 111 21 Praha 1

• DENMARK
Munksgaard, Book and
Subscription Service
PO Box 2148
DK 1016 Copenhagen K.
Tel.: +45 33 12 8570
Fax: +45 33 12 9387
Website: www.munksgaard.dk; e-mail:
subscription.service@mail.munksgaard.dk

• REPÚBLICA DOMINICANA
CUESTA - Centro del libro
Av. 27 de Febrero, esq. A. Lincoln
Centro Comercial Nacional
Apartado 1241, Santo Domingo
CEDAF - Centro para el Desarrollo
Agropecuario y Forestal, Inc.
Calle José Amado Soler, 50 - Urban. Paraíso
Apartado Postal, 567-2, Santo Domingo
Correo electrónico: fda@Codetel.net.do
Sitio Web: http//www.fda.org.do
Tel.: +001 809 544-0616/544-0634/
565-5603
Fax: +001 809 544-4727/567-6989
Sra Altagracia Rivera de Castillo,
Directora Ejecutiva

• ECUADOR
Libri Mundi, Librería
Internacional
Juan León Mera 851
Apartado Postal 3029, Quito
Correo electrónico:
librimul@librimundi.com.ec
Universidad Agraria del Ecuador
Centro de Información Agraria
Av. 23 de julio, Apartado 09-01-1248
Guayaquil
Librería Española
Murgeón 364 y Ulloa, Quito

• EGYPT
The Middle East Observer
41 Sherif Street, Cairo
Tel.: +202 393972
Fax: +202 3606804
E-mail: book-order@meobserver.com.eg
Website: www.meobserver.com.eg

• ESPAÑA
Librería Agrícola
Fernando VI 2, 28004 Madrid
Librería de la Generalitat
de Catalunya
Rambla dels Estudis 118 (Palau Moja)
08002 Barcelona
Tel.: +34 93 302 6462
Fax: +34 93 302 1299
Mundi Prensa Libros S.A.
Castelló 37, 28001 Madrid
Tel.: +34 914 36 37 00
Fax: +34 915 75 39 98
Sitio Web: www.mundiprensa.com
Correo electrónico:
libreria@mundiprensa.es
Mundi Prensa - Barcelona
Consejo de Ciento 391,
08009 Barcelona
Tel.: +34 934 88 34 92
Fax: +34 934 87 76 59

• FINLAND
Akateeminen Kirjakauppa
Subscription Services
PO Box 23, FIN-00371 Helsinki
Tel.: +358 9 121 4416
Fax: +358 9 121 4450

• FRANCE
Editions A. Pedone
13, rue Soufflot, 75005 Paris
Lavoisier Tec & Doc
14, rue de Provigny
94236 Cachan Cedex
Site Web: www.lavoisier.fr
Mél.: livres@lavoisier.fr
Librairie du commerce
international
10, avenue d'Iéna
75783 Paris Cedex 16
Site Web: www.cfce.fr
Mél.: pl@net-export.fr
WORLD DATA
10, rue Nicolas Flamand
75004 Paris
Tél.: +33 1 42 78 0578
Télécopie: +33 1 42 78 1472

• GERMANY
Alexander Horn Internationale
Buchhandlung
Friedrichstrasse 34
D-65185 Wiesbaden
Tel.: +49 6121 37 42 12
S. Toeche-Mittler GmbH
Versandbuchhandlung
Hindenburgstrasse 33
D-64295 Darmstadt
Tel.: +49 6151 336 65
Fax: +49 6151 314 043
Website: www.booksell.com/triops
E-mail: triops@booksell.com
Uno Verlag
Poppelsdorfer Allee 55
D-53115 Bonn 1
Tel.: +49 228 94 90 20
Fax: +49 228 21 74 92
Website: www.uno-verlag.de
E-mail: unoverlag@aol.com

• GHANA
SEDCO Publishing Ltd
Sedco House, Tabon Street
Off Ring Road Central, North Ridge
PO Box 2051, Accra
Readwide Bookshop Ltd
PO Box 0600 Osu, Accra
Tel.: +233 21 22 1387
Fax: +233 21 663347
E-mail: readwide@africaonline.cpm.gh

• GREECE
Papasotiriou S.A.
35 Stournara Str., 10682 Athens
Tel.: +30 1 3302 980
Fax: +30 1 3648254

• GUYANA
Guyana National Trading
Corporation Ltd
45-47 Water Street, PO Box 308
Georgetown

• HAÏTI
Librairie «A la Caravelle»
26, rue Bonne Foi
B.P. 111, Port-au-Prince

• HONDURAS
Escuela Agrícola Panamericana
Librería RTAC
El Zamorano, Apartado 93, Tegucigalpa
Oficina de la Escuela Agrícola
Panamericana en Tegucigalpa
Blvd. Morazán, Apts. Glapson
Apartado 93, Tegucigalpa

• HUNGARY
Librotrade Kft.
PO Box 126, H-1656 Budapest
Tel.: +36 1 256 1672
Fax: +36 1 256 8727

• INDIA
Allied Publisher Ltd
751 Mount Road
Chennai 600 002
Tel.: +91 44 8523938/8523984
Fax: +91 44 8520649
E-mail:
allied.mds@smb.sprintrpg.ems.vsnl.net.in
EWP Affiliated East-West
Press PVT, Ltd
G-l/16, Ansari Road, Darya Gany
New Delhi 110002
Tel.: +91 11 3264 180
Fax: +91 11 3260358
Oxford Book and Stationery Co.
Scindia House
New Delhi 110001
Tel.: +91 11 331 5310
Fax: +91 11 371 3275
Oxford Subscription Agency
Institute for Development Education
1 Anasuya Ave., Kilpauk
Madras 600010
Periodical Expert Book Agency
G-56, 2nd Floor, Laxmi Nagar
Vikas Marg, Delhi 110092
Tel.: +91 11 2215045/2150534
Fax: +91 11 2418599
Bookwell
Head Office:
2/72, Nirankari Colony, New Delhi-110009
Tel.: +91 11 725 1283
Fax: +91 11 328 13 15
Sales Office:
24/4800, Ansari Road
Darya Ganj, New Delhi - 110002
Tel.: +91 11 326 8786
E-mail: bkwell@nde.vsnl.net.in

• IRAN
The FAO Bureau, International
and Regional Specialized
Organizations Affairs
Ministry of Agriculture of the Islamic
Republic of Iran
Keshavarz Bld, M.O.A., 17th floor
Teheran

• IRELAND
Office of Public Work
4-5 Harcourt Road, Dublin 2

• ISRAEL
R.O.Y. International
PO Box 13056, Tel Aviv 61130
E-mail: royil@netvision.net.il

• ITALY
FAO Bookshop
Viale delle Terme di Caracalla
00100 Roma
Tel.: +39 06 5705 5688
Fax: +39 06 5705 3360
E-mail: publications-sales@fao.org
Libreria Commissionaria
Sansoni
S.p.A. - Licosa
Via Duca di Calabria 1/1
50125 Firenze
Tel.: +39 55 64 8 31
Fax: +39 55 64 12 57
E-mail: licosa@ftbcc.it
Libreria Scientifica Dott. Lucio
de Biasio "Aeiou"
Via Coronelli 6, 20146 Milano

• JAPAN
Far Eastern Booksellers
(Kyokuto Shoten Ltd)
12 Kanda-Jimbocho 2 chome
Chiyoda-ku - P.O. Box 72
Tokyo 101-91
Tel.: +81 33 265 7531
Fax: +81 33 265 4656
Maruzen Company Ltd
PO Box 5050
Tokyo International 100-31
Tel.: +81 33 278 1894
Fax: +81 33 278 1895
E-mail: h_sugiyama@maruzen.co.jp

• KENYA
Text Book Centre Ltd
Kijabe Street
PO Box 47540, Nairobi
Tel.: +254 2 330 342
Fax: +254 2 22 57 79
Inter Africa Book Distribution
Kencom House, Moi Avenue
PO Box 73580, Nairobi
Tel.: +254 2 211 184
Fax: +254 2 223 5 70
Legacy Books
Mezzanine 1, Loita House, Loita Street
Nairobi, PO Box 68077
Tel.: +254 2 303853
Fax: +254 2 330854

• LUXEMBOURG
M.J. De Lannoy
202, avenue du Roi
B-1060 Bruxelles (Belgique)
Mél.: jean.de.lannoy@infoboard.be

• MADAGASCAR
Centre d'Information et de
Documentation Scientifique et
Technique
Ministère de la recherche appliquée
au développement
B.P. 6224 Tsimbazaza, Antananarivo

• MALAYSIA
Electronic products only:
Southbound
Sendirian Berhad Publishers
9 College Square, 01250 Penang

• MALI
Librairie Traore
Rue Soundiata Keita X 115
B.P. 3243, Bamako

• MAROC
La Librairie Internationale
70 Rue T'ssoule
PO Box 302 (RP), Rabat
Tél./Télécopie: 212 7 75 01 83

• MÉXICO
Librería, Universidad Autónoma
de Chapingo
56230 Chapingo
Libros y Editoriales S.A.
Av. Progreso Nº 202-1º Piso A
Apartado. Postal 18922
Col. Escandón, 11800 México D.F.
Mundi Prensa Mexico, S.A.
Río Pánuco, 141 Col. Cuauhtémoc
C.P. 06500, México, DF
Tel.: +52 5 533 56 58

Fax: +52 5 514 67 99
Correo electrónico:
1015452361@compuserve.com

• NETHERLANDS
Roodveldt Import b.v.
Brouwersgracht 288
1013 HG Amsterdam
E-mail: roodboek@euronet.nl
Tel.: +31 20 622 80 35
Fax: +31 20 625 54 93
Swets & Zeitlinger b.v.
PO Box 830, 2160 Lisse
Heereweg 347 B, 2161 CA Lisse
E-mail: infono@swets.nl
Website: www.swets.nl

• NEW ZEALAND
Legislation Services
PO Box 12418
Thorndon, Wellington
E-mail: gppmjxf@gp.co.nz
Oasis Official
PO Box 3627, Wellington
Tel.: +64 4 499 1551
Fax: +64 4 499 1972
E-mail: oasis@clear.net.nz
Website: www.oasisbooks.co.nzl

• NICARAGUA
Librería HISPAMER
Costado Este Univ. Centroamericana
Apartado Postal A-221, Managua

• NIGERIA
University Bookshop (Nigeria)
Ltd
University of Ibadan, Ibadan

• PAKISTAN
Mirza Book Agency
65 Shahrah-e-Quaid-e-Azam
PO Box 729, Lahore 3

• PARAGUAY
Librería Intercontinental
Editora e Impresora S.R.L.
Caballero 270 c/Mcal Estigarribia
Asunción

• PERÚ
INDEAR
Jirón Apurímac 375, Casilla 4937
Lima 1
Universidad Nacional «Pedro
Ruiz Gallo»
Facultad de Agronomía, A.P. 795
Lambayeque (Chiclayo)

• PHILIPPINES
International Booksource
Center, Inc.
Room 720, Cityland 10, Tower 2
H.V. de la Costa, Cor. Valero St
Makati, Metro Manila
Tel.: +63 2 817 9676
Fax: +63 2 817 1741

• POLAND
Ars Polona
Krakowskie Przedmiescie 7
00-950 Warsaw

• PORTUGAL
Livraria Portugal, Dias e Andrade
Ltda.
Rua do Carmo, 70-74
Apartado 2681, 1200 Lisboa Codex

• SINGAPORE
Select Books Pte Ltd
03-15 Tanglin Shopping Centre
19 Tanglin Road, Singapore 1024
Tel.: +65 732 1515
Fax: +65 736 0855

• SLOVAK REPUBLIC
Institute of Scientific and Technical
Information for Agriculture
Samova 9, 950 10 Nitra
Tel.: +421 87 522 185
Fax: +421 87 525 275
E-mail: uvtip@nr.sanet.sk

• SOMALIA
Samater
PO Box 936, Mogadishu

• SOUTH AFRICA
David Philip Publishers (Pty) Ltd
PO Box 23408, Claremont 7735
Tel.: Cape Town +27 21 64 4136
Fax: Cape Town +27 21 64 3358
E-mail: dpp@iafrica.com
Website: www.twisted.co.za

• SRI LANKA
M.D. Gunasena & Co. Ltd
217 Olcott Mawatha, PO Box 246
Colombo 11

• SUISSE
Buchhandlung und Antiquariat
Heinimann & Co.
Kirchgasse 17, 8001 Zurich
UN Bookshop
Palais des Nations
CH-1211 Genève 1
Site Web: www.un.org
Van Diermen Editions
Techniques
ADECO
41 Lacuez, CH-1807 Blonzy

• SURINAME
Vaco n.v. in Suriname
Domineestraat 26, PO Box 1841
Paramaribo

• SWEDEN
Wennergren Williams AB
PO Box 1305, S-171 25 Solna
Tel.: +46 8 705 9750
Fax: +46 8 27 00 71
E-mail: mail@wwi.se
Bokdistributören
PO Box 301 61, S-104 25 Stockholm
Tel.: +46 8 728 2500
Fax: +46 8 31 30 44
E-mail: lis.ledin@hk.akademibokhandeln.se

• THAILAND
Suksapan Panit
Mansion 9, Rajdamnern Avenue
Bangkok

• TOGO
Librairie du Bon Pasteur
B.P. 1164, Lomé

• TUNISIE
Société tunisienne de diffusion
5, avenue de Carthage, Tunis

• TURKEY
DUNYA INFOTEL
100. Yil Mahallesi
34440 Bagcilar, Istanbul
Tel.: +90 212 629 0808
Fax: +90 212 629 4689
E-mail: dunya@dunya-gazete.com.tr
Website: http://www.dunya.com

• UGANDA
Fountain Publishers Ltd
PO Box 488, Kampala
Tel.: +256 41 259 163
Fax: +256 41 251 160

• UNITED KINGDOM
The Stationery Office
51 Nine Elms Lane
London SW8 5DR
Tel.: +44 171 873 9090 (orders)
        +44 171 873 0011 (inquiries)
Fax: +44 171 873 8463
and through The Stationery Office
Bookshops
E-mail: postmaster@theso.co.uk
Website: www.the-stationery-office.co.uk
Electronic products only:
Microinfo Ltd
PO Box 3, Omega Road
Alton, Hampshire GU34 2PG
Tel.: +44 1420 86848
Fax: +44 1420 89 889
Website: www.microinfo.co.uk
E-mail: emedia@microinfo.co.uk

• UNITED STATES
Publications:
BERNAN Associates (ex
UNIPUB)
4611/F Assembly Drive
Lanham, MD 20706-4391
Toll-free: +1 800 86534
Fax: +1 800 865 3450
Website: www.bernan.com
E-mail: query@bernan.com
UN Bookshop
The United Nations Bookshop
General Assembly Building Room 32
New York, N.Y. 10017
Tel.: +1 212 963 7680
Fax: +1 212 963 4910
Website: www.un.org
E-mail: bookshop@un.org
Periodicals:
Ebsco Subscription Services
PO Box 1943
Birmingham, AL 35201-1943
Tel.: +1 205 991 6600
Fax: +1 205 991 1449
The Faxon Company Inc.
15 Southwest Park
Westwood, MA 02090
Tel.: 6117-329-3350
Telex: 95-1980
Cable: FW Faxon Wood

• URUGUAY
Librería Agropecuaria S.R.L.
Buenos Aires 335, Casilla 1755
Montevideo C.P. 11000

• VENEZUELA
Fundación La Era Agrícola
Calle 31 Junín Qta Coromoto 5-49
Apartado 456, Mérida
Fudeco, Librería
Avenida Libertador-Este
Ed. Fudeco, Apartado 254
Barquisimeto C.P. 3002, Ed. Lara
Tel.: +58 51 538 022
Fax: +58 51 544 394
Librería FAGRO
Universidad Central de Venezuela (UCV)
Maracay
Librería Universitaria, C.A.
Av. 3, entre Calles 29 y 30
Nº 29-25 Edif. EVA, Mérida
Fax: +58 74 520 956
Tamanaco Libros Técnicos
S.R.L.
Centro Comercial Ciudad Tamanaco
Nivel C-2, Caracas
Tel.: +58 2 261 3344/261 3335
Tecni-Ciencia Libros S.A.
Torre Phelps-Mezzanina
Plaza Venezuela
Apartado Postal: 20.315, 1020 Caracas
Tel.: +58 2 782 8698/781 9945
E-mail: tchlibros@ibm.net

• ZIMBABWE
Grassroots Books
The Book Café
Fife Avenue, Harare;
61a Fort Street, Bulawayo
Tel.: +263 4 79 31 82
Fax: +263 4 72 62 43

• Other countries/Autres pays/
Otros países
Sales and Marketing Group
Information Division, FAO
Viale delle Terme di Caracalla
00100 Rome, Italy
Tel.: +39 06 57051
Fax: +39 06 5705 3360
E-mail: publications-sales@fao.org

11/98